DATE DUE

Stalin's Apologist

Stalin's Apologist

Walter Duranty
The New York Times's Man in Moscow

S. J. TAYLOR

New York   Oxford
OXFORD UNIVERSITY PRESS
1990

Oxford University Press

Oxford   New York   Toronto
Delhi   Bombay   Calcutta   Madras   Karachi
Petaling Jaya   Singapore   Hong Kong   Tokyo
Nairobi   Dar es Salaam   Cape Town
Melbourne   Auckland

and associated companies in
Berlin   Ibadan

Copyright © 1990 by S. J. Taylor

Published by Oxford University Press, Inc.
200 Madison Avenue, New York, New York 10016

Oxford is a registered trademark of Oxford University Press

Library of Congress Cataloging-in-Publication Data
Taylor, S. J. (Sally J.)
Stalin's apologist : Walter Duranty, the *New York Times*'s Man in Moscow /
S. J. Taylor.
p.   cm.
Includes bibliographical references.
ISBN 0-19-505700-7
1. Duranty, Walter, 1884–1957.   2. Foreign correspondents—United States—Biography.
3. Foreign correspondents—Soviet Union—Biography.
4. Soviet Union—Politics and government—1917–1936. I. Title.
PN4874.D87T39   1989   070.4'332'092—dc20   [B]   89-16108   CIP

9 8 7 6 5 4 3 2 1
Printed in the United States of America
on acid-free paper

For Herbert L. Fink, graphic artist

Acknowledgments

The research for this book and my fascination with Walter Duranty began more than a decade ago, when I jotted down a short note to myself that he would make an interesting subject for a full-scale biography. Recently, I came across that note and paused to reflect how far I have traveled since writing it—to New York, Florida, and California; to London and Liverpool; and finally to Moscow and the Ukraine— in search of this complicated man, who attracted so many admirers and detractors alike.

My early reflections on Duranty's character and on the accusations leveled against him might have remained inconsequential had it not been for Robert Conquest's study of the Ukrainian famine of 1932– 33, *The Harvest of Sorrow*. Conquest brought into the public domain a detailed and scholarly record of this monstrous crime, which had been so successfully concealed and for all intents and purposes consigned to oblivion. Fully aware of the heavy personal toll such a topic inevitably exacts, I remain deeply indebted to Conquest for his work.

An invaluable aid to my book was the study grant provided by the National Endowment for the Humanities in Washington, D.C. This allowed me to conduct extensive research, particularly at the Public Record Office in Kew, England, and at the British Newspaper Library in North London, without which it would have been impossible to establish which of the journalists who claimed to have covered the famine did in fact do so and where the truth of the matter lay.

Harrison E. Salisbury, former Moscow correspondent and associate editor of the *New York Times,* provided access to critical materials I would otherwise not have been able to view, as well as sustained encouragement for my project. He read an early draft of the manuscript and made many useful suggestions for amplification.

I am no less indebted to Jane Perry Gunther, the widow of John Gunther, for painstakingly collecting from her husband's voluminous personal papers entries relating to Duranty, as well as giving me her own candid impressions of Duranty in his later years.

In Orlando, Florida, Parker E. Enwright not only gave me access to Duranty's personal papers, which formulated the basis for this study, but also shared with me his memories of Duranty as he neared the end of his life. Enwright's recollection of events was flawless, and I remain deeply obligated to him.

The late W. Averell Harriman, who was U.S. Ambassador to the Soviet Union, Ambassador at Large, and Governor of New York, knew Duranty in the mid-Twenties in Russia, and I found his precise recollections of Duranty extremely helpful.

Of the American journalists who knew Duranty personally and who shared their recollections with me in interviews, I am particularly grateful to author William Shirer, who frequently used Duranty as a commentator in his early broadcasts from Europe for CBS; and to Henry Shapiro, retired United Press Moscow Bureau Chief and honorary fellow at Harvard Institute for Russian Studies. My thanks go also to the late Robin Kinkead, formerly of Reuters; to the late Joseph Alsop, syndicated columnist for the *Washington Post–Los Angeles Times* Press Service; to Drew Middleton, former Moscow correspondent and retired military correspondent for the *New York Times;* to C. L. Sultzberger, author and retired correspondent of the *New York Times;* and to the late William Stoneman, reporter for the Chicago *Daily News.* In addition, Walter Kerr, former editor of the Paris *Herald Tribune,* and Robert St. John, retired correspondent for the Associated Press, both shared their time generously with me. The incisive and often witty remembrances of George Seldes, author and former correspondent for the Chicago *Tribune,* were extremely valuable and always amusing.

The lively accounts of Duranty in Hollywood given to me by

author and screenwriter Mary Loos were of great help, and her patience in "putting me into the picture" is much appreciated. Mrs. Sylvan Hoffman, sister of writer Marjorie Worthington, shared her remembrance of Duranty and gave me access to the correspondence between Worthington and him during the 1940s and early 1950s. Mrs. Agnes Walker, the widow of journalist H. R. Knickerbocker, and his brother, Dr. Kenneth L. Knickerbocker, retired Chairman and Academic Vice-President of the University of Tennessee, both gave extensive interviews. And although he did not wish to be interviewed, George F. Kennan, of the Institute for Advanced Studies at Princeton, sent me highly informative accounts of Duranty in Moscow in the 1930s.

I must also thank Richard Edes Harrison, retired free-lance cartographer and member of the Coffee House, for his impressions of Duranty in New York in the 1940s, as well as W. Colston Leigh, retired owner of Colston Leigh, Inc., booking agency for lecturers, and former agent of Walter Duranty and H. R. Knickerbocker.

On the other side of the Atlantic, I would like to thank Richard Ingrams, former editor of *Private Eye* and the official biographer of Malcolm Muggeridge, who used his good offices with the retired journalist on my behalf; and most especially Malcolm Muggeridge himself, who overcame his initial reluctance to renew bitter memories and finally agreed to talk with me. But for Muggeridge's eyewitness accounts of the famine in the spring of 1933 and his stubborn chronicle of the event, the effects of the crime upon those who suffered might well have remained as hidden from scrutiny as its perpetrators intended. Little thanks he has received for it over the years, although there is a growing number who realize what a singular act of honesty and courage his reportage constituted.

Clare Hollingworth, former war correspondent for the *Daily Telegraph* and *Daily Express,* now defense correspondent for the *Sunday Telegraph,* spent an afternoon with me recounting her memories of Duranty in Bucharest in 1940, for which I am grateful. I have benefited likewise from a most interesting discussion with the late Professor Colonel Gerald Draper, former Senior War Crimes Prosecutor of the British Military Courts at Nuremberg, and recently a member of the International Commission of Enquiry into the Ukrainian Famine of 1932–33. By the same token, I am indebted to James E. Mace, Staff Director of the Commission on the Ukraine Famine in Washington,

Acknowledgments

D.C., who gave me important information about the response of the U.S. State Department to the famine.

Of the many archivists and librarians on both sides of the Atlantic who provided assistance, none was more diligent and enthusiastic than A. D. Nightall, Secretary of the Old Bedfordian Club, who, among other things, tracked down for me photographs of Duranty as a schoolboy. Also extremely kind were Chester M. Lewis, retired Archivist for the *New York Times;* Robert C. Christopher, Administrator, The Pulitzer Prizes; Kenneth A. Lohf, Librarian for Rare Books and Manuscripts at Butler Library at Columbia University; Jean Holliday, Special Collections Assistant, Princeton University Library; Edwin Kennebeck, who made available to me the private files of Viking Press, Inc.; and Matt Clark, Acting Secretary of the Coffee House in New York, who gave me access to records and helped to put me in touch with many who knew Duranty. Others who were kind enough to answer inquiries and give me information include P. Cain, Archivist at Reuters, Ltd.; W. Myers, Assistant to the Bursar at Harrow School; Professor Derek Brewer, Master at Emmanuel College, Cambridge; E. S. Leedham-Green, Assistant Keeper of the Archives at the University of Cambridge; P. Hunter Blair, Archivist of Emmanuel College; D. A. Ruddom of the London Borough of Barnet Library; M. J. Callow of the Foreign and Commonwealth Office; J. A. Ryden of the City Estates of Liverpool; Gordon Read, archivist of the Merseyside Maritime Museum; J. Dunbar of the National Westminster Bank, Ltd.; and Martin Starr of the Teitan Press, Inc.

On a more personal level, I wish to thank Murray Park for giving me his impressions of what it was like to be a student at Bedford School; Pauline Duke, who typed an early draft of my manuscript; and Dr. Tom Fiddick, who suggested a number of additional sources of information; and Dr. Robert Trager for advice freely given.

Dr. M. E. Lamb patiently read early draft chapters of my manuscript and offered valuable advice, and Kyril Fitzlyon, author and former official of the U. K. Ministry of Defence, was kind enough to read a later draft and make a number of helpful suggestions. Lawrence Jackson also read a late draft, giving much attention to detail.

I owe a special debt of gratitude to Lisa Corbin for her many hours spent meticulously copy-editing the final manuscript; her patience and skill were invaluable to me.

Acknowledgments

Finally, I must thank Dr. George Brown, retired Director of the Honors Program and Chairman of the Journalism Department at Southern Illinois University. It was he who, a dozen years ago, said, with characteristic enthusiasm, "Wouldn't it be *great* if you could find some of the guys who knew Duranty in his heyday, and talk to *them*?" I did, and this book is the result.

February 1989   S. J. Taylor

Contents

Prologue   3

    I   *Liars Go to Hell*   9

   II   *Maggots upon an Apple*   28

  III   *For You But Not for Me*   49

  IV   *A Sea of Blood*   63

    V   *A Mad Hatter's Tea Party*   80

  VI   *"Luck Broke My Way"*   97

 VII   *A Roman Saturnalia*   117

VIII   *The Mysterious Fatalism of the Slav*   135

  IX   *Applied Stalinism*   154

    X   *Dizzy with Success*   172

  XI   *A Blanket of Silence*   193

 XII   *The "Famine" Is Mostly Bunk*   210

XIII   *The Masters of Euphemism*   224

XIV   *Getting Away With It*   241

Contents

XV   *Hypocritical Psychologists*   256

XVI   *A Citizen of the World*   273

XVII   *Hollywood*   293

XVIII   *I Write As You Please*   312

XIX   *Midnight Minus One Minute*   328

XX   *Death Is the End*   347

Notes   357

Select Bibliography   391

Index   399

Stalin's Apologist

WALTER DURANTY

The greatest of foreign correspondents to cover Moscow
WILLIAM L. SHIRER

The greatest liar of any journalist I have met
in fifty years of journalism
MALCOLM MUGGERIDGE

Prologue

When he wasn't in Berlin having his wooden leg readjusted, or in St. Tropez basking in the sun, or in Paris at the races in the Bois de Boulogne, the *New York Times* man in Moscow could usually be found among the throngs at the bar of the Metropol Hotel. A veteran correspondent of World War I and a Pulitzer Prize winner, Walter Duranty was widely recognized as the top authority on the Soviet Union. His shrewd assessments of Bolshevik power struggles were front-page news for at least a dozen years.

On the 7th of November 1933, the Soviets began celebrating the sixteenth anniversary of their October Revolution with a 101-gun salute, followed by a display of military might that proclaimed their stubborn perseverance in a world divided by economic disparities and international rivalries. For two-and-a-half hours, Joseph Stalin reviewed waves of resolute Russian troops in Red Square, the "Internationale" echoing through loudspeakers. Seasoned reporters from the West, wearied by all the saber rattling, stood in the bitter cold, trying to figure out a fresh angle for the stories they would send to the readers back home. When at last the parades ended, the journalists retired to the warmth of the nearby Metropol and a rehash of the day's events.

On an occasion such as this, Duranty would usually be at the center of the discussion, pounding his cane against the floor to emphasize a

3

point, mowing down his less-gifted colleagues with a turn of phrase, often witty, not always kind, not always truthful. But tonight, Duranty's spot at the bar was conspicuously empty.

Two weeks before, he had cabled his editors in New York, asking their permission to accompany Soviet Foreign Minister Maxim Litvinov to Washington, D.C., where, it was suspected, Litvinov might bring about what the Soviets had been seeking for seventeen years— diplomatic recognition of the world's first Communist state by the United States of America.

A reporter who had scooped some of the best newsmen in the business, Duranty was an old hand at doping out a story ahead of his competitors. At about the time his colleagues stood in the Moscow hotel listening to the strains of American jazz, played Soviet-style, Duranty was standing in the Oval Office of the White House, covering what he would consider to be the single most important story of his career. Paraphrasing the title of John Reed's famous account of the October Revolution, Duranty described the event as "the ten days that steadied the world."

Later in life, Duranty would remember the press conference as the single moment of greatest satisfaction he had ever experienced. As the other reporters were filing out after President Franklin D. Roosevelt's announcement of recognition of the Soviets, the President held Duranty back for a moment, asking him confidentially, "Well, don't you think it's a good job?"

A few days later, at the dinner held to celebrate the event in New York's Waldorf-Astoria, Duranty was introduced to the fifteen hundred dignitaries in attendance as "one of the great foreign correspondents of modern times," and as the little Englishman with the cane stood to acknowledge the introduction, the crowd "rose for the first time and cheered." For Duranty, it was the crowning glory of an already brilliant career—a personal triumph for the man who had predicted that the Bolshevik regime, against all odds, was here to stay.

Duranty seemed an unlikely candidate for such heroic stuff. Short, balding, and unprepossessing in appearance, his one outstanding characteristic was a limp, which resulted from the loss of his left leg in a train accident in France some years before. That and his keen gray eyes were what saved him from the commonplace. No one, though, who had ever seen him animated, his eyes glittering, could forget the engag-

4

ing and provocative style of his conversation, even if they did some-how forget exactly what it was he had said.

Perhaps it was the way he talked that made him such a hit with the ladies, for Duranty possessed this extraordinary attraction for women. His sexual escapades were legion, despite the loss of the leg—or, as some believed, because of it. The rumors were fed by his keeping a Russian mistress discreetly at home in Moscow and a French wife, even more discreetly, in a villa in St. Tropez.

Coeds from Eastern schools, departing from European tours to wit-ness the building of Paradise, adored the *Times* correspondent and his titillating banter. He told them tales about the dangers of opium, to which he had briefly become addicted, so went the story, in the painful days following the loss of his leg. He chain-smoked Camels and sipped Scotch as he talked, making no apologies for his admiration of V. I. Lenin and his successor Joseph Stalin, whose methods, he be-lieved, would ultimately prove successful in the backward Russian state.

For them, and for his readership in America, Duranty created the leaders of the Soviet Union, much as a novelist creates a set of mem-orable characters. In his own unmistakable, personalized style, he viv-idly recounted the conflicts among them, the dramatic ebbs and flows of their struggles for power. Lenin: cold, logical, and wise. Trotsky: brilliant, but erratic; fatally flawed. Stalin: man of steel; "a Franken-stein monster."

Two exclusive interviews with the reclusive dictator gave the impression that Duranty was Stalin's Western confidant. The first was in 1930 at Duranty's request; the second, at Stalin's, on Christmas Day 1933—a seeming reward for Duranty's part in helping to achieve U.S. recognition.

As Fascism rose in Europe and Japanese Imperialism threatened the East, Western powers sank deeper into the quagmire of the Great Depression, unable, it seemed at the time, to protect themselves from these forces. Against this background, Duranty touted the accomplish-ments of Stalin's Five-Year Plan, ushering in what would come to be called "the Red Decade." His stubborn chronicle of Soviet achieve-ments made him the doyen of left-leaning Westerners who believed that what happened inside Soviet Russia held the key to the future for the rest of the world.

The brutality of Stalin's policy of collectivization that displaced millions, his establishing of the Gulag Archipelago that sent untold numbers of Soviet citizens to work and to die in unimaginable degradation and squalor—these were lightly glossed over by the Soviet Press Office, in a policy of propaganda that succeeded even beyond the expectations of government officials. The bloody purges that would expunge Stalin's opponents from every sphere of Soviet life were but a dark shadow against the future.

But in 1933, the watershed year, when Stalin finally achieved U.S. recognition, disquieting rumors had begun to surface. There was a growing number of reports about a famine, purported to have taken place in the grain-growing districts of the Ukraine, the Northern Caucausus, and across the nomadic cattle country of Kazakhstan: a disaster that cost the lives of millions of peasants, a calamity of incalculable dimensions.

For later generations, as the sheer magnitude of that event began slowly to emerge, questions would arise as to why nobody knew, why the American public hadn't been told. How did Stalin manage to conceal the greatest man-made disaster in modern history, when perhaps as many as ten million men, women, and children were allowed to die by slow starvation as a result of their refusal to conform to Stalin's plan to collectivize agriculture?

Had this been a deliberate act of genocide against the Soviet peasantry, or, as Duranty characterized it, an example of anti-Communist propaganda promulgated in "an eleventh-hour attempt to avert American recognition by picturing the Soviet Union as a land of ruin and despair"?

Throughout his career Duranty would claim his only object as a journalist was "to find the truth and write it as best I could." Yet despite this high-minded goal, by 1957, the year of his death, Duranty would be labeled "the No. 1 Soviet apologist in the United States"; and in the years that followed, he would become the prototype for the dishonest reporter: "a fashionable liar," some would call him, "a journalistic shill," others would say.

What were the loyalties of this complicated man? What motivated the line of action he adopted?

"What I want to know is whether a policy or a political line or regime will work or not," Duranty once said; and he refused "to be

6

sidetracked by moral issues or to sit in judgment of the acts of individuals or of states."

It was a tough-minded stance, clear-headed and uncompromising: a philosophy that carried Duranty from anonymity to celebrity. Whether it brought him any closer to the truth than others in the profession was another matter—one still worth considering.

CHAPTER I

Liars Go to Hell

Walter Duranty fancied himself a Citizen of the World, a man of knowledge and influence, culture and wit, born, symbolically, on the Isle of Man,[1] and this particular bit of fluff he obligingly spun out for anyone who cared to listen. It sounded good and enhanced his image. But it wasn't true.

It was less a lie, perhaps, than the smokescreen of an imaginative talker who invented a public self for the amusement of his listeners, even as he buried his past from any real scrutiny for reasons he kept to himself. Duranty was actually born, a fact more symbolically apt than anything he could have invented, in Liverpool, the "Cradle of Socialism," as it came to be known, a city "with as high a proportion of paupers as could be found in any town in England."[2]

Duranty's family was not among them. Instead, he came from the affluent middle class, merchants for some hundred years before his birth, perhaps of slaves. There was always that shadow of a suggestion—as with all "the gentlemen of Liverpool"—that taint, so ostentatiously flung at the city early in the nineteenth century by the hotheaded actor George Frederick Cooke. Encountering some offense during a performance, Cooke rounded on his audience and cried out that Liverpool was "a place accursed of Heaven and abhorrent to nature," its wealth, "the price of human misery," and there was not a brick in their houses that was "not cemented with human blood."[3] Until the abolition of the slave trade in 1807, it flourished, nurtured by the city's connection with the West Indies, the number of Liverpool ships engaged in the traffic approaching two hundred with a cargo of nearly 50,000 Africans in that last year alone.

Alexander Duranty, Walter Duranty's paternal grandfather, was born in the West Indies and immigrated to Liverpool either in 1842 or 1843, accompanied by his wife Jane.[4] A vigorous and substantial man in his early thirties, he established a household in Hamilton Square in Birkenhead, a respectable suburb of the city, first at Number 7 and then at Number 60, each of them fine houses, especially for a young couple just starting out. Almost immediately they began their family. In 1844 a daughter, Catherine Emily, was born; within a year, their first son Charles, within two, William Steel Duranty, named after a close family friend. It was this youngest boy who would eventually become the father of Walter Duranty. Later on, there would be a last addition to the family, Selina Jane, born ten years after her elder brother. The family was eminently respectable, prosperous, and genteel, at least at this stage, and staunchly Protestant, pillars of the Presbyterian Church.

In the next decade Alexander Duranty would advance from employment in W. Rose and Company to be the proprietor of his own firm, Alexander Duranty and Company. As his sons grew to manhood, they would join the business along with Duranty's German-born son-in-law Theodore Ruete, husband to Catherine: a growing family concern then, alternately described as merchants of oil, of cotton, of commodities, and finally as commissioning agents for the Red D. Steamer Line. For a time during the mid–1860s, Alexander Duranty held the post of Vice Consul of Venezuela, while retaining full control of the business.

As Britain's second largest port, Liverpool accounted for at least a third of the country's commerce, with more foreign or overseas trading than any other city in the world. It became a world market for cotton and grain, and controlled the world manufacture and trade in sugar, soap, salt, and oxygen.[5] Iron, steel, machinery, pottery, and textiles passed through the port daily. At the Queen's and Coburg docks, the tall masts stretched upwards against the horizon, the steamers' smokestacks belching out black clouds of smoke. During the nineteenth century the crude and makeshift warehouses were replaced by magnificent commercial and industrial buildings—the India Building, the Cotton and Corn Exchanges.[6] Taxes on income and property were higher in Liverpool than in any other city in the English provinces.[7]

The high level of prosperity permitted a singularly decorous lifestyle, one envied by other northern cities. The traditional contrast was between industrial Manchester and the seaport Liverpool, the former hamstrung by the latter's privileges. These resulted, in large part, from a charter granted by King John in 1207, which allowed Liverpool to collect port dues on the products of Manchester and other industrial outposts in the north of England. The inequity resulted in a bitterness that found its way into the popular culture of the age. What would happen, a music-hall song asked, if the charter were withdrawn?

> Alas then for poor Liverpool, she'd surely go to pot, Sir. . . . They might come down to Manchester, and we could find them work to do, Sir.[8]

The contrast between industry and commerce, celebrated by these lyrics, has since become blurred, but the advantages enjoyed by men like Alexander Duranty were very real indeed.

By 1871, five years before his death, the elder Duranty owned two impressive houses, one on Princes Road, another, "Melbreck House," on Allerton Road in Birkenhead. His daughter Catherine and his stolid, dependable son-in-law lived next door, their household only slightly less imposing than the patriarch's. There were in Duranty's house on Princes Road his wife Jane, his two sons, now grown to manhood and active members in the family business, and his remaining daughter, the baby of the family. Duranty also supported his sister-in-law, who had accompanied him and his wife from the West Indies. In his employ were almost as many servants as family members—a Scottish nurse who had been with the family for years, a cook, a butler, two scullery maids. It was a prosperous household, where the Victorian values of hard work and moral rectitude were reflected not only in the age's obsessive commitment to money making but also in the certain belief that prosperity rewarded the righteous.

By the time of his death at the age of sixty-four, Alexander Duranty had amassed an impressive fortune, at least the equivalent of a modern-day millionaire, with an estate valued at just under £30,000, including his real estate, his insurance policies, and his stocks, shares, and securities. His scrupulous attention to business matters was exem-

11

plified by his Last Will and Testament, a document no fewer than nine pages in length. Its guiding principle was the preservation of all that he had accumulated during his lifetime for the use of his wife and many progeny. To his dear Jane, he left £500 in cash as well as the income from his rents, stocks, shares and securities, and the major portion of his "household furniture plate linen china glass books works of art . . . all my Carriages and Horses and the Stock of Wines liquors provisions and consumable Stores."[9] The rest was parceled out—in income from trusts, to his two spinster sisters-in-law, Mary and Jeanette Greenshields, and not forgetting "my old Servant Julie Campbell," an outright gift of £100. To his children, he left equal portions in trust, £10,000 each; and finally, for his children's children on their twenty-first birthdays, equal portions of his residuary estate.

Thus, whatever the excess or failures of his father, the future of the unborn Walter Duranty was to some extent secured, with sufficient funds to allow him to fritter away the first nine years of his adult life in a manner unanticipated, and undoubtedly abhorrent, to the elder patriarch who had paved his way—if not in perfect comfort, well then, with enough money to patch together the fly-by-night lifestyle the young man was to elect.

Within a year of her husband's death, Mrs. Jane Duranty had changed the name of the family firm from "Alexander Duranty and Company" to "Widow Duranty and Sons," thus establishing herself in a tradition of strong women that was at odds with the prevailing Victorian stereotype of fawning dependency, yet not all that uncommon in the days of Empire. It was too much for her son-in-law. A short time later, he deserted to another firm. The family disintegration had begun.

In 1881, the Widow Duranty's youngest son William moved out of her home in order to marry, but he remained in the family business, along with his elder brother Charles.

William Steel Duranty's wife came from a household less impressive and certainly more beleaguered than that of her husband, yet perfectly respectable. Emmeline Hutchins's father, Charles Hutchins, had been a craftsman, an engraver by trade. Born in Stirling, Scotland, in 1816, he lived for a time in Seacomb, Cheshire, before setting up shop in Liverpool. At the age of thirty-five, he was the sole support of five children, all under eight years of age. Emmeline was his youngest. When she married William Steel Duranty in 1881, her father had already died, perhaps worn out from the effort. The bride was fully thirty-three years old, hardly girlish, her escape from spinsterhood remarkable in a city where she had already outlived by one year the average life expectancy.

The couple moved into 10 Falkner Square, taking their place as members of the Establishment. It was a graceful, multi-story town house in a tree-lined square, located in Mount Pleasant, known for its rolling green lawns, its gardens, its secluded and leisurely way of life, easily the most fashionable area within the city's boundaries. In the streets stood handsome carriages with their attendant grooms; in the drawing rooms, impressive works of art and opulent furnishings reflected the good taste of their owners. The houses surrounding that of the newlyweds were inhabited by brokers and high-level civil servants, accountants, and merchants of tea, carpets, timber, cotton, and wine. Thus, William Steel Duranty and his wife Emmeline joined the city's elite, no doubt supporting, as did the majority of their neighbors, the theater, the literary clubs, and the debating societies of the city.[10]

Those living in the fine hilltop avenues around Falkner Square seldom acknowledged another segment of society, one that could be glimpsed out their carriage windows as they swept past the infamous areas around Scotland or Vauxhall Roads, or other unsightly spots along the waterfront—wretched and barefoot children, begging mothers, vagrants, unsavory prostitutes who had long since ceased to be ashamed of the way they earned their living. The poor were everywhere. Altogether, the neighboring slums shared "some 2,000 public houses and grog shops—'drunk for a penny, blind for twopence'—many of these the scene of nightly disorder comparable with the riotous behavior of privateersmen a century before."[11]

The day Walter Duranty was born, the 25th of May 1884, the weather was unseasonably cool, about 42 degrees Fahrenheit, with strong southwesterly winds.[12] Usually there would be some letup in the cloud cover that depressed northeast England throughout the winter, but this year the clouds were sticking even into the last days of spring.

The year was shaping up ominously in terms of the world economic outlook. A scant ten days before Duranty's birth, the New York Stock Exchange had dwindled downward, creating a full-fledged panic, "the worst since Black Friday in 1873."[13] Banks were closing all over New

13

York, the doors locking shut. The worst was the suspension of the Metropolitan National Bank. At a loss for what else to do, milling crowds gathered on the streets of the city.

In England, in the industrial North, iron production was falling,[14] the result of prolonged depression, and the panic in distant New York was viewed only as the latest crisis in a long string of economic woes. Under the continuing strain, "shipyards lay idle, factories closed their doors, farmers could not pay their rents, and agricultural laborers flocked to the cities to swell the ranks of those already without work."[15] In Liverpool itself, there had been a recent fall, though slight, in the price of cotton, described in the newspapers as a mere "loss of tone, though demand has been holding up."[16]

With the state of the world markets irrelevant, it seemed then, to his security, Duranty's early childhood was one of privilege. He took his place in that bourgeois, peculiarly Victorian middle-class matrix out of which evolved a commitment to cultural achievement, to individual attainment. His was a family of "doers," of rigid conformity; there was that contempt for the drones of both the upper and lower classes alike. In later life, Duranty would openly flaunt his low regard for the aristocracy: "nincompoop anachronisms" who thought they were "the reincarnation of allegedly able ancestors."[17] And when a prominent socialite once asked whether he was from the landed gentry or aristocracy, he couldn't resist snarling that he was from the lower middle class.[18] That was stretching it a bit—downwards—but it illustrated the full distance he was prepared to put between himself and a class his family evidently despised.

He was of that segment of British manhood upon which fell the full responsibility, as he would later write, "of Empire and Kipling and the White Man's Burden." His earliest memories reflected the typical Victorian horror show.

When I was a child in England secular books were not considered suitable reading for the young on the Sabbath Day, and their place was taken by improving works, like *Pilgrim's Progress* or, as in my home, by Foxe's *Book of Martyrs*, profusely illustrated. There was one picture which always puzzled me. A nude saint (or martyr) was stretched upon the ground, his middle covered by a tin basin from which protruded the tail of a cat, all fluffed and bushy, as cats' tails are in moments of stress. Two hard-faced men were piling red-hot coals on the top of the

14

basin, but what this meant I could not understand. As time passed and my knowledge grew, I worried out the letter-press and learned that the cat also had to worry out its way from the impromptu oven, through the poor martyr's living flesh. I cannot believe that such things are "good" for children, but . . . no child who has absorbed Foxe's *Book of Martyrs* with his morning porridge—and survived it—need blench at anything he saw in the jungles of Africa.[19]

These early years helped to condition the young Duranty to find, between himself and the inhabitants of wherever he might be, a chasm, as deep and wide as can exist between a backward people and the British Ruling Class. His responsibility would be to define, to describe, to delimit—a foregone fact of his upbringing. There could be no identification with the masses, any more than he saw anything of himself in the plight of the poor children of Liverpool.

Despite the distancing, however, he must have been aware of the queer little creatures—they could hardly be called children—running wild in the city. At one time there were as many as 23,000 of them in the dockland area alone; one of every two children born in the city died before reaching the age of eleven.[20] It was in Liverpool that Dickens had observed the street life for some of his novels: barefoot girls atop tables, reciting jingles for pennies in public houses; street urchins huddled together on steps, puzzling out the pictures on a handbill; naked boys bathing in the Leeds and Liverpool canal beside the Burlington Street bridge; the shoe blacks; the chimney sweeps; all of them so different from the young Duranty. His was a world of nannies and French maids, of long, slow Sunday afternoons in Sefton Park, near his Uncle Charles's house, where young boys in dark suits with stiffly starched collars stood beside their fathers in their cravats and bowler hats as they watched fine toy replicas of sailing yachts skim the glassy surface of the lake.

The contrasts at work in Liverpool were singularly representative of the extremes of poverty and wealth resulting from industrialization, or, as it is more euphemistically known, "modernization"—the sometimes bitter fruit of the revolution that had its beginning a century before.

In Liverpool it was the Irish who first crossed the sea in order to find work on "the Manchester-Liverpool railway line across the treacherous marshlands of Chat Moss." Later, they came to escape the potato famines, hundreds of thousands of them, crowded onto the decks of the "coffin ships." Fully a quarter of these refugees from starvation would stay in the port city to make a life in the back alleys and doorways, finding lodgings in cellars that were as often as not flooded with stagnant sewage.[21] City officials routinely ordered the cellars filled with sand to prevent their use as shelters by the poor.[22]

Those who could made their passage to America to try for the good life. Those who couldn't joined the throngs of unemployed who peopled the streets. By the year of Duranty's birth, Liverpool had become a city whose population exceeded 600,000, at least a tenth of them in a state of destitution.

Despite the general attitude of the middle class into which Duranty was born—whose response to the growing ills was distinctly anti-Catholic and anti-Irish—various societies sprang up to help the poor, to try to prevent the cruel neglect of children and violent acts against them, which were the inevitable result of fathers out of work and on the streets while their wives labored in the grim factories. These early charitable societies laid the foundation for the modern welfare state, and thus Liverpool became, in its attempt at dealing with the ravages of the Industrial Revolution, "the cradle of Socialism."

The year before Duranty was born, the Utopian society of Sidney and Beatrice Webb, H. G. Wells, and George Bernard Shaw—the original Fabian Society—was organized, and began its advance from crackpot status to political viability after the full effects of virtual manhood suffrage, granted in 1884, were realized. The parties needed the laboring man's vote, and the laboring man was joining "the tide against laissez faire." When the Fabian Society joined forces in 1900 with the Independent Labour Party, the trade unions, the Marxist Socialists, and rival and more radical Marxist groups, the Labour Party became an important new force.[23]

These were the events of Duranty's youth, events that would shape his life and, to some extent, color his interpretation of what was to follow.

Duranty first became aware of Russia, he was fond of recounting, at an English country fair at a show entitled *Herr Parizer's Penny Novelties*, where he was taken by his nurse at the age of four. "There were three principal items," he remembered.

16

First, a stout woman in a white night-gown wore a golden crown slightly askew and sang *Rock of Ages Cleft for Me*, while the screen bore a colored picture of another woman—or was it, I wonder, the same woman—clinging to a black rock surmounted by a white cross in the midst of raging waters.

The second scene was acted. We saw the Squire and his Lady at dinner, attended by a minion in a red waistcoat. Its climax was the hasty consumption by the minion of a mass of broken bread behind his master's back. The Squire turned and caught him, whereupon, in confusion, he regurgitated everything upon a silver tray. This repulsive playlet roused the audience to roars of enthusiasm, fully shared by me.

Having thus purged our souls, as Aristotle said, by religion and laughter, the Parizer genius next produced tragedy, a grim picture—or rather a series of colored "stills," entitled, with appalling subtlety, *A Russian Ride....*

The first picture showed the Russian family—father, mother and five babies of tender years—going off for a sleigh ride across the snowbound steppe. In the second appeared a wolf-pack, hundreds of hungry beasts with slavering jaws and fiery eyes. In the third picture, captioned "Pursuit," the wolves were gaining. The fourth picture was shocking. The wolf-pack leaders were abreast of the foam-flecked horses, which the driver, erect, was lashing with all his strength. In the fifth, which froze our blood, the father tossed a baby to the wolves. Sixth, ditto; seventh, ditto; eighth, ditto. In each the driver stood erect and flogged his foaming horses, while the wolf-pack surged around them. The ninth and last picture let us breathe again. "Saved" was the title in large black letters. The sleigh was at rest before a wooden building, and the breath of the panting team smoked in the frosty air. The driver sat huddled on his seat, and behind him the distracted parents embraced their surviving child. In the background a squad of soldiers fired a volley at the wolf-pack.[24]

The show, Duranty said, marked his mind "with error and prejudice about Russia." It implied that Russia was a "wild and barbarous country where savage animals could still menace man" and that "Russians, through callousness or necessity do not hesitate to sacrifice lives of others, however dear to them, to save their own...."[25]

The other event of his youth that made a significant impact on him was typical Victorian Gothic, the kind of sin and guilt dispensed to youngsters as a matter of course, almost like tonic. In Duranty's case, it seems to have remained the central memory of a man who didn't remember much about his early days.

Once as a young boy, when he lied to his grandmother—"a woman of rigid virtue and a pillar of the Presbyterian Church, and generous withal"—she pressed his finger against a hot bar in the fire grate, and when the young Duranty cried out, she said, "Liars go to hell, and in hell it burns like that forever."[26]

Is it surprising that Duranty chose to reject the theological baggage of John Knox, the hell-fire tradition of guilt and sin and fierce retribution that ruled and motivated the older generation?

As for his grandmother, he never really loved her after that.

The movement was outward, away from the city, middle-class flight to suburbia, and William Steel Duranty took his wife, son, and infant daughter, along with his household of servants, and left the town, although he continued the commute to the firm. They set up housekeeping in Westraydun, Blundell Sands, Waterloo, in a temporary move that stretched out into six years; it was pleasant, bucolic, but not exactly what they were after. At last, in 1893, a further commute, to Belford Freshfield, Formby, some ways distant from the center of the city, in a countrified environment: here they bought a dwelling more a mansion than a house, with a drawing room for entertaining, multiple bedrooms, servants' quarters, and a long sweeping drive that curved around to the back. William Steel Duranty took the new railway line into the city while his son Walter was groomed for Harrow.

Something about the mature Walter Duranty belied an exclusive upper-class education, and there was that suspicion among his colleagues that Duranty had never, in fact, attended the well known public school. The Harrow-Eton thing seemed somehow "above his station,"[27] his detractors would say.

But Duranty was indeed a Harrow boy, complete with top hat on Sunday, straw hat during the week; ample Latin, more Greek, and the "steady drill in accidence and syntax, the acquisition of vocabulary, and the accurate if painful translation of simple sentences from one language to another."[28] Along with French, this was where Walter Duranty would excel. He had that facility for language.

Later, his fellow correspondents would be impressed by the fact that Duranty could pick up any local newspaper and rattle it off, translating rapidly into perfect French, Latin, Greek, or eventually, after a

few years in Moscow, Russian.[29] "Walter Duranty was the most cultivated, brilliant, civilized, best-educated reporter in all Europe, except
for perhaps his friend William Bolitho, from South Africa,"[30] a colleague would say, one of Duranty's supporters.

It was only in mathematics that the young Duranty fell down, turning in a mediocre performance.

Life at Harrow "was primarily a toughening or hardening process
in which children learnt to conceal or repress their more tender emotions, and to create for themselves a fairly cheerful and self-controlled
existence away from their homes."[31] Duranty disliked it. As an adult
he complained that the British "treat their ruling class far rougher and
more harshly than they treat the proletariat."[32]

The boys were up early, in chapel by seven, with only a cup of coffee in their stomachs. They had an hour's lesson before breakfast,
another four hours of steady work before lunch. Then, there were three
more grueling lessons to be got through before tea, still more study
time afterwards. Sunday brought little relief, with as many as three
compulsory chapel services, one before breakfast.[33]

Sports were mandatory. The boys were required to participate in
the "games"—cricket, of course, and two codes of football—learning,
above all, good sportsmanship, teamwork, and discipline. Always
there was that unstated Victorian fear that boys left idle would get into
trouble: free time was regarded as *suspicio sexualis*.[34]

The subject of sex was taboo, and the only information the boys
could glean came from illicit sources, full of misinformation, or
through the Bible or the classics. And then, regardless of all the
attempts to prevent it, there was the early "buggery." Some said the
public school system engendered the tendency among British males.
But Duranty sensibly pooh-poohed such nonsense. He was, as an
adult, frank, open, cosmopolitan in speaking about sexual matters,
much more so than his newspaper colleagues from the United States,
who were unaccustomed to such frankness. They were quite honestly
shocked at Duranty's declaration that homosexuality was part of a
young person's development and that public school experimentation
was little more than "mutual masturbation," nothing at all to worry
about.[35] All his life, Walter Duranty would take up controversial points
of view, showing, as the years increased, less and less patience with the
insular and the provincial. He would become opinionated, outspoken,
cocksure—he was a public school boy, all right.

Then, suddenly, in 1899, when Duranty was fifteen, it came to an end. He was pulled out of Harrow, without explanation, and the family vacated the house in Formby. For reasons never made clear, his father dropped from sight entirely, leaving his mother to take up modest lodgings on her own, with only her fourteen-year-old daughter, for company. "Widow Duranty and Sons" disappeared without trace, victim to the uncertain times.

Duranty found himself hastily shuttled from Harrow to Bedford Grammar School. He was registered there as Number 4161, his mother's name written out in full, the space reserved for his father's name left blank.[36] William Steel Duranty would not rejoin his wife for several years, and when he did, it would be a pinched existence, in a modest home owned by his daughter.

When Walter Duranty was transferred from the prestigious Harrow to the respectable Bedford, he was the only boy of his year to suffer such a come-down. Most of the others were listed as "taught at home." Many were substantially subsidized by the Harpur Foundation, a charitable trust that helped some of the needier boys with their school fees which were, in any case, attractively lower than those in other schools of like quality. Duranty joined the ranks of the more heavily sponsored boys, easily soaring through the highly selective admission requirements. Undaunted, it seemed then, by his family's reversal, Duranty quickly took his place as one of the better students, his record at school something of a model.

The bow on the school rowing team, he was one of "Our Eight," described at one time as much improved "in the use of his slide, but he tumbles badly over the stretcher."[37] He went in for rugby, avoiding cricket, but never distinguished himself much on the team. He "was rather light," but made up for it "by always playing well."[38] Despite his mediocre record, he would later identify "the day he got his 'colors'" as the happiest moment in his life, in one of the few references he ever made to his childhood.

His best physical skill was speed, and he distinguished himself only once in his sporting career at the school, in the House Steeplechase. The annual event took place on March 25th 1903, "in very favourable weather. The Seniors was won by Duranty . . . who thus takes the Steeplechase Prize."[39] The first sixty in the race had their names listed in the school magazine, *The Ousel.* Walter Duranty's stood at the top.

Then, too, he was senior monitor. There were six of them who headed the various boarding houses, taking the collection to the altar on a Sunday, maintaining discipline, and generally "running everything." Part of it, of course, was expected to include the infamous activity of "fagging." At school, corporal punishment resulted from serious infringements of discipline, like intentional damage of school property, but in the boarding houses like Mr. Barnes's, where Duranty was a monitor, there was a higher degree of discipline, the slipper giving way, more often than not, to the cane.

The system included a series of fines for minor infractions, which were kept account of. When he got too many, a boy was liable to be beaten. It was a ritualistic affair: the caning was recorded in a book by a "referee" who stayed to witness the punishment, just to be sure things didn't get out of hand. The boys thought of it as "a game of forfeit." None would have thought of complaining. As senior monitor Duranty was in charge of such punishment. In exchange, he was accorded special privileges.

It was easy to spot the senior monitors on a Sunday, decked out in special clothes, fancy waistcoats, blue ties, bowler hats. If they liked, they could carry a silver-tipped cane.

Otherwise, on weekdays, they were indistinguishable from the other boys, in navy blue jacket, black tie, starched stiff collar, and white shirt. Bedford boys wore the school cap on the back of their heads, the badge a dark navy blue with a gold eagle crest.[40]

In the young Duranty, now growing to manhood, there suddenly appeared this flair for the dramatic, this love for the theatrical. In his last year at Bedford, he appeared in the school production of *The Grand Duchess*. His "utterance," according to the school magazine, was "exceptionally clear and sonorous" as he made "his flying visits to the scene, [giving] individuality to the minor role of Aide-de-Camp."[41]

But comedy was Duranty's forte. On "Speech Day," the final ceremony of his last year at Bedford, Duranty appeared in two skits, the first "the French Scene," where he took part in a short duologue by Verconsin, *Infanterie et Cavalerie*, as Mathias, the old infantry sergeant. Along with his partner, he was, the magazine said, "capitally got up," maintaining "very creditably the tone and motions of senility."[42]

In "the Greek scene," an episode "very freely adapted" from *The Birds* by Aristophanes, "Special praise [was] due to *Prometheus* (W. Duranty) for the clearness of his enunciation. . . . He inflected his voice

21

as though speaking in his mother tongue; this very ease occasionally resulted in a rapidity which may have baffled all but alert 'Grecians.' His get-up, too, was remarkably good."[43] Again, then, this unusual aptitude for language—it would place him far in the lead once he started his journalistic career.

But that "clear and sonorous" enunciation—a characteristic of his rather high-pitched voice—would later disqualify him from a career in broadcasting. It simply wasn't thought appropriate for serious work as a radio commentator, especially in those early days of primitive transmission.[44]

The special responsibilities his intellect imposed upon him were defined for Duranty and the other boys at that ceremony on "Speech Day," held on the 23rd of July 1903, when he was leaving Bedford. The headmaster of the school emphasized the necessity for self-reliance and concentration in his final address:

> In a school like this which draws boys from all corners of the British Empire, and sends them out again to make their way to every corner of the globe, these are the most valuable lessons which can be learnt (hear, hear).
> [Each boy] should feel that he is a member of a great society to which he owes duties, for which he has to do something, and whose welfare depends upon his conduct and his character . . . and feel he is a part of a larger whole to which he owes the sacrifice of some convenience and some liberty.[45]

This was the burden the boys were expected to assume as the new generation of rulers of the British Empire.

In the class lists for May 1903, Walter Duranty was rated third overall in a form of fourteen. In Classics, he finished second; third in French, fourth in History and Divinity. He took the Top Award in Classics, and his teacher, T. P. Gordon Robinson, helped Duranty proceed to an open Classical Scholarship at Emmanuel College, Cambridge.

And so, in the autumn of 1903, despite his family's reversal in fortune, Duranty arrived at Cambridge more as a result of ability than of social connections, which once having been respectable, perhaps even formidable, were now of the sort that the less was said about them, the better. He formed the habit of saying less and proceeded in good form. But there must have been some feelings of resentment, even of shame for the young man, now entering manhood.

The university town of Cambridge was built primarily of gray stone and red brick enclosing colleges of impressive architectural design. In the marketplace, the bells of Great Mary's chimed out the hour in that lonely way of small towns where time seems to pass more slowly than in the hectic cities. The streets in those days were often thin of people, except for a few townsfolk and, of course, the inevitable students. These were mainly men, generally of privileged backgrounds, who affected a "somewhat dowdy appearance, it not being quite the thing to look smart."

> Cloth caps in winter, straw boaters in summer, would be in evidence, and bowler hats on a Sunday; walking-sticks and gloves being essential appendages for visits to Newmarket or Lords.[46]

The young men favored gray flannel trousers, "stiff collars pitched rather high under the chin and Norfolk jackets."[47] In Duranty's case, any pretensions to dress would have been an affectation. He wasn't good looking, so why bother?

He had a mug face, his hairline high, receding a bit already. He wore his hair cropped short in an abbreviated Roman style. His thick-lipped, sensual mouth seemed to have a slightly cynical twist around the corners. The nose was fine-chiseled but a shade too large, that bit too flat. The only relief in this none-too-handsome face was a pair of clear, gray eyes, slightly hooded, twinkling, letting it be known some-how that one was in the presence of a keen intellect, a man with an unusual sense of mischief and of humor. At full height, Duranty was no taller than five feet six inches; this as well as the look of youthful idealism he conveyed in his more serious moments made him look a good deal younger than he was. And his lively manner, his outrageous talk, added to the impression.

Duranty matriculated at Emmanuel College on the 21st of October 1903, "having already, earlier in the same month passed the second part of the Previous Examination."[48] During that first year, he paid for his own room, board, and tuition. But during his second year and again in his third, he received financial assistance, the sort generally reserved for students in need.[49]

Emmanuel had been founded as the result of a Charter of Queen Elizabeth I, sealed on 11 January 1584. The grounds of the College had been acquired from the Cambridge priory of the Dominicans, and its "half-ruined buildings" had been converted into "the hall, the buttery, and the Fellows' parlour, with the Master's Lodge above."[50] Later Sir Christopher Wren designed the chapel, its cloister, and the surrounding gallery, which was the most striking architectural feature of the court. The interior of the first-floor gallery was handsomely wainscoted and later furnished with a couple of dozen chairs and two settees of walnut in the Chippendale style. Behind the chapel were prospects of open grass, flowers, and an ornamental pond with mallards and moorhens paddling in the gray waters. In the Fellows' Garden a gigantic and ancient Oriental plane tree dominated rolled lawns trimmed by flower beds and hedgerows.

The original purpose of the college is clear from the statutes. It was intended to be a "school of prophets," and "[f]rom the first the College was reputed a Puritan establishment."[51] Indeed, of the first one hundred settlers with a university education in New England, fully one-third were Emmanuel men; the best known, John Harvard, is credited with the founding of the first university in the New World. Throughout the years, Emmanuel College maintained a reputation for excellence, its distinguished graduates including such men as Thomas Young, known for his work in areas as diverse as the wave theory of light and the deciphering of Egyptian hieroglyphics, and Sir William Gell, the classical archaeologist, "whose work on Pompeii was standard throughout the nineteenth century."[52] Generally speaking, the College remained primarily a center for religious studies, with many of its young men destined for the church.

In those days, just after the turn of the century, the young men still addressed each other by their surnames. It was the fashion to smoke pipes and stay up talking into the early hours of morning, especially since they weren't allowed to be out past midnight, Dean's rules. At Emmanuel the talk centered on theological questions, always a bore to Duranty whose interest in the classics stemmed from a love of drama and narrative and whose commitment to religion had been from the start perfunctory. He fancied himself a literary type, a poet, or perhaps

24

a novelist. He wouldn't have minded writing short stories in the style of Saki (H. H. Munro), whom he admired and who had preceded him at Bedford. One of Duranty's classmates at Emmanuel, Hugh Walpole, would also succeed at writing fiction, a craft that somehow remained out of reach for Duranty, despite his considerable rhetorical skills.

Until his last year at Emmanuel, Duranty continued with his rowing. The team practiced on the Cam, the lingering river that winds its way through the city with hardly a ripple, the bent branches of the willow trees that line its banks drifting atop the calm water. Surprisingly, the Cam was "in a state of flood" during Duranty's first year, and the crew's poor start was blamed on the unusual circumstance.[53] The bad luck continued, however, and the crew never amounted to anything, at least not while Duranty was at Emmanuel.

He continued to excel in his studies, perfecting the classical grounding that would later show in many of his dispatches. He would use many of the stories he learned at Emmanuel to give substance to his newspaper writing, making literary allusions a hallmark of his personal style. His Cambridge education also, as he liked to recall in later years, "trained [his] mind," taught him how to "meet people without embarrassment" and to "get up on [his] feet and talk" in debating societies, as well as to play bridge and poker.[54]

In the only anecdote of his student years that Duranty ever published, he credited his education as the means by which he acquired a bit of business acumen. When he was twenty, he got a lucrative job during the Christmas vacation giving lessons in Latin and Greek to the son of a wealthy lace manufacturer in Nottingham. While there, he chanced to get into an argument with a rich and obnoxious friend of his employer—in Duranty's words, "a fat-faced, purse-proud, arrogant son of Satan"—who dismissed the practical value of a college education out of hand. The young Duranty impulsively bet that he could double an investment of five pounds within twenty-four hours. Once having put himself on the spot, he came up with the bright idea of selling 160 bottles of "cheap but violent perfume" at a stall in the marketplace at Leicester. But by five o'clock in the afternoon he had managed to sell only seven bottles. He was saved when "a thick-set ugly fellow" running a neighboring stall showed him how to do it. Duranty had the right product, he was told, but not the right selling manner.

25

So he began yellin' and yippin' and taking out the atomizer and squirting it at couples and saying how good it was, and you might be surprised to hear that he sold two dozen bottles in five minutes.[55]

With the help of a little urchin, who also joined the act, Duranty had sold, by half past eight, his full stock, bringing him a profit of 120 percent and enabling him to win his bet, after all.

Despite his quick wit, however, and undeniable brilliance, beneath the impressive academic record and promise of a fine career, there was in the young Duranty a character flaw. It was isolated early by one of his instructors, recognized even by Duranty himself as a threat to his future. He saw, he himself admitted, "too many sides of a question to be sure which one of them was quite true," and in his "heart of hearts" he was "rather inclined to pity single-minded people as being somehow deficient in unbiased judgment."

I once said something of the kind to a master or teacher . . . and he replied severely, "You, Duranty, are afflicted by the curse of Reuben—instability. You may flatter yourself that you are seeking for truth, but the fact is that you cannot make up your own mind. Remember the curse of Reuben, "Unstable as water thou shalt not excel." I was much cast down by this reproof until one day I thought to myself that I did not particularly want to excel. What I wanted, I thought, and what I still want, I know, is to see and hear new things, and to find out—to find out the great things of world affairs and the small things in people's minds, not for any profound purpose, good, bad, or indifferent, but for my own interest, entertainment and, in latter years, amusement. It is perhaps a selfish philosophy and somewhat negative, but it is neither greedy nor cruel; nor is it foolish or frightened.[56]

So quite early on, and quite cheerfully, Walter Duranty opted out. He would observe events and people as a source of interest and entertainment, following a philosophy of detachment somewhat at odds with the customary idealism of youth.

And then there was the family thing. Those years when the young Duranty was testing his mettle, first at Bedford, then at Cambridge, learning the boundaries of his intellect and his academic ability, his father had simply disappeared, while his mother scraped by alone. Reunited after a lengthy interval in the modest house in Golders Green, a suburb of London, they would recede further and further from Duranty's consciousness. He learned he could leave the complicated past behind if he went forward fast enough.

When his mother died in 1916, there was no word from Duranty. Fourteen years later, his sister died at forty-five, a spinster. Her life had been devoted to her father, who outlived her by three years. And when in 1933, plagued by senility and the diseases of old age, William Steel Duranty died, he left a personal estate valued at merely £430, besides the house his daughter had left him—a pathetic come-down from his early days of opulence and plenty. Walter Duranty's only acknowledgment of his family in all of these years was a curt document notarized in Moscow, authorizing his father's solicitors to sell the house, take their fee, and send him the proceeds.

Publicly, he solved his problem once and for all in his autobiography, *Search for a Key,* by killing off his parents in a railway accident and orphaning himself at the age of ten, an only child.

It put an end to any unwelcome questions.

CHAPTER II

Maggots upon an Apple

Whenever Aleister Crowley stepped out of line, and somehow that turned out to be fairly often, his mother fell into the habit of calling him "the Beast," based upon the text from Revelation: "And I saw a beast coming up out of the sea, having ten horns and seven heads, and on his horns, ten diadems. . . . And he opened his mouth for blasphemies against God. . . ."

She and her husband, until his premature death from cancer of the tongue when "the Beast" was only eleven years old, were active members of the exclusive sect known as the Plymouth Brethren—a group of strict fundamentalists, whose tenets included more than a passing preoccupation with the nature of sin and death,[1] good stuff for the training of their boy.

For a while the young Crowley followed in the path of the Brethren, but sometime after the death of his father and about the time of the onset of his own puberty, Crowley made a signal discovery: that the mention of torture or blood aroused him sexually. The young Crowley "even liked to imagine himself in agony and in particular, degraded by and suffering at the hands of a woman whom he described as 'wicked, independent, courageous, ambitious.'"[2] He became fascinated by the Book of Revelation, dwelling morbidly on the False Prophet, the Scarlet Woman, and the Beast, with whom he now identified. There were other early signs of an unusual sensibility, coupled perhaps with an abnormal imagination, which led him to test beliefs others were satisfied to accept at face value. Told a cat had nine lives, for example, the young Crowley

> caught a cat, and having administered a large dose of arsenic . . . chloroformed it, hanged it above the gas jet, stabbed it, cut its throat, smashed its skull, and, when it had been pretty thoroughly burnt, drowned it and threw it out the window that the fall might remove the ninth life. The operation was successful.[3]

In 1896, when he was twenty, Crowley went up to Trinity College, Cambridge. There, he occupied his time with reading and the writing of verse. It was not in the common style:

> All degradation, all sheer infamy,
> That shalt endure. Thy head beneath the mire
> And dung of worthless women shall desire
> As in some hateful dream, at last to lie;
> Woman must trample thee till thou respire that deadliest fume;
> The Vilest of worms must crawl, the loathliest vampire's gloom.[4]

Although Crowley never fully lost his interest in female defecatory functions, later in his life his focus changed abruptly to the expulsion of semen—or "elixir," as he called it—often in novel or bizarre situations. The poem "With Dog and Dame," a celebration of bestiality, remains perhaps the outstanding example of his preoccupations. By the time he came to write his poetic anthology White Stains, Crowley had begun signing his name in a large, childish scrawl, the capital "A" being so enscribed as to represent a thick penis with curlicues at the base resembling large testicles. He also formally adopted his mother's pet name, commonly referring to himself as "Beast 666," the great Anti-Christ predicted in the Book of Revelation.

His powers had resulted, Crowley believed, from a mystical revelation that had come to him on the last day of the year 1896, when, waking from a particularly troubling nightmare in the afternoon, he came to the realization that he could in fact control reality with magic.[5] The discovery inspired him. And at once he accepted in himself the desire to become "an Adept in the Secret Arts, a Magus." It was not

29

your everyday occupation; nevertheless, Crowley had found, like many a young man before him, his life's work.

In the early teens of the twentieth century, at the age of thirty-eight, Beast 666, the Great Magister, "the Wickedest Man in the World," as Crowley alternately called himself, was going through something of a crisis. He had just crossed over from London to Paris, there to practice the black arts and magico-sexual rituals to which he had dedicated the preceding dozen or so years of his life. He now found, as he put it, "inhibition,"[6] and along with it, the threat that his chosen path might close before him. Fortunately, he was saved when he made the acquaintance of a man some eight years his junior, but wise already in the ways of the world.

That man was Walter Duranty.

Since leaving Cambridge, Duranty had for several years been beating a path back and forth from New York to Marseilles to Paris, experimenting with a fly-by-night sort of existence he found exhilarating. Financed at first by the trust his grandfather had provided, then by the occasional sale of a short story or by "pumping Latin into some birdbrain son of the rich,"[7] he boasted he had spent more than one night on the banks of the Seine when he didn't have a sou for the price of a room.[8]

Crowley, struggling with his conscience for what was perhaps the only time in his life and in the grips of something approaching a depression, had begun to think of abandoning his great quest. It was Duranty who helped him, as he put it, "win out."

The relationship between the two men was cemented by the pair's common interest in smoking opium and in a woman, said to be a former artist's model, who represented to Crowley throughout his life the epitome of the Scarlet Woman, Crowley's ideal of femininity. About Jane Cheron, he wrote

> She is like a flower washed up
> On the shores of life by the sea of luck,
> A strange and venomous flower. . . .[9]

Cheron was also "a devotee of that great and terrible god, Opium,"

30

and later in his novel *The Diary of a Drug Fiend*, Crowley based a character on her, the strange and alluring Haidée Lamoureux:

> [She] was a brilliant brunette with a flashing smile and eyes with pupils like pin-points. She was a mass of charming contradictions. The nose and mouth suggested more than a trace of Semitic blood, but the wedge-shaped contour of the face betokened some very opposite strain. Her cheeks were hollow, and crow's feet marred the corners of her eyes. Dark purple rims suggested sensual indulgence pushed to the point of weariness. Though her hair was luxuriant, the eyebrows were almost non-existent. She had pencilled fine black arches above them.[10]

Haidée Lamoureux makes a quick cameo appearance in this loosely structured and self-indulgent account of a drug addict, who is, of course, Crowley himself. In the particular scene where Lamoureux appears, a nightclub in Paris, Crowley also introduces others of his acquaintance, among them the notoriously high living Frank Harris, who appears as the character Jack Fordham, and Lord Alfred Douglas, identified as the figure of "a young-old man." Indeed, the enterprising Crowley sold the novel on the promise that he would base the characters on real individuals he knew personally.[11]

But even among these colorful characters, Lamoureux stands out. It would be difficult for her to do otherwise, dressed as she is, in a revealing evening gown decorated with blue and silver sequins, bound with "a yellow sash spotted with black." Over this apparel, she has "thrown a cloak of black lace garnished with vermilion tassels." Her crooked fingers, which are "covered with enormous rings of sapphires and diamonds," are unexpectedly filthy.[12]

Lamoureux has a "monotonous" voice of "ecstatic detachment," which apparently derives from her continuous use of the drug heroin. "You mustn't expect to get the result at once," she explains about her addiction. "You have to be born into it, married with it, and dead from it before you understand it."[13]

For the beginner, Crowley explains that the "philosophical types of dope [are] morphine and heroin," and in his novel, he substitutes heroin for opium, which Cheron actually favored. She apparently remained an addict throughout her life. Certainly, there is ample evidence that she still smoked the drug some dozen years later, although she managed to free herself temporarily from time to time. And in

Crowley's fictionalized account, at least, his "heroin heroine" had few regrets:

> "Before I started heroin, year followed year, and nothing worthwhile happened. . . . [N]ow that I've gotten into heroin life, a minute or an hour—I don't know which and I don't care—contains more real life than any five years' period in my unregenerate days."[14]

There is also the suggestion of early promiscuity, before the drug took its place as the central interest in Lamoureux's life, a fleeting reference to herself as the "chief of sinners in my time, in the English sense of the words." Now, she explains, those few times she remembers the act of love, she is overcome by "a faint sense of nausea."[15]

These are apparently the characteristics that helped make Cheron Crowley's ideal of womanhood. Her stain of "inexpressible evil" makes her the perfect partner for "the wickedest man in the world." And despite what he termed "her complete lack of fascination," Crowley did remain fascinated by Jane Cheron, and for a good many years.

He and Duranty routinely shared the favors of "the fair damozel J.C." just as they shared an interest in dope. It was an affable *ménage à trois*: sex with the one partner, drugs with the other, a little magic on the side. Duranty patiently tutored Crowley upon the rather startling side effects of continued use of the drug opium.

To his initial distress, Crowley found his "Baculum . . . hard to lift and impossible to discharge," during sexual intercourse, "although almost continuously on the point of so doing."

> Brother W.D. records similar effects from prolonged opium smoking. The condition is intensely enjoyable, once the mind has dismissed its impatience or mistrust of a good Chinese. The pleasure goes and grows. It becomes Joy in the present, in the Way itself. It is childish after all, to lust for Result. I've proved it in High Magick, in all holy things; so also in this holiest.[16]

It is not uninteresting to envisage Walter Duranty in this last year before the war idling away an hour in the dank basement of Crowley's apartment, or perhaps more comfortably in a sidewalk café on boulevard du Montparnasse, chatting avidly about his penis, the miraculous effects of opium upon it, and the inevitable similarity between it and

Crowley's own "stick, staff, or rod," as he was wont to call it. And this was after Duranty had turned thirty.

He was highly sexed from the beginning, and it is little wonder that it was Duranty who, in the end, attracted the enduring affection of Jane Cheron, for whatever that turned out in the long run to be worth.

Early in life, Duranty had acknowledged his intense attraction to the opposite sex and had come to accept quite realistically that, unattractive as he was physically, he would have to do something if he was to be able to indulge his inclinations. What, he asked himself seriously, could *he* do that other men could not? He was intelligent, had brains, he decided, and he set out to make himself interesting by dazzling women with his conversational abilities.

He boasted later in life that he taught himself, by careful study, how to be interesting, inventing a distinctive style of talk.[17] One woman would later say, "He had a kind of magic. . . . He could make you laugh. An evening with him was like an evening with no one else."[18]

"It was the things he talked about," another friend said, "the way in which he talked. His voice would sink into a whisper, then get louder, but never very loud, his voice thin, quiet, with hardly any resonance at all."[19] When he hit upon a fascinating topic, like sex or politics, Duranty's eyes would sparkle with a tiny gleam, at once humorous and intriguing. And part of the charm was that Duranty, unlike other reputed raconteurs, was also a good listener, always allowing the other person to talk as well. It was in this way, despite his looks, that he was able to develop an attraction for women, to the extent that a distinguished journalist in summing up Duranty's achievements during his lifetime would call him "one of the great lady's men of his generation."[20] Long after he had lost his leg and loped as best he could into old age, one of his ladies would confide to one well-known New York socialite that his sexual prowess was "simply amazing."[21]

The ladies might have been surprised to discover that Duranty always said he liked them dumb and in a recreational mode. He was, moreover, an early adherent to the theories of Otto Weininger,[22] whose 1906 dissertation *Sex and Character* disqualified women from any serious contention in the intellectual or creative realms, provinces reserved strictly for men, since a woman was unable to take any interest in a thing for itself, "only in proportion of how much she wants to be loved."[23] Weininger, it may be remembered, also dismissed the Jewish race along with women in that the former's basic "femininity" placed its members permanently beyond the pale of serious achievement. Upon publishing his tract, which initiated something of a cult philosophy among the intelligentsia in the early days of the century, Weininger promptly committed suicide.

A short time before he became drama critic for the *New York Times,* Alexander Woollcott, on his first trip abroad, met Walter Duranty on the *terrasse* of La Closerie des Lilas, a "rather scatterbrained young ne'er-do-well" who had about him "a faint air of skullduggery." Like many others before and after him, Woollcott fell prey to the peculiar charm Duranty could always exercise by virtue of skillful conversation: "No other man . . . could make a purposeless hour at the sidewalk café so memorably delightful," Woollcott would say.[24]

Duranty had worked up some harebrained scheme that the drama critic found amusing. There was a night at the Bal Bullier nightclub "when Duranty went among the dancers distributing yellow hand-bills which proclaimed the debut of the 'neveu du dieu Oscar Wilde' with the legend 'On parlera, on chantera, on boxera.'" Duranty planned to take the pretty young man to Bucharest and sell him there as Bombardier Wells, leaving town before the Rumanians discovered the truth.[25] In fact, at the time Duranty was pushing his outlandish scheme at the Bal Bullier, sometime during the summer of 1914, he had already been reporting for the *New York Times* for about six months, and he was still heavily involved with Crowley and with Cheron, as well as with the sticky substance of the poppy.

Wythe Williams, the head of the Paris bureau of the *New York Times*, was sitting in his office, a dingy little cubicle up five flights of stairs on the rue Louis le Grand. Williams had been in Paris only a short time, making out as best he could, with few acquaintances and no command of the language. Unexpectedly, a couple of young men came rushing into his office babbling about a Frenchman who intended to fly upside down in an airplane. The feat was to take place somewhere near the city. Did Williams want the story?

The younger one, a "pale and carelessly dressed" Englishman, said he intended to write it; the older man, an American, would take photographs. Williams turned them down, explaining there were no provisions in his meager budget to pay for such a piece. But the Englishman was persistent. They were the only outsiders who knew about the event, he insisted, and he bubbled with such good-humored enthusiasm that Williams gave in.

The next morning, the young man returned as he had promised, with his manuscript—an impossible piece of work, the "story just as upside-down as the airman had flown." In that first attempt at writing for the newspapers, Walter Duranty showed "no sense of journalism," Williams remembered. When he told Duranty that, however, it didn't seem to faze him. Duranty's eyes "never wavered," and he answered, "'I know that. . . . You please rewrite it and let me watch how it is done.' I did so," Williams said, "with Duranty looking over my shoulder, and gave this well-known journalist his first lesson in preparing copy for a newspaper."[26]

The story the pair put together chronicled the "extraordinary aerial acrobatics" of the famed airman Alphonse Pégoud, and the event—one of the earliest demonstrations of "looping the loop"—was heralded as "an epoch-making experiment."

"At Juvisy this morning," their story began, "the aviator Pégoud performed the astounding feat of flying upside down in an aeroplane."

Several days ago he left his machine in midair and came to earth in a parachute. While dropping to the ground he saw his aeroplane fly upside down by itself and land safely, right side up. He then conceived the idea of making the machine repeat the performance, with himself in it. . . .

At the moment of his departure he was by far the calmest person present.

He rose to a height of 3,000 feet and then turned the nose of the machine earthward. For 200 feet it fell like a stone. It then turned inward till it was flying on its back, after which it rose perpendicularly upward. Then it completed the circle by regaining its normal flying position, having accomplished an apparent impossibility.[27]

The story marked a turning point for the aspiring reporter. Duranty was unemployed, without a sou to his name, but was somehow managing to survive in the Latin Quarter, a section of Paris that Williams knew little about. He himself had tended to stay with the moneyed and exclusive American colony who—unlike the expatriates who replaced them after the war—preferred in those days to stay on the Right Bank. Duranty kept coming back, again and again, insisting he wanted to become a journalist. "He called every day," Williams remembered later, "his eyes always shining as he asked questions about what made up the news." Williams told him that the *New York Times* paid little, that "a part of the payment was the glory." But Duranty said he didn't care about money. "He finally talked himself into a position," Williams said, "because he talked so much I could no longer refuse him and arranged with the *Times* to give him a salary."[28]

The Pégoud feat had taken place on the lst of September 1913. Walter Duranty went to work three months later for the *New York Times*, on December 1st.

On December 31st, "the last day of the vulgar year 1913," Aleister Crowley began the first of twenty-three ritualistic happenings called "the Paris workings." They were aimed at evoking the gods Jupiter and Mercury. The first ceremony toward achieving this end was to receive the sacrament "from a certain priest, A.B." which Crowley proceeded to do at 5.35 p.m., as recorded in his diary, a precise account of his varied and excessive life. Priest A.B. was Walter Duranty,[29] and what receiving the sacrament meant, in effect, was "that Crowley received his semen."[30] Precisely how this was accomplished was never fully disclosed; nevertheless, it was recorded that participants in "the Paris workings" were given over to painting "prime pantacles" in various preordained places, jumping from one spot to another vigorously, and chanting "*Sanguis et Semen! Sanguis et Semen!*" (Blood and Semen! Blood and Semen!) along with more lengthy Latin recitations. Duranty translated most of the verse concocted by the pair, "he being the better Latinist."[31]

> Every drop of semen which Hermes sheds is a world. . . . Those worlds are held in chains, but invisibly. People upon the worlds are like maggots upon an apple—all forms of life bred by the worlds are in the nature of parasites.[32]

The sixteenth "working" was perhaps the most impressive of the twenty-three. Crowley "became inspired and entered a trance," in which he was given instructions to place a wax phallus, carved earlier, into "a besica" (a shallow dish in the shape of "the yoni" or female pudendum) and that a sparrow or pigeon should be slain before the Accendat, the sacrifice taking place while chanting these words, *Nunc flavi Jovi spumantem sanguine saevo Passerem* (Now I have blown to

Jupiter a sparrow foaming with fierce blood) or "other such words as may be suggested by the Art-Bachelor W.D."

Then, during the ceremony, Crowley cut the figure four on the breast of another partner named Victor Neuburg, encircled his head with a chain, and flogged him on the buttocks. The pair recited another of Duranty's verses in Latin before attempting to commit sodomy. Since neither man was in actual fact homosexual, the attempt was a failure—as were presumably the "Paris workings" themselves in their goal of raising the specters of Jupiter and Mercury in Crowley's apartment.

Of these activities Duranty would later say little, only that he no longer believed in anything. "But wouldn't it be funny," he once remarked to a woman friend of his in Russia, "if all the magicians went to heaven."[33]

In that last year before the war, Walter Duranty was a chameleon-like figure darting in and around the crowds that thronged the boulevards of the Latin Quarter, at once a member of that strange underground that has always been an invisible layer in Paris and simultaneously a member of growing importance in the American establishment.

He showed Wythe Williams a new Paris, one where painters and their models—"*les petites fleurs* of Paris"—sat at sidewalk cafés darning the socks of their lovers. Here on the Left Bank, the boulevardiers still strolled along the beautiful avenues past the homely domestic array, creating the perfect scene for *La Bohème*: struggling writers, sculptors, painters, creative artists of all kinds, came to the cafés with their dogs and sipped wine in the declining light of afternoon.[34] Drinks were a franc apiece, beer or champagne.

Young women carrying parasols paraded in their pale garbs beside the Seine. The Paris stage was still graced by the presence of the Divine Sarah Bernhardt, and by a revival of Shakespeare's *Antony and Cleopatra*, produced by Firman Gemier and including a scene in which the revelers were nude.[35] It was a Paris of extravagant beauty and outlandish behavior—*la belle Époque*, something a good deal more than a rarified atmosphere of frail pastels.

Duranty made his headquarters the Café du Dôme on the boulevard du Montparnasse, at the time a small café with only two small rooms, very few tables, and a bar. Wythe Williams, who had become charmed by the scene and fast friends with Duranty, would sit along-

37

side him, occasionally chatting with Jo Davidson or Cecil Howard, the well-known but hopelessly impoverished sculptors, or the painter A. G. Warshawsky. Williams was a heavy-set, baby-faced family man with a pugnacious tilt to his head—a man's man—who had no difficulty discerning in Duranty a like sensibility. At worst, Duranty seemed an irrepressible scamp; at best, a mirrored reflection of the values of those around him. Besides, he knew so much, he was in touch with so many different sets in the city that he was becoming more and more invaluable.

By now, Alexander Woollcott had joined them in his brief spring sojourn that would stretch into the beginning of summer 1914. The previous autumn, Woollcott had been offered the Paris office of the *New York Times*, which, for reasons undisclosed, he declined. By the winter of 1914, he would have returned home to New York to take up the position of drama critic at the newspaper.[36] But now, he relaxed with his "old pal of the Paris office," Walter Duranty.

Woollcott was known for his easy living, conspicuous consumption, and inclination to gamble. A story made the rounds that purported to show the character of the *bon-vivant*. Once, Woollcott "cleaned out Walter Duranty at bézique in the days when the famous correspondent was an impecunious reporter in Paris." When Duranty asked for a two-franc loan for cab fare home in the early hours of the morning, Woollcott, it was said, "became the steely-eyed gamester. 'I won that money fairly, Duranty ... and I keep it as I won it.'"[37] Despite the incident, Woollcott remained a firm friend of Duranty's, always describing him as "an exhilarating companion of my youth."

After Woollcott reluctantly returned to the States, in the few weeks just before the start of the First World War, Duranty and Williams continued with their friendship, the former avoiding mention of his pal Crowley, who perhaps by this time was turning into something of a liability for the upwardly mobile Duranty.

On a raw afternoon in March 1914, Madame Henriette Caillaux, wife of the former premier of France, walked into the office of Gaston Calmette, pulled out a revolver, and fired six shots at close range, killing the editor of *Le Figaro* instantly.

On a stifling morning in July of the same year, 142 newspaper correspondents crowded into a small courtroom at the Palais de Justice to witness the trial of Madame Caillaux for murder, in what had become an international *cause célèbre* that had forced the resignation of her husband as Minister of Finance and embarrassed the French government. Some of the reporters, it was rumored, had paid as much as $200 apiece for their seats. The courtroom suffered from poor ventilation. One of the newsmen complained, and an official of the court cracked two of the seven windows slightly. It promised to be a hot afternoon.

"As the hands of the courtroom clock pointed to 11:30, Wythe Williams became aware of a small commotion in the crowded aisle nearby. A court attendant was elbowing a passage through the spectators in the rear, making way for a reporter for *Le Petit Parisien*."[38] The new arrival was "a fat, perspiring man," who had come as a temporary replacement for his colleague whose lunch break had just begun. The pair crawled awkwardly in opposite directions over the laps of the seated reporters. Just as he squeezed into his colleague's empty seat, the fat man leaned over to an acquaintance and said in a low voice: "There is a panic on the Bourse." The Englishman seated beside Williams, whom Williams had earlier written off as the smug, "superior" type, whispered that the bankers must be frightened by the Austrian demands on Serbia.[39]

A month before, on the 28th of June, the Archduke Franz Ferdinand and his wife Sophie, heirs to the monarchy of the Habsburgs, who for centuries had been rulers of the Austro-Hungarian Empire, had been assassinated in Sarajevo, capital of the small southeast European state of Bosnia. The assassin was a young Serb extremist, one of a group of conspirators who wanted Bosnia to separate from the Empire in order to join Serbia, their national state. Although the Austrians found no proof that the Serb government had been involved in the conspiracy, they nevertheless sent an ultimatum to Serbia. On the 25th of July, the Serbs accepted the ultimatum, listing only a few reservations, these obviously an attempt at saving face.

It was to these events that the English journalist was referring when he whispered to Wythe Williams at the trial of Madame Caillaux. At lunch in the basement of the Palais de Justice, the pair took seats beside one another. Williams remembered the Englishman saying, "'It will be jolly annoying if this Bourse business develops into war, you know.'"[40]

When Williams returned to the *New York Times* bureau that night, Duranty was full of the hubbub that had hit the Bourse. He excitedly told Williams that the financial house that had started all the frantic selling had "connections in Vienna"; it was the same one that only a couple of years before had "made millions just before the onset of the last Balkan war."[41] The pair looked at one another for a long minute before returning to their work on the Caillaux trial. After about an hour, Williams turned to Duranty and commented that the story was running at about 2000 words. He thought it would probably lead the *Times* the next morning because of "all the direct testimony." He told Duranty to mark the cable file "rush."

"But about this panic on the Bourse story. Don't you think we should send a special on that?" Duranty asked. Before Williams could answer, the men heard something outside. "Listen!" Duranty said sharply, and the pair stood up, rushed over to the windows, and looked down on the boulevard des Italiens, which lay just below one side of the building. Williams thought the approaching crowd was yelling "Down with Caillaux!" but Duranty said no, it was something else.

The Austrians had broken off relations with Serbia, declaring war on the tiny nation. Everyone knew what that meant. Soon Russia, the patron and protector of Serbia, would join in the fray, in turn dragging in other countries. Williams and Duranty could now make out what the approaching mob was yelling: "À Berlin! À Berlin! Alsace! À Berlin!"[42]

Williams quickly ordered Duranty to halve the Caillaux story, and, warning him that it was now "a race with the censor," he said "to crowd everything possible on the cable before he gets on the job." The two of them worked feverishly, pasting everything from the late editions onto the cable forms to be wired to New York. Duranty wanted to carry it down to the Bourse himself, just to see whether "there were any signs of the censor."[43]

He returned, some time later, looking dishevelled and roughed up. Williams would remember that he had been "trembling with excitement." On his way back from the Bourse, where he had seen no evidence whatever of a censor, Duranty had decided on the spur of the moment to stop by the Gare du Nord, where vast crowds of Americans were assembling. Thousands, Duranty said, were "fighting for places in the trains for England." Suddenly, someone in the crowd recognized

40

Duranty as a foreigner, and they turned on him. After a fracas, Duranty found himself arrested by a policeman, who, looking over his identity papers, released him immediately.

As Duranty finished telling this story to Williams, there came again the sound of cries and shouting in the street below. Duranty and Williams rushed for a second time that evening to the window. A man had yelled "Vive l'Allemagne" out of one of the upper-story windows, and now the mob was ripping off the boards that had been nailed across his shop's windows earlier in the day. He was a German art dealer. As the mob tore off the boards, they used them as "battering rams through the plate glass," destroying everything inside.[44] Duranty rushed down, but came back a few minutes later. Breathing heavily, he reported that

> "A man came out holding a marble Adonis by the arm . . . and [a] cop said to him, 'Be good now—be good!' and the chap replied, 'Well, if I can't smash it, you smash it!—So the cop took it and leaped upon it with both feet."[45]

The crowds beneath the window continued to gather until there were well over ten thousand people in the streets below the *Times* bureau, singing the "Marseillaise" for hours, Williams reported, "with a solemn hatred of their national enemy sounding in every note."[46] At last cuirassiers moved in on the mob with their horses, breaking it up for the night.

When the singing began to die down, the two men lit up their pipes, and Duranty asked whether they shouldn't "cut it out for a few hours?" As Williams nodded his assent, they heard a wild cry from outside. They were in time to see the sickly sight of "a broken body across the saddle of one of the cuirassiers," the man who had earlier given the cheer for Germany.[47]

He was the first casualty of the war.

Late that night the two men took a long walk, ending up at the great golden dome of the Invalides, which shelters the tomb of Napoleon. "The same thought was in both our minds," Williams said. "Did France then have a general comparable to the one sleeping there?"

> We wandered back across the Seine, staring into its waters glinting in the early sunlight, and then went to a Turkish bath for a few hours'

41

rest, in prep for another hectic day and night. The complete stillness of that luxurious marble-lined room, except for a tinkling fountain and the soft padding of barefoot attendants, was unreal, apart from the new nightmare of life.[48]

Then, on their way home in the early hours of the morning, they spotted "a poster beside the Tricolor of France that draped the entrance to the newspaper, *Gil Blas*: 'Every employee of this paper is of military age and therefore is now in the service of France. *Gil Blas* necessarily suspends publication, perhaps forever.'"[49]

The days following witnessed a wave of destruction across the city, which took place in the name of patriotism. No one with a German name was safe as the mobs roamed the streets, systematically demolishing the houses and shops of the "spies," destroying their belongings, or claiming them as booty. "Suspected German sympathizers were hounded and beaten. There were cheers for Britain, for Belgium, for the United States. . . ."[50]

American tourists in Paris found to their dismay that the banks were refusing their drafts for money. Stranded and desperate to leave, they lined up by the thousands in front of the American Embassy, trying to find a way to get the cash for their passage home. Williams decided this was a big story and set about to get a list of their names and addresses to be published by the *New York Times*. He hired a virtual army of "fledgling" assistants to carry out the immense task. When at last the list was completed, he carried it to the cable office, only to find that the censor refused it on the grounds that it might contain some secret code that could in some way give aid or comfort to the enemy.[51] It was Williams's first run-in with the French censors, but it wouldn't be his last.

He regretted, he told Duranty, having delayed in setting up an alternative method of submission to the New York office other than through official channels. He had talked much about such a project with the *Times* editors in the New York office, but never actually got around to putting it into operation.

Now it was too late.

Events led quickly and irrevocably toward a war that would engulf all of Europe, and much besides. Immediately after the Austro-Hungarian government's declaration of war against Serbia, Russia began a retaliatory mobilization, which, once begun, was not easily halted. Austria's allies, the Germans, sent an ultimatum that demanded Russian demobilization within twelve hours. When the Russians refused, Germany declared war against them. Two days later, the Germans declared war on France and, on the 2nd of August, demanded free passage through Belgium.

When Belgium refused, Germany invaded its territory, bringing into operation the so-called Schlieffen plan, envisaged "as a sort of funnel through which German armies could pass, then flood out beyond the French armies and encircle them."[52] After brief consideration, Great Britain declared war on Germany, the only Allied Power to do so, instead of having war declared upon it. In a curious anti-climax, Austria-Hungary at last declared war upon Russia on the 6th of August.

Thus it was that when the verdict of "not guilty" was delivered at the murder trial of Madame Caillaux, nearly two-thirds of the original group of journalists present during the arguments were no longer there to hear it.

By the beginning of September 1914 the tourists were scrambling out of Paris like insects caught in a sudden flash of bright light. They were joined in their exodus by many of the French bourgeoisie, who had gathered together what belongings they could and fled. Those journalists who were married sent their wives and children out with the others, they themselves staying on in the city. On the 5th of September the Germans crossed the Marne.

The American and British correspondents gathered where they always had—on the *terrasse* of the Café Napolitain—and waited. It was a warm afternoon, Indian summer, the sun "casting straight shadows of the full leaves, down on the tree-lined sidewalks." The city had frozen. No one appeared on the streets. Communications with the outside world were practically non-existent: no telegraph, practically no telephone. Paris was "a city detached—apart from the rest of the world." That night, "every auto-taxi in the city was conveying a portion of General Maunoury's army out of the north gates, to fall on the enemy's right flank," and the next morning all through the city were heard "the opening guns of the Battle of the Marne."[53]

It was the world's most decisive battle since Waterloo. Had it ended differently, the history of the twentieth century might have taken a radically different course. At its end, more than half a million men had been killed, wounded, or captured. The battle presaged the massive casualties that lay ahead, in a war that came to be called "Armageddon" by the correspondents who covered it.

The battle was a strategic victory for the Allied armies, and importantly for French morale, Paris was saved. But the Allies' immediate counteroffensive quickly bogged down, halted by a defensive line made up of holes scratched hastily into the ground and manned by "[o]ne man with a machine gun . . . more powerful than advancing masses. Trench warfare had begun."[54]

An unexpectedly severe system of censorship locked quickly into place as French officials sputtered out a series of rules under which men might "accompany the armies of France and write about the war."[55] The first rule, that war correspondents had to be citizens of one of the Allied nations, had the immediate effect of disqualifying any American reporting in France. In addition, correspondents had to have "perfect knowledge of the French language." It was said that the test devised to determine this facility was on a level that "would baffle a Sorbonne professor."[56] Moreover, all dispatches were to be written in French for the convenience of the censor.

It was also required that war correspondents sign a pledge of loyalty to the French army. They were to wear white armlets with their names and nationalities and that of their newspapers clearly written in black letters, and they were to be accompanied to predetermined locations by specially detailed officers, all of them lodged and transported at the expense of the French government.[57]

The atmosphere of rumor and misinformation that resulted from the virtual suppression of accurate news led to a kind of frenzy when word of defeats and casualties did finally leak out. Meantime, the propaganda machine churned out stories of German atrocities against the French and the Belgians. "The Bureau de la Presse, which controlled war news in France . . . disseminated atrocity stories at such a rate that the French press ceased to put individual headlines on them and simply ran them week after week under the same title: LES ATROCITÉS ALLEMANDES."[58] There were tales of babies whose hands and feet had been cut off, nuns whose breasts had been hacked away, a Canadian soldier who had been crucified, and the most bizarre, "the solemn assertion that the Germans had tied [a] village priest to his bell and used him as a live clapper."[59]

Wythe Williams said later that Duranty was one of those most willing to believe in the wickedness of anything German. Upon hearing the atrocity propaganda, Duranty set off on his own, without any particular authority to do so except his own solemn belief in the veracity of the stories, to determine their truth. He duly returned, Williams reported, admitting "that none of the rumours of wanton killings and torture could be verified."[60]

During these first years of the war, Duranty remained too much a novice to be considered for use as a war correspondent, and he stayed mainly in Paris, picking up what news was current in the capital. At home his countrymen were queuing up to enlist. In later years, there would emerge several myths—the sort that always surround celebrity—that purported to explain why Walter Duranty never served in the armed services himself during World War I. Some would say, mistakenly, that he was exempted from service because of his leg. Others had the notion he had lost his leg in the war, taking it as a matter of course. But it was still several years before Duranty would have the accident that cost him his left limb. Finally, a cult of pacifism grew up around the famous Duranty: in his obituary it would be said that "he was of the generation which was rigidly pacifist on political grounds."[61]

Realistically speaking, it would hardly have been in character for the self-interested Duranty to rush home to join the throngs volunteering for what would become the most futile slaughter in the history of warfare. What Duranty really needed was an excuse, and the eloquent apologia he devolved later in life lent dignity to his rather conspicuous decision not to fight. He had known, he estimated, some 3,000 boys during his schooling, and "pitiless statistics" showed him that two-thirds of them were dead. "So that," Duranty wrote, "if you will forgive me, is why I don't talk of the friends of my youth and why I am not overproud to think I'm still alive."[62]

Wythe Williams, on the other hand, volunteered to drive an ambulance, disgruntled by a censorship system that prevented him from reaching the front. He was "determined to do something useful and served under fire at Amiens";[63] anything seemed better to him than sitting uselessly around the Paris bureau. By early 1915, the French relented. They had realized at last that depriving a potential ally like

America of news was a tactical error. Williams thus managed to get himself accredited by the beginning of February that year, sending the *New York Times* "the first authentic detailed description of the French forces after the battle of the Marne."[64]

In the meantime, Duranty developed into that kind of reporter who takes "unholy glee" in the discomfiture of the political figures he was reporting—a type common among correspondents who deal daily with local corruption. By the time he had been with the *Times* a couple of years, he had begun to view the events he reported with the detachment of the cynic.[65] This changed radically when he got a first-hand taste of wartime death.

It came in his first big war story—the Zeppelin raid over Paris in early 1916, which he later said "was more horrible than the Russian famine of 1921, when millions died."[66] No doubt it was, to a green reporter unexperienced in the wages of war. It seems to have impressed his mind more significantly than any of the events to follow.

Six hundred and sixty feet long, the Zeppelins were ten times larger than a blimp. Their rigid framework was covered with fabric, the inside filled with gas bags. The original strategic bombers, they wreaked havoc on many European cities, their threat extending as far north as the English Midlands, as far east as Moscow. More terrible still was the hysterical reaction they engendered among the target population. Rumors abounded that the Germans were using the bombers to release poison gases and even deadly bacteria. In one case, the high incidence of gangrene in the surviving victims of an attack over London led British doctors to charge that a virus had been released along with the bombs.[67] The charges were publicly denied by German officials. But the fear and terror continued unabated.

On the 30th of January 1916, Walter Duranty and a friend were strolling near the Place de la Concorde when they noticed Lloyd George and Bonar Law entering the Hôtel de Crillon. Lloyd George later that year became Prime Minister of England, and Bonar Law, his Chancellor of the Exchequer. Duranty's companion remarked that the "Zeppelins could have a good bag if they could drop a bomb now." It was a grim joke, not all that funny considering the recent attack made by the unwieldly but deadly bombers upon the city of Epernay.

Three hours later, Duranty was sitting at a sidewalk café when "police and firemen began extinguishing lamps and the whisper passed, 'Zeppelins signaled approaching the city.'" The reaction of the crowds was unexpected. They rushed into the streets, almost as if it were a holiday, "excited and light-hearted, watching the aeroplanes darting across the sky like shooting stars." Then a rumor passed through the crowd that hits had been made in the suburbs.

Duranty somehow made it to a telephone to call the bureau, discovering that "some fifteen bombs had fallen near the fortifications in the populous tenement district." He grabbed a cab and headed in the direction of the stricken area. He arrived near midnight, according to the newspaper account he wrote about the event.

> Around each doorway was gathered an excited group of children half dressed and running about shouting. From the whole quarter arose a murmur like the buzz of a huge and angry hive of bees. As I stumbled through the darkness—the taxi was not allowed to pass—I heard constantly one word, "reprisals," as the keynote of every conversation and shouted in every gathering. . . . At the smitten street . . . the firemen and police were busy amid the ruin, and bodies awaiting removal to the Morgue were lying on heaps of rubbish in the narrow courtyards. The houses that had been hit looked exactly like the photographs of gun-ravaged towns. Here half the front of a house had been torn away, leaving a child's cot hanging over the edge. Its occupant was somewhere under the ruins, and the neighbors were trying to comfort the frantic mother in the next-door kitchen.
>
> The worst case of all was a five-storey tenement at the end of a cul-de-sac. . . . Here the family of a zouave, Auguste Petitjean, were celebrating the father's leave from the front. His wife and 15-year-old daughter, Lucie, his old father-in-law . . . and his sister . . . with her two little boys . . . had gathered around a table to hear stories of the war. Suddenly the war struck them. All seven were killed instantly. When I left there four bodies already had been recovered.[68]

The story, as Duranty wrote it, was in a style that would become easily distinguishable with its dramatic attention to detail, its use of the personalized "I," Duranty himself a character in the action. There would develop in his work an epic sweep upwards toward literary climax; he never permitted downward motion. At the end of the Zeppelin dispatch, he spoke of stern faces, savage voices, advancing his moral to the tragic story: "Germany must pay."[69]

For Duranty, the news event was the vehicle for dramatic action.

He was more writer than reporter. Whatever happened, Duranty would somehow convert it into a good story. And there would always be that mingling of truth and the elements of fiction in his work, a certain liberty—poetic license, if you will—more interpretative, less objective, at times, some would say, fatally flawed by constant wavering and equivocation.

And then there was the straight request that he lie to support the interests of the war effort. The circumstances have been lost but the fact of one falsified story was recorded by Duranty himself. In the summer of 1917, he said, he was called upon to write a fake story for the Allied propaganda machine. "I was young and inexperienced, but I had to decide the question alone," he recorded afterwards. His first thought was the competition. His colleagues, called upon to do the same thing, might not, he mused, be as honest as he. Then he tried on another idea: that the story *might* be true in a world where all things were possible. But it wouldn't wash.

Finally, he found himself in a bar with Navy men, and after "a bleary session" he at last wrote his "eyewitness account" of a naval battle in which the Allied naval forces thwarted a German submarine attack.

Walter Duranty was thirty-three when he wrote the falsified story, and during that period of his life, he fancied himself a poet in the e. e. cummings style, an idea he would never completely abandon. He recorded his misgivings over the faked dispatch in a poem, which depicted his moral dilemma: "i sat and wondered whether the End justified the means/as many another reporter had wondered before me/ and whether that meant any end justified any means/i decided it didnt," he wrote.

It was the question that would haunt his career from the beginning, the same question that would plague the Bolsheviks later, as they invented the Soviet Union—it would become the catchphrase of the Thirties as the West entered the Great Depression and the Soviets seemingly created paradise on earth.

The young Duranty was sure "any end" did not justify "any means" all right. But "whether a noble end justified any means/i wasnt so sure about that."

Finally, Duranty asked himself whether "a noble end" justified "somewhat doubtful means," and on this question he just "fancied it might."[70]

CHAPTER III

For You But Not for Me

One of the more unpleasant side effects of smoking opium to excess is a kind of hallucinatory insomnia, and in February of 1917 Duranty's lover Jane Cheron was having a hard time getting a decent night's sleep. Not for the first time in her life (nor would it be the last) she decided to go to the south of France for the cure. With the hardcore user, there is always the question whether taking the cure is a bona fide attempt to break the habit; or whether, the pleasurable effects of the drug having been diminished, eradicated, or even reversed from excessive use, the aim is simply to purge one's body of the drug so as to renew the intensity of the pleasure when its use is resumed.

Whatever the case, Cheron went south, probably to St. Tropez, one of her favorite haunts. She went with her "young man," who was also in need of the cure.[1] It is not known whether this young man was Walter Duranty, and Cheron's relationships were sufficiently casual that there is no way to be sure. What is known is that she and Duranty were locked in a relationship that would lead to marriage, and despite the difference in their ages—Duranty was said to be considerably her junior[2]—they would remain paired at least nominally for many years to come. All of Duranty's colleagues identified her as his wife, and on several occasions, she played hostess to his host in a variety of social situations, some more stimulating than others.

On this particular occasion, Cheron rid herself of her insomnia more quickly than she had expected. To her complete surprise, she fell almost immediately into a deep and nourishing sleep, and "in the morning, she found that she had—between sleeping and waking—copied the pantacle of Ankh-f-n-Khonsu on a great sheet of paper. . . .³ This was one of Aleister Crowley's great magical emblems.

Although Cheron and Crowley had been frequent bed partners, she had never shown an interest in his magic, much to his disappointment. But in this case, Cheron cared enough about what had occurred to have the pantacle embroidered in silk upon a cloth some four feet long. She saved it for several years, until she saw Crowley once more and could show it to him.

From Aleister Crowley's point of view, the event was of major importance since Cheron was a Nonbeliever, and when he saw the pantacle, he openly rejoiced. It was, he realized, "an unmistakable sign." In Crowley's world, however, there was rarely any shortage of signs. He remained certain all his life, for instance, that "the Paris workings," which he had initiated on New Year's Eve, 1913, and continued into the early months of 1914, had in fact been the basic cause of the First World War.⁴ Responsible though he may have been for that great holocaust, he was one of the first out of Paris once it had begun.

One of the first ones back in was a man who seemed an unlikely candidate—Duranty's old pal Alexander Woollcott, or Aleck, as he preferred to be called by his friends. Pudgy and artistically inclined, the *New York Times* drama critic didn't seem cut out for the vicissitudes of soldiering, but immediately after the United States declared war on Germany in April 1917, there he was, lining up to share in all of the rights and privileges extended to a private in the U.S. Army. He hoped, he explained somewhat shamefacedly to his friends, that basic training would run some of the fat off him, and it must have done so because he good-humoredly made it through the ordeal and thus across the Atlantic, making light of any inconvenience or embarrassment he had suffered. What he had intended was to join the fighting men at the front, but he ended up on the "bedpan brigade" at a hospital in Savenay. Not surprisingly, he was immensely popular, not only with the string of celebrities who found their way into the orderly room at the hospital but also with his patients and fellow workers. Somehow, he always managed to have a bottle of something drinkable on hand for anything that could be construed as an appropriate occasion. Duranty turned up there regularly.[5]

And of course, when Woollcott wasn't on duty, he traveled to Paris, where he managed, despite the hardships imposed by the war, to live characteristically high. "His special haunts were the Café Napolitain, where he stood drinks to all comers and held forth oracularly to all listeners in alternate French and English, and the Cornille . . . in the Latin Quarter. . . ."[6] There, he initiated "a convivial poker game" that continued intermittently throughout the war. At Christmas in 1917, Woollcott, Duranty, and Wythe Williams managed to get together for "a real reunion" at the Parisian flat of Heywood Broun of the *New York Tribune* and his wife Ruth, who lured them all with the promise that they would "collapse from overeating" if they contrived to get there.[7]

Surprisingly, Aleck Woollcott became one of the best-known war correspondents at the front. A few months after the Christmas feast at the Brouns he was drafted for work on *Stars and Stripes,* the U.S. military newspaper, where he met Harold Ross, later the editor of *The New Yorker* and one of the original founders of the Thanatopsis Club that met at the Algonquin Hotel in New York. Ross was running *Stars and Stripes*, and Private Albian A. Wallgren of the Marines was working up the cartoons. Wallgren took one look at Woollcott and created the character that would make Woollcott the most beloved mascot of the American enlisted man. Soon, this new cartoon character appeared on the pages of *Stars and Stripes*: the figure of a "chubby soldier in uniform and a raincoat, his gas mask worn correctly across his chest, and a small musette bag at his side, tin hat placed correctly, straight across his head, puttees rolled beautifully, prancing with that almost effeminate rolling gait of Aleck's."[8]

Meantime, Woollcott made his way fearlessly in and around the front, gathering material for the kinds of things the fighting men wanted to read: stories about rotten cooks, nosey dogs, leaky boots, and other common nuisances of life at the front. He was well known as "Our Intrepid Hero, Med. Sgt. Alexander H. Woollcott—A War Correspondent For Whom The Front Never Had No Terrors."[9]

Wherever Woollcott went, light-hearted stories followed. He wrote to a friend that he was "on Montmartre not long ago with my dear Walter Duranty, than whom no one can have a warmer spot in my foolish heart."

> As we were skating home in midnight darkness, a polite young lady
> (who was out shopping, I suppose) linked arms with us and walked all
> the way bantering to the opera. Walter urged her on me as one pas-
> sionate as a lion. I whispered to her that he was passionate as a rabbit,
> which is much more to the point. In leaving, she confided to the stars
> her private opinion that we were both passionate as two plates of
> noodles.[10]

Theirs was a madcap world of enforced frivolity and steel-hearted
foolishness, a tacit determination to keep at bay the real madness that
surrounded them, and threatened to envelop and destroy an entire
continent.

During this time, Duranty made the acquaintance of a young man who
had just begun reporting for the Manchester *Guardian*, a South African
who had worked his way up from his homeland to England, where he
enlisted in the British Army. He became a junior lieutenant and fought
at Ypres,[11] a scene of some of the most ferocious fighting in the war. It
could be said that William Bolitho was the only reporter in Europe at
that time whose education matched Duranty's own.[12] Certainly Bolitho (his full name was William Bolitho Ryall) would have a prolific
literary output in the coming decade.

Duranty credited Bolitho with teaching him "nearly all about the
newspaper business that is worth knowing." According to Duranty,
Bolitho "could see further through a brick wall" than anyone he ever
knew.[13] "He possessed to a remarkable degree . . . the gift of making a
quick and accurate summary of facts and drawing therefrom the right,
logical and inevitable conclusions."[14] Among other things, Bolitho told
Duranty grim stories about the superstitions of men at the front, who
feared they were soon to die. At one of the hot spots where Bolitho had
fought, an Irish captain terrorized the men in his regiment by accurately predicting their deaths. Whenever he mentioned that he had
found one of their names in "me little black book," they knew their
time had come. Ironically, Bolitho told Duranty, the day before the
captain himself died, he found his own name written in the book.[15] It
was Duranty's kind of story, exactly the sort of thing he found
intriguing.

With the coming of the war, Paris had undergone a fundamental
change—from a city of dilettantes and down-at-heels adventurers to

the gathering place for a new generation of intellectual leaders, young men whose ideas would radically transform the twentieth century. Now, they filled the sidewalk cafés talking earnestly of the events taking place, the eventual outcome of the war, and what it would mean in the years ahead. They had come streaming in from England, from America, from all parts of the globe either to do their part, like Ernest Hemingway or William Bolitho, or to report the fighting for the presses of the world. Sooner or later, they all turned up in the French capital for a few drinks, a game or two of poker, an exchange of news about what was really taking place at the front.

By 1917, on the Western Front, Germany occupied most of Belgium and the northeast of France, forming a more or less permanent trenchline—defended by the so-called Hindenburg line—that, once established, had moved very little. With the introduction of poison gas at the second battle of Ypres in 1915, the character of warfare had changed significantly. This was a squalid war where hundreds of thousands of casualties were squandered over a few feet of land: Mons, Verdun, the Somme, Ypres—or "Wipers" as the British soldiers called it—these were the names of places that quickly came to symbolize the futility of the fighting. Wythe Williams, among other correspondents present at the General Headquarters in Chantilly, recorded the words of the French commander-in-chief, General Joseph J. C. Joffre, who, speaking of the battle that had lasted throughout most of 1916, said: "I do not speak of the wounded. At Verdun, our losses were 460,000 killed and the Germans 540,000. It is a field of a million dead."[16]

At the Battle of the Somme which began in the summer of the same year, the first day of fighting saw 60,000 British casualties, 20,000 of them dead, in what was "the heaviest loss ever suffered in a single day by a British army or by any army in the First World War."[17] By the end of the fighting, in late November, they had advanced little more than eight miles. More than any other battle, the Somme influenced the way men came to regard the Great War: "brave helpless soldiers; blundering obstinate generals; nothing achieved."[18]

On the Eastern Front, things were no better. If possible, they were worse. It quickly became apparent that the Russians were plagued by a wholly incompetent leadership, some of whom hadn't read a military manual for decades. They also suffered from inadequate communications and from an incomprehensible shortage of war material. The battle of Tannenberg, which took place at the end of August 1914, with

53

Russian losses exceeding German at the rate of ten to one, shattered Allied confidence and presaged events still to come.

A surge of patriotic feeling had briefly unified Czarist Russia at the onset of the war, but the rally was short-lived, as defeat piled upon defeat. The German figures of Russian casualties were set at something between five million and eight million men.

Throughout the war, Russian soldiers had been routinely sent to the Eastern Front without boots, without proper clothing; all too often without even rifles or ammunition. Disorganized railroad transport and inept planning compounded the problems. With a poor industrial base from which to wage the war, the Russians depended heavily upon the Allies for even the most basic of equipment. But after their ill-fated defeat at Gallipoli in the Dardanelles, the Western Allies had been forced to give up hope of establishing a workable supply passage. As the war continued, grave shortages of food, both at the front and in the cities, heightened to crisis proportions, and the Russian people began to clamor for peace.

For the British the war had begun as a moral crusade against the Savage Hun. In the first month alone, more than half a million volunteers had enlisted to fight for King and Country, with a hundred thousand each month thereafter. Inspired among other things by the ubiquitous posters of a sternly pointing Lord Kitchener, and of women in brave profile clutching their children and saying "Go!," British volunteers for the war would number more than three million.[19] For the initial wave of idealists, it was "a war to make the world safe for democracy," a "war to end war."

This belief was shared by many of the war correspondents themselves. They remained unshakably convinced of the intrinsic rightness of the struggle. Even a veteran war reporter like England's Frederick Palmer later admitted he had believed "deep down" that this war was different from those that had gone before it. "After this exhibition of mass murder," he later wrote, "we would relegate war to past savagery in common with witch burning, imprisonment for debt, drawing and quartering, the torture chamber and hanging for thievery. Foolish dream!"[20]

Contributing to the attitude had been the initial carnival atmosphere created in part by the belief that the war wouldn't last beyond Christmas 1914, and in part by the highly publicized antics of big media names. One of the first reporters in at the onset had been the American glamor boy Richard Harding Davis, called "the hero of our dreams" by H. L. Mencken. War had been good to Davis. He was even credited with having started one—the Spanish-American War—at the behest of his boss, William Randolph Hearst, the newspaper magnate who had created an empire based on sensationalism. As a result of this and his enormous fame, Davis was the highest paid correspondent in the world, with a salary of $32,000 per year plus expenses, an immense amount of money at the time.[21] His stylish appearance and self-conscious good looks—even at the age of fifty-one—couldn't have hurt either. Davis had a strong, masculine jawline with a cleft-chin, emphasized by the high collars of the time. His hair was neatly clipped, with only the suggestion of a curling forelock across his high forehead.

He and his second wife, the former Bessie McCoy (better known as the "Yama Yama Girl" of the Ziegfeld Follies), occupied a $1000-a-day suite on the *Lusitania* on their highly publicized crossing, before Davis safely tucked Bessie away in London and set out for Belgium.[22] He managed to get a story out of Brussels before he fell into the hands of the Germans. They mistook him for a British officer out of uniform and submitted him to a summary court martial, very nearly executing the man who until now had seemed invincible, most especially to himself. He said later he had never been so frightened. Until then, war had been something of a game to Davis. Now, with his own mortality looking him in the face, Davis sank quickly into the background, licked by a war that made no provisions for media stars. He left in a huff after a decent interval, saying he wasn't "about to write sidelights."[23]

Still, Davis's belief in the rightness of the war never wavered. When he died at fifty-two of a heart attack the following year, he had on his desk the outline of a story urging American entry into the war on the Allied side.

In early 1917, the United States was still uncommitted, and Floyd Gibbons was credited with writing the story that helped to persuade the Yanks to come in. In the same tradition of flamboyance as Davis, but with something more substantial to back it up, the "nervy 29-year old Chicagoan" booked passage for Europe on the *Laconia,* a ship he and his newspaper, the Chicago *Tribune*, believed likely to be torpedoed. "When he went aboard, the *Tribune* saw to it that he was provisioned with a special life preserver, flasks of brandy and fresh water, and several flashlights."[24] Eight days later, the *Laconia* was sunk by a

German U-boat just as Gibbons had foreseen, and the survivors were picked up out of the water by rescue vessels. Gibbons, his "eyes bloodshot from wind and lack of sleep," nevertheless got off a cable warning the *Tribune* of a story to follow and began immediately typing "one of the most vivid, arresting, and detailed dispatches of the war."[25]

In Gibbons's dispatch, one of the survivors from Lifeboat 3 told about an encounter with the German submarine that sank the *Laconia*. The "black hulk" of the submarine, "glistening wet and standing about eight feet above the surface of the water," came alongside the lifeboat to ask in a distinctly German accent, "What ship was dat?" The survivors gave the name of the ship, along with its weight, and the number of passengers it held: "seventy-three . . . men, women and children, some of them in this boat."

"Vell," Gibbons reported the captain as replying, "you'll be all right. The patrol will pick you up soon," and the U-boat slid back down into the black waters. Gibbons's story was acclaimed throughout the United States, and "was read from the floor of both houses of Congress." To the readership in America, the exchange between the survivors of the *Laconia* and the submarine captain added to a growing body of evidence that the Germans' unrestricted policy of submarine warfare, even against neutral shipping, was a convincing reason why Americans could no longer stay out of the war.[26]

Gibbons was in a category all his own; a flamboyant type, yes, but a believer all the same. In a short time he would prove his mettle in a way that earned the respect of every other newsman in the field. Among them would be a newcomer, Walter Duranty, who, for all his faults, knew how to recognize the real thing when he saw it. And when Gibbons later upstaged him in the Soviet Union, Duranty still wouldn't hesitate to credit him with being the better man.

By now the English censors, like the French before them, had been forced to bow to pressure from home, this time exerted by the British Cabinet itself. At last, British Headquarters had allowed in a number of "writing chappies," among them such men as Philip Gibbs writing for the *Daily Telegraph* and the *Daily Chronicle*, Percival Phillips of the *Daily Express* and *Morning Post*, W. Beach Thomas of the *Daily Mail* and *Daily Mirror*, H. Perry Robinson of the *Times* and *Daily News*, and Herbert Russell of Reuters. Outstanding among them was the thirty-seven-year-old Gibbs. Described by his colleagues as "frail" and "sensitive," the "slender, thin-faced" Gibbs proved nevertheless to have a moral stamina that few of his colleagues could match, and despite the pressures resulting from a rigorous censorship, he immediately took the lead on the British side.

The British rules of censorship barred any mention of regiments by name and prohibited the mention of places or names of the men as well.[27] These rules were never broken by the British gentlemen who reported the war. As Gibbs put it,

> We identified ourselves absolutely with the Armies in the field. . . . We wiped out of our minds all thought of personal scoops and all temptation to write one word which would make the task of officers and men more difficult or dangerous. There was no need of censorship of our despatches. We were our own censors.[28]

When the United States entered the war on the 6th of April 1917, the rules for accreditation to the American Expeditionary Force were escalated, raising the stakes of the game. First, the correspondent had to swear to the Secretary of War or his authorized representative that he would refrain from giving any information that might be of aid to the enemy. He had to give a detailed itinerary of where he planned to go after he joined the force, the area where he intended to carry out most of his reportage. Moreover, his paper had to post a $10,000 bond "to ensure that he would comport himself 'as a gentleman of the Press.'" If a reporter did break any of the rules, the money was forfeited to charity.[29]

Many Paris-based American correspondents were already reporting the war under the censorship of the French, among them Wythe Williams for the *New York Times*, Paul Scott Mowrer of the Chicago *Daily News*, and Stoddard Dewey of the New York *Evening Post*.[30] Now, with America's entry, correspondents started pouring in from abroad. Reuters eventually had 115 men in the field, the Associated Press a smaller but substantial team of veterans. The *New York Times* would arrange a coverage "larger than any British newspaper's," and the editor, Carr Van Anda, papered his office walls with maps to keep track of his men in the field.[31]

Unlike the British, who perceived it as their duty to report favorably about the Allied cause, the Americans were not gentlemen. Wythe Williams, who had always chafed at the French censorship, was dis-

missed from the press corps "for willful violation of the censorship."
The authorities accused Williams of violating "the spirit of his accreditation agreement" by sending an article to *Collier's Weekly* without
first submitting it for approval. More damning, the article openly
attacked French politicians, blaming them for the failure of the Nivelle
offensive on the Chemin des Dames in late April 1917.[32] Very nearly
expelled from France in disgrace, Williams was saved at the last minute by Georges Clemenceau, himself a former journalist before he
became premier of France.[33] Williams's position in the press corps,
however, was considerably eroded by the incident, his reportage never
again attaining the same degree of self-confidence.

He was transferred to Pershing's headquarters about six weeks
later, clearing the way for a new man to cover the French armies for
the *New York Times*. Thus it was that Walter Duranty, still a relative
novice as a reporter, entered the mêlée of idealists, adventurers, stunt-
men, egoists, and hard-core newsmen who had elected to cover this
war. Somehow, he would be like none of them.

By June of 1917 the Anglo-American Press Mission attached to the
French General Headquarters consisted of three French officers, four
British, and four Americans. At the end of the month, Walter Duranty,
who had been handling stories emanating from the Paris bureau,
joined these front-line veterans. It was obviously a try-out for the eager
Duranty, and he wanted to do well.

At their quarters, the correspondents "dwelt in monastic luxury,
served by ... orderlies and eating the choicest foods."[34] The cook was
a soldier who, formerly having been assistant chef at the Ritz in Paris,
was now comfortably sitting out the war in a lucky assignment. Duranty found himself housed in a chateau located "about two miles out
of town on the Paris road" in opulent surroundings. "The fittings were
modern and elegant," one of his fellow reporters would write, "even
to a squash court adjoining the stables. The peacocks that paraded the
lawns, spreading their tails and blowing their shrill tin trumpets, were
typical of the place."[35] Rumor had it that the chateau belonged to a
handsome French playboy, who in peacetime kept several mistresses.

The correspondents had put up a big map at their quarters, which
provided a detailed outline of the front. Army reports were issued each
morning, their content abridged, then printed neatly on paper squares
that were attached to the map to be cross-referenced to the map's key.

Every trench, every road, any expanse of woods, each local landmark was depicted clearly. As soon as the army reports were inserted, the correspondents reviewed the map for any noticeable changes from the day before.[36] Each had been assigned a conducting officer who now accompanied him to the corps headquarters in a chauffeur-driven car.

There, the maps were even more detailed. At corps headquarters, officers each morning would run over once more the previous day's events with reporters: "Every wood and village, every viewpoint, we knew, and every casualty clearing station and prisoners' enclosure."[37] The idea was to get "as close to the front as possible," watching any shelling that was taking place, and interview anyone they possibly could talk to. Later they would piece together a story based on this pretty much second-hand information.[38] Then too, if they could, they wangled lunch with the officers, who were always full of information about the moves anticipated from high command.

On mornings when big battles were expected, the correspondents "divided up the line of the front," as Philip Gibbs explained it, drawing lots for "the particular section which each man would cover."

> Then, before the dawn, or in the mirk of winter mornings, or the first glimmer of a summer day, our cars would pull out and we would go off separately to see the part of the line alloted to us by the number drawn, to see the preliminary bombardment, to walk over newly captured ground, to get into the backwash of prisoners and walking wounded amidst batteries firing a new barrage, guns moving forward on days of good advance, artillery transport bringing up new stores of ammunition, troops in support marching to repel a counterattack or follow through to new objectives, ambulances threading their way back through the traffic, with loads of prostrate men, mules, gun-horses, lorries, churning up the mud. . . . Tired, hungry, nerve-racked, splashed to the eyes in mud, or covered in a mask of dust, we started the journey back to our own quarters. . . .[39]

But any discomfort suffered by the reporters was minor in comparison with the hardships commonly endured by the fighting men, hardships that increased in proportion to the rising casualty figures until it became almost impossible to absorb the perpetual nightmare life had become. It took its toll on the newsmen whose task it was to watch the suffering of others, "the duration of all the drama of death that scarred one's soul as an onlooker; the frightful sum of sacrifice . . . [recorded]

59

day by day."[40] Gibbs said that "the whole organisation of that great machine of slaughter . . . the effect of such a vision, year in, year out, can hardly be calculated in psychological effect unless a man has a mind like a sieve and a soul like a sink."[41]

Others shared Gibbs's reactions. Frederick Palmer, who started out the war as a correspondent, but from a sense of duty became a censor for the American forces, said the correspondents "went and came always with a sense of incapacity and sometimes with a feeling that writing was a worthless business when others were fighting."[42]

Duranty himself would later say: "There were things I saw in the War which won't bear telling, but after a time you became hardened or callous or maybe a little crazy for the rest of your life."[43]

The gas rattles and strombos horns sounded the death knell of the early idealism associated with the war, and the fighting had turned into a grim struggle of attrition. Movement was continually hampered by the use of poison gases: tear gas was common, and sneezing gas, nuisances at worst; but then came the mustard, phosgene, and chlorine gases that hung on in the ditches, around the barbed wire and along the rocky crevices long after they were first released into the air. Men at the front looked like strange cartoon-like figures—blind mice dressed as soldiers, feeling their way into battle.

The roads of the armies were blocked by thousands of refugees: children hysterical with fright, mothers whose milk had dried up, marching as long as nineteen hours without food or water, the unbelievable stench of it all.[44]

In these conditions, even getting basic supplies through to the armies was hazardous. Hot food was carried to the men in open bucket-like containers, sometimes contaminated by impurities that had dropped in along the way. During battles, there would be no hot food at all. The men were forced to scavenge for something to eat or drink, as often as not stealing even their drinking water from the dead.

In the winter months, mud seeped continuously into the trenches, and had to be painstakingly removed with awkward, long-handled scoops. At times men stood in the mud knee-deep, sometimes for days, even for weeks with no change of socks or of boots. This could cause "trenchfoot," which could lead to gangrene. In "the butcher shops," as they were called, amputations were routine, a result of the filth and of the grisly wounds caused by shrapnel. During a battle, the operations continued almost around the clock.

With grim humor the men joined in the chorus of a jaunty music-hall song that caught the spirit of their lives in the trenches:

> The bells of hell go ding-a-ling-a-ling
> For you but not for me,
> And the little devils have a sing-a-ling-a-ling
> For you but not for me.
>
> Oh, Death, where is thy sting-a-ling-a-ling?
> Oh, where thy victory?
> The bells of hell go ding-a-ling-a-ling
> For you but not for me.[45]

By the war's end and in the years that followed, a bemused disbelief would rise into a tide of anger and frustration at the staggering number of casualties, the gratuitous waste of human life during these four years.

The suffering had been unanticipated, unrelieved—and largely unreported.

Looking back at the war, the idealists would ask themselves where the dream had gone wrong. The promise of the future, a generation of young men, had perished in the trenches. The pockets of the war profiteers were bulging with loot. And while the men had huddled, cold and wet in the trenches, the correspondents had in large part taken it easy, enjoying the unexpected windfall of luxury provided by the war.

Disillusioned idealists would become cynics, and a period of savage soul-searching began, the bitterness setting in like a thick fog. It was generally agreed that the press's performance during the war had amounted to one of the most thoroughgoing cover-up jobs in the history of wartime coverage. The blind censorship of the military apparatus and the unthinking obedience of the press corps were held responsible. C. E. Montague, first a soldier, then a censor, at last an editor on the Manchester *Guardian*, believed the problem stemmed from the fact that the war correspondents lived "in the staff world, its joys and its sorrows, not in the combatant world."

> The staff was both their friend and their censor. How could they show it up when they failed? . . . They would visit the front now and then, as many staff officers did, but it could be only as afternoon callers from one of the many mansions of GHQ, that haven of security and comfort. . . . Their staple emotions before a battle were of necessity akin to those of the Staff, the racehorse-owner or trainer exalted with brilliant hopes, thrilled by the glorious uncertainty of the game, the fascinating nicety of every preparation, and feeling the presence of horrible fatigues and the nearness of multitudinous deaths chiefly as a dim, sombre background that added importance to the rousing scene.[46]

Montague condemned the attitude "that a battle was just a rough, jovial picnic," the men eager to get into the fray to show what they were made of. He hated "the jauntiness of tone" that marked the work of the average war correspondent. There was on the face of it, he believed, a certain viciousness, an undaunted optimism that betokened the work of the propagandist more than the reporter.

Others disagreed. Admitting that the communiques were often overly optimistic and one-sided, even misleading, they pointed to the vital necessity of keeping up spirits "in a struggle of world magnitude."[47] Frederick Palmer readily accepted the conflicting roles of the correspondent and the censor. He had been both during the war. Palmer admitted to having had "moments of acute consciousness" in which he realized he operated on two separate levels. Essentially, he believed, there was no escape from the duality of his motives and the layer of hypocrisy that cast him "for the part of a public liar to keep up the spirits of the armies and the peoples of our side."[48]

Once you were there, you were there, as irrevocably as the men in the trenches, and with about as much choice in the matter.

Duranty—who would make the giant leap from obscurity to fame during the last few months of the war—found the argument irrelevant. It did not trouble his mind. He had never entertained idealistic notions; there was no reason now at the war's end to resort to disillusionment. The fighting he reported in the spring and summer of 1918 would teach him, in his own words, "a measure of indifference to blood and squalor, and fear and pity. Sudden death [would] become a commonplace, and vermin a joke."[49]

CHAPTER IV

A Sea of Blood

In long, slow columns the troops made their way across the fields of northern France, heavy kits on their backs, as much as they could carry, even frying pans; their movement heavy and sluggish much as the rivers they walked beside.[1] The weather was hot, dusty, the roads baked into a hard chalky surface that threw up clouds of dust and lightly layered everything in sight. Horses and supply wagons rumbled along beside the exhausted men, weaving in and around their ragtag columns and the other vehicles on the road, in disorderly and disorganized movement. On a hill close by, an artillery unit was casually firing field guns, causing great booms of sound overhead and frightening the horses. The men smoked cigarettes and pipes as they went through the synchronized movement of loading and firing the great cannons. The scene reminded Duranty of something he had read somewhere, maybe in the States, and he made a note of it before hurrying from the hill where he made the observation.

The correspondents assigned to the French armies had moved to new quarters, this time a grand chateau just outside Provins.[2] Duranty sat at a table, smoking heavily—by now he was onto American cigarettes—deciphering the notes he had taken during the day, churning out the copy with spectacular speed; confident, part of it and loving it.

General Erich F. Ludendorff's offensive began at 5 o'clock in the morning, dawn, in thick fog, a stroke of luck for the Germans. With the Americans on their way over to join in the fighting, Ludendorff now believed the only chance the Germans had of winning the war was a knockout strike before the Yanks could actually get into the action. With this in mind, he developed his best men into "shock troops"— the spearhead, as it were, of the massive assault.

After several hours of "hurricane shelling, in which it is probable that a great deal of gas was used . . . the German infantry advanced and developed attacks against a number of strategical points on a front of about twenty-five miles between the Scarpe and Hargincourt, ten miles north of St. Quentin."[3] In his dispatch dated the 22nd of March 1918, the day after the offensive began, Philip Gibbs said that forty divisions had been identified, "and it [was] certain that as many as fifty must be engaged. In proportions of men, the British are much outnumbered, therefore the obstinacy of the resistance of the troops is wonderful."[4]

In their "ruthless sacrifice of life," Gibbs wrote, the Germans hoped to overwhelm the Allies by "sheer weight of numbers," but he predicted the attack would ultimately fail because of

> . . . the spirit of those men, their confidence, their splendid faith, their quiet and cheerful courage, their lack of worry until this hour should come, the curious incredulity they had that the enemy would dare to attack them, because of the strength of their positions and of the great British gunfire.[5]

The front page of the *New York Times* carried Gibbs's story in full, its columns crammed with related news, including a story on the bombardment of Paris with long-range guns, a "daylight air raid" that tapped the morale of the usually unflappable Parisians.[6] Later, the "monster cannon" would be given the nickname "Big Bertha" in an attempt at reducing the fear the shelling produced in the civilian populace. In London, "the feeling was one of supreme confidence" in the men at the front. In Berlin, the Germans were claiming victories "near Monchy, Cambrai, St. Quentin, and La Fere." In Washington D.C., officials were "absorbed throughout this beautiful Spring Day in the great events taking place in the theatre of war across the Atlantic."[7]

Regardless of the impression the page gave of extensive and thorough coverage, however, there was no getting away from the fact that the *New York Times* had produced no stories of its own. It looked uncomfortably as if there had been no *Times* man at the front when the offensive was launched. The gap widened during the next few days, as the French started falling back into what Gibbs termed a "retreat without haste," and Lloyd George called for aid from America. Finally, six days later, the *Times* issued a statement explaining the situation: "*Since the beginning of the Great Battle Mr. Gibbs' reports . . . have been the only special dispatches from the front transmitted to America without one or more days' delay.*"[8]

Backstage, Carr Van Anda was jockeying to put together what would become one of the most impressive news teams covering the offensive. Edwin L. James, better known as "Jimmy," had been accredited to the American army only ten days before the offensive got under way, Duranty was in Paris, and G. H. Perris and Charles C. Grasty were moving into place. Meanwhile, "Van Anda kept cabling Walter Duranty . . . to send everything at the 'double urgent' message rate . . . 75 cents a word" in an attempt to get the news from the battlefield to New York as close as possible to the date the events were taking place.[9]

At the same time Van Anda was scrambling, the Allies were at last making a serious move toward unifying their armies. Less than a week after Ludendorff sent in his troops, in an emergency meeting of the Supreme War Council at Doullens, General Ferdinand Foch was appointed "co-ordinator" for the Western Front. It was a dubious title, a try-on to maneuver one man into a leadership position. But it stuck, mainly because of Foch's intelligence and tact. Within a few days, he was appointed commander in chief of the Allied forces in France. The U.S. commander, Major General John J. Pershing, who by then had eight available divisions in France, agreed to the appointment, and Grasty wrote an enthusiastic biography of Foch for the *Times*.

With the Americans on their way and Foch at the helm, morale on the Allied side was rising, despite the initial success of Ludendorff's incursion. The French premier Georges Clemenceau rallied his people in words that anticipated another great orator of the twentieth century:

I shall fight before Paris, I shall fight behind Paris. The Germans may take Paris but that will not stop me from carrying on the war. We shall fight on the Loire, we shall fight on the Garonne, we shall fight even on the Pyrenees. And should we be driven off the Pyrenees, we shall continue the war from the sea. But as for asking for peace, never![10]

By the end of May the *Times* was ready. James had caught up with the American army, whose 1st Division was just about to get its first taste of action at Cantigny. Walter Duranty was back with the French armies, and Charles C. Grasty and G. H. Perris were in place, one in Paris, the other at the front. The system to relay the dispatches by extra-charge transmission from the battlefield to New York was also set up. Everything was ready—except the Germans.

"Questions as to when the enemy will attack or where the blow will fall have given place to another—why doesn't he attack? . . . Is it in hope of affecting the nerves of the Allied soldiers by continued tension?"[11] The questions were those of Walter Duranty in his first by-lined story for the *New York Times*—a page-one think piece that placed him securely beside the top men on the paper. Confident, energetic, eager, he concluded the story on an upbeat note: "Something must break soon. It will not be France or her allies."

This was the first of more than a hundred by-lined dispatches filed by Duranty between July and October, each about 1000 words long, some considerably longer, the great majority of them written from the front. Most appeared either on the front page of the paper, or on the second, only the sidebars falling as far back as page three.

Within three days of his first piece, another page-one story appeared, this time with an important new angle:

> Everywhere on the front the poilus say: "A half million Americans—that's the best news yet," or "Your divisions are in line now in the big battle. C'est magnifique!" One feels what a tremendous moral force to the French Army is the knowledge that America's millions are backing it up just when the enemy is "scraping his bucket" to the very dregs to get every available man, young, old, or half crippled, into line for a last great effort.[12]

For the first time during the war, the action at the front involved the Americans more than the French, whose tactical retreat Duranty described as "orderly and planned." Simultaneously, he wrote, Foch was moving up his reserves "to make the enemy pay a heavy price for his gain of ground." One of Foch's strategies was to allow the Germans to outrun their artillery, and Duranty must have got wind of it from somewhere, for his stories stressed the high number of casualties the Germans were suffering in the drive forward. "Each mile [the German] advances weakens his striking force and increases his fatigue and difficulties of communications and transport," he wrote. "Each mile exposes him more completely to the fire of the French artillery and machine guns."[13] Even the refugees' movements showed no signs of panic as they had earlier, when they formed the "flotsam" of the March retreat. They now seemed "surprisingly calm and confident," as they slowly flowed along the back roads reserved for them by the military, their "farm carts piled high with hay and bedding, with furniture underneath, or driving cattle. . . ."[14]

On the battlefields, it was open warfare, "such as the Americans knew in the Civil War."

> . . . the observer might be watching a reproduction of one of the battle stories of Ambrose Bierce. Here is a battery position at the edge of a wood. A little further machine guns are installed to sweep the river bank, and among the trees behind them a battalion of infantry is under cover. . . .
>
> On the heights to the left sudden smoke clouds leap up incessantly where the shells are obstructing the advance of the German infantry toward Chateau Thierry. From time to time one catches sight of them scurrying forward like ants across an interval of meadow between the woods that cover most of the country. . . .[15]

Duranty observed it all from on high, recording what he saw with a lofty, measured style, not uninfluenced by his classical education; homely now in the opening scenes but with that undercurrent of excitement that would spill over into thrilling epic prose.

Another war correspondent, Floyd Gibbons, the young Chicagoan who had made his big hit with the dispatch about the torpedoing of the *Laconia*, was on the lookout for another scoop. Already warned several times by the censors to stay out of unauthorized places, Gibbons routinely ignored them, calling his more cooperative colleagues "lazy louts who won't get out after their own news."

Gibbons had heard that there was "a hot corner" at Lucy-le-

Bogage, not far from Belleau Wood, where the U.S. 2nd Division was engaged in heavy fighting. Accompanied by a Major Berry, a frequent companion of his, he found there a large company of U.S. Marines, inching forward through a field of wheat under a steady stream of enemy machine-gun fire.[16] Gibbons and Berry advanced slowly, waist high in wheat.

> There was a sudden whish and bits of wheat were clipped off, by a spray of machine gun bullets. [Gibbons] dropped. He got up again at once, feeling his arm, where he was hit slightly. But he dropped again, turned over, and his companion saw his eye, exactly like a whole small raw egg, roll slowly down his right cheek. There it wobbled and swayed, but stayed, held by greyish-red filaments: they looked like "nerves." [Gibbons] had to lie in the wheat all day, holding his eye there, low on the cheek.[17]

The machine gun fire was so blistering that nobody could get near the men, until, at last, Lieutenant Oscar Hartzel, a former *New York Times* writer, managed to reach them and help them to safety.[18]

The story that Gibbons had been hit made the rounds among the correspondents, who waited to see if he would make it. Word came back: Gibbons would survive, but he had lost his left eye. Legend had it that Gibbons was "a marvelous patient. When told the eye was gone, he quipped from bed, 'Well Doc, I won't have to squint down the neck of a bottle anymore, like you guys.'"[19]

Gibbons received the Croix de Guerre with palm for gallantry. The French citation crisply described the events surrounding Gibbons's injury, and continued: "Rescued several hours later and carried to a dressing station, he insisted on not being cared for before the wounded who had arrived before him." It was signed simply "Pétain."[20]

The correspondents gave a party for Gibbons before he sailed for home. There were "champagne, coffee, cigars, and brandy" and the usual after-dinner tributes. Then Gibbons stood up. His arm was in a sling; he was wearing for the first time the black patch that would become his trademark. He stood there, looking surprisingly vulnerable, visibly shaken. He cleared his throat. "Now," he said slowly, "I'm going to show you two-eyed bastards how to make a speech."[21]

Duranty also had a narrow brush with death, not long after Gibbons was injured at Belleau Wood. Fascinated by the new weaponry of modern warfare, Duranty made it a point to visit the French tank corps to see for himself how they worked. The bulky weapons, he quoted one young officer as saying, looked "like a herd of elephants running amok."

One afternoon in June he talked to the young crews who manned the tanks, taking lunch with them in the afternoon. They asked him if he wanted a ride, and he jumped in with enthusiasm, going up to an advance post behind the lines. Duranty stayed with the crew, chatting through lunch, and they all decided it would be fun "to go on together to a point in the front trench from which they were to attack next morning." But the officer at the advance post objected, saying he thought Duranty might miss his ride back to headquarters that evening and so not be able to write his story. "So they went," Duranty wrote, "and I stayed and talked with the rest of the tank detachment."

They were full of stories, because the tank corps "saw life," as they say in the Marines—and death. I do not know about the other armies, but with the French it was not considered tactful to ask after friends in any tank or battle-plane outfit who were not around when you came to visit. They might be on leave or just sick or slightly wounded, but the odds were they were dead. The tanks lost sixty per cent killed of their effectives in the French Army, which is the highest mortality for any branch of any fighting service in the War.

While we were talking, there came a phone message from the line ahead saying that a stray shell had hit one of the tanks, which had gone up in flames. The commanding officer said quietly, "That's too bad . . . I wonder which it was. Can you get the number?" Five minutes later they phoned again to say it was number seventeen, which was the one I had ridden in, and that they were sending back the bodies because there was not much firing, just an occasional shell or so. So I saw them and felt sick . . . black and incredibly shriveled, like three little faceless nigger boys.[22]

Later, Duranty would admit to having been so "bitterly scared" by the dangers he faced in the war—"air-raids, shells, bullets—that . . . intangible perils did not bulk large anymore."[23]

The first half of June saw some of the bitterest fighting of the war. As the battles of Château-Thierry and Belleau Wood raged, Ludendorff launched the fourth of his five major attacks, sometimes called the

Noyon-Montdidier Offensive. This time Foch was ready, having been warned by deserters from the German army. Although the Germans made some gains, a Franco-American counterattack on the 11th of June halted the advance.

This was the battle that inspired Duranty to write his most epic dispatch on World War I, singled out at the time by *Current History Magazine* as one of the outstanding examples of American journalism written during the war.[24] In it, Duranty called the second week of June "one of the bloodiest and most decisive periods in the world's history. . . . the veritable climax of four years of struggle."

> In the last twenty-four hours the violence of the fighting has increased still further. The limit of human endurance has been forced yet another notch higher. Along a front of nearly twenty miles the Germans are driving more than a quarter of a million men forward through a sea of blood. The defenders say that it is as though the whole of the German Army is engaged against them; no sooner is one battalion annihilated than another takes its place and another and another. . . .
>
> The grassy slopes of the hill bore a hideous carpet of thousands of German dead, over which new forces still advanced with the same madness of sacrifice as the Carthaginians of old, flinging their children, their possessions, and themselves into Moloch's furnace. The bloody religion of militarism that Germany has followed for forty years has led its votaries to culminating orgies of destruction.[25]

He wrote of the French defending their positions calmly, registering counterattacks just at the moment when the Germans had exhausted themselves. They had paid in blood, he wrote, for each foot of ground, then lost the positions after all. "In the villages thus retaken, the poilus say, gray-clad corpses lay heaped up as though they had been collected for a gigantic funeral pyre, and more than once the advancing enemy was screened from the defenders' fire by a rampart of his own dead."[26] The French had met the enemy's advance with "a stubborn resistance," and now the German dead lay on the hard earth "thick as fresh-cut wheat."

There could remain no doubt, Duranty wrote, that the appointment of Foch had been correct and that his strategies were inspired. Try as they would, the Germans could not make it back to their immediate objective, a hollow in the land that would have made for them "a natural fortress with an infinity of cover for guns, men, and machine guns against which no fury of sacrifice might prevail."

At last, Duranty spoke of an observation post he had passed through only a few days before where he had seen "a great natural amphitheatre in a sort of mountain."

> At one side the Germans had carved a huge eagle, colored blood red, on a slab of rock above a grotto that had been their headquarters. Beneath it in Gothic letters was the Brandenburg motto, 'On Brandenburg, on!' The artist who designed the bird that is the symbol of German violence was well inspired. The Kaiser's eagles are red, indeed, clotted and stained from beak to claw with the crimson of countless slaughters.[27]

It was rousing prose, heroic in form to match the momentous events he was describing. The ebullience and energy of his style were incomparable, even on the staff of the *New York Times*, and it brought him growing fame as a page-one war correspondent.

With success, however, came the resentment of the men he had displaced. Internal jealousies and hard feelings were not untypical of the highly competitive *Times* staff, and for Duranty they would grow more serious. But for now, he was riding high.

At roughly the time Duranty was spinning out the greatest of his dispatches on the Western Front, in the small village of Ekaterinburg in the Urals, a group of revolutionaries, fearful Nicholas II might be liberated by counterrevolutionary forces, assassinated the deposed Czar of Russia. The act was the culmination of a series of tumultuous and chaotic events in Russia.

A splinter political group known as the Bolsheviks had overthrown a Provisional Government that had been set up to rule Russia after the forced abdication of Nicholas II. With few policies and little power, the Provisional Government strongly supported one general objective—to keep Russia in the war. Ironically, it was the same policy which had forced the Czar's resignation, the policy opposed by a majority of the exhausted Russian population.

In Zurich, Vladimir Ilich Ulianov, better known as N. Lenin, was sitting out a long and bitter exile. With the news of the Czar's abdication, he tried to arrange his passage home, but receiving rebuffs from the Allies, he turned without hesitation to the Germans, who allowed him to cross their territory in a sealed train on the 8th of April 1917.

Arriving at the Finland Station in Petrograd eight days later, he began hammering away at the Provisional Government and its unpopular decision to continue fighting. After several unsuccessful attempts, he managed finally to ramrod through the soft political core of the Provisional Government, at a stroke gaining control of Russia and creating for himself the image of a decisive, strong-willed leader. The date was 7 November 1917, according to Western calculations; by the Russian calendar, Old Style, the 25th of October—hence, the October Revolution.

By the 3rd of December, Lenin had declared an Armistice with Germany, and on the 3rd of March 1918, Leon Trotsky concluded negotiating with the Germans the notorious Brest-Litovsk Treaty, with terms so unfavorable to Russia that it convinced many in the West the Bolsheviks were little other than German agents.

"At French headquarters . . . ," Duranty wrote, "it was an axiom that the Bolsheviks were enemies of God and Man, and sold to Germany—a loathsome union of anti-Christ and Judas."[28] Without the withdrawal of the Russians from the Eastern Front, so went the logic, Ludendorff could not have launched his March offensive on the Western Front. In a state of anger and confusion at Russia's separate peace with Germany, a decision was made—one which would set the tone of relations between Soviet Russia and the West for decades to come. In April of 1918, Britain sent troops it could ill afford into Russia, along with contingents from France and the United States, in an attempt to retrieve Allied munitions and supplies, support the anti-Bolshevik counterrevolutionaries, and keep Russia in the war.

The news of all this, Duranty said, "touched me slightly"; at least that was his view at the time. But in fact, these distant occurrences would have significant bearing on Duranty's career as a journalist, and indeed upon his entire life and reputation. Random events had slotted into place, like beads on a string, and whimsically, everything seemed to conspire to affect the career of Walter Duranty. In Russia, a chronology merged and remerged in such a way as to confound and distort Western perceptions. On the Western Front, Duranty's remarkable success in reporting the war meant that his colleagues wouldn't in the least mind seeing him stationed safely in some out-of-the-way place where he would pose less of a threat to their own ambitions. If these were the elements of good fortune, then Duranty was a lucky man.

In the meantime, the Allies were preparing for what would come to be known as the Second Battle of the Marne, later recognized by historians as the turning of the tide. Ludendorff's five offensives had all been brusquely rebutted by a successful unified operation from the troops of four nations—France, Great Britain, the United States, and Italy. After July, Ludendorff would be forced to withdraw from the Soissons-Château-Thierry-Reims salient in order to reduce the front for his depleted and demoralized forces. In the five months of his offensive, Ludendorff had sustained half a million casualties. Even worse from the German point of view, the American troops were now pouring into France by the hundreds of thousands.

During the days that led up to this event and throughout the battle itself, Duranty seemed strangely energized by what he was seeing and reporting. Too close for comfort perhaps, his dispatches appeared frequently on page one in the columns immediately to the left of lead position, vying with Jimmy James, who, assigned to the American army, dominated that space. On several occasions, Duranty actually managed to dislodge the talented James.

James's writing epitomized the clean objective reporting that would formulate the model for the next five decades in American news reporting. Duranty had an all-stops-out style that at times swept slightly over the top, enough to make the reading riveting without actually slipping from fact into fiction.

With the kind of deliberate honesty later depicted as the movie stereotype of American masculinity, Jimmy James clipped out his lean prose with compelling clarity: "The close of the second day of the great German offensive," he wrote on the 17th of July 1918, "finds the Kaiser's troops held, and in some places repulsed, on that part of the line over which Americans are fighting."[29]

Beside James on page one, Duranty's lead showed what James was up against:

"The crossing of the Marne is worse than hell," runs a German message found on a captured pigeon. Could there be better evidence of the success of the Franco-American resistance against the terrific drive?

As to the American troops, a French officer said to me last night: "They fought with the skill and élan of one of our crack divisions."[30]

73

It was the unmistakable flair of the virtuoso, and along with it, Duranty had this ability: to figure out what readers would be curious about, what they would want to know. If other writers considered themselves too good "to write sidelights," Duranty was happy enough to pick them up. Facile, imaginative, observant, he made a feast of the leavings of the other correspondents.

He traveled along the crowded roads in his chauffeured car, looking out the window at the dusty leaves on the trees. Debris was piled high all around. Artillery trucks, resembling covered wagons, transported the shells in woven baskets, like eggs. Along these important supply lines, mules slowly dragged massive cannons, their long shafts carved with the names of the men who had fired them: immortality, their only crack at it.

Model-T cars, like thin-legged insects, picked their way through the traffic and past the men on foot—walking wounded, returning from battle; fresh troops going in; everyone smoking, pipes and cigarettes everywhere.[31]

Duranty pictured "a day's march to a modern battle," taking his reader along. "Imagine you form part of a unit just ordered into the line," he wrote.

> After a long night trip of broken, jolting sleep on the straw-covered floor of a cattle truck you detrain at a tiny depot, of which you know nothing save that it is "somewhere in France." If you are lucky there will be coffee in the station canteen. More likely you munch a biscuit or sandwich and get a drink of water from your own bottle.[32]

Afterwards, "you pile yourself and your equipment into a big square camion" which is "camouflaged with patches of green and brown." You may be lucky enough to get a real breakfast later on up the road. Otherwise, you try to sleep through some of the journey. When you can't sleep anymore, you look out the back of the truck. There you witness "a continual nightmare of dust and heat." Through the heat, which by now "is stifling and the dust fog almost impenetrable . . . you see dimly ambulances flit past or camions rumbling ponderously, like your own, some empty, others bearing wounded, motionless in morphine's lethargy, on stretchers arranged crosswise."[33]

You are shocked by the first "terrific burst of sound" which seemed to be right beside you. But it is only guns being fired at the "boche" some ten miles distant, "not an air bomb or a German shell" as you had imagined. You are close to the front, and now you leap down from the camion for your evening meal. Afterwards, with the cool of evening coming on, you march forward. "Someone starts a chorus, and you go forward more cheerfully." You are nervous, but it is "mixed with a strange thrill of exhilaration. You know you will do your utmost, and your comrades beside you likewise. The rest is in the hands of the god of battles."[34]

Back in corps headquarters, Duranty noticed some recently arrived American magazines, picked them up, read the "highly colored stories of the horrors and danger of German gas."[35] The result was a dispatch that aimed at correcting "a very erroneous impression on the subject" prevailing at home. The gas, he explained to his readers, was little more than "a very serious nuisance which hampers [the men's] defense by forcing them to wear masks." He reassured them that the masks afforded the troops "absolute protection against all gases, even during a period of hours." He then described the blisters "as if by boiling water" that could be caused by touching any object impregnated with mustard gas. He described a corporal "whose nose was swollen like a tomato because he incautiously sniffed the fragment of a hyperite shell."

> To show what veteran soldiers think of the matter, let me quote this remark of a German prisoner taken on Monday by the Americans at Vaux. He was a meagre specimen, but has been forty months at the front, four times wounded, and decorated with the Iron Cross.
> "What do the Germans think of gas?" I asked him.
> "We don't mind it in the least," he replied with a grin. "Our lungs have been trained to stand worse than that by the infernal mixture they have given us the last twelve months in place of tobacco."[36]

The most bizarre story Duranty reported during the war also involved the reactions of Germans, this time of U-boat crews. Near the end of the war, Duranty was one of the first Western correspondents into Bruges after its liberation. The young crews of the German U-boats had dominated that city throughout the occupation. Duranty described them as "the spoiled darlings of the German forces in Belgium," who were allowed "unlimited license." With offers of high pay, rapid promotion, plentiful decorations, and huge awards of prize money, the German military sought to encourage men to stay in the dangerous service. In the "finest houses in Bruges" where they were quartered, the crews requisitioned "the cream of the famous Belgian wine cellars." For amusement, they demolished the glasses, crockery, and furniture in their drunken revelries, setting fire to several of the houses.

Duranty visited the rathskeller of one mansion left standing and observed the strange frescoes that had been drawn on the walls, with a "vulgarity of tone . . . typically German." Mostly anti-English, the pictures showed John Bull being blown out of the water by a torpedo, or off the white cliffs of Dover by a champagne bottle's hitting him square "on the seat of his trousers." The mottoes urged the submarine crews to "Enjoy wine and women while you can. You live but once and will be a long time dead." Another said, "Drink deep of wine, ye heroes . . . [to] make you forget the dark days of hardship." What haunted the men was the "coffin fear." Duranty said it seemed "to have been a common feature of their lives—a form of nerve trouble akin to what doctors call claustrophobia, the fear of a shut room."[37] It was said to be easy to recognize a member of a U-boat crew "by his haggard and slovenly appearance"—one of the signs of "coffin fear."

> A Belgian civilian doctor said he had treated many cases of morphine and ether poisoning among mere boys, who did not dare reveal the vice to their own medical officers, or, for that matter, the Admiral of the U-boat men. They might stagger, yelling in drunken ribaldry in the streets, with the lowest women on either arm, break windows, or molest civilians; they might even insult officers of the army—they were never punished.[38]

Duranty wrote a good many other "sidelights," some that lionized the American fliers who daily risked their lives to give "the boches a foretaste of hell"; or of civilians toasting the bravery of the American soldiers in makeshift banquets held in cellars. Nor did Duranty miss the courage of the ordinary French poilu. In one sad story, he chronicled the heroism of 4000 French soldiers who held off over 30,000 Germans for twelve hours. In full communication with corps headquarters as they fought, they sent back messages that revealed their certain knowledge of their own fates: there would be no rescue. "Then at five minutes after noon came the last message: 'Done for.'"[39]

At the end of July, when it was clear that Ludendorff's offensive had been successfully halted, Foch rapidly turned the tables on the enemy with the Aisne-Marne Offensive. He struck the German lines in a series of quick hammer-blows all along the front, pushing the Germans back, despite stiff resistance. With defeat dogging his heels, Ludendorff now lost another 30,000 as prisoners to the Allies, who, pushing forward, found abandoned hundreds of German mine throwers and thousands of machine guns. Allied morale surged upwards as the shattered German troops began their historic retreat. On the 28th of July, in the lead story, Duranty adopted a terse style of reporting to emphasize the importance of the moment.

> The Germans are retreating in the Marne salient.
> The Allies have already gained several kilometers.
> It is a frank admission of defeat.
> The second battle of the Marne may pass into history as the beginning of Germany's downfall.[40]

And three days later, in a more characteristic style of writing, he counted the cost when "war's destruction reaches the acme of horror ... the confusion of twisted iron, splintered wood, hundreds of stricken horses stiffened in the incredible postures of their death agonies, and the still ghastlier remains of what once had been men." A lieutenant standing beside him pointed to something in the distance, and Duranty felt that strange recognition that the living have for the dead. What he saw was "a German hand outstretched from a huge stone heap as if in final supplication. Such," Duranty wrote, "is war as Germany has brought it upon the world."[41]

Some two weeks later, in Champagne, men, women, and children filled the streets, welcoming the victorious troops back in the bright sunlight, the men substituting straw hats for the usual cloth ones, the girls in aprons and sunbonnets, the women wearing stiffly starched white collars against dark dresses. The flag bearers marched past the respectful onlookers, holding before them the flags of their countries, now in tatters. As the troops passed by them, the men took off their hats in respect. Then the officials of the city gave the soldiers bouquets, bowing with gratitude and respect, the black American troops honored along with the rest. Around them the city stood, damaged but intact.[42]

At last Foch began the Meuse-Argonne Offensive—his final drive. Duranty watched the attack from a high plateau, staying there the entire night.

> As far as the eye could see the northern sky was split up with flashes that winked out continuously along the whole line. Nearly all were the sudden, broad glare of French "departures." But now and then a tiny triangle of light marked the explosion of a German "arrival."
>
> Right ahead a crimson glow now rising high above the horizon, now scarcely distinguishable, told of a huge German munition dump that blazed for three long hours. . . .
>
> At brief intervals a white star shell or colored rocket would soar up from a German position. One could well imagine the desperate plight of some German commander as he called in vain for his own artillery to protect him against the inferno of destruction.
>
> As the bombardment swelled in volume toward the dawn, the words "drum fire" exactly expressed the sound. All night the air had been filled with an enormous and irregular tumult, in which the deep drone of the allied aircraft passing, as it seemed, in an unbroken stream, to add their part to the work of destruction seemed the leitmotif of the cannon's thundersong.
>
> But when the climax came it was like nothing so much as the roll of a titanic drum, explosion so thick upon explosion that no separate sound could be distinguished.[43]

Then it was the end—the victory so bitterly wrested from enemy hands. In its aftermath, desolation and destruction remained as a reminder of the four long years of suffering and of death. Traveling through some of the war's most devastated cities a few days before the signing of the Armistice, Duranty passed through Ypres, where some half-million men had been lost. The worst of the battles there had ended with the futile struggle over Passchendaele, "the battle of the mud," Lloyd George had called it.

Duranty remembered Ypres as it had been, its central square, "once a thing of beauty, flanked by the marvelous Cloth Hall and the thousand-year-old houses. . . ." Then he tallied the costs of the war.

A Sea of Blood

Grass and weeds are the tragedy of Ypres; one cannot even tell where the houses stood or the roads once ran. But the appalling shell-torn waste that is the battlefield of Flanders surpasses the wildest visions of Doré in ghastliness and gloom. For nearly four miles the road of rotting planks that is the sole passage across the ridges winds amid acres of shell holes merging one into another.

No single tree or bush or hedge or building remains to tell that human beings once cultivated this desert. Here lies a rusting tank and three broken caissons. Further on is a hole that was a dugout where men lived and died. Everywhere are shattered concrete barbed wire in crazy festoons, convex roofs of corrugated iron that gave some shelter against the elements, planks by millions for roadways, and faded crosses that mark innumerable graves.

This frightful realization of Macbeth's "blasted heath" is the resting place of tens of thousands of brave men to whom death must have been a relief from more than mortal hardship. Now only rats—huge, gaunt, and hungry since the humans have departed—inhabit the accursed spot. . . .[44]

CHAPTER V

A Mad Hatter's Tea Party

There was trouble in the office, and Duranty was at the center of it. Charles A. Selden, assigned to the Paris bureau sometime near the end of the war, had been offered the job as bureau chief. Selden wanted the position and eventually did accept it. But in spring 1919, he was dithering. His reason: Walter Duranty.

On April 9, Selden wrote to Carr Van Anda that "if Duranty [was] to be attached to the Bureau as assistant or in any other capacity," he, Selden, would not feel comfortable taking over the operation. It was one thing during the war, he wrote, when Duranty came into the office only on the odd afternoon. It was another now that things were operating on a more or less normal basis. Duranty was "most unreliable and tricky," and Selden "should hate to work with him or be responsible for him on any phase of the correspondence or business of the Paris office."[1] As his parting shot, Selden added a postscript saying that senior *Times* staffer Richard V. Oulahan, in Paris for the Peace Conference, had read his letter and agreed with the sentiments expressed in it.

But Oulahan and Selden weren't the only ones working out of Paris. Jimmy James was still there, grabbing the plum assignments as quickly as they came up in the French capital, or more often, in the cities of Western Europe; C. H. Grasty was still around, and there were others who floated in and out from time to time. In evaluating Selden's indictment of Duranty, it would be difficult to dismiss the simple question whether there was enough to go around, and if there wasn't, who was going to get what there was?

Duranty was British in an office of Americans, with a better education than any of them, and possessing a remarkable talent for writing and reporting, a trait certain to irritate his close associates. No doubt Duranty's unconventional set of mores also contributed to Selden's dislike of him. Described in later years as "reliable and respected,"[2] Selden was a careful and meticulous company man who no doubt found personally distasteful Duranty's inclinations toward pleasure-seeking. There may also have been a new and perhaps unpleasant sense of self-importance in the recently elevated Duranty based on his highly successful war reporting, which had placed him alongside the best writers of the period. He had inevitably developed a taste for page one, and the kind of crumbs he was now being tossed—small scandals, franc devaluations, penny ante crime stories—were probably difficult to swallow.

Despite the presence of Selden and Oulahan, and more significantly, the ambitious Jimmy James, Duranty was still managing to squeeze some page-one and page-two clips out of the deal. On the day the Peace Conference opened, in fact, Duranty produced a prominent front-page story, using again what would become one of his standard writing techniques: the "imagine-you-are-there" story.

> Imagine that you are standing in front of the French Foreign Office on the Quai d'Orsay, beside the Seine, at 2:30 this afternoon. Before you stretches a long, low building with the Tricolor on its summit waving in the bright Winter sun. The courtyard is thronged with soldiers and officers in picturesque uniforms.[3]

Alongside them were "soldiers in khaki, Americans and Australians for the most part" plus the crowds lining the streets. Duranty described the surrounding buildings, the ceremonial pomp and circumstance, shrewdly noting that in this "hour of France's triumph, Russia alone among her friends [was] unrepresented."

The close of the Conference would find Duranty and Selden in direct competition, Selden inside for the signing, Duranty stuck at the gates of Versailles, straining for a glimpse of the distinguished guests as they arrived. Even then, he managed to upstage Selden with the story of an ancient woman, supported on either side by her two sons, who begged and received admittance without a ticket: "I shared the defeat," she cried, "let me share the victory."[4]

Duranty's story ran fifteen column inches to Selden's five. It was run at the top of page two, Selden's buried at the bottom. It must have felt like something of a rebuke to Selden, who had so recently lodged his complaints about Duranty in the New York office.

For his part, Duranty made short shrift of a bureau head who "became an executive instead of a reporter" and who allowed his time to be "taken up with office detail." Duranty was irked by the way Selden ran the bureau, although he never referred to Selden by name. Instead, he spoke of his dislike of "showy, expensive offices" filled with reporters "who trod on each other's feet, stenographers, filing clerks, messengers and attendants" and the resultant bookkeeping department, with its officious accountants.[5] Later on, he would describe these years as "dreary after the excitement and independence" of reporting at the front.[6]

> I have always thought that a foreign correspondent's office ought to be under his hat, with a cubby-hole somewhere to park the hat and a typewriter, and meet people on occasion. A desk and a telephone and one or two assistants and a good man for night work—that's all an American newspaper really needs in any European capital.[7]

Duranty figured the Paris bureau's overhead at something in the neighborhood of $2000 per month, before counting the salaries of the men doing the real work—a goodly sum in the years just after the war, when the franc was in perpetual decline. Furthermore, he couldn't see any practical reason for regular office hours, where there was nothing to do except "sit and chew the rag" with the other reporters. Duranty thought a foreign correspondent should be out on the streets, talking to people, keeping his eyes and ears open. The only time he needed to be in the office was when he was actually writing up his story. He also hated the idea of a reading-room where reporters were constantly admonished to keep the files in order. The whole operation, he maintained, was little more than "show business" designed to gratify "the big shots of the home office" who wanted "to come and find large expensive premises in the center of town, and an air of bustling activity. . . ." Duranty would have preferred to keep the bureau small, and take the difference in an increase in salary.[8]

With his wholly uncorporate attitude and his unrelenting competitive drive, it was no wonder he did not fit in under the regime Selden imposed. The two men seemed to be able to agree on only one thing: that Duranty should go elsewhere. Thus it was that Duranty applied for permission to enter Soviet Russia, a request quickly granted by the New York office. It was the Bolsheviks who brought a halt to his efforts, automatically denying him entry along with most other Western correspondents. From the Bolshevik point of view, the West had shown only hostility toward their continuing fight for survival. They had no intention of granting admission to a group of newspapermen whose first order of business was no doubt to spotlight their most glaring failures.

Since their original incursion in spring of 1918, the Allies had continued to send troops into Soviet Russia. In fact, contingents were sent in from Britain, the United States, France, Italy, Japan and seven other countries in all, who thereby became enmeshed in a policy that had no clear objectives other than providing support to counterrevolutionary forces. Taken altogether, their numbers remained comparatively small, but the Bolsheviks viewed this invasion of their territory as indicative of Western hostile attitudes in general.

In late summer of 1918, a British and French contingent moved into Archangel and, with the help of anti-Bolsheviks there, easily seized the port, expelling the Soviet garrison and creating a defense radius around the city of about 100 miles. In Siberia, U. S. troops were dispatched to guard the Trans-Siberian Railway from Vladivostock to Lake Baikal, to stop it falling under the control of the Japanese. Improbably enough, they were able to support a legion of Czech soldiers who, determined to fight alongside the Allies, had crossed Russian territory *eastwards* intending to return to Europe by boat from Vladivostock; in so doing, the Czechs helped to precipitate an uprising against the Bolsheviks by supporters of a short-lived Volga Republic. Other Allies were positioned in the south, near the ports of Odessa and Batum.

With the outbreak of Civil War in the summer of 1918, the Allies openly collaborated with the "Whites," as the counterrevolutionaries came to be known, despite the widely divergent political groups the term encompassed. The efforts of the Whites were almost wholly unco-ordinated, and a number of groups emerged on the basis of regional interests and under the direction of local leaders who happened to be at hand. In the south, anti-Bolshevik movements tended to unite under the general leadership of Anthony Denikin, leading to the emer-gence of the White Volunteer Army. In the north, a former populist, Nikolai Chaikovsky, set up a government that was supported by the intervening British and French in Archangel. From Siberia, Admiral Alexander Kolchak, joined by the confused but eager Czech soldiers, advanced steadily, taking Perm in the north and almost reaching the Volga. From the West, General Nikolai Yudenich established a White base in Estonia.

Although the Bolsheviks had anticipated a German threat from the Baltics and moved the country's capital from Petrograd to Moscow, it was with the gravest of misgivings that Lenin watched the approach of Yudenich from Estonia to the very outskirts of Petrograd, where, so it was reported, the Whites were successful on 16 October 1919 in seiz-ing Gatchina, only thirty miles away. In the Western press, the event was jubilantly reported as a complete rout of the Bolsheviks, and the front page of *The New York Times* reported with equal gusto the fall of Petrograd to Yudenich's forces on the 20th. The only problem was that the report was entirely false: Yudenich's forces had actually been defeated on the outskirts of the city and were falling back rapidly to their position inside the borders of Estonia.

By that date, Walter Duranty was already well on his way into the Baltic States, where Yudenich was making his last stand. Duranty would later describe this episode in his career as being more akin to "a Mad Hatter's Tea Party" than to a conventional reporting assignment, and he maintained the confusion of events and authority he found there was a good introduction to how things were done in that part of the world.[9]

In October 1919, only a short time before Yudenich made his unsuc-cessful foray into Soviet territory, the United States appointed its first High Commissioner, Naval Commander Gade, to the Baltic States. According to the terms of the Brest-Litovsk Treaty, Latvia, Estonia, and Lithuania had been ceded to Germany. But now, with Germany's defeat, the three countries were making a bid for their independence, and the Allies were supporting them. Gade was to have his headquarters in the Latvian capital of Riga, and C. H. Grasty, attached to the *Times* Paris bureau as a roving correspondent, was assigned to accompany the commander to his new mission. But Grasty, a somewhat older man, could find little to appeal to him in Baltic regions in the winter, and he eased himself out of the assignment, which in turn was transferred to Walter Duranty.

Fed up with office politics and highly desirous of his independence, Duranty was eager enough to go, and he was assigned a place with Gade's party on the naval cruiser that would carry them to Riga.

It was an appointment Duranty never kept. He gave the excuse that he had come down with a bad case of the Spanish flu, the same illness, he said, that had killed so many in the last year of the war and just afterwards. He suggested to his office that he catch up with the cruiser at Copenhagen, and they agreed. The plan was for Duranty to travel up through Germany to Hamburg, taking the train-ferry across to Denmark and on to Copenhagen.

But in Germany, Duranty found the railroads shut down, and he was forced into continuing his journey by leapfrogging from city to city by whatever means he could find. Completely undismayed by this turn of events, Duranty seemed on the contrary to welcome the freedom of the open road, far away from the eagle eye of the Paris office. One of his first discoveries was "a new racket, which was then popular in Eastern Europe."

> A man with nerve, some pull and a little money could, it seemed, get a courier job in some of the smaller countries and carry official mail at his own risk and peril. He would also take a suit-case full of silk stockings, underwear, cosmetics, vanilla extract, and so forth, and if he was sufficiently unscrupulous, cocaine or heroin. He would sell his "cargo" on reaching his goal, then buy jewels or furs or *objets d'art* or even platinum, which had leaked out of Russia.[10]

But the existence of small-time smuggling was not Duranty's only discovery. He managed to get stories out of practically everything he encountered on his trip to the Baltics. In Finland, he reported on the famous White Guard, who had defeated a Red Revolution inside Finnish borders with the help of German troops.

More important, he learned of the defeat of the Yudenich forces and gave a cogent description of the battle in the middle of a long dispatch describing the situation in Finland.[11]

His continuing maze of travels was to lead him to other important stories. Aboard one small coasting vessel traveling from Helsingfors (Helsinki) to Reval, he met a Dutchman who told him that the prominent Bolshevik Maxim Litvinov was on his way to Estonia, ostensibly to arrange for the exchange of prisoners and hostages, but in fact to introduce thinly veiled peace negotiations with the Finns and Estonians. Duranty decided to stay put in Dorpat to witness the meeting between Litvinov and representatives of the Baltic States. In fact, he was able to pick up the scoop that the Soviets would offer new reconciliation treaty terms to the Baltics, recognizing their complete independence and offering important new trade agreements. And for a second time, he reported that Yudenich's White Russian Army was withdrawing toward the Estonian frontier at Narva, "thoroughly beaten."[12]

The same Dutchman whom Duranty had met on the boat hunted Duranty down in Dorpat because he "admired and coveted [Duranty's] coat"—a "pseudo-Burberry with a kangaroo collar and a lining of rabbit dressed to look like sealskin." Duranty said the coat had cost him a mere $40 at Galeries Lafayette in Paris, and the style—"flashy without dignity and pretentious without warmth"—was popular with second-rate French aviators.[13] When the Dutchman mentioned having had a long interview with Litvinov concerning an exchange of Dutch and Russian prisoners, Duranty offered his coat in return for information.

The result was an interesting outline of Litvinov's attitudes and intentions—another feather in Duranty's cap. One of the topics Litvinov had discussed with the Dutchman concerned Duranty himself, along with a number of correspondents from news organizations like the Associated Press, the Chicago *Daily News,* and the Chicago *Tribune,* who had asked to be admitted into Russia to cover events unfolding there. Litvinov had told the Dutchman he was unwilling to receive members of the American press in Dorpat, let alone admit them to the Soviet Union. "If there were any 'good' newspapers represented, like the London *Daily Herald* or Manchester *Guardian,* it would be different," Litvinov said. "I am willing to talk to them."[14]

After hearing various accounts of Yudenich's campaign, Duranty privately formulated the opinion that the anti-Bolshevik forces were "rotted by incompetence and jealousy, or worse." It was hardly the prevailing Western view of the defenders of Russian democracy. In fact, Duranty would write later, the army led by Yudenich, forced back and in a state of utter disarray, was finished off by a typhus epidemic, "which killed 11,000 out of 15,000, in circumstances of despair, filth, starvation, misery and lack of medical aid so frightful that the *New York Times* would not print [his] account of it. . . ."[15] Yet, he maintained, his story was taken directly from the report of the American Red Cross to High Commissioner Gade. The *Times* did, however, run a short, sanitized version of the story in a page-four report in late December.[16]

Duranty found conditions in the Baltic States primitive and difficult. The population was close to starvation, transport "so shattered that there were only five working locomotives in the whole of Latvia."[17] Especially disconcerting was the plenitude of lice, the carrier of typhus, a disease common, if not epidemic, throughout the three countries.

Politically, the situation in Latvia mirrored to some extent the problems of each of the small Baltic States. They had all been dominated throughout their history by the stronger and larger countries that surrounded them. In 1919, Latvia was still occupied by the Germans who had been, since Brest-Litovsk, the controlling faction.

In the capital, Riga, the German leader Graf Rudiger von der Goltz had maintained order since the end of the war, at first at the direction of the Allies. But it soon became clear that he intended, if he were able, to take over both Latvia and Lithuania permanently, despite the defeat of his country. By the time Duranty made it onto the scene, von der Goltz had just been persuaded by the recently arrived British to withdraw as far as Mitau.

But there, Duranty reported, "the Germans showed the same bestial cruelty, the same wanton destructiveness" as they had during "their victorious advance through Belgium and France. . . ." He wrote of their destruction by fire of two of the town's most famous landmarks—"a magnificent seventeenth century castle built by Rastrelli, architect of the Winter Palace in Petrograd and the College Library, which dates from the reign of Catherine the Great." He talked to the peasants, listened to their stories of German atrocities, saw the bodies of a group of men the Germans had used for target practice—one of them a "wretched half wit [who] stood dazed without even attempting

87

to escape." His body lay "huddled almost at the roadside." Another man's head was blown away, a "gruesome sight" even the "drifting snow" couldn't hide.[18] For Duranty, the Germans hadn't changed since the war ended, and his reportage on their conquests in the Baltic was substantially a continuation of his war coverage.

With the Germans' withdrawal, the British became the most important force in the region, operating under the leadership of the British High Commissioner for the Baltic Provinces, Stephen Tallents. As it happened, Tallents had been at Harrow the same time as Duranty, and Duranty fitted himself easily into the old boy network, establishing a warm rapport with Tallents. It was another lucky break, and Duranty was quick to expand his relations to others in the British contingent, forming the habit of taking lunch at the British Mission.

> . . . one day, about a week after my arrival in Riga, I found sitting by the fire in the big club-room, a young British officer in khaki uniform with the insignia of a Colonel, but wearing Russian high boots; beside him there was a gray astrakhan cap, of the type worn in the Cossack regiments. This was Lieutenant-Colonel Alexander, a regular officer in the Irish Guards, now detached by special order to command the Baltic Landeswehr. . . . Alex, as everyone called him, was the most charming and picturesque person I have ever met, and one of the two soldiers I have known who derived a strong, positive, and permanent exhilaration from the worst of danger.[19]

Duranty immediately recognized in the young Alexander, who, incidentally, had also been at Harrow, those organizational and leadership characteristics that would eventually carry him to fame in World War II, first at Dunkirk where he was put in charge of the evacuation of the British troops, and then as commander of the historic Tunisian campaign. It would be Alexander who informed the Prime Minister in 1943: "Sir, it is my duty to report that the Tunisian campaign is over. All enemy resistance has ceased. We are masters of the North African shores." Now at twenty-seven years of age, he was as handsome and dashing as he was competent, and he and Duranty became close friends.[20]

Alexander's first goal after taking over the Latvian fighting force, known as the Landeswehr, was to establish a sense of self-worth and discipline among the common soldiers, an objective which, as Duranty reported to the *Times,* he achieved with remarkable speed.[21] Lavishing

praise on the young military leader, Duranty recorded the early victories of Alexander and his inherited army against the Bolsheviks,
whom Alexander drove from Latvia in a matter of three weeks.

With a modesty of tone that would become a familiar characteristic, Alexander attributed his success to the flexibility of his small force.
"In Russia," he told Duranty, "God is on the side of the small battal-
ions, not the big ones. . . . That is, if they have the right spirit and are
properly trained. I believe that if Napoleon had had 50,000 men
instead of 500,000 the retreat from Moscow would have never
occurred."[22] It was unusual for Duranty to become so genuinely enamored of anyone he reported, but even at this early date, Alexander
apparently had about him an aura of courage, good cheer, and sheer
professional competence, which inspired unsolicited respect from
those around him.

It was later said that Walter Duranty was the only newspaperman
Alexander would ever speak to,[23] and throughout the next two decades
he and Duranty were often seen together, whenever the two men found
themselves stationed in the same place.

Duranty's contacts among the British continued to pay off, giving him
an exclusive which he was later to call the best break he ever had in
twenty years of reporting—"a cracker-jack story on a plate, so to
speak."[24] Looking forward to two weeks of festivities over Christmas
and New Year's, Duranty willingly abandoned his plans when he was
tipped off that the local authorities had discovered a Red conspiracy
to overthrow the Latvian government, along with the apprehension of
a courier from Soviet Russia. The literature carried by the courier gave
conclusive proof of Bolshevik intentions of espionage in the United
States. The story Duranty wrote about the affair netted him the only
bonus that he ever received from the *New York Times*.

The courier was a Russian sailor, who was "betrayed by some girl
with whom he had unwisely slept," Duranty later recalled. He had
been captured by the Latvians in Libau carrying some $8000 worth of
diamonds concealed in the heels of his boots, a seventeenth-century
miniature surrounded by diamonds, and a vast sum of cash.

He was also bearing seditious literature that gave instructions to the
Communists in America to try to enlist American soldiers returning
from the war to revolt—materials Duranty in retrospect found "silly,
inflammatory stuff," but at the time worth a front-page lead.

A great Bolshevist conspiracy has just been discovered here, and the leaders with the principal subordinates have been arrested to the number of 100. The object was to overthrow the Government and establish Bolshevist rule.

Last, but not least, a Russian sailor was taken bearing large sums of money and jewels of great value concealed in the soles of his boots and a letter from one of Lenin's closest satellites to "comrades" in America. . . . It is said to contain minute directions for the conduct of the Bolshevist campaign in America, for the organization of various centres, and the methods to be followed subsequently.[25]

A few days later, Duranty was given an interview with the courier "for an hour . . . in company with allied and Lettish officers and an interpreter." When Duranty described the courier as having a "brutal face, but decidedly not stupid," he was to some extent relying on the typical news-writing conventions of the time of over-emphasizing physical traits to increase reader interest.

But in his zealous account of the incident, Duranty somehow overreached himself. The sailor's story was that he had been approached by the Bolsheviks and asked to convey the literature and valuables he was carrying to a prearranged destination, and the Bolsheviks would in return pay the expenses of his passage. There was no doubt in Duranty's mind "that the man was a typical Bolshevist agent." In addition to having a "half-digested education," Duranty said, he showed the typical Bolshevik cunning in evading questions. "There was, too, a sullen mulishness at times which went well with the gorilla jaw and receding forehead."[26] Seemingly, these were all qualities of the typical Bolshevik.

In retrospect, it seems difficult to understand why an overwritten story such as this made such a hit in New York. The United States, however, was then in the grip of a national hysteria over what was viewed as the growing threat of Communism. "The Red Scare," as it came to be known, gave the courier story a context of national importance as an example of Bolshevik intentions in America.

Since the beginning of 1919, a national media campaign inspired by official U. S. attitudes had fanned natural suspicions about the Bolsheviks into an atmosphere of hatred and violence. A number of strikes across the country added to the prevailing view that these were in reality Communist-inspired attempts at the violent overthrow of the U. S. government.

The Seattle general strike in February, the series of bombs sent to public officials in April, the Boston police strike in September—these and other events incited a volatile fear of Bolshevik revolution. In response, numerous state legislatures passed syndicalist and sedition laws to prohibit membership in organizations advocating violent overthrow of the government, while mobs destroyed socialist offices and beat up or lynched IWW members. As a grand climax to the Scare, Attorney General A. Mitchell Palmer launched his famous Red raids, arresting for deportation 450 supposed Communist aliens in twelve cities on November 7, 1919, and then seized 4,000 more suspects in thirty-three cities on January 2. On December 21, 1919, 249 persons were actually deported on the "Soviet Ark," the *Buford,* including the well-known anarchists Emma Goldman and Alexander Berkman.[27]

Duranty's Red Courier story, which broke in the Christmas Day issue of the *Times,* landed squarely in the middle of those events. The story offered confirmation from abroad that the extraordinary actions being taken at home were essential measures of self-protection against destructive and sinister outside forces. Never one to miss out on an opportunity, Duranty continued writing about the conspiracy, milking the story for all it was worth and probably a good deal more.

The story had an unexpected side effect that Duranty found extremely gratifying. About three days after it broke, the acting head of the American Mission in Riga received a cable from his superiors in Washington asking why he hadn't informed them of the big "Courier-Spy-Document story" that was splashed across the front pages of the *New York Times.* As Duranty later explained, "The chief reason was that he did not know about it. The British might have told him, but I had asked them not to; and I might have told him, but I didn't. . . ."

Duranty's reason for keeping the diplomat in the dark was simple revenge. It seems the man stole away a girl Duranty had escorted to some party. The American was tall and handsome; Duranty was neither. And the diplomat danced extremely well. "He was the kind of man who would never have any trouble about any girls, so why grab mine?" So when the American *chargé d'affaires* summoned Duranty to his office to ask why he hadn't been informed of the story, Duranty asked:

"Can't you guess?" He looked as if he did guess. "Yes," I added, "and I hope that the cable you received from Washington was the kind of cable Van Anda sometimes sends me, I mean the sort of cable that makes you think you've been scalped by a troop of Indians." He said it was, which made me feel better; and he said he was sorry, which made me feel better still. He said, too, "If you've got any more of this stuff, will you let me see it?" So I let him see it; the hatchet was buried, and I felt magnanimous. But the girl always danced with him at parties, and gave me only a pleasant smile.[28]

Within a month of Duranty's hit story, the Estonians signed the Treaty of Dorpat with the Soviets, bringing freedom to Estonia through Russian recognition of the country's independence. In Latvia, where the Bolshevik troops had been expelled by Alexander and the Landeswehr, an armistice was declared between Latvia and the Soviets. With this settlement, Duranty returned to Paris, where he continued to write for several weeks about the events he had witnessed on his trip to the Baltic. None of his reports, or any of the stories he wrote from Riga, ever mentioned Commander Gade, the American High Commissioner he was sent to cover.

In March of 1920, only a few weeks after Duranty's return to the Paris bureau, a Communist rebellion took place in the German Rhineland. With his recent successes in the Baltic, Duranty seemed to have become the *Times* resident expert in anything to do with Communism, and Van Anda instructed that Duranty was to cover it. With his customary enthusiasm, Duranty immediately jumped on a train to Duisburg, where things were "hotting up," as he put it. There, he ran into his old friend William Bolitho who was still reporting for the Manchester *Guardian*.

The pair were soon picked up by the local German authorities and taken to the military commander, who recognized Duranty's name immediately, since he had served under von der Goltz in Latvia. "Oh, yes, I know you, Duranty," he said. "You're the man who wrote filthy lying stories about atrocities we committed in the Baltic." According to Duranty's own version of the story, he became frightened, and when frightened, he became angry. Rounding on the German officer, Duranty insisted in inflamed language that he had witnessed the atrocities personally. He described the bodies he had seen with his own eyes, remembering specifically the incident in which the Germans had used local peasants for target practice. Then he enumerated other atrocities he had not reported, but which had struck him forcibly at the time as being particularly barbaric. Strangely, the stories, along with Duranty's fury, seemed to amuse and pacify the German commander, and he carelessly issued free passes for both Bolitho and Duranty, telling them to go out and see for themselves if the same sort of things were going on in Germany.[29]

Bolitho had just come from Alten Essen, where he had been with the Communists and watched their ultimate demise there. He was indignant because of what he called "the fatalism" of the revolutionaries, their acquiescence in their own defeat, and he and Duranty compared notes.

In the case of the Reds he had just been with, Bolitho figured out early on that they were sure to be annihilated by the superior forces that were closing in around them like a net. He told the leaders they had only one chance, and that was to threaten to blow up all the key mines and factories in the area, then go ahead and blow one up to show they meant to do what they threatened. Bolitho advised them that they could then bargain for certain political and economic concessions, as well as their own pardons.

"Do you think they'd do it?" Bolitho asked Duranty with disgust. They had told Bolitho that if they blew up the mines, they would have nowhere to work afterwards. They preferred to throw themselves on the mercy of the authorities, who, Bolitho told Duranty, had already begun executing the men even before he could get out of town. Bolitho was so impressed by the incident that he later wrote a play about it.[30]

By the same token, Duranty had watched some men die before the firing squad when there were enough of them to overpower their guard, if they had decided to make a run for it. Instead, they shared a cigarette before going meekly to their deaths, an event that fascinated Duranty. Neither he nor Bolitho could fathom the motivation of men who accepted their own deaths passively, when they could have given themselves a chance, however remote, at living. Bolitho had his own theory, which he now introduced to Duranty for the first time:

> "Don't forget ... that the majority of people and the majority of opinions are nearly always wrong about everything, not always, but nearly always, and if you ever are in doubt and can't make up your mind, and have to make it up, there are long odds in favor of your being right if you take the opposite view from the majority. All this talk

of Democracy and the 'Sovereign Peepul' and *vox populi* being *vox Dei*
is just a trick by cunning demagogues to kid the masses."[31]

It was an elitist philosophy that would make its appearance again
and again in Duranty's writing. In a way, Duranty took Bolitho's idea
to heart in ways Bolitho himself never anticipated. By following the
credo in reporting Russia, Duranty thought he had found an inside
track on the truth. Somehow, he believed, merely by taking the minority view, he would be able to see through the outward hypocrisy of
men's actions and into their innermost motivations.

Duranty also came up with another hypothesis of his own: that if
he put himself in another man's shoes and asked himself what he
would do if he were in that man's situation, he would somehow be able
to see further and deeper into the man than others, and in many cases
be able to predict the future.

While the world Communist revolution predicted by Lenin was failing
to materialize, the Soviets had at last gained the upper hand in the civil
war raging within their own borders. In late 1919, Allied forces had
withdrawn from the north and from the Odessa area. In the spring of
1920, the American troops in Siberia were withdrawn as well. And by
the latter part of 1920, even the southern Whites had been successfully
suppressed by the Red Army. With their defeat, the episode of Allied
Intervention in Soviet Russia was effectually at an end, leaving a residue of hostility that would continue on the Bolshevik side for many
decades to come.

For their part, the Allies stepped up their propaganda campaign
against the Bolsheviks.

One of the chief contributors turned out to be Walter Duranty. At
least a year before he made his big hit in New York with the Red Courier story, Duranty was reporting the Bolsheviks in a less than favorable
light, referring to the feeling in Paris that the dangers of Bolshevism
were growing "daily stronger." It had led, he complained, to a highly
overcharged atmosphere where information was being distorted "as
the newspapers avoid alarming news on the one hand and on the other
are over-ready to feature exaggerated stories."[32]

With the success of his Red Courier story, however, Duranty now
seemed ready to abandon all caution, jumping into the fray feet first
and writing stories studded with his own opinions and beliefs—all of

which were strongly anti-Soviet. He picked up catchy phrases like "bacillus Bolshevismus," and called the Soviet leadership "this Bolshevist gang at Moscow."[33] Bolshevism became "a compound of force, terror and espionage, utterly ruthless in conception and execution";[34] a quotable quote indeed, and as it happens, one of the statements that seems to have gone down as Duranty's watchword on the Soviet system.

Of course, many of Duranty's anti-Bolshevik stories were simply the result of one-sided press releases issued in Paris by the French. During the six months' war between Russia and Poland, for example, Duranty painted a rosy picture of Polish prospects, emphasizing the incompetence of the Red Army. The Poles' drive into the Ukraine in the winter and spring of 1920 seemed certain to Duranty to succeed, just as Alexander's defeat of the Bolsheviks in the Baltics had been a matter of only three short weeks. But Duranty, along with others who favored the Poles, was caught short by the strong counterattack of the Soviets, who turned the tables on their enemy in a series of rapid advances that carried them to the very outskirts of Warsaw. Trotsky's brilliant reorganization of the Red Army very nearly resulted in the annexing of a huge segment of Poland, a fact disputed at the time by Duranty.

Duranty later admitted he had done a poor job of reporting the Soviet-Polish war, excusing himself on the grounds that he had been trying to report it from Paris and had only French press releases for most of his information.[35] But that could not account for the tone or the zeal of his anti-Soviet writing.

Only a short time later, when the Bolsheviks cautiously initiated a white-flag policy in the propaganda war with the West, Duranty moved in again with his sensational prose, which now seems frankly overwrought. Was this attempt at healing the rift between East and West the voice "of a devil luring the world to destruction, or of a great-hearted brother in liberty eager for self sacrifice that the world may again find happiness?"[36] In formulating his dramatic question, Duranty suggested that civilization itself hung in the balance. Then, too, he wrote frequently of the imminent downfall of Soviet Russia, adding his own flourishes to the reports issuing forth from the French press office.[37]

Twenty-four years later, in 1944, when he was sixty years old, Walter Duranty would lament the bad name given to the Bolsheviks, pointing out that no other country in history had been subject to such consistent misinterpretation by other countries as had the acts and policies of the Soviet Union during the first quarter-century of its existence.[38] Ironically, he had been one of the most active writers during the period to do just that.

In early August of 1920, he and the other writers who had been issuing wildly anti-Bolshevik reports suffered a severe shock.

A pair of young researchers, Charles Merz and Walter Lippmann, published the results of a content analysis they had been conducting on the nature of *New York Times* coverage of Soviet Russia. Their research extended from March 1917 to March 1920, covered 36 months and 1000 issues of the newspaper. All in all, the pair had examined between 3000 to 4000 news articles, some of them written by Walter Duranty, although he was not singled out by name. Despite his youth, Lippmann had already established a formidable reputation, won on *The New Republic*, which was something of a house organ of President Wilson's New Freedom. It was in this influential magazine that he and Merz published their thoroughly damning article.

From November 1917 to November 1919, they wrote, "it was stated that the Soviets were nearing their rope's end, or actually had reached it" ninety-one times.[39] Twice, it had been reported that Lenin planned retirement, three times he had been thrown into prison, and once he was killed. The *Times* had four times reported that Lenin and Trotsky were planning flight. Three times, they had already fled. The authors of the article finished by saying that the news reports had been motivated more by the hopes of the editors than by the facts themselves. It was a case of seeing not what was before their eyes but what they "wished to see."[40]

Although the *Times* did not publicly acknowledge the report, it was badly stung. It had never before suffered this kind of harsh criticism, nor would the paper experience it in the future.[41] Getting a man into the Soviet Union now became a matter of the utmost importance and one of Van Anda's first priorities.

CHAPTER VI

"Luck Broke My Way"

In the summer of 1921, "luck broke my way," as Duranty put it, "in the shape of the great Russian famine, which then threatened to cost about 30,000,000 lives, and probably did cost 5,000,000 or 6,000,000 including deaths from disease."[1]

It was an opportune moment for Duranty, human suffering aside, because the Bolsheviks intended to admit a number of correspondents to cover the débâcle, and Duranty hoped to be one of them. Allowing Western news coverage was not a decision the Bolsheviks made willingly, but by this time, mere survival had necessitated the compromise of many of the original ideals of the Revolution.

By the end of 1920, the Bolsheviks had met a series of unexpected calamities more or less successfully. The Civil War had ended, with the Whites decisively defeated, their troops dispersed, as many of them as could fleeing to the West. Allied Intervention had fizzled out, mostly of its own accord, after the defeat of the counterrevolutionaries. The six months' war with the Poles had been terminated, if not favorably, at least on terms basically acceptable and less than humiliating.

But the cost had been enormous. Food shortages had resulted in forcible requisitioning, at first considered by the Bolsheviks a temporary measure justified by their need to feed the army and the workers in vital industries during the Civil War. However, it quickly turned into a general policy of rationing and supervision of food distribution.

War Communism, as it was called, came to rely more and more upon repression and outright violence as the main methods of securing meat and grain from the peasants. Essentials like salt, kerosene, and matches were in short supply; important manufactured goods, such as boots and farming implements, were not forthcoming. With few rewards for their labor, the peasants showed little interest in growing more than what their immediate needs required. Now a ruinous drought in the grain-growing districts added to the misfortunes of the already depleted countryside, and the entire nation lay exhausted, in a state of virtual collapse.

The Soviets had little recourse other than to appeal for help from abroad, and Herbert Hoover's American Relief Association at once agreed to meet them in Riga to discuss the terms under which they would undertake to meet the disaster. One of their stipulations was that news correspondents from the West be allowed to report on the relief work, and Van Anda cabled Duranty instructions to go to the Latvian capital to cover the negotiations and be prepared to enter Russia when they were concluded.

As soon as he arrived, Duranty discovered he stood less chance than any of the other correspondents of being admitted into the country. Characteristically, he managed quickly to ingratiate himself with the Soviet press officer, a young man by the name of Markov, who, like Duranty, had been educated in England. Markov told Duranty confidentially that Duranty was being rejected by the Soviet representative Maxim Litvinov because of the Red Courier story he had written in Riga two years before and because of the dossier of anti-Bolshevik stories he had written from Paris.

George Seldes of the Chicago *Tribune*, who was among the dozen or so reporters waiting alongside Duranty, said that nobody expected Duranty to get a visa.

"Litvinov singled Walter Duranty out—didn't want to admit him," Seldes remembered nearly sixty years after the event. "But Walter said he got all the false stories mentioned in 'A Test of the News' from the highest government officials in France and that everybody else, even the Associated Press, had been picking up the same false stories as he had from the same sources."[2]

What actually reversed Litvinov's decision, so Duranty believed, was an exclusive Duranty wrote from Riga on the subject of Lenin's New Economic Policy. Duranty's newly acquired friend in the Soviet press office alerted him to the decree published in *Pravda*, translated it for him, and explained its importance to him. Without Markov's help, Duranty said later, he would never have succeeded in gaining admission.[3] The story began with the kind of high drama typical of Duranty's work, but went on to explain the new policy seriously, without hyperbole and without affixing blame:

> Lenin has thrown communism overboard. His signature appears in the official press of Moscow on August 9, abandoning State ownership, with the exception of a definite number of great industries of national importance—such as were controlled by the State in France, England and Germany during the war—and re-establishing payment by individuals for railroads, postal and other public services.[4]

If Duranty was in fact accepted on the basis of this story, the reason is probably that the article objectifies the NEP and represents an honest attempt to explain it, rather than glorying in what amounted to a straightforward admission of defeat on the part of the Bolsheviks. In that sense, a potentially explosive reversal in policy became the action of reasonable men instead of latter-day demons intent on destroying the world—an image Duranty would have hardly hesitated to use earlier in describing the Bolshevik leadership. In effect, the story called a moratorium on that sensational style. His comparison of the New Economic Policy with measures instituted by the Allies during World War I also put the Soviets in good company, a fact Maxim Litvinov could not have failed to notice. Thus, with this token of good will was Duranty admitted provisionally to the Soviet Union, in what George Seldes would later call "a pleasant surprise to us all."[5]

Seldes and Duranty hit it off, so much so that Duranty confided to him some of the inner workings at the *New York Times* Paris bureau. In particular, Duranty made a frank admission of being on the outs with Jimmy James, the correspondent whose work flanked his own on page one in the last few months of the war.

"He and James had a feud on," Seldes remembered. "Why they didn't like each other, I don't know. I can understand why Walter couldn't stand him, though. He was Walter Duranty's nemesis."[6] Seldes was here referring to a persistent dislike the two men felt for one another which lasted throughout their lifetimes. Somehow, in talking over the old days, Seldes managed to convey the impression that he hadn't had much use for Jimmy James himself.

"He was not a nice man," another of James's colleagues said of him in later years, "but don't quote me on it."

It was a slow train, five days plus, with no electricity, no food, no provisions for sleeping. The correspondents carried suitcases, sleeping bags, boxes of canned food, and portable typewriters, everything they thought they might need once they got into Moscow. There was the tacit assumption, which seemed at the time rather exciting, that they were being watched, that the Soviet secret service had marked them for surveillance; then the rude awakening: they weren't even important enough to be met at the station. After a long wait in which no one appeared, the men eventually located a porter who said nobody ever met trains in Moscow because nobody ever knew when they would arrive.

At last, the newsmen were picked up by a truck sent over by the Foreign Office, with a few young Cheka soldiers who helped load the baggage while they good-naturedly cadged American smokes. Then the whole entourage made its way through the potholed streets into a derelict area where the Press Office was located. It stood on the corner of Theater Square in the center of town behind the Metropole Hotel, "a seedy spot," Duranty called it.[7]

The men climbed five flights of dirty steps to the Press Office, perspiring a bit from the climb, out of breath, and at "a physical disadvantage in bearding the Bolshevik press lions in their dens."[8] One of the officials, a New Yorker, recognized Duranty's name and pointed out he had nearly been sent to prison as a result of Duranty's anti-Bolshevik reporting, especially the stories that came out of Riga. Duranty was face to face with one of the aliens flushed out by the Red Scare two years before. Duranty told him he was now in a position "to turn the tables," but the man retorted that in Soviet Russia, at least, innocent men were not sent to jail.

The reporters immediately began pressing to go to the Volga to see the famine, and the press officer seemed cooperative, promising vaguely he would see if it could be arranged within a few days. Meanwhile, they should settle into Moscow and become acquainted with the city. There were objections, telephone calls, a lot of talk, and then they were landed in the Savoy Hotel, a lodging somewhat at odds with all that its name implied.

The rooms the correspondents were given were swarming with rats and mice, and insects of all kinds. They had electricity and the telephones actually worked, but there was no running water. Every morning, a kettle of hot water was delivered to the room for making tea. Otherwise, there was no place in the hotel or close to it to grab a bite to eat. As quickly as he and the others had settled in, they began the long walk to the only "private restaurant" in Moscow and had, to their surprise, a reasonable dinner.

As they were making their adjustments to the privations of the Soviet capital, the men were given a rude awakening by the first of many "anguished and peremptory cables from [their] home offices" giving them the unwelcome news that, while they were sitting around in Moscow, Floyd Gibbons had made his way into the stricken region, and was "beating [their] heads off and scoring one of the biggest newspaper triumphs in post-War history."

Duranty later wrote, "All we could do was to run bleating . . . to the Press Department and be told, 'We are making arrangements; there will doubtless be a train for you to-morrow.' It was an agonizing experience, but there was nothing we could do about it but gnash our teeth and wait."[9]

Floyd Gibbons, now a dashing figure with his black eye patch, had chartered a plane and told Litvinov he planned to fly into Red Square in it, giving his paper a big scoop. Appalled at the prospect, Litvinov instead offered Gibbons the chance to go early into the area stricken by famine, exactly what Gibbons had been after all along. Once into the Ukraine, Gibbons sent his dispatches back by messenger and by train to Moscow, where they were cabled directly to the United States. In this way he gave his newspaper a ten-day lead on the others. Duranty said Gibbons "fully deserved his success because he had accomplished the feat of bluffing the redoubtable Litvinov stone-cold . . . a noble piece of work."[10]

For the *New York Times* though, it was a case of having to buy what they had already paid for—and from a rival newspaper. And so Gibbons's first dispatch, copyrighted by the Chicago *Tribune*, appeared in the pages of the *New York Times* on the 1st of September 1921. In it, he described the empty streets and sidewalks of a small village inside the state of Samara. The people, he reported, were

101

exhausted by malnutrition and no longer had the energy to go about the streets. Instead, they holed up inside their houses, eating cakes made from dried melon rinds which were ground up, then used as a kind of flour. The concoction provided no nourishment, only filled the stomachs of the starving. Hunger, Gibbons reported, had already claimed the lives of one-third of the inhabitants of the village.[11]

In the days that followed, Gibbons would be the only reporter to document the horrifying prospect of the deaths of as many as fifteen million people from starvation, one million of whom Gibbons believed were "doomed to die in spite of any relief measures that America or the world may take." He wrote of walking through the camps along with the others of his party with heavy towels wrapped around their faces to protect them against the rampant cholera and typhus, the diseases that accompany starvation. All around them, the Russian peasants lay upon the bare ground, slowly dying.

Gibbons's dispatches were stark and presented a picture of relentless misery:

> I talked with a doctor who saw a dog tearing the flesh from a dead man lying here in the market-place. The commandant of our train tells me of a woman with two children in her arms who threw herself under the train preceding ours. Women with puny weazened babies biting at their flat breasts wander through the streets, shouting wild gibberish, and with a wild light in their eyes. Every day the city authorities find rotting bodies in cellars, attics, lofts, sheds and out of the way places, where misery crawls away to gain the privilege of dying alone rather than in the midst of the city's filth and confusion.[12]

Perhaps the most affecting of his dispatches concerned the description of a dying child. The mother had beckoned Gibbons over and lifted up a cover to show him the naked youngster lying beneath. The body, he wrote, had been stuffed with a "black, greasy clay called 'eel,'" which could be found locally. The stuff had no grit and clung to the teeth, and the children grabbed it up and ate it in order to "still the gnawing of hunger in the stomach." Because the clay could not be eliminated by the system, it remained in the children's intestines. "Then comes the swelling of the abused 'innards,'" he wrote, "together with masses of worms, and the horrible distension that changes the likeness from that of a man to that of a superinflated goblin."[13] The only escape from the resulting agony was death.

102

He wrote of the docility of the victims, who often lay within sight of small markets where meager but sustaining supplies of food were on sale, speaking of his surprise that "the pangs of hunger so far have not driven the starving hordes to storm the market place and take the food there displayed for themselves."

> It may be because they are too weak; maybe it is because starving men will not fight, for these men and women do not fight—not even the latter to save the lives of their children. . . . I witnessed no fight between any of the sufferers over food.[14]

Faced with such overwhelming human suffering, Gibbons and the other three Americans accompanying him, "who had brought promises only to this land of need," bought all of the food they were able from the nearby markets and carefully rationed out 372 chunks of black bread, watching to be sure each piece went to a different person. But after the bread gave out, sixty of those who had waited patiently for their share had still not received any food, "and we sent a man on horseback to a town four miles away where we managed to buy thirty pounds more which we distributed an hour later."

> It was the first distribution of American relief in the Volga country, but we had no mistaken ideas about the good that it did. We could only feed that mite to some who had passed the food craving period and it would only renew the tortures that they had already gone through. We, who gave the bit of food, received more good from it than those who received it because in a measure it atoned for the fact we had in our bodies the warmth of ample food and were wearing whole clothes and were housed on a boat while 400 fellow-humans of our color and belief in our God were dying miserably within a stone's throw.[15]

Gibbons steadfastly recorded the suffering he witnessed, without glossing over ugly facts or resorting to sentimentality. His stories offered no easy solution to the horrors of the famine.

Duranty finally made it into the famine-stricken area, five or six days behind Gibbons. With Gibbons far in the lead on the major stories, Duranty was left to cover the sidelines. In contrast to Gibbons's graphic and emotional coverage, Duranty's reporting seemed precise, professional, even mannered. His first dispatch concerned the starving children who had been deserted by their parents, and in it he fell back on straight technique—his "imagine-you-are-there" device—which had served him well in the past:

> Imagine yourself standing at the corner of a dusty street through whose humps and hollows runs a car line with cars every ten minutes. The houses are mostly low, wooden structures with dirty window panes or gaping holes like bleared and sightless eyes. . . .[16]

In this town, Duranty wrote, were children whose "fingers are positively no fatter than a good sized match, for I compared them." The arms were "no wider than rulers. . . ." One boy's face was "shrunk to the size of a woman's hand and the blue eyes are utterly disinterested. The body may weigh fourteen pounds—just skin tense over the wasted little skeleton."[17]

A month before, when Duranty was still in Riga, he had written of the frenzied mobs "united in a brief orgy of pillage in such meagre stores as the towns possess."[18] Now he realized that this story had been pure fiction. Like Gibbons, he was surprised by the passivity of the people who were truly starving as they waited for death to claim them. Somewhere, in the shadows of his surprise was silent disapproval, something akin to what he and Bolitho had felt in Germany when they talked about the men who went obediently to their deaths instead of making a run for it. The peasants were touched by the taint of fatalism, vaguely related in Duranty's mind to superstition.

The only actual emotion he recorded was that of anger. Confronted by the passivity of a matron in charge of a makeshift orphanage, which was really nothing more than a "pest house" where the children were kept before they died, Duranty attacked her for not trying to keep the children clean, "even without soap." The woman shrugged it away, answering, "What is the use? They would die anyway. . . . God has hid his face from Russia. . . . We are being punished for our sins." Duranty went away, he said, "feeling sick, and hating [himself] for being healthy and well fed."[19] But there was just a trace of contempt for people who seriously entertained such backward notions, and in time, he would come to respect the Bolsheviks for trying to rid the peasants of their religious superstitions.

Otherwise, for all the vividness of his accounts, he seemed personally untouched by the suffering he was witnessing, bringing precision and exactitude to his work instead of emotions. He made much of the distinction that most of the people died not of hunger but of the diseases related to hunger, a fact that turned up in his work with great frequency. "Few, save the children," he wrote, "died of actual hunger, but typhus, cholera, dysentery, typhoid, and scurvy, the diseases of malnutrition, took their plenteous toll."[20]

As quickly as he possibly could, he changed his focus to a more upbeat subject—the work of the American Relief Administration and its distribution of the first food into the famine-stricken areas.

> Loads of white flour sacks, some on big motor trucks, stirred the Tartar population from its usual Oriental calm. Slant-eyed women wearing round skull caps, colored scarfs, short skirts and high embroidered leather boots, paused in their bargaining at the market stalls, pointing in surprise. The children ran eagerly forward. The wild little Tartar horses plunged in terror. A gleam even came to the lustreless eyes of a dying boy on the sidewalk, long past help, and the gaunt old crone beside him raised her skinny fingers to shade her eyes that she might see better.
>
> One figure only paid no attention to the approach of relief—that of a dead man lying with his feet in the gutter.[21]

There was about this narrative a story-book quality, effective and immediate if somewhat theatrical; almost stagey in its treatment of actual people. It was difficult to realize they were real individuals and not simply characters in a story or a play.

What is certain is that unlike Gibbons—who felt compelled to try to alleviate the suffering he saw even though he realized it was futile—Duranty distanced himself. He was watching from the back of the stalls, recording the drama. He was not part of it, and he never would be.

One week later, Duranty was back in Moscow, blandly reassuring his readers that it was still possible to dine well, if only you knew where to go and if you had the right money. He described the meal it was possible to get: "fresh Astrakhan caviar, with pre-war vodka; white bread and butter, delicious borscht soup, with old sherry; grilled salmon and roast partridge, with vintage burgundy or champagne; cakes of every kind, cream, sugar, custard, fine Russian cheese, hothouse grapes, old port and older cognac."[22]

Prohibition was still in force in the Soviet Union, just as in the

United States, but spirits were available for the knowing. In addition to the vintage stuff, the same "familiar game of buying superproof alcohol at the drug store and mixing it according to taste with non-alcoholic wine is played here as in New York." Even the bootleggers were the "same shifty individuals with the same backstair method."[23]

It was comfortable to be back in Moscow, away from the pitiful famine victims, even though the city itself was down and out. Moscow reminded him of Lille after its liberation by the French during the war: bedraggled, but full of hope. These were "the hard years," when the country was trying to get back on its feet, and the inhabitants of Moscow were a strange looking lot. Many of the people were wearing only sheepskin with the tanned hide on the outside, their inner garments made from blankets, curtains, carpets, or canvas. One little girl, Duranty noted, was dressed in a Persian rug that had been cut up to make a skirt, with the fringe hanging down as trimming around the hem.[24] Many of the people in the streets were barefooted, a few wore sandals, and some were wearing "home-made carpet slippers, with their ankles swathed in rags and bound round and round with cords."[25]

As he walked around the streets of the city, he noticed that there were hardly any shops open for business. Only three kinds had opened their doors: barber shops, shops with surveying materials, and dingy stores with shriveled produce.[26] The other shop windows were boarded up, deserted. The streets of the city were full of potholes or holes where water-mains had burst or there had been digging to clear choked drains. Moscow had once had fine buildings, but all had now fallen into a state of disrepair. The wooden cottages built as long ago as the seventeenth century seemed to have suffered least. Such amenities as steam heat had been missing in Moscow for a long time, and the more modern buildings were marred by the makeshift stovepipes that stuck out of the windows. In contrast, the street cars were doing a brisk business, and many buildings still had electric lights and telephones.

In his early dispatches back to the *Times*, Duranty described the coarse and crude foods of the general populace and the desperate fuel shortage that in the winter had caused people first to destroy their furniture, then pull up the floorboards, leaving bare ground beneath. He also described the typical lifestyle of the city's inhabitants, taking a young professional couple as an example.

The husband is working, say, in a Government office and the wife teaching in a Government school. If they are lucky, they have been able to procure two rooms, one for sleeping and one for living, cooking, etc. Their combined wages are insufficient, but plus their rations of food and fuel they are able to keep body and soul together. The wife does the cooking before going to school, using a homemade system of fireless cooker with the aid of cushions which keeps the food hot for a single big meal—no one takes more than one in Moscow—around 3 or 4 o'clock, with bread and tea or cocoa in the morning and at night.

The husband spends his off days in trips to the country, where he buys flour, butter, eggs, etc., to sell at a profit in Moscow and buys fuel and clothes with the proceeds.[27]

At first Duranty's own situation did not seem much better than the young couple's, and there were other complaints as well.

He and the other correspondents were each permanently assigned a free room in the Savoy, but it was the filthiest room, he attested, he had ever been in. Duranty was reduced to putting the legs of his bed in saucers of kerosene to prevent the lice and cockroaches from making their way up onto the bed during the night.[28] The majority of the hotel's staff were spies from the secret police, at that time called the Cheka. George Seldes said that all the correspondents were put under surveillance both day and night. "Go to the window of the crawling, rat-infested, Soviet official hotel ... and across the street in a shadowed hallway was a Cheka agent. Leave the hotel and he followed you everywhere. Our consciences may have been clear, but our nerves were soon unravelled."[29] Appalled by the circumstances, Duranty began to look around for someplace else to live.

But the surveillance did not stop with their personal lives. Seldes quickly found out that even his assistant, assigned him by the Soviet press office, was gathering information for the Cheka. So too were interpreters employed by the Soviet secret service. In that "supercharged atmosphere," fact-gathering quickly dwindled to a matter of keeping an eye on the official decrees or what was published in *Pravda* or *Izvestia*, by Tass or broadcast by the official radio station.[30]

The correspondents were also hindered by serious censorship. One of the early official Russian press officers was a graduate of Columbia University. He didn't use a blue pencil to strike an offending passage, Seldes reported; he used scissors and actually cut the words from the pages of the copy.[31] He and the other censors insisted they did not censor facts or "the truth" but the "tone" or "attitude" of the information before them.[32] They would leave "facts" but were liable to cut anything that smacked of "interpretation."

Duranty, the others felt, had a distinct advantage over them because the *Times* allowed him to write long dispatches, sometimes more than a thousand words. He was able therefore to use more words to mask what he was saying and add coloration to his story intended to tip off his readership. Looking back, Seldes remembered Duranty as being "particularly Machiavellian," so much so that sometimes the public wouldn't get it.

At last, the press office came up with the idea of a kind of "bookkeeping debit sheet." It was intended to turn reporters against one another, and in large part, it succeeded. The debit sheet added to the hard feelings that newsmen in direct competition with one another inevitably harbor.

The process worked this way. The correspondents were always confronted by the censors alone, never as a group. Once they had them isolated, they would hold up another reporter's work as an example to them. "A's work," they would say, "shows more loyalty than yours." It was a simple trick, but once it was instituted, the censors were able to maintain better control on what went out of the Soviet capital. From that point on, one reporter said,

> ... the journalist in Moscow had to become master of a new art: the art of telling three-quarters, a half, still smaller fractions, of the truth; the art of not telling the truth in such a way that the truth would be made apparent to a thoughtful reader; or conversely, the art of telling the whole truth up to the point where its negative or positive significance would become apparent.[33]

The decisions of the censors were final, and the experienced correspondent grew with time to understand "what would and would not be allowed to pass and saw no gain in a fruitless wrangle with the censor."[34] Duranty seemed less intimidated by the censorship system than the other correspondents, having worked during the war under French censorship, which he believed to be worse than that instituted by the Bolsheviks. He also took the trouble to learn Russian so that he could read the newspapers himself instead of being dependent upon an interpreter who was no doubt under instructions to report to the Soviet secret service. Eventually, he would be able to read beyond the literal meaning and between the lines.[35]

Nevertheless, Duranty complained that, just before the foreign correspondents entered the Soviet Union in 1921, Maxim Litvinov had promised there would be no censorship of news destined for foreign newspapers, except as pertained to military matters. Yet, as time elapsed, that principle was less and less respected. By the time Duranty had been reporting for nearly two years, he said that censorship had become "a definite and concrete thing with the usual characteristic faults." Duranty wrote up his complaints in an article published in the *New York Times* on the 13th of September 1923, when he explained in very simplified terms the nature of Soviet censorship.

"Freedom of speech," he explained to his readers, "as the term is understood in America, does not exist in Russia. Newspapers are all state-controlled and nothing may appear that does not meet the approval of the censorship." The Bolsheviks defended their position, he said, by emphasizing that the country was too backward to understand what they were attempting, so the leaders of the country were obliged to control the reading material of the masses for their own good. In an incredibly naive statement, the Bolsheviks pointed to the fact that their political group remained a minority, and that if they permitted free expression, they would surely lose control of the government.

But what concerned Duranty most was the censoring of the dispatches of the foreign correspondents stationed in Moscow. He shrewdly advanced his complaints by way of criticizing the French censorship during the war. The Bolsheviks, he implied without stating outright, were making the same mistakes. The problems, he said, were "overnervousness," "overzeal," and "overtenderness." But the most damaging was the inevitable tendency on the part of the censor to feel that somehow he was responsible for the news passed by him, that his stamp somehow gave it a sort of official standing. This line of reasoning, Duranty emphasized, was false, as the whole reason for censorship is the suppression of information that may injure the state, and that alone.

Finally, he said that the censorship had been tolerable until the Butchkavitch spy trial, when "panic and fear" began to dominate the Russian censors. "In plain English," Duranty wrote, "the fear complex dominated their usual prudence," resulting in an atmosphere of suppression that was becoming intolerable.[36]

Duranty's mention of the extreme censorship that appeared during the Butchkavitch affair was perhaps an example of the cunning Machiavellian reporting that George Seldes thought typified his work. But in this case it was not simply a matter of trying to get something past the censors and across to his readers. It seemed more as if Duranty were trying to off-load onto the censors what had for Duranty been the sorriest episode thus far in his reporting career.

Van Anda had been particularly disappointed by Duranty's performance and had severely criticized his inadequate reportage of the execution of Butchkavitch. Duranty now seemed to be saying: "Don't blame me for what happened. Blame the Soviet censors."

The Butchkavitch affair centered on the trial of the head of the Roman Catholic Church in Russia, Archbishop Zepliak and his Vicar General, Father Butchkavitch, who were accused, along with others in the Church, of spying for Poland. Duranty, it appeared to Van Anda, seemed to accept without question the Bolshevik version of events, without delving further into the matter. After the men were found guilty, the event became an international *cause célèbre*. But Duranty remained oblivious to world reaction.

The fact is, regardless of the newsworthiness of the event, he reported the story only once, and then only briefly, giving as his opinion the prevailing belief, shared by all the correspondents, that "no death sentences will be pronounced—or at any rate, if they are pronounced—will certainly be commuted."[37] World opinion rallied strongly behind the church men, and Western governments lodged formal protests requesting that the death sentences be commuted. But, as the days ticked off, it seemed less and less likely that this would happen. At last, the archbishop's sentence was commuted to ten years' hard labor. In the case of Butchkavitch, however, the execution was actually carried out.

Duranty did not report it, and the *Times* was forced to pick up the story from the Associated Press.

Years later, Duranty admitted the fault had been solely his own, and he blamed his error in judgment not on the censors, as he seemed to earlier, but on his isolation.

Honesty compels me to add that from a newspaper point of view I mis-
handled the whole trial. To begin with I underestimated its news value
at home, which is an unpardonable sin for a reporter to commit; sec-
ondly, I was convinced that it was a more or less formal affair which
would end quietly with an exchange of prisoners. At the outset I may
have been right in this opinion but I held on to it too long and played
down a story that I should have written up. My New York office dealt
with my shortcomings more in sorrow than in anger, but I realized that
I had failed them and asked myself why.[38]

The answer he came up with was that he had been buried too long
in the Soviet capital, and as a result, had lost his sense of news judgment. From that time, so Duranty wrote, he made it a point not to
spend more than four consecutive months in the Soviet Union before
going "out," as it was called, and in this, he was fully backed by his
newspaper. There was no doubt some merit to this line of thinking.

From a more cynical point of view, however, it was almost as if the
wily Duranty had turned his own error in judgment to personal
advantage.

On the night of the 31st of August 1918, Lenin was shot by a young
girl in Moscow where he was addressing a workers' meeting. He
seemed to make a complete recovery, and it was thought unnecessary
to remove the bullet that had lodged in the back of his neck. By 1922,
however, he began to suffer from severe headaches, and doctors
believed the cause to be the bullet, which appeared to be pressing
against a nerve. On the 23rd of April, the bullet was removed, and in
the aftermath of the operation, Lenin suffered a paralytic stroke.

The following November, Lenin addressed the opening session of
the Communist International Congress, which was held in the former
Kremlin throne-room. Duranty, attending the event, believed at that
time he could detect no sign of Lenin's recent stroke, which had caused
an outbreak of wild rumors in the Soviet capital. A week later Lenin
spoke at a special session of the Moscow Soviet held in the Grand
Opera House. The Western press corps was given seats in the orchestra
pit, and this time, Duranty believed that he could detect "a slight
thickness of speech and slurring of diction, as if Lenin's tongue was
too large for his mouth."[39] He wrote this into his story about the occasion, but the censors changed the passage to read simply that Lenin's

111

voice "seemed rather thicker and less clear."[40] Nevertheless, from this time onwards, correspondents stationed in the city began to consider the question of who would succeed Lenin in the event of his death.

Duranty later claimed that he had been one of the very first to single out Joseph Stalin as the next leader of the Soviet Union. He pointed to a column he wrote on the 18th of January 1923, in which he assessed the various political contenders.

> Trotsky is a great executive, but his brain cannot compare with Lenin's in analytical power. Djerjinsky goes straight to his appointed goal without fear or favor and gets there somehow, no matter what are the obstacles, but he is also inferior to Lenin in analytical capacity. Rykoff and Kameneff are first-class administrators, and hardly more.
>
> But during the last year Stalin has shown judgment and analytical power not unworthy of Lenin. It is to him that the greatest part of the credit is due for bringing about the new Russian Union, which history may regard as one of the most remarkable Constitutions in human history. Trotsky helped him in drawing it up, but Stalin's brain guided the pen.[41]

Almost a year before, in March of 1922, Stalin had been made General Secretary of the Central Committee of the Communist Party, and this influenced Duranty's opinion of Stalin's potential.[42] Mainly, though, he based his opinion on Stalin's obvious strength and stability in comparison with Trotsky's sometimes diffused and erratic brilliance. Later, in a curious gesture of generosity, Duranty credited Ernestine Evans, one of his erstwhile colleagues, with making the first prediction that Stalin would be Lenin's successor. When Stalin became General Secretary, Evans had singled him out in an article written for the *Atlantic Monthly*.[43] But if Evans had been the first to spot Stalin, Duranty had been quick to put his money on the same horse: "Stalin is one of the most remarkable men in Russia," he wrote in that early column, "and perhaps the most influential figure here today."

When the facts later proved Duranty correct, he would make much of that early assessment. It was the first of many references in which Duranty would identify himself with the Soviet dictator, Joseph Stalin.

For the most part, Duranty's first two years of reporting in the Soviet Union had been concerned with economic issues, in particular, Lenin's New Economic Policy—the set of economic reforms put into place just before Duranty had entered the country. In this area of reportage, Duranty excelled himself.

As early as September 8, 1921, Duranty reported that the encouragement of petty industry was necessary if the peasants were to have an incentive to produce enough food for the general population. In 1921, cultivated land was only 62 percent of the pre-war acreage, the harvest little more than 35 percent of the normal output.

The need to halt the requisitioning had become obvious earlier that year in March, to Lenin at least, when the mutiny at the Kronstadt Naval Base took place, followed quickly by a revolt in the Province of Tambov. In plain words, Duranty wrote, either the peasants would have something to buy, or they would grow no more food than was necessary for their needs.[44] For the worker, there was the high cost of bread, the absence of meat from his diet. And another problem was the "steady issue of new paper money, which has caused incessant disputes and even strikes over a wage that a month before seemed at least acceptable."[45]

The New Economic Policy aimed at restoring the ruined economy, even though it did represent a radical departure from the pure Communism originally envisioned by the Bolsheviks. The most radical change from NEP was the "reorganization of all national economy on a straight money basis."[46] In addition, the State retained control of large industry, medium industry connected with foreign trade, and all wholesale commerce. Private enterprise was allowed to flourish in small industry, that is, in plants employing fewer than twenty workers each. Toward the peasants, the government initiated a tax in money or in kind, which averaged between 10 and 15 percent—a direct departure from requisitioning and an incentive to them to produce more.

The rampant inflation in the economy had at first been thought naively by the Bolsheviks to be evidence that money was no longer necessary under Communism. But they were quickly disapprised of this notion as the economy declined immeasurably. And in 1922, they began issuing a gold-backed currency—the chervonetz, which was given the value of ten pre-war rubles. Duranty later explained the effects of this new currency upon the Soviet populace:

> The chervonetz notes were . . . secured by the bank's gold reserve of
> not less than twenty-five percent of the total emission. For a time they

113

circulated side by side with *sovznaki* ... whose depreciation had reached astronomical figures. It had actually become the practice to lop off three or more noughts from the sovznaki at the end of each year, so that the million-rouble notes of 1923 represented a million million roubles in terms of 1921.... the ratio between the stable gold-backed chervonetz notes and the vertiginously falling sovznaki was officially announced from day to day, which caused much confusion and dispute and greatly hampered business. ... in May [of 1924] they were completely withdrawn from circulation on an exchange ratio of twenty million roubles for one chervonetz. Allowing for the above-mentioned removal of noughts, the true conversion rate of the original Soviet rouble would have been about fifty million million roubles for one American dollar.[47]

The peasants were the last to get the chervonetz, and the weeks' delay to market caused them huge losses. Industrial prices increased at a rate three times higher than agricultural prices, because state trusts and cooperatives had "blithely raised rates to meet the insatiable demand for manufactured goods." The major result was that the peasants were once again unable to buy any industrial products. "The crisis grew so acute," Duranty said, "that the peasants hoarded their produce and refused to buy goods from the cities, which threatened industrial stagnation."[48]

During this period, Duranty's lucid and simplified explanation of economic problems was exemplary, and some of his best work in the Soviet Union was economic reporting. His lead on the subject of increasing industrial prices is a model of clarity:

> Russia is now facing a crisis whose gravity is not diminished by the fact that it is potential and latent rather than immediate and acute. The source of this trouble is the purchasing power of the peasant which is almost wiped out by the huge disproportion between prices of food products and manufactured goods as compared with before the war. The result is increasing business stagnation.[49]

In addition to his newspaper reporting, he applied his narrative skills to the problems of the Soviet economy in an unexpected way. He wrote short stories, in something approaching the style of his idol "Saki," showing the immediate effects of rampant inflation upon the behavior of the "backward Russian peasant." The stories weren't all that bad.

In "The Thrifty Peasant and the Precious Mattress," a competent peasant who learned proper farming methods as a prisoner of war in Germany finds that he can command huge prices for his produce in Moscow. So he grows fresh garden vegetables and carries them into the city, where he sells them for very good prices. Eventually, he makes a small fortune, all of which he stuffs into his mattress. He plans to reinvest the money in more land, with the result that he is very stingy and won't even buy his children shoes.

When he sets out to purchase his land, however, he discovers that his paper money is worth less than the horsehair that was originally stuffed into his mattress. In a rage, he goes out and sells more foods in Moscow, but with these profits, he immediately buys bootlegged vodka and gets stinking drunk.

The early days of NEP witnessed the dawn of an age of commercial freedom as the small businessman cashed in on the opportunities now open to him. A restaurant proprietor of Duranty's acquaintance showed how it went. He had begun with a small restaurant, which grew as the new freedoms increased. He then began speculating in real estate and antiques, making a lot of quick money. He managed to amass "a fine eight-room apartment of his own, no less than three automobiles, two mistresses, and a large amount of gold, foreign valuta and jewels."[50]

At the same time, a number of bars, nightclubs, and "gaming hells" began to open their doors around the city. These operations were tolerated by Soviet officials because they paid huge taxes to the government, which in turn used the funds to make repairs to "the streets, sidewalks, drainage and lighting systems."[51] One of the biggest gambling establishments was "a place called Praga at the corner of Arbat Square . . . [with] two roulette tables both with zero and double zero, two baccarat tables and a dozen games of *chemin de fer.*"

It was a strange sight, this Praga, in the center of the world's first Proletarian Republic. Most of the men looked like what they were, the low-class jackals and hangers-on of any boom, with fat jowls and greedy vulpine features; but there were others of a better class, former nobles in faded broadcloth and Red Army soldiers in uniform . . . eager

115

for Moscow's fleshpots and a flutter at the tables. A smattering too of foreigners, fixers, agents and the commercial vanguard of a dozen big firms attracted by Lenin's new policy of Concessions, hurrying to find if the report was true that Russia might again become a honey-pot for alien wasps.[52]

Seedy establishments known for their corruption also appeared. One of them, a place simply called "Bar," began as a restaurant but quickly moved into the illegal businesses of prostitution and the sale of alcohol and dangerous drugs.

Along with this welcome end to "the hard years" came an ethos that seemed to endorse more freedom in sexual matters. The radical intelligentsia of the Revolution had originally viewed women as an exploited group; the family, an extension of capitalism. In this context, the husband was considered the bourgeois, his wife the enslaved proletarian. Laws had been passed "that made divorce easily attainable, removed the formal stigma from illegitimacy, permitted abortion and mandated equal rights and equal pay for women."[53] A chance remark made by Lenin that the act of love should "be as simple and unimportant as drinking a glass of water" had become the rationale for unlimited promiscuity, causing free sexual relations to become one of the fringe benefits of the Revolution. Adding to the trend were the early writings of the sometimes feminist, sometimes sexual liberationist, Alexandra Kollontai, who had herself been involved in a number of highly publicized affairs. The Soviet state had even shown a desire to assume unprecedented responsibility for the country's youth. All these things, along with the new economic freedoms, created a wide-open atmosphere, and Moscow became something of a center of corruption, where personal behavior tended to become more and more excessive.

Duranty found nothing amiss in such a setting, and he now nestled in comfortably, making plans to stay in Soviet Russia for the duration.

CHAPTER VII

A Roman Saturnalia

Lenin's New Economic Policy reminded Duranty, he later remarked, of "the old Roman Saturnalia, when for three days each year slaves and underlings might usurp with impunity the pleasures and privileges of their masters."[1] By this, he meant that during the NEP years, the entrepreneurial types who had been bound by the principles of extreme Communism were, in a manner of speaking, freed from their chains and permitted to indulge their natural inclination toward profit-making. It permitted them to indulge other inclinations as well.

The way Duranty was telling the story many years later, he and another correspondent threw in a thousand or so dollars in order to put a small house into good order sometime in April of 1922. During those first few years after the Revolution, there was a provision that anyone who made certain improvements to delinquent and ruined property could then live there rent free. So, Duranty said, he and his colleague put in new windows and a new floor and "fixed the stoves and plumbing, and generally put [the place] in good repair as dwelling quarters." He thereby secured snug and comfortable housing which would provide him with rent-free accommodations while he was in Moscow. That was the story.

George Seldes remembered it differently. It was not, Seldes said, a fellow correspondent that Duranty lived with but his wife, Jane

Cheron Duranty—whom Seldes referred to as "Jeannot." Seldes was the couple's frequent guest at dinner, and became fairly intimate with them over the years.[2]

It was unclear when the couple were married, or where, but in some ways the Jane Duranty of a decade before remained unchanged. She was still given over to rather flamboyant tastes in her clothing, and she draped her body with beads whenever she entertained the visitors who made their way to Duranty's little house. By now, however, she was less than the stunningly handsome young woman who had so attracted Aleister Crowley before the war. In fact, she looked a good deal older than her husband, who always retained a youthful appearance which belied his actual years. Duranty apparently admired his wife, though, and later in life, in the late 1940s or early 1950s, whenever he made one of his infrequent references to Jane Duranty, there was a tone of some respect, even of affection, friends remembered.[3]

But the overriding impression of George Seldes was that the couple had been married for a long time—long enough at least to be on the lookout for something new. Duranty especially seemed the kind of man who wouldn't hesitate to attempt sexual conquests with his wife present.

Soon after moving in and getting the place into shape, Jane Duranty hired a young cook, "a very pretty peasant girl," Seldes said, "pretty and young and vivacious and all of that; and tall, for a Russian." The young girl very quickly became Duranty's mistress, and "Jeannot" didn't appear to Seldes to be terribly upset by the arrangement.

"There was no reason he wouldn't have a mistress living in the same house with his wife," Seldes said. For her part, Jane Duranty was preoccupied by her interest in taking drugs—"smoking dope," Seldes called it—"and it wouldn't surprise me if *he* was smoking . . . marijuana or *something . . . before* his leg accident." Seldes couldn't remember exactly what it was. "I still remember the pretty servant girl though," he said. For the record, Duranty affirmed that in this period life became extremely agreeable to him in the Soviet capital. He was able to obtain the little luxuries of life, he said, like "candy, American cigarettes and razor blades" from the American Relief Administration canteen. He had a number of good friends who dropped in from time to time. And in addition to all that

I had a little T-model Ford and a chauffeur who was not too Russian
for safety, a comfortable apartment and an excellent cook, whom I had
taught to prepare meals as I like them, which is simple but good.[4]

The cook's name was Katya, and she had grayish blue eyes and an
upturned nose, with prominent high cheekbones, and a remarkably
fine figure. Obviously from a peasant family, she had all the physical
characteristics of a Slav.[5]

Everything had fallen comfortably into place, and Duranty decided
to stay on permanently at the end of 1922. Later, he would call the
next two years the pleasantest of his entire stay in Moscow.

Most of the visitors to Duranty's little house came there because he
had installed, in addition to three tiled stoves, an open English fireplace in one of the smaller rooms. On cold winter nights in Moscow,
Duranty remembered, people liked to sit before the fire, warming
themselves and talking over the events taking place in the country. His
visitors came from both the Left and the Right, and Duranty learned
a good deal from the continuous discussions and arguments that took
place before his big fireplace. Ironically, among the frequenters to his
house were the leftovers from the Red Scare, who appeared to bear
him no ill will for the part he played in helping to create the atmosphere that had led to their expulsion from the United States.

"Big Bill" Haywood came there often, a lost soul among the
bureaucratic Soviets. He had been sentenced, along with a number of
other members of the Industrial Workers of the World, known as the
"I.W.W.s," to a long jail term in the United States during the anti-Red
drive, but he had skipped bail and escaped to Russia. It hadn't made
Haywood very happy, though, for he never fully adjusted to the Soviet
Union. He told Duranty he was used to fighting scabs and police and
mine-guards, but he couldn't really tolerate the continuous talk of the
Russian Bolsheviks and their preoccupation with "this *ideelogical* theory stuff." He believed one day, the Bolsheviks would come to blows
over it. Duranty found the idea farfetched and unrealistic.

Unable to speak Russian with any fluency, Haywood grew more
and more isolated. Duranty believed that he would have gone home
to the United States if he could have managed it without going to jail.
Haywood made a stab at trying to organize a group of American rad-

119

icals to work in the Kusnetzk iron basin in Western Siberia, but failed. Alienated and disillusioned, Haywood stayed on for want of some-place else to go, until he died a few years later.[6] A short time after his death, Haywood's prediction that the Bolsheviks would destroy one another over theoretical principles started to come true, an event Duranty duly acknowledged.

Another of the American radicals, Bill Shatoff, fared better, becom-ing "in rapid succession a banker at Rostov, the director of an oil trust in the Caucasus, and head of a steel plant, all in the service of the State."[7] Shatoff's enthusiasm for the Bolshevik Revolution never failed him, not even when chided by his old compatriot Emma Goldman, the anarchist, who early in 1920 met him once more inside Soviet bor-ders and was openly shocked by his ready adaptation to a regime Gold-man quickly dismissed as completely corrupted.[8] Citing the obvious abuse of civil and human rights, Goldman wasted little time before departing the country. She left Russia in 1921, three months after Dur-anty entered, but the two would not meet one another for many years, and then only briefly, after she had moved to her house in the south of France.

Goldman's reaction to the Bolshevik regime was a common one among the American radicals who had been forced to leave their homeland. During these early days they were still willing to discuss their disillusionment in the quiet confidence of Duranty's parlor, and for a time, Duranty was a student to their views and to those of others who grew to hate the regime. In large part, however, he played the devil's advocate, thrashing out the issues in debates that lasted until the early hours of the morning and which he believed helped him to clarify his own ideas. Eventually, he would find his own way, spinning out a distinctively personal version of Bolitho's elitist philosophy. The opinions of others would become less and less interesting to him.

Despite the official state policy of Prohibition, everybody managed to keep drinking, and bootleggers continued to flourish at every level of society. As in the United States, there was "the same confidential passing around of the best receipts for producing 'a drop of the real stuff' from a mixture of raisins, sugar, yeast, and warm water."[9] Dur-anty also reported that although there was a law against selling liquor, foreigners could often procure high quality French champagne or Rhineland wines at bargain prices.

And then there arose the odd phenomenon, which still occurs today

in the Soviet Union, of the sudden appearance of an unheard-of luxury, as in the case of a big shipment of "first-class chocolates," which
went on sale in October of 1921 in the large department stores opened
after NEP was put into operation.[10] Otherwise, things remained very
difficult to get, and extremely expensive—except for caviar, which was
a real bargain at about a dollar a pound.[11]

Artistic license accompanied the new freedoms of the NEP, and suddenly Moscow was alive with enclaves of painters, musicians, dancers,
and writers, all of whom claimed to be the true representatives of the
Revolutionary Spirit. It was the age of what Duranty's friend William
Bolitho came to call "pretentious nonentities, the first crop of thistles
of the great plowing up of the century. Lunarcharskys, Mariengoffs,
Imagists [*sic*], belated Futurists, all the band."[12]

The past quickly became *passé*, experimentation *de rigueur*, and
bold new types saw their artistic movements as the wellspring of political change.

> Sentiment, spirituality, human drama and undue interest in individual
> psychology were out of fashion, often denounced as "petty-bourgeois."
> Avant-garde artists like the poet Vladimir Mayakovsky and the theatre
> director Vsevolod Meyerhold saw revolutionary art and revolutionary
> politics as part of the same protest against the old, bourgeois world.
> They were among the first members of the intelligentsia to accept the
> October Revolution and offer their services to the new Soviet govern-
> ment, producing propaganda posters in Cubist and Futurist style,
> painting revolutionary slogans on the walls of former palaces, staging
> mass re-enactments of revolutionary victories in the streets, bringing
> acrobatics as well as politically relevant messages into the conventional
> theatre, and designing non-representational monuments to revolution-
> ary heroes of the past.[13]

Other groups, like the off-beat nudists or the reform-minded advocates
of Esperanto, vied for a place in what they thought would be an open
society that would freely accommodate them and their heretofore
unacceptable beliefs.

In the spring of 1921, Isadora Duncan had been invited by the Soviet
government to come to Russia to found a dancing school for Bolshevik
children. As Duncan recorded it in the florid account she wrote of her

life, the telegram inviting her affirmed that, "The Russian Government alone can understand you. Come to us; we will make your school."[14]

Duncan agreed at once, professing to be exhausted from "bourgeois, commercial art. . . . I want to dance for the masses, for the working people who need my art. . . . I want to dance for them for nothing. . . ."[15] She was given a large house in Prechistenka Street, previously occupied by the Russian ballerina Balashova, who had emigrated to Paris. The house was decorated in the rococo and Empire styles, embellished with cupids and Napoleonic emblems, which Duncan disparaged and tried to cover up.

The house quickly became a center for Duncan's spectacular soirées, or "orgiastic nights," as they came to be called, which were frequently attended by the American community in Moscow and included members of the American Relief Administration and journalists like Bessie Beatty, Ernestine Evans, and, of course, Walter Duranty.

Before very long, Duncan made the acquaintance of the poet Sergei Esenin, who had recently become associated with the Imaginists, a group of poets who insisted upon the primacy of "image" in their poetry. Part of the school of "urban bohemia," the Imaginists represented a marked departure from the celebrated pastoral poetry of the Russian countryside. The group had also adopted unusual destructive overtones, which led them to strange anti-social antics. Esenin, who had heretofore been the poet of the village—dressing always in the simple style of the peasant —now became a "tender hooligan," adorning himself in the manner of a self-conscious dandy. He and his entourage—most prominent among them Anatoly Mariengov, with whom Esenin was rumored to have a sexual arrangement—delighted in blasphemy, obscenity, and drunken revelry, which often ended in orgies of destruction.

The famed Esenin's excesses seemed to result from this unfortunate connection with the Imaginists, whose anarchistic behavior was carefully calculated to create a sensation in any setting. Disillusioned with the course of the Revolution, Esenin lamented the "iron, and the machine, and the power of 'death.'"[16] The peasant paradise he had hoped for and foreseen was now impossible, he realized. The emphasis upon industrial production and blackened and sooty cities repulsed him, driving him to disillusionment and the brink of self-destruction.

He seemed to sense that the philosophy he entertained as an Imaginist was not one that would be tolerated for long. Soon decadent movements like his would be replaced by the State-sponsored school of Social Realism. But for now, he and his cohorts were able to cavort with impunity.

The meeting between Duncan and Esenin was indicative of the nature of their future relationship. Esenin burst into the room surrounded by the other Imaginists from whom he was rarely separated. Sighting the handsome young poet, Duncan rose sedately from her divan and asked the pianist to play a waltz by Chopin, one "that she felt would appeal to the lyric soul of the golden-haired poet." She then began a seductive but "rapturous" dance, coming forward to Esenin, "her eyes radiant, her hands outstretched. . . ." The poet said something brutal about her sensuous movements to his friends, then began himself to whirl around the room in a grotesque parody of her dance.[17]

This was the man Isadora Duncan was soon to marry, her first and only husband—the lover she so desperately sought for "the 'autumn' of her life."[18] The fact he was nearly two decades younger than she seemed only to increase her attraction to the emotionally unstable, but brilliant Esenin.

Walter Duranty had seen Isadora Duncan dance when he was a young man still at Cambridge, "and ever afterwards the memory of her grace and beauty and slim, flashing limbs stayed with me as something rare and wonderful." By the time he met her personally, she was a "stout middle-aged woman married to this pimply Esenin." He found her irresistible nevertheless, because of what he called "a flame inside her whose brightness had nothing to do with her body."

> I knew that she was fat and lazy and drank to excess and did not much care whether she was ill-kempt or sloppy, but I knew also that she had a hole in her heart which excused everything. In all human experience there is nothing so devastating as a hole in the heart, no matter what it comes from. In Isadora's case it was caused by the tragic death of her children in Paris when a taxi-driver drove them and their governess and himself suddenly into the Seine, because his steering gear went wrong on the corner of a bridge, and all of them were drowned. After that Isadora did not care much about anything. She told me so herself and I said, "Did you ever care much about anything?

123

You're an artist, aren't you? What do artists care about anything ever?"
Isadora said, "You're damn clever, Walter Duranty, and you're a damn
fool. Can't you understand that there's all the difference between what
you feel as an artist and what you care about as a person?"[19]

To Duranty, Duncan remained an attractive force, and they became
intimate friends, Duranty acting as confidante to the fading dancer as
she began her downward slide.

On the night of the 26th of November 1923, he sat in Duncan's
dressing room as she prepared to perform with her students as part of
the festivities of the Fifth Anniversary Congress of the Women's
Department of the Communist Party. Also present was the famous
Bolshevik, Alexandra Kollontai, the world's first woman ambassador
and a controversial but popular figure in her own right.

Kollontai had made her reputation as a strong defender of the
rights of women. Her serious studies of the inhumane working conditions suffered by women and children in factories, along with her tracts
attacking prostitution, greatly influenced the Communist Party's early
attitudes, as reflected by the wide-ranging reforms regarding women
which had been enacted into law. This was not what interested Duranty, however. Like others, he was fascinated by Kollontai's controversial attitudes toward the relations between the sexes.

In a series of works that included pamphlets, academic articles, and
novels, Kollontai advocated "erotic friendships" among Party regu-
lars, later developing the concept of a "Winged Eros." This was the
idea of a "spiritual interaction" between the sexes with emotional
commitment that could "function as part of communism by forging
bonds of 'comradely solidarity' between the members of the collective.
. . . The 'Winged Eros' was eroticism with the possessiveness removed,
it was the attraction of equals that enhanced the harmony of the group
rather than isolating the couple in self-absorption."[20] Although she did
harbor these idealistic views on human sexuality, Kollontai was not,
as is often thought, an advocate of the "glass of water" theory of sex,
which amounted to little more than promiscuity.[21] She firmly believed
in love and mutual responsibility between the sexes. But the result of
Kollontai's writings was a growth of hostility toward her among the
Party's most powerful members, and it was generally believed she was
appointed ambassador in order to separate her from a rapidly changing
political climate.

Elements within the Party now blamed Kollontai personally for many of the excesses of the age. Her popularity and the popularity of her writings were thought responsible for the general marital instability, which had brought well over 100,000 divorces in 1922 alone. The conditions led to an army of prostitutes that in Petrograd was as large as ever it had been before the Revolution.[22] She was also held to account for the millions of orphans and waifs who roamed the streets in gangs—the *bezprizornye*, who were more like wolves than children. Rationally, no one could deny that the Civil War and famine had been the main causes of the parentless children. But Kollontai's views made her an easy scapegoat for any problem that seemed related to instability between the sexes.

Because of her open manner, Isadora Duncan had made Duranty aware of the suffering she had experienced as a result of the death of her children. He seemed to know nothing, however, about the reversal of Kollontai's fortunes and the hardships she had suffered. Nevertheless, on the night of the Fifth Anniversary Congress, the two women did not seem to mind Duranty's remaining in the dressing room as they began speaking to one another candidly. Delay followed delay in the program, and Duncan became wildly impatient for her dance to begin, "her eyes, her hair, her robe one fierce red storm of flame."[23] Finally, she turned to Duranty and sent him out for some vodka. When he returned with the bottle, he found Duncan and Kollontai talking of "life and love and men and what they thought of them."

As he told the story, Duranty "sat tight and listened" to a conversation "delivered at high tension by two past masters in the Art of which they spoke"—the art of love. In the spirit of the English gentleman, he later professed not to be able to remember anything he had heard that night, but admitted "rarely [having] an hour of greater entertainment, and I am certain that the transcript of their dialogue would have made a marvelous book."[24]

For the record, he wrote up the performance as something of a triumph for Isadora Duncan. And despite his professed inability to remember the conversation he overheard beforehand, during the stage performance he was sufficiently alert to see the irony of the pantomime in which a baby was given to Communism, like the Christ child—a strange anomaly in an atheist state. He also spotted the "eight-year-old Mary Peters, baby daughter of Karl Peters, one of the most terrible of the Cheka zealots, her wisp of red tunic like blood in the spotlight."[25]

Duranty's tendency to be indulgent toward a middle-aged Isadora Duncan was not shared by everyone. Only a few years later, Duranty's friend William Bolitho, by then a successful writer, would describe her Russian years thus:

> The naive sparrowishness of her claims on humanity, in step, changes into a more and more definite socialism. No doubt her adherence to Leninism was never very intellectual; still the flag-waving, the red-tunicism, this was disagreeably nearer, by whatever the distance, the hysterical earnest of a woman with a cause, than to the exciting day-dreaming of the other Isadora. I find the account of her visit to Russia, her marriage to Esenin, . . . more distressing than interesting . . . Incident after incident, as set down by her dearest friends, makes us uneasy. She accepts the use of a flat belonging to an artist, a dancer (ballet, it is true), exiled from Moscow, and criticizes the furniture glee-fully and without amenity. She goes to select a fur coat from the vast store of those commandeered from middle-class women, and is snubbed by the very official when she chooses one, thinking it was free of charge. The Communist conductor leads his orchestra out disdain-fully when she reminds him she has sacrificed a great deal to come to "help the children of Russia."[26]

A first-hand account of her dancing in this period reinforces Boli-tho's brutal summing up: she was, to one disappointed young man sit-ting in the audience, "a woman who looked over fifty . . . wearing a transparent *giton* over a naked, flabby body, massive and shapeless, hopping and tripping with rudimentary movements whose range was limited in the extreme."[27] If Duranty himself shared such sentiments, he kept them quiet, remaining for all intents and purposes her devoted friend and admirer.

His indulgence did not extend to her young husband Esenin, whom he classified as "an extremely worthless poet." It was unlike Duranty to sit in judgment on others. He usually took the attitude of "live and let live." Still, he found it pleasant to mix with the Imaginist clique, attending frequently the drunken orgies held either at Duncan's house or more usually at the "Stable of Pegasus," the nightclub owned by Esenin and his friends—a hideaway for the rowdier members of the intelligentsia.

It may have been here that, according to one story which was passed down by correspondents over the years, an "immurement" took place. In the middle of one wild party Duranty attended, involving drugs and copulation, with alternate couplings, a Russian boy and girl were bricked up behind a wall, to everyone's delight. They were at last released, so went the story, before the party broke up. This incident greatly amused Duranty, who later boasted about it in confidential conversations.[28]

On another night, though, finding the drunken Esenin more offensive than usual, Duranty fell into an argument with Duncan. Duranty insisted Esenin was not only a lewd fraud, but also a terrible poet and asked Duncan "why on earth she married that one." Just at that moment, Duranty remembered, over the drunken rabble in the café, Esenin began to recite a poem he had recently written—"The Black Man."

> The poem was raw and brutal but alive and true. It described the feelings of a drunkard on the verge of delirium tremens, who was haunted by the face of a negro grinning at him. . . . As his voice rose there came utter silence in the café. Line after shattering line banged the consciousness of that motley crowd and froze them into horror. It was tremendous and terrible to hear the agony of the haunted wretch, and Esenin made us share it. . . . Then Isadora, whom nothing could dismay, said to me quietly, "Do you still think my little peasant boy has no genius?"[29]

A little over a year later, two days after Christmas, 1925, Esenin wrote a farewell poem in his own blood, then hanged himself in his room in the Angleterre Hotel in Leningrad. He was at the time estranged from Duncan by mutual agreement, after a flamboyant Western tour in the United States and Europe that left the reputation of both the poet and the dancer in tatters. Duncan herself would die only two years after Esenin, as a result of her loose and flowing style of clothing—"Flou," it was called by the French—when her scarf caught in the wheel of her car and instantly broke her neck.

Duranty never got over his dislike of Esenin, even after his suicide, and he wrote a short story based loosely upon his character called "The Crazy Poets and the Distant Star." Just as there was often an element of fiction in Duranty's reporting, there was usually an element of fact in his fiction. The story was about a gang of crazy poets, who, under

127

the influence of drugs and alcohol, were tricked into trying to kill Party officials at Lenin's tomb in the Red Square Parade. They were found out just in time. The story was based on a factual incident that had nothing to do with Esenin, but that hadn't prevented Duranty's using the poet as the leader of the gang.[30]

Duranty enjoyed particularly the period of time when he ran with the artistic groups in Moscow because he still nurtured the desire to become a fiction writer, and he wrote a number of short stories centering on these early days in the Soviet Union. Many of the stories chronicled the changes in the country and their effect upon the common people.

In one, "The Brave Soldier and the Wicked Sorcerer," a Red soldier overcomes the evil spell of the village sorcerer and priest and is rewarded by the government, demonstrating the Bolshevik regime's wish to undermine the superstition and religion that continued to play a big part in village life. In another, "The Wife Who Lost Her Patience," a wife kills her husband who kept squandering their meager earnings on drink, and is found guilty of murder. Her appeal to the court is dismissed—not because she killed her husband, but because she had paid for a last mass for his soul, thus committing the offense of "gross superstition."[31]

Ever since the Butchkavitch affair, Duranty had formed the habit of going out of the country at regular intervals, ostensibly to regain his perspective on the news values of the Western world. In reality, these forays often turned into extravagant holidays—sometimes to Paris, where he mixed with expatriate writers, sometimes to New York, where he saw his old friend Aleck Woollcott.

In New York, the Algonquin Round Table was in full swing. It included Woollcott, of course, now a famous playwright and drama critic, as well as Harold Ross, the editor of *The New Yorker*; the writer Dorothy Parker, known for her pungent witticisms; and Duranty's old friend from Paris days, Heywood Broun. A casual institution that grew to legendary proportions, the club was called "The Young Men's Upper West Side Thanatopsis Literary and Inside Straight Club—or more properly Thanatopsis."[32]

The club occupied a second floor suite, provided free of charge by the Algonquin. Duranty's friendship with Woollcott made him a regular whenever he was in town. It was here that he enjoyed long sessions of poker with another well-known member of the club, the comic Harpo Marx, an inveterate gambler, who drove up the stakes. The game usually started about five o'clock in the afternoon on a Saturday, lasting into "the gray light of Sunday morning." Harpo was appearing on Broadway in *Cocoanuts*, and he was permitted to drop out of the game, go do the show, then rush back in costume and continue play.[33] At one of these sessions, Duranty and Woollcott had a bit of a falling out, not an uncommon event between Woollcott and his friends. Whatever it was that caused the problem, they managed to thrash it out, because Duranty returned, grumbling about "that villainous Ross," and playing furiously into the night.[34]

The acquaintanceship between Duranty and Harpo Marx formed at the card table in this period would even extend to Moscow, for, as Duranty recalled a decade later, Harpo came there sometime "to give a little private performance," one which Duranty thought was the funniest thing he had ever seen.

> His hosts were a few of the greatest Soviet theatrical people. He played his harp, dropped knives and forks. They thought he was a sublime genius. I did, too.[35]

For now, Thanatopsis was the height of New York City high life, its participants frequenters of glamorous and expensive nightclubs like "21." Woollcott had a hideaway on Long Island as well, where his closest friends often escaped for a weekend of relentless pleasure.

Altogether, for Duranty, this period in New York put the seal on an obsession that would show up often in his work—an idealization of New York City, the place where smart people lived smart lives—following a style that seemed just out of reach of the Moscow correspondent. Again and again in Duranty's work, there were references to New York City as a kind of center of the universe. Later, after the start of the Great Depression, a Russian told Duranty he wondered how the press managed to suppress news of the horrific epidemics and starvation he was certain must have accompanied the crash. Furious, Duranty "got a picture of New York in the *Times* rotogravure section, taken from an aeroplane, and shoved it under his nose. 'When you can build a city like that, you may talk about America. Until then, shut up.'"[36]

For the present, Manhattan had become the haven of the fashionable. Always at the forefront, Woollcott now affected a certain characteristic manner of dressing which distinguished him from other New Yorkers on the street. It is entertaining to picture how he must have looked, with his cape flung carelessly across his massive bulk, the huge, black, big-brimmed hat he always wore slanted at a rakish angle, a black walking stick in his hand—acceptable trademarks for a man of the theater. It must also have been a novel sight to watch the short and limping Duranty unevenly bumping along the streets beside Woollcott, leaning heavily on *his* cane.

For, by now, Duranty had been in the train wreck that cost him his left limb. Like Woollcott, who always managed to make his rotund figure an asset, Duranty made his cane a distinctive trademark. But the idea to do so originated not with Duranty, but with William Bolitho.

The accident had occurred in November of 1924 when Duranty was taking the boat train from Paris to Le Havre. He heard a hell of a crash as the train "ran off the rails in a tunnel and another train ran into it. . . ." Duranty found himself flying "twenty-five yards through the air, with no worse injury than a splintered shin."[37] Getting his bearings, he found that his left foot was wedged between two pieces of metal and some wood, "with white pieces of bone sticking out above [his] shoe."[38] At first, he thought he was lucky because the others around him were so much worse than he. One of the last ones to be carried away, Duranty felt no pain and believed his injury to be minor.

In an apparent attempt to save the leg, the surgeon set it in a cast and gave Duranty a tetanus shot. That in turn caused a terrible itching, which drove Duranty into a frenzy, reminding him, he said, of the trials of Job.[39]

After all this the terrible pain began. When at last they took off the cast, there was the feared gangrene. The surgeon had no recourse but to remove the leg between the ankle and the knee.[40] A friend of Duranty's later said he believed Duranty remained secretly bitter over the incident because he believed he didn't have to lose his leg. Openly, Duranty claimed that the pain was so bad that if he had had any poison, he would have taken it.[41]

Duranty now felt overcome by a weary sense of futility, and for the first time in his life, he felt the fatalism he had seen in others. Never a religious man, Duranty had no belief in an afterlife. Once you get close to death, he believed, and you understand clearly that it is inevitable, you stop caring. "To human beings," he wrote, "Death is the End."

> One may think one believes in a life after death, but it is generally a vague sort of belief, rather a hope than a belief, and death is the End. If you come very near to death and get familiar so to speak with death, you begin to feel that you have reached ultimate issues and that you don't give a damn.[42]

Faced with this perception, Duranty comforted himself with the thought that he probably *was* going to die. But if he didn't, he promised himself, he would "act differently in the future." He reckoned that he had been frightened over trivialities too many times during his lifetime. Now that he was facing the great void, he made a private vow:

> None of the things I have been afraid of before, complaints by my boss or the loss of my job or the opinion of my friends or any danger, are as bad as the thing I am facing now, which is death by slow torture. Than that there is nothing worse; if I escape it I can say to myself that I at least can no longer be frightened by anyone or anything. Now, facing death, I regret few of the things I have done, but I regret not doing a great many things I might have done and not saying or writing things I might have said or written. "Henceforth," I thought to myself, "If I *do* get back I shall do as I please and think as I please and write as I please, without fear or favor." I was half delirious, but that was a good thought, which stayed with me and strengthened me. Of course it was impossible, as I found out later.[43]

And so evolved the philosophy of Walter Duranty, a hybrid of the elitist credo of William Bolitho and of his own experiences of near death after a train wreck near Rouen. After a so-far remarkably eventful life, his only regret: that he had not done more.

Duranty made a regular practice of explaining, in strictest confidence, to an amazingly large number of people, his predilection for smoking opium. They all seemed to believe the information was a secret they shared with him exclusively. In each of the personal versions and in all his public writings on the subject, Duranty dated his addiction to the drug from his accident on the boat train, the accident that cost him his left leg.

Who could blame him? He was in terrible pain, he found that morphine made the pain bearable, the morphine led to opium: "I have seen some unpretty things, and enjoyed many lovely things," he would say, in one way or another, "but opium is the best . . . and by God, I don't regret it."[44] In this way, Duranty used the accident to mask his earlier drug use, giving himself a wholly justified excuse both for his addiction and for talking about it—something he apparently loved to do.

When at last he got out of the French hospital, Duranty went to St. Tropez to recuperate. It was there that Jane Cheron Duranty had purchased a house, where she continued to live for many years after she left Moscow. It is not known when Duranty's wife left Russia to make her permanent home in St. Tropez, but it is quite possible that she made the move when Duranty had his accident. There is no doubt she nursed Duranty back to health.

Duranty never mentioned her help during this period, but he mentioned the opium. He wrote two sets of memoirs, both featuring the drug and both an uneasy mixture of fact and fiction. The first was a semi-fictionalized autobiography entitled *Search for a Key*, in which he identified a man named Clifford Hawtrey as the individual who supplied him with drugs. Again, in an article in the *Atlantic Monthly*, which was published in 1943, the same year as *Search for a Key*, Duranty named the same man as the individual who brought the drug to his hideaway in St. Tropez. The magazine article, which is entitled simply, "Opium Smoking," indicates that it was delivered to him whenever he needed it to alleviate the pain from a broken hip and an injured sciatic nerve after a wreck in a taxi in rue Montmartre in August 1918: a fictional story, but close enough to Duranty's actual accident.

The opium poppy, he wrote fondly, is white before it blossoms. It is nicked under "the fat green bud," and white stuff oozes out. In the morning, it has changed to a brown color, and that is the opium. You then cook the brown drops to a boil and strain them through cloth. The remaining residue is what you smoke.[45]

The effects of the drug are "a clarity of perception" and a seeming "novelty of vision" strangely Oriental, wherein mere "supposing" makes it true.

After a while, you are thoroughly hooked, and the horrible nightmares begin, and you find you are "stuck like a fly on flypaper." The effects of addiction finally become as horrible as the pain from the original affliction, he reported.

Again, it's difficult to sort out what's true and what isn't. Many years later, Duranty told a friend's wife that he loved opium and that the period during which he was taking it was the happiest time in his life. He said if he had any money at all, he would go right straight back to it. The woman was John Gunther's wife, and she asked him how he got the opium. He answered, "Well, I was living in France at the time, and it simply came by mail every week from London in a little envelope." He confirmed to Jane Gunther that his wife also smoked the drug. To another acquaintance, he confided he continued smoking the drug for six months after the loss of his leg. He gave this advice to the young man: "If you ever get the chance, smoke opium two times. The first time, it will make you sick. The second time, smoke to enjoy it. And then, don't *ever* smoke it again!"[46]

The days after he left St. Tropez were pleasant ones for Duranty. He rented a studio apartment in Montparnasse, setting up headquarters at the Café Select on the corner next to the Rotonde. That year, 1925, the Select was like "an Anglo-American Club where every one knew each other."[47] The life he described was an easy one. The expatriates would meet about noon for an aperitif, then go along together for lunch. The afternoon would perhaps be passed on the Seine or at the races at Longchamps. "[T]hen perhaps cocktails on the Right Bank, and dinner, followed by hours of conversation on the Select Terrace once more. It seemed a rendezvous for all the most interesting people I knew." Ernest Hemingway frequently turned up there, as well as Floyd Gibbons, who stayed on for a couple of weeks before going off somewhere on one of his gigantic schemes. Bolitho joined them for a short time.

Despite the lazy pleasure of each passing day, the truth of the matter was that Duranty had fallen into a depression over the loss of his leg, even though he had received the equivalent of $10,000 compensation from the French government. Notwithstanding this, Duranty was sinking. It was Bolitho who pointed out that it could become a lucky break, if Duranty took the right attitude.

Anyone was bright enough to make the most of a lucky break, Bolitho said: "Any fool can do that." To profit from your losses, he insisted, that was something that required intelligence, marking the dif-

133

ference "between a man of sense and the damn fools." Before he lost his leg, Bolitho said, Duranty had been an average man, a bit under-height and of course a good deal brighter, but indistinguishable from anyone who might walk in the door. Nobody had ever noticed him particularly. "But now you are lucky, and I'm not trying to comfort you, I'm stating facts. Henceforth people will say, 'Who's the little man with the limp who asked an intelligent question?'"[48] As for the money, it would give him a measure of independence, and rightly invested, provide a nest egg against difficult days.

The cane became Duranty's trademark, and he quickly learned to emphasize his points by gesturing with it in the air, or hitting it against the floor or a piece of furniture.

As to the advice about the money, it didn't work out quite the way Bolitho envisaged. No sooner had Duranty received the compensation than he spent it, frittering it away on fancy living. If the truth were known, Duranty hadn't changed all that much since the early days.

CHAPTER VIII

The Mysterious Fatalism
of the Slav

A winter holiday late in January 1924, heavy snowfall, with a temperature of 20 below zero Fahrenheit: the streets of Moscow were virtually empty. Late in the day, at about 6 o'clock, a special fly-sheet edition appeared, informing the city's inhabitants of the death of Lenin. News spread slowly. The flags, which had been lowered to half-mast, were barely visible through the blur of snow.

Nobody expected it to be Lenin. At the first glimpse of the black borders on the news sheet, a few cried out Trotsky's name. Then, the gradual realization: the great Bolshevik leader was dead.

From now on until after the funeral, time lost all meaning for Duranty. His life became "a roundabout of chasing the news, writing it, and writing it and chasing it." Outside, the temperature steadily declined from 20 below, to 28 below, finally, down to 35 degrees below zero, a cruel Arctic wind driving sheets of snow through the city's streets. Inside, Duranty drank hot mulled wine and worked through the "[f]everish, flurried hours blurred by lack of sleep, overwork, and the thrilling excitement of being able to report one of the moments in human history. . . ."[1] The stories seemed to write themselves.

Moscow, January 23, 1924—Premier Lenin died last night at 6.50 o'clock. The immediate cause of death was paralysis of the respiratory centres due to a cerebral haemorrhage. . . .

At 11.20 o'clock this morning President Kalinin briefly opened the session of the All-Russian Soviet Congress and requested everyone to stand. He had not slept all night and tears were streaming down his haggard face. . . .

"I bring you terrible news about our dear comrade, Vladimir Ilyich."

High up in the gallery a woman uttered a low, wailing cry that was followed by a burst of sobs.

"Yesterday," faltered Kalinin, "yesterday, he suffered a further stroke of paralysis and—" There was a long pause as if the speaker were unable to nerve himself to pronounce the fatal word; then, with an effort which shook his whole body, it came—"died."

The emotional Slav temperament reacted immediately. From all over the huge opera house came sobs and wailing, not loud or shrill, but pitifully mournful, spreading and increasing.[2]

Duranty, rising to the occasion, would in these days write what are now considered classics in the field of journalism, clearly the best dispatches of his career. The day after Lenin's death, he led with "[t]wo unforgettable pictures . . . from this day of Russia's sorrow."

First, Lenin lying in state—such simple state amid such grandeur—in the columned hall of the former Nobles' Club; second, the face and shoulders of Kalinin helping to bear Lenin's coffin from the station, when two steps down from the platform its weight was suddenly thrown on him in front. Kalinin was a typical Russian peasant driven by misery like millions of his fellows to work whole or part time in a city factory. During these moments of strain he symbolised the struggle of Russia's 140,000,000 peasants against the blind enmity of nature and human oppression. For two nights he had not slept and, as the level ground relieved part of the burden, he staggered from sheer exhaustion. But on he went like an old peasant ploughing the stubborn earth, with sweat pouring down his cheeks in an icy snow-flecked gale, until he reached a gun caisson with six white horses waiting in the station yard to carry the coffin to the Nobles' Club.[3]

Duranty followed the cortège as the winter storm raged around the dark figures lining the streets. Troops stood "shoulder to shoulder," pressing back the crowds, and the Red flags posted along the way danced wildly in the wind. The "procession, marching slowly with linked arms twenty deep across the street," kept time to the solemn funeral music. Finally, they reached the Opera House Square. Along with the honored Old Bolsheviks, who had all been at one time or another political prisoners, Duranty stood waiting in the bitter cold until at last they were allowed to enter the Nobles' Club.

In the center of the room Lenin lay on a high couch with four columns that gave the effect of a sort of old-fashioned four-poster bed without curtains. Over his feet was a grey rug with something stencilled on it, over his body a dark red blanket; and his head rested bare on a white pillow. The face was a yellow-white, like wax, without the slightest wrinkle and utterly calm. The eyes were closed, yet the expression was one of looking forward seeking something beyond his vision.[4]

By the day of the funeral, a Saturday, the temperature had plummeted to 35 degrees below. In this desperate cold, the air clung to the vast multitude of people gathered in Red Square and congealed into "a fog . . . like a smoke sacrifice."[5]

For those who took part in the historic days surrounding Lenin's death, one question remained unanswered: Where was Trotsky? He had been ill, was said to be recuperating in the Caucasus. Whatever the circumstances that detained him, however, Duranty always believed this was the actual beginning of Trotsky's decline in the eyes of the masses; the people, Duranty thought, never forgave this slight to their dead leader.

At first and under the influence of the emotion of those days, Duranty kept up a steady stream of what he would later call pure "sentimental twaddle." Well-informed sources, he had written on the day of the public funeral, now believed that "Trotsky, Radek, and other insurgents will join hands with the 'machine' leaders, Stalin, Zinoviev, Kamenev, and Bukharin, over Lenin's grave." It was, Duranty predicted, "the first step toward reconciliation."[6]

What Duranty was referring to was the gradual emergence of internal factionalism among the top Communist leaders that had, this cold winter, developed into a direct confrontation between Trotsky and Stalin. Duranty himself "put his money on Stalin." Nevertheless, it was not until the spring months, after Lenin's death, that it became apparent the Party apparatus Stalin had erected behind the scenes since taking over as General Secretary was, in fact, unbeatable. Trotsky was an outspoken critic of NEP, and wanted the early suppression of

137

the "kulak"—the middle-ranked peasant whose competence in agricultural matters and whose general resistance to Communism was
retarding the path to Socialism. Thus, Trotsky became known as the
"Left" wing of the party. The Rightists, epitomized by Nickolai Bukharin, did not believe in forcing the pace of Socialism, favoring instead
the slow assimilation of Socialist principles. By aligning himself first
with Kamenev and Zinoviev against Trotsky, and later moving against
all three, Stalin managed to defeat the Left wing of the party.

He had done so by joining up with the Party's Right wing. Later,
when he was strong enough, Stalin would suppress Bukharin as well.

But these political maneuvers were not at all obvious to the early
watchers of the Kremlin; only slowly did they become apparent, and
then only to the cleverest. William Henry Chamberlin, reporting for
the *Christian Science Monitor* and later for the Manchester *Guardian*
as well, interpreted these internecine struggles as the Bolshevik state's
first few feeble steps toward a democratized form of government.
Chamberlin came to the Soviet Union highly enamored of the world's
first Communist state, and he excused the excessive zeal of the Cheka
on the grounds that it had been forced upon the Party by the Civil War.
Now, with the opening up of debate within the highest party ranks, he
believed in "the ultimate victory of the democratic forces within the
party. . . . Time is unmistakably on their side."[7]

The machinations of Stalin's party apparatus inevitably sank into
the background for Duranty, however, for it was in the middle of Stalin's intrigues that Duranty had the train accident that cost him his leg.
It caused his absence from the Soviet capital for almost a full year.

When he returned to Moscow in August of 1925, Duranty found himself confused by the events then taking place in the Politburo. In his
absence from Moscow, he had read everything he could lay his hands
on. Returning, he now tried to employ Bolitho's elitist philosophy and
prove that he could think better than the herd. He sat down, he rec-
ollected later, listing everything about which he felt fairly certain.
What he came up with were a few conclusions which, although not
earthshattering, would formulate his accurate assessment of the situation, leading to a period of highly informed reportage. His judgment
about events in the Soviet Union during this time reached its highest
point.

Duranty believed that Socialism was here to stay. Unlike others who continued to make rash predictions about the Bolshevik state's imminent downfall, Duranty took the view that the Bolsheviks were firmly in control of the country, and that this control would not be shaken. With this in mind, he now came to think of NEP as only a temporary expedient. He expected the Soviets to return to a more militant Socialist path. The "kulak" or peasant problem at the heart of so many of the disagreements between Trotsky and Stalin was the central question, Duranty thought, and its resolution was the most important concern of the next decade. Whoever led the way in the Party struggles would determine how this and other pressing problems would be dealt with. Duranty believed that ultimately Stalin would lead the way.[8]

His reportage of the period shows the steady revelation of these ideas, developed in an orderly progression of thought. By the middle of summer, 1926, Duranty was insisting that despite Trotsky's brilliance as a "far abler and more popular" leader, Stalin, "the administration 'boss,'" as he put it, had "more political sense than the rest of the Communist Party put together."

> He is a remarkable personality, this son of a Georgian cobbler who veils his cold-blooded astuteness behind an apparent brusque simplicity.
> "I am a plain, rugged fellow," he told the Communist Party Congress last Winter. "You must forgive my lack of tact or delicacy."[9]

By autumn, Duranty was reporting, with the kind of satisfaction of one who correctly predicts the outcome, the "complete defeat for Trotsky and his associates."[10] It was not a matter of Duranty's preferring one Socialist leader to the other. It was a matter of being right.

In the early days of NEP, W. Averell Harriman, who would later become U. S. Ambassador to Russia and afterwards governor of New York, was one of a few American businessmen awarded a concession in the Soviet Union—an arrangement whereby foreign capitalist firms were permitted to exploit rich mineral deposits in the country in return for capital equipment and foreign currency. Economically, the plan was expected to yield certain economic advantages in those early days of struggle. But the original purpose of the plan had been political. In the days immediately following Allied Intervention, Lenin had thought the presence of foreign capitalists would contribute to better

139

relations with the outside world and help to prevent the threat of further military incursions.[11] With a twenty-year contract in hand, Harriman and his company had undertaken "a concession from the Soviet Union to exploit manganese deposits at Tchiaturi, near Tiflis, in the Caucasus," which had been one of the largest producers in the world before the war.[12]

In December of 1926, Harriman was inside the Soviet Union trying to figure out what was really going on. He saw Trotsky and spoke with him, but the talk was of limited value since, as Harriman put it, "Trotsky was on his way out." It was Duranty who tipped off Harriman that Stalin was the man to watch.

Even then, Harriman remembered, Walter Duranty was something of a controversial figure simply because of his prediction that the Bolsheviks would remain the governing force in Soviet Russia. "If you said it was going to last," Harriman said, talking over the old days, "you were accused of being pro-Soviet, because all the outside experts said it *wouldn't* last." On the other hand, Harriman didn't get the impression that Duranty was particularly pro-Soviet. "I simply didn't find that to be true," Harriman said.

The two men had a number of "very free talks," and Harriman found Duranty "particularly well-informed." Making the rounds, Harriman believed then that Duranty's analysis of "present and future was the most penetrating of any reporter's of the time." After his talks with Duranty, Harriman decided that NEP was not going to last, and that the concession looked shaky as well. At the end of his trip, Harriman decided to withdraw from the arrangement, a decision that turned out to be the right one—and he returned to the United States frankly grateful for the information Duranty had given him.

Half a century later, Harriman's opinion of Duranty hadn't changed, and he wanted to make that very clear. Unhurried and deliberate, he picked his words precisely, exercising all the caution of a former diplomat and politician: "Penetrating ... good judgment ... sound judgment ... accurate ... wise. ..."[13] The words added up to high praise.

There had been another reporter along at some of the talks between Duranty and Harriman—H. R. Knickerbocker. "Red" to acquaintances and "Knick" to his best friends, Knickerbocker had a shock of red hair that made him easy to recognize even at a distance. He had been reporting as an assistant correspondent in Berlin for the New York *Evening Post* and the Philadelphia *Public Ledger* when he accepted a position as Moscow correspondent for the International News Service. In the two years he was in the Soviet capital, Knickerbocker and Duranty became close friends, closer in some ways than Duranty and Bolitho. Knick was among a slow but steady influx of correspondents into Moscow. Interest was growing, but not at a particularly rapid rate.

In the United States, as prosperity led to a feverish consumerism, the tendency, as always, was to look inward. Self-absorbed by nature, Americans racing through the Roaring Twenties found little to distract them from matters at home, and attention to foreign affairs declined markedly. In one analysis of forty daily newspapers in 1927, the average percentage of space devoted to happenings abroad ranged from 9 percent to 2.5 percent, the latter figure representing inland coverage.[14]

Indeed, although Duranty's reporting during this period was clearly delineated, extremely well-informed, and mature, it seemed that very few American readers cared, absorbed as they were by their own affairs.

In 1927, Knick was posted back to Berlin, and for the next few years he and Duranty kept up a lively correspondence, Knick doing a host of little favors for Duranty—exchanging money at favorable rates and sending it back by friends, or picking up things Duranty needed that were unavailable in Moscow.

Besides, Knick and Duranty shared another interest—writing fiction. Before Knick left Moscow, the two began collaborating on a series of short stories, actually managing to finish six of them before Knick left. They had a weekly wager whereby whoever didn't finish his story had to pay the other one. Then, they exchanged their stories and edited one another's work.

The plan was to submit the six they wrote together under Duranty's name, since it was better known than Knick's and since both of them thought it looked better to have only one name on a story. If things worked out, the second six were to be in Knick's name.[15] For Duranty, it was the first of several attempts at collaborating. A sociable type, Duranty never did enjoy working by himself.

On the lst of April 1927, Duranty wrote Knick telling him that he had revised the six stories, retitled them, and sent them off sometime around the 10th of March to an agent in New York, whose name he had apparently got from Wythe Williams or Aleck Woollcott. The stories, Duranty wrote Knick, were "not awful good but not so bad. ...." and he expected "to hear something pretty soon from New York." Without Knick in Moscow, Duranty admitted that he had started playing bridge in the evenings instead of writing. He wished Knick would come back right now because he had "a corking idea [for a play] and a red-hot title. But thats hardly enough for Broadway."[16]

By June, however, when Duranty came back from a three-month trip to China, he found bad news waiting for him. "I have just had a foul and bitter disappointment," he wrote Knick. "That lousy bastard in New York wrote me a pompous and idiotic letter the upshot whereof was that he was sending the stories back without even trying to place any of them. I still dont really understand why, because he said they were splendidly written but 'resembled episodes from real life rather than short stories and also deal with persons and events alien to American life.'" Duranty called his comments "highbrow nonsense about the form and function of the short story. I suppose the blighter has never heard of Maupassant or disapproves of him." Duranty was sure that he knew what the public wanted "better than this fish, but it's furiously irritating. The point now is what to do." In closing, Duranty restated his determination to write more short stories—"Chink slant this time"—as soon as he had any free time.[17] Meantime, he bundled up the stories a second time, sent them to other agents in New York and London, and settled down to wait.

Duranty's junket to China in 1927 did lead to one short story with a "Chink slant," as he put it, called "The Spirit Within." It deals with the confrontation of ideologies between a dedicated Christian missionary and an idealistic Red Army Communist, who are both captured and face torture by a cruel Chinese bandit, but who are unexpectedly freed because of their bravery.[18]

Perhaps of more interest was an eerie incident Duranty experienced on the trip, which, some years later, he recalled as being the strangest thing he ever saw.

It was simply a detachment of a Red Spear battalion I saw one night on the south side of the Yellow River, on the road to Lo-yang, in China. They weren't Communists, not really—just peasant rebels, who had suffered misery and torture. They were not in uniform, had few rifles. They were dangerous only from fear, and they barred our way to Lo-yang. They were just a lot of men grouped around a row of campfires, like the stories you read of American Indians. I had an interpreter, a boy who could speak their outlandish language. Nothing happened. Nothing at all. They wouldn't let us go to Lo-yang, so we just had to go back. They did us no harm.[19]

Explaining the significance of this seemingly harmless incident, Duranty said:

There was just something else there besides the men—a strange presence, the strangest I had ever known. I didn't see it. I sensed it. Something happened later, but not to me. About two weeks afterward, a correspondent from a London paper went down there, and that was the end of him.

In short, Duranty had encountered a sense of Death.[20]

Duranty's visit to China had been prompted by recent Communist uprisings there which would soon lead to the beginning of the twenty-two-year Chinese Civil War. The New York office, Duranty wrote to Knick, "seemed to think I had cleaned up." He had been given the option of staying, but decided to return to Moscow because "things were fizzing here—and may fizz some more though personally I rather doubt it. I only got back last week and am not yet quite sure of my 'line.'"[21] As it turned out, Duranty missed the big event. A bare three weeks after he had left in mid-July, the Communist-influenced Hankow government purged Chinese Communists from its ranks, expelling Russian political and military advisers.

Hankow had been regarded by the Communist world "not only as the most conspicuous success of revolutionary technique since 1917, but as the test case: If its success could be extended and made permanent, the victory of the international (Trotskyist) tendency was assured; but if Hankow failed, the militant world-revolutionists failed as well, and even in Russia the future became obscure."[22]

The event, seemingly removed from the immediate affairs of the Soviets, would be one of several factors that Stalin would manipulate in order to disgrace Trotsky and his so-called Opposition, driving them into exile by the end of the year. Trotsky had been the prime adherent of the international Communist movement, and world revolution now seemed impossible. The Stalinists had always been more inward-looking, believing that Socialism in Soviet Russia did not depend upon the success of a world revolution. To Western observers in Moscow, it seemed that the Russians most interested in Hankow were Trotsky, Radek, Bukharin, and a few of their friends, "while the official (Stalinist) Russians, although uniformly courteous to their visitors, could not help giving the impression that China was only one of their many problems, and not one of the most important."[23]

For his part, Duranty privately admitted to being unrelievedly bored by the Trotsky-Stalin affair, and he insisted he didn't care a whit for the theory and economics of Stalin. What he was really interested in, he told a group of Americans at a dinner party in November of 1927, was writing fiction.[24] Only a few days before, he had received the gratifying news that one of the short stories he had written with Knick had been accepted for publication. This was an improbable tale about an inquisitorial old witch attached to the Red Army who awes superstitious townsfolk by determining guilt on the basis of whether or not a parrot bites the fingers of the accused. The story was entitled "The Parrot."[25]

"Talk about dreams coming true—" Duranty wrote to Knick on the 4th of November. It had been one of "the foulest, coldest, blizzardest days even Moscow can produce." But when he received Knick's news about the story, he could see "the blue sea of the Azure Coast twinkle gaily in the hot sun." He was especially pleased because it corroborated his own judgment of his work, "about which I was beginning to be shaky." This proved that the agent, "that mouldy Liveright," was dead wrong in his literary pronouncements. Duranty himself had been sure all along that the stories were "smoothly written and adequately constructed." He suggested that Knick's wife Laura could now start looking for sable coats, saying that "four hundred seeds of encouragement" were all it took to call forth steady effort, "even from a sluggard like myself."

In his enthusiasm, Duranty proposed this scenario for Knick. For the next two months, they should try to turn out "at least four more stories and have them on the way." Duranty told Knick that he had already informed Birchall at the *Times* Paris office

> that if things here were quiet Id like to turn the work over to Cholerton
> at Christmas and take three months leave of absence without salary.

144

He wasnt overjoyed but agreed in principle. I want to learn German anyway, so would come to Berlin and rent me a small apartment, and I having nothing else to do we shouldnt find it impossible to produce about ten pieces in that time. . . . By the end of March, then, we might be in a position to kiss the newspaper game goodbye except for a special stunt every now and then.[26]

Duranty closed the letter, babbling about movie rights and German translations. Knick fired him back a letter affirming that he too was "still uplifted."

Upon receipt of your letter I went into a trance during which I consumed half a bottle of Scotch, and upon coming out was surprised not to find a completed short story a[t] hand. . . . By God it would be great to get out of this grind of newspaper work. Once we have sold, say, twelve in a row, we could afford to talk about throwing up our jobs. But not until then.[27]

Knick had taken on a number of extra free-lance jobs, and he was holding down the office on his own, since one of his colleagues had gone on vacation. But his own note of caution whirred into a wildly unrealistic optimism by the end of his letter, when he asked Duranty if he knew that Theodore Dreiser had received $95,000 for the movie rights of *An American Tragedy*. On that note, Knick wrote, "Let the congregation rise and sing." Knickerbocker, the son of a Methodist minister, signed off, "Yours in the worship of Mammon."[28]

On the night of the dinner party at which Duranty professed a growing boredom with Soviet affairs, he was still basking in the warm afterglow of the news about the sale of "The Parrot." Soon, he must have been thinking, he would be able to leave his position on the *Times* and give himself over to full-time "literary" writing, thus fulfilling the dreams of his youth.

The novelist Sinclair Lewis was at the time traveling to Soviet Russia, and he planned to stop off in Berlin along the way. In a postscript to one of his letters, Duranty had asked Knick to talk "Red" Lewis, as everyone called him, into bringing coffee when he came. Lewis's wife, Dorothy Thompson, was already in Moscow, doing research for a book on Russia. Duranty, she wrote later, showed her how Bolshevism was an *emotional* force by telling her about a young girl who went to Lenin's tomb to stand, meditate, and "get new strength."[29]

It had been Thompson who had carried the letter containing the news of the success of "The Parrot"—first to Knickerbocker in Berlin, where she stopped off for a few days, then on to Duranty. Her presence in Moscow was the occasion for a good deal of socializing, which included meeting other reporters in the Soviet capital. Among them was United Press correspondent Louis Fischer. Like William Henry Chamberlin, Fischer was a sympathizer with the Socialist cause, "a fellow traveller," as it was called. To show his enthusiasm for the regime, Fischer affected simple Russian dress, often appearing in a roughly cut peasant shirt. In the summertime, he wore hand-crafted leather sandals with stockings.

Fischer now referred to Duranty as the "dean of Moscow foreign correspondents," but he remained alive to the fact that Duranty was, even then, "a bundle of paradoxes." Duranty saw drama in politics, he believed, "but detest[ed] the theatre and rarely attend[ed] a performance of the opera or ballet." As Fischer saw it, Duranty didn't much care what happened to the world, and he chalked down Duranty's "interest in politics" to "his love of spectacle." At social occasions, he reported, Duranty tended to dominate the conversation by talking "about wars, blood, and women," which he did very well.

It was true that Duranty had become the unofficial social host of Moscow, a role he was to relish over the next few years. To come to Moscow without checking in with Duranty was unthinkable for those in the know. Only a short time after Dorothy Thompson arrived, Duranty would play host to Sinclair Lewis, introducing him to "the American colony." Lewis and his wife were the guests of honor at a dinner given at Duranty's apartment. Always known for his outrageous behavior, Lewis discoursed wisely on this occasion, did a brilliant reading of his own work, and then, dead drunk, fell asleep on Duranty's couch. Finally, not knowing what else to do, everybody just went home. Duranty always held it against Lewis, believing that Lewis had behaved deplorably.

Also at the party was a likable young man of twenty-seven, who, like Knickerbocker in Berlin, would become a life-long friend of Duranty, despite the difference in their years. Vincent Sheean noticed right away the attractive cook who was serving the meal. "Nice cook you have, Duranty," he said. "You leave that cook alone," Duranty snapped back. He was wearing a smile to soften the effect.[30]

Vincent Sheean, "Jimmy" to his friends, was a young journalist

hired by the North American Newspaper Alliance (N.A.N.A.) to have
"personal adventures in the tradition of Richard Harding Davis," and
report them for the arm-chair enjoyment of their readers. He was one
of several refugees from "the experiment" in Hankow who had, after
its failure, made his way to Moscow. At the moment, Sheean was in
the doghouse with N.A.N.A. for writing political analyses of the situation in China instead of giving them the kind of "personal adventures" they craved.

With him was a young and attractive red-haired woman named
Rayna Prohme, also just returned from Hankow. Unlike Sheean,
Prohme was a Communist and had been employed as the Soviet representative's assistant when "the revolution" had been halted. She and
the other Communists had had to escape by stealth from Hankow to
avoid torture, perhaps even execution, since the Nationalist troops had
shown no tendencies toward mercy in dealing with their enemies.
Now, Rayna Prohme sat beside Jimmy Sheean, having only recently
made a daring escape from a premature and painful death, or so it
seemed at the time.

Jimmy Sheean first heard of Rayna Prohme when he was in China:
"Red-headed gal," someone had said, "spit fire, mad as a hatter, complete Bolshevik."[31] A few minutes after that, he met her—a Chicago
girl a long way from home.

> She was slight, not very tall, with short red-gold hair and a frivolous
> turned-up nose. Her eyes were of the kind anthropologists called
> "mixed," and could actually change colour with the changes of light, or
> even with changes of mood. Her voice, fresh, cool and very American,
> sounded as if it had secret rivulets of laughter running underneath it all
> the time, ready to come to the surface without warning. All in all, she
> was most unlike my idea of a "wild Bolshevik," and I told her so. She
> laughed. I had never heard anybody laugh as she did—it was the gayest,
> most unself-conscious sound in the world. You might have thought
> that it did not come from a person at all, but from some impulse of
> gaiety in the air.[32]

Prohme had gone to the University of Illinois, Jimmy Sheean to
the University of Chicago, and they hit it off immediately. Her sincerity, Sheean wrote, "floated over her like a banner." She was a type, one

of those who hungered for a cause, like the suffragettes, "the kind of thing that made so many nice American girls go out and get themselves cracked over the head by policemen. . . ."[33]

From the beginning, it had been obvious to Sheean, as to others, that the Communist coalition in Hankow would end in catastrophe, and he cabled his bosses that he wanted to stay to cover it. His instructions came back, "a longish cablegram," the gist of which was that Sheean was sending them "entirely too much about politics . . . what we expect of you is something quite different, and we want you now to 'have personal adventures.'"[34] Reluctantly, Sheean had gone off in search of a "personal adventure" just as the government was collapsing, leaving the others to escape ten days later, in the middle of July. He had no idea what had happened to Prohme until he worked his way to Moscow and found that she had made it there as well.

Prohme had decided to enter the Lenin Institute "to be trained as a revolutionary instrument." By now hopelessly in love with her, Sheean was very much against it. He was convinced the Communist Party was "a false cloud," and he hoped to save Prohme from it. They took rooms together, arguing late into the night about her decision. But she found the debates tiring, and often had trouble getting out of bed the following morning. Then, on the morning of November 12, she went to see Dorothy Thompson and fainted in her hotel room. The event aroused little interest at the time, but within twenty-four hours, she had become extremely ill. In a state of delirium, she was taken to the Hotel de l'Europe, where she continued to worsen.

That night a winter storm hit Moscow. After a sleepless night of worry and torment, Sheean made his way in the early hours to Duranty's house to ask his advice, since Duranty was "the only person I could appeal to with any confidence," Sheean wrote later. Duranty was asleep, but he sat up in bed, and they tried to decide what to do. A friend dropped by, and hearing the problem, suggested the German Embassy's doctor. He went along with Sheean, since Duranty found it difficult to walk on the ice with his wooden leg.[35]

The German doctor went to the hotel, and quickly diagnosed the illness as fatal. Prohme was confined to a dark room, waiting to die, although she didn't know it. When Sheean was allowed in to see her, she told him what frightened her the most.

> "The doctor thinks I am losing my mind," she said, "and that is the worst thing of all. He won't say so, but that is what he thinks. I can tell

by the way he holds matches in front of my eyes and tests my responses. He doesn't think I can focus on anything. . . ."

She had spoken vaguely of the fear before, and all I could do was say that I did not believe it was well founded. But on the next day . . . she felt certain that this was the case, and it kept her silent and almost afraid to speak, even to me. I sat beside her hour after hour in the dark, silent room, and blackness pressed down and in upon us. Two or three times she raised her voice to say: "Don't tell anybody."[36]

Rayna Prohme died of encephalitis, or inflammation of the brain, on Monday, 21 November 1927, "thus literally, and all too aptly, burning away," Sheean would write. After publishing his autobiography, in which he recorded her death, Sheean became something of a cult figure, and Prohme "the heroine of our youth" for a generation of serious readers.[37] Despite the fame and success that came his way, Jimmy Sheean never quite got over the death of the young and idealistic girl, as all of his friends were very much aware.

Everybody left town: Sheean out of Moscow for good, "Red" Lewis and his wife continuing with their tour, Duranty remaining behind to nurse fantasies about his fiction. Lots of snow and ice—it was going to be a hard winter. Duranty had received a none-too-encouraging letter from his agent in New York indicating he was having trouble selling the other stories Duranty and Knick had written.

Undaunted, Duranty wrote Knick that he didn't "want to see the blue Mediterranean only from a bath chair." If Russia wouldn't sell, he would turn his hand to other topics. He had plans to write two more short stories, which he would then send to Knick. He would have them there in no time "unless things fizz here too much."[38]

The stories never got written. On the 18th of December, the Fifteenth Party Congress expelled the seventy-five leading members of the opposition from the Communist Party. Trotsky was sent to Alma Ata, on the borders of China in southeast Kazakhstan. In a letter dated the 23rd of January 1928, Duranty wrote Knick: "I saw Trotsky off the night of my return. . . ."[39]

Duranty and Paul Sheffer, the highly respected correspondent of the *Berliner Tageblatt*, received a telephone call that Trotsky would be leaving for internal exile on an afternoon train, and Duranty and Sheffer were both there, watching Trotsky, his wife, and two assistants make their departure. The large group of onlookers assembled there behaved well, "a large force of police" and special secret service troops present just to make sure.

Sheffer and Duranty went home and filed their stories—orderly departure, "sympathetic" crowd sort of stuff. It was fully two days before they found out it wasn't Trotsky.

Sheffer turned up at Duranty's apartment, excited. He told Duranty that "there was no Trotsky at the Kazan Station."[40] The real Trotsky and his wife had been dragged, resisting, from their home earlier and placed on a single railway carriage, which, some fifty kilometers from Moscow, was "hitched to a train bound for Central Asia."[41] The authorities had been taking no chances. They wanted to avoid any disturbances, so they had deliberately arranged a "Potemkin" Trotsky. Duranty heard later "that the central figure was an actor who had impersonated Trotsky in one of the Civil War films."[42]

For Duranty, it was another reminder not to trust the judgment of others in Soviet matters. In some cases, he couldn't even trust his own.

Emerging from the Kremlin's internal power struggles was the outline of a policy that indicated the direction the Stalinist majority would take in the future. In March 1928, a public announcement was issued that a group of saboteurs in the mining industry from the Shakhty region of the Donbass would be tried publicly. There were charges of conspiracy between the defendants and "foreign capitalist powers." Figuring prominently in the prosecution's case was the concept of "class enemies," or "spoilers," intent on destroying the system from the inside. The Western correspondents made plans to give the trial full coverage. Indeed, the highly publicized trial would be featured in the Soviet press in a kind of carnival atmosphere designed to entertain the masses.

Earlier, in 1924, Duranty had covered the *in camera* trial of the arch-terrorist Boris Savinkov, writing a highly dramatic account of it. A Social Revolutionary, Savinkov had been an early supporter of Kerensky and the Provisional Government and was known to be behind the assassination of several officials under the Czar. It was thought he had been the moving force behind the attempt on Lenin's life in 1918, as well as attempts on other prominent Bolshevik officials. In a highly charged speech delivered just before his sentencing, Savinkov openly confessed his guilt, professing no remorse.

Duranty wrote then that he would always think of the Savinkov

150

trial as "the greatest theatrical performance I ever attended. . . . Savinkov's final speech was the greatest piece of oratory I have ever heard. . . . like the last speech from the scaffold with which condemned criminals about to die in old Britain, whether they were kings or highwaymen or poor devils who had stolen a sheep, used to regale an appreciative audience."[43]

Now, covering an equally dramatic trial four years later, in 1928, Duranty brought to bear a similar attitude, his love of spectacle overcoming his critical faculties. Of the trial's opening, he wrote: "Half a hundred pallid prisoners today faced the bar of bleak-faced, grim proletarian justice to answer for their alleged sins against the sovereign people in the 'class war trial' of the technicians of the Donetz coal region."[44] The walls of the courtroom were "stark white, livid in the morning daylight," and the defendants looked tired and weary, white-faced. Duranty wondered whether he could not discern a sense of fear whenever the prosecutor, Nikolai V. Krylenko, looked at the men who were on trial for their lives.[45] The circus would drag on for weeks: a practice run for the future, only nobody knew it then. It would alert the Soviet Public to a new enemy—the worm inside.

A very young John Gunther, twenty-six years old, filling in for their regular correspondent Junius Wood, was sent by the Chicago *Daily News* to the Soviet capital. It would be a short sojourn, but long enough to cement a friendship with Walter Duranty; paternalistic, perhaps, at the beginning, since Duranty was some seventeen years Gunther's senior. Gunther was full of the enthusiasm of youth. Moscow was "a night-owl city"; the *Daily News* office "the center of drinks, gossip, and intrigue for all of American Moscow." The bureau had a bathtub, and sooner or later, most of the American colony made it over there to indulge in the luxury of a real bath.

The Duranty Gunther described was a "queer animal," bumping along "over the cobbles" beside the younger man in the early hours of the morning. He made an entry in his diary that Duranty had "a very fine mind," but looked "like a shrivelled monkey." He found Duranty's domestic arrangement intriguing:

When one dines with him in Moscow, an extremely pretty girl, smart in semi-evening frock, opens the door, shaking hands. She then disappears again, and late in the evening, asks Walter if he wants to get to work, she has finished the *Izvestia* proofs. Then they go to bed together. In the morning, she shines the shoes. Mistress, secretary, servant. An unholy trinity for you! Of course, by Moscow law, since they share the same residence, she's his wife, too. . . .[46]

On the 4th of July, Gunther went to Duranty's house, for "caviar, bright new red crabs, tiny individual new chickens, strawberries. At about 5:00 the next morning everybody in town was still coming." At 7:15 they all moved to someone else's apartment for breakfast.

It was the morning of the day that the verdict in the Shakhta trial was delivered. The first announcement came that the verdict would be read at 4:00 p.m. It was delayed to seven, then to nine. "Everybody in the world just kept running between hotel and court; standing in the wind; watching the slick coppers on white horses; listening to the mob arguing, gesticulating, wondering."

The American journalists assembled at Duranty's house to wait, his place being the nearest to the tribunal.[47] In the early hours of the following morning, they all filed in to the court to hear the verdict.

"The great 'Shakhta' trial ended at 1:30 a.m. today with eleven death sentences, thirty-eight imprisonments. . . . [in] a drama that has gripped the Soviet Union for the past six weeks," Duranty wrote.

The defendants "met their fate impassively. . . . only their eyes seemed to be living." They stood, in motionless rows, "pale and exhausted but upheld by the mysterious fatalism of the Slav. Through the whole hour and a half that followed none of them weakened or whimpered."[48]

Abroad, accusations were flying that the confessions of the defendants had been wrung out of them by torture or lack of sleep. Many years later, reports emanating out of the prison-camp system would confirm the worst. The trial marked the first use of the "conveyor," a system of uninterrupted interrogation, alternating with long periods of solitary confinement, in cells with "hot or cold floors." The confessions had been "in large part, fake."[49] Shakhta was the prototype for the future, the harbinger of things to come. For Duranty, schooled in skepticism, there seemed to be an irresistible force that drew him in, causing him to accept at face value the verdict of the Soviet court. "Most of the accused, I am convinced, deserve their fate," he wrote ingenuously.[50]

It was a strange stand, especially coming on the heels of the Trotsky episode. Duranty's assessment of the first Soviet show trial violated his own most important rule as a reporter in Moscow: "to believe nothing that I hear, little of what I read, and not all of what I see."[51]

Then, at the end of 1928, there came the fraud of his own perpetration, albeit unintentional. None of the stories he had written with Knick had made it into publication—with the sole exception of "The Parrot"— which had done very well and was selected for inclusion in the O. Henry volume of the best short stories of the year. When the volume was published, Duranty got a shock. "The Parrot" was actually named the best short story of 1929, with all the public praise and congratulations that that entailed.

Duranty made the decision to bluff it out rather than admit the work published under his name was not his alone. In all probability, it was Knick who had written the original draft, making Duranty's position even more embarrassing. Knick took it well. On the 14th of December 1928, Duranty wrote, telling him that he was "a noble and honest citizen. To write me such a nice letter about what, as you know well, was your work as much as mine." Duranty was now sorry they hadn't published under both names, since it seemed "awfully unfair that I should get the credit alone. . . . honestly, Knick, it is a dam shame, and I'll be glad to sign any letter to the O. Henry people you care to suggest, when I come to Berlin."[52] Knick never asked him to write it.

A later tally made the entire affair seem preposterous. When all the expenses were taken into consideration, the proceeds from the story, cash-money, turned out to be "a sadly meagre $40."[53]

CHAPTER IX

Applied Stalinism

In early October 1929 the cover of the *Worker's Gazette* featured a picture of a train pulling into a city that looked very much like New York. Stamped across the photograph were the block numerals "1933." The photograph imprinted pictorially the new Soviet policy under Stalin. By 1933, the last year of the recently initiated Five-Year Plan, Soviet Russia intended to match, and perhaps exceed, the industrial capacity of the United States.[1] It was a "hurry-up-and-catch-up" program of lock-step modernization that would carry the backward Russian nation into the front ranks of international leadership during the twentieth century.

The Party used heroic war imagery—complete with "shock workers" and an industrial "front"—to characterize the venture. A preoccupation with output in metals led to a full-blown cult of iron and steel, as various parts of the nation vied with one another for the installation of new factories. In the countryside, a new requisition of grain and livestock was expected to yield the surplus necessary to cover the costs of industrialization. Peasants were urged with renewed intensity to join the State-run collective farms, where cultivation methods were more efficient than on outdated single plots. In the city, the mixed economy of NEP was at first severely curtailed, then halted altogether with the arrest and deportation of the most prominent of the speculators, the legal and financial harassment of more modest practitioners. The march of progress toward the Communist millennium had begun.

Then, on the 24th of October, "Black Monday," came the headlong crash of the New York Stock Market. Week followed week with no sign of recovery, and bad news turned into worse as the full extent of the catastrophe made itself felt, first in the chaotic American banking system, then in the currency markets, and finally in the international investment world.

Chipper as always, Duranty wrote Knick in late November to say he hoped Knick hadn't suffered "particularly from the recent deplorable events in New York, which have given me small cause for self-congratulation." Duranty had lost only $2000, not much, and it certainly didn't alarm him unduly; he believed the money and the market would soon "come back." Maybe, he joked, Knick's new baby son Hubert Conrad had some ideas on the subject.[2] Duranty quickly moved on to other issues, not recognizing at first that the rules of the game had changed dramatically—in his favor.

A few days later, he sent New York a dispatch that played up the optimism of the Five-Year Plan, the Marxist credo, and the basic faith "that human nature is plastic, that the life-ways of nations or individuals can be turned into fresh channels, that the new and unknown may successfully replace the old and familiar, in short, that environment is everything and heredity nothing."[3] Duranty wrote the story almost without thinking, automatic reflex heralding epic events, as per usual, all in a day's work.

It wasn't until two years later that he fully understood the change in direction Soviet propaganda had taken: "The world depression," he wrote then, "has played the role of forming and directing Soviet public opinion, which is not the least part of the Stalinist program. . . ."[4]

Indeed, the growing optimism of the Soviets was reflected by the popular ditty sung in the State schools at the time:

Capitalism's falling down,
falling down,
falling down,
Capitalism's falling down,
so said Lenin.
Communism's going up,
going up,

155

going up,
Communism's going up,
so said Stalin.[5]

Meanwhile, in the United States, the crisis had reached the lives of the ordinary people. Banks were failing, unemployment increasing, shanty towns called "Hoovervilles" springing up across the nation. The stock market crash set into motion a downward spiral that would lead eventually to fifteen million unemployed in the United States alone. Until now, the Soviet experiment had attracted mainly contumely and the curiosity of contempt. With prospects for their own future now bleak and unpromising, Western intellectuals began to cast about for alternatives to the system that had failed. Stalin's Five-Year Plan seemed to offer renewed hope for achievement and self-respect.

During 1929 only 2500 Americans had shown enough interest in the Soviet experiment to visit the country, but by 1930 the number had doubled, and by 1931 as many as 10,000 had made the pilgrimage to witness the energetic building of a nation by an enthusiastic army of workers.[6] American leftists, always wary of the path Socialism had taken in the Soviet Union, now cited the achievements of the regime. The list of men willing to reconsider their position included intellectual leaders like Waldo Frank, Clifton B. Fadiman, Granville Hicks, Sherwood Anderson, and Edmund Wilson. The change in the climate of opinion was perhaps best epitomized by the reaction of novelist Theodore Dreiser, who, after visiting the Soviet Union in 1928, returned with mixed feelings, expressing his doubts about the effects of a dictatorship upon thought and art. By 1931 he was praising the "individualism" of the Soviet state, holding Stalin's Five-Year Plan up to America for emulation.[7]

In the same year, a new best-seller hit the lists and stayed there for seven months—*New Russia's Primer*.[8] It was a book originally designed for use in the Soviet classroom, a primer for school children ages eleven to thirteen. It found its way onto the American market in a version translated in part by American educational visionary George S. Counts. In the English edition, it was transformed into a simply written propaganda piece that praised the importance of the Five-Year Plan and the usefulness of the drive to collectivize agriculture.

The primer explained in easy-to-understand terms the inefficiency of the current system of agriculture in the Soviet Union. It said there was much waste in the country now, and this waste should be stopped in order better to feed the Russian people. The book praised the "sov-khozes" and the "kolkhozes" (the state-operated and the collectivized farms). These "grain factories," the book said, were amazingly efficient, preventing waste and providing good food for Soviet children. "On the kolkhoz the cultivation of the soil is superior: the yield of grain and straw is greater. . . . the cow gets better food and gives more milk. . . ." The process of collectivization would culminate in a productive new agricultural system to replace the old.

> No matter what side you approach the question, the conclusion is clear: a change is necessary. And this change is already going on. It has embraced one-half of all the peasant farms, and in a few years, in place of poverty-stricken individual households, we shall have one mighty Union of grain factories.[9]

Acceptance of a planned Socialist economy was becoming increasingly fashionable in the United States. Aesthetes who had formerly dabbled in Dadaism and other *avant-garde* movements outside the mainstream of artistic expression now turned eagerly to Communism. By September of 1932, a group of influential American leaders subscribed to an "open letter" which declared their support for the Communist Party in the United States. It was signed by such notables as John Dos Passos, Edmund Wilson, and Lincoln Steffens, along with fifty others.[10] At about the same time, *The New Republic* editor Bruce Blivens, in comparing the Soviet Union with the United States, wrote that "he wanted to cry for his own citizens."[11]

A few of those who visited the Soviet Union objected to what they saw there: men like the poet e. e. cummings, who believed the Soviet State "had enthroned impersonality, mechanization, and dogma, all the enemies of self, sentiment, and spontaneity in which he believed."[12] Economist Charles A. Beard said the Five-Year Plan was "an afterthought at the end of a series of economic improvisations," its success still to be demonstrated. The Plan's only un-American aspect, Beard believed, was the brutality with which it was forced upon the Soviet citizens.[13]

At the same time, foreigners out of work in their own countries, particularly skilled workers and specialists, were able to find employment in the U.S.S.R. They flocked in, hoping to find a better life than the one they were leaving—golf clubs and all.[14]

In Soviet Russia the pace of industrialization quickened, feeding upon the unbounded enthusiasm of the Russian workers. In the countryside, the drive toward collectivization turned into a rout, Party workers forcing more and more peasants onto the State-supported farms and requisitioning their belongings, including livestock. In January 1930, Duranty wrote to John Gunther, who was now back in Paris for the Chicago *Daily News*, that he was glad he didn't "dodge out" of Moscow for the holidays

> because yesterday we got something quite definite, nothing less than the deliberate intention to socialise the whole of agriculture at the earliest possible occasion, anyway not later than the harvest of 1932, which is really rather exciting. I ran a story—plus some remarks by His Nibs himself about the revision of NEP—as marking a definite return to the militant communism which Lenin chucked in '21. Of course, they are taking a big risk and most of the gang here think its must or bust, that having got the bull by the tail they can't let go. Personally, I believe just the opposite—they think they are getting away with it and do not see why they should not strike while the iron's hot. But it's rather a toss-up.[15]

The story Duranty was referring to in his letter to Gunther had been written just two days before. It greeted the dramatic news with an equally dramatic, if unconventional, lead.

> On August 9, 1921, I wrote "Lenin has thrown Communism overboard:" That was overstatement. But now Stalin in my opinion marks the beginning of a new militant phase—like "militant communism"—and is out to accomplish what Lenin could not—collectivization of the peasants.[16]

This, Duranty wrote, marked a "radical change" from the days of the New Economic Policy, and gave a "smashing reply to critics who thought 20 percent [collectivization] was too fast by 1933." He predicted that Stalin's new policy would be as far-reaching as the NEP announcement had been in August 1921.

158

If the story marked a watershed for the Communist Party, it also delineated the growing importance of Walter Duranty himself. Like any man rising to the top of his profession, he was accruing enemies: both external opponents who took umbrage at the tone of his reporting and also, inevitably, men on the inside, who for one reason or another, disliked him and wanted to see him replaced. Beginning 7 January 1930, and continuing for three months, Duranty's writing would be monitored inside the New York offices of the *Times*, scrutinized by staffers looking for signs of corruption.

Simeon Strunsky, a prominent anti-Bolshevik who wrote an unsigned column on the editorial page, and Joseph Shaplen, an émigré Russian Social Revolutionary who had actively opposed Lenin, both believed Duranty to be pro-Soviet, and Strunsky took Duranty's stories apart piecemeal in an effort to prove it. The report he compiled fell short of proving Duranty's guilt. Certainly, there was the over-blown style Duranty assumed as he careened from one point of view to another, now praising the accomplishments of the regime, now criticizing. In one story, he proclaimed that the peasantry wholeheartedly supported collectivization, the next admitted there had been resistance involving bloodshed. At the same time, official Soviet figures were themselves wildly undependable, veering from a high of 96 percent collectivization to a low of 31.7 percent.

But Duranty could hardly be held responsible for citing figures published in *Pravda*, as he simultaneously pointed out that they were unreliable. In the end, Strunsky was reduced to mere knuckle-rapping: "It should be possible," he wrote in the report he submitted to the acting managing editor, "to maintain a more objective attitude to official claims or official figures."[17]

What the survey did signify was the lengths to which individuals were prepared to go to jettison Duranty from his post.

By 1930, Frederick Birchall, who had known Duranty in Paris and was now acting as managing editor, recommended Shaplen replace Duranty in Moscow. His recommendation fell by the wayside.

In the meantime, Duranty became the focal point for public debate, at the center of the East-West controversy. Reaction to dispatches which, in earlier days, had met with indifference, now became violent. If Duranty were absent from the Soviet capital, as he frequently was, his supporters accused *Times* editors of suppressing him. His critics, on the other hand, wanted him suppressed permanently, and "the phrase 'Uptown Daily Worker' was coined by the anti-Duranty-ites to categorize the *New York Times*."[18]

"A handful of people," one of his critics wrote to the editor, "have made a slaughterhouse of a country with 150 million people. That bloody demonstration is spreading poison and decay all over the world, calling into existence monsters like Italian, German, and Austrian Fascism, China's banditism, Palestine pogroms and other dark forces. . . ." Duranty, the writer said, was trying to bring about a unity between a democratic America "with a country which is dreaming of establishing an international Cheka." It was an act "no intelligent man" would commit.[19] Representatives of the ousted Social Democratic Party also wrote, condemning Duranty's "onesidedness in shedding light on fearful tactics."[20]

His supporters applauded the Stalinist regime for its attempt to bring civilization to a backward country, maintaining it was "probable that the Soviet system in Russia is here to stay indefinitely." Realistically, it would take "fifteen years to bring better living conditions to the Russian worker." In the meantime, one contributor wrote, "I must admit that Mr. Duranty's information is most reliable and correct under the circumstances. He gives clearer views of the situation than any foreign observer can obtain."[21] Another pro-Duranty-ite complained that the "gigantic social experiment now taking place in Russia" had yielded great achievements and that he would like to see some recognition of Duranty's reportage in *Times* editorials.[22]

That letter pointed up the wide discrepancy between Duranty's dispatches and the editorial policy of the newspaper. In one, most curious report given by Duranty in confidence to the American Embassy in Berlin, he would go so far as to say that "'in agreement with the *New York Times* and the Soviet authorities,' his official despatches always reflect the official opinion of the Soviet régime and not his own."[23] The truth of Duranty's statement dubious at best, the *Times* itself remained unflaggingly conservative and staunchly anti-Stalinist, with an editorial policy at direct odds with the tolerant attitude of its Moscow correspondent. As one carefully conducted content analysis showed, the overall impression the newspaper gave was to reinforce the values and goals of a democratic, capitalistic system. Those who read over the years what the newspaper had to say about the Soviet question would probably have the impression that an eventual conflict between the U. S. and the U.S.S.R. was likely, and should it occur, would probably be justified.[24]

Despite any differences between his "line" and that of the editorial staff, Duranty believed implicitly in his own powers of observation and deduction. He quickly learned to squelch the wild rumors that emanated regularly from Riga, where a large community of White Russians watched and waited for signs of impending disaster for the Bolsheviks. And although it stung at times, he eventually became inured to criticism from inside. Early in 1927, in an argument with another staff member who was reporting a non-existent revolt in the Ukraine, Duranty wrote to Knick, complaining: "You know already its not over easy to work here without having life complicated by a battle with ones own office. Ive heard nothing on the subject for four days so imagine hes accepted defeat at last."[25] He reached the point where he automatically defended himself on all sides, discrediting anyone who criticized him.

"If a foreign correspondent is looking for a bed of roses," he grew fond of saying, "he would do well to go into floriculture."

The announcement of the all-out drive to collectivize agriculture, which had been published in *Pravda* in January 1930, was a belated admission of events that had been taking place in the countryside for almost two years. In the grain-growing districts in the Ukraine and the North Caucausus, the extraordinary measures employed during the requisitioning period had been played down in sanitized and misleading news releases in the official press. What had actually occurred was the systematic exploitation of the peasantry through methods of harassment.

There was a mobilization of cadres. 30,000 activists were sent to the grain growing regions. In the villages emergency "troikas" were set up, with full power to overrule local authorities. The village, district and provincial party organizations were harassed with purges of "weaklings." The grain markets were closed. The amount of grain which peasants could have ground in the mills was limited to a minimum for their own consumption. In effect, though the Centre from time to time deplored "excesses," the requisitions of the Civil War had indeed returned.[26]

Behind these events was the unsolved peasant problem and the stubborn question of how to coordinate the agricultural with the industrial sector. Earlier crises had proved to the Party that the poorer peasants, with their backward farming methods and single-plot cultivation, could barely feed themselves, let alone contribute to the needs of the nation. The exiled Trotsky had advocated rapid collectivization to bring the agricultural sector in line with the industrial, and Stalin had objected, joining the Right Opposition, who wanted a continuation of NEP and the gradual alignment of the two sectors. Then, in an about-face, Stalin abandoned the Rightists, led by Nikolai Bukharin, gradually purging them during 1928 from leadership positions, just as he had earlier with Trotsky's Leftists.

According to Stalin, it was the kulak—the prosperous middle peasant whose agricultural surpluses in effect fed Soviet Russia—who held the country to ransom by clinging to the concept of a free market. The term "kulak" meant literally "fist," stemming from the function of some of the most prosperous kulaks as moneylenders in the village. Since the Revolution, the Party had known that these high level peasants were not motivated by the goals of Socialism. Attempts at imposing Socialist principles had been met by steady resistance, sometimes by violence. Stalin had rejected the idea of offering major concessions to the kulaks in return for their cooperation, choosing instead to speed up the collective farm movement. The choice to follow the latter course essentially meant all-out war in the countryside. The enemy was the kulak.

The prevailing belief was that the villagers continued to hold in their hands vast hoards of grain, which were controlled mainly by the kulaks, and from 1929 the "Ural-Siberian method" was adopted by the Politburo and put into operation on a nation-wide basis. The village was called together and induced to accept the higher collection figures of the authorities, applying a system of "self-taxation" to grain as well as money, and to decide which "kulaks" were holding out. Whoever spoke against the Party's proposals was denounced as a kulak, and this was sometimes followed by "'arrests, house-searches, fines, confiscation of property, or even shooting.' The meetings were kept in session until those remaining voted acceptance."[27]

As a result of these methods there had been instances of armed insurrection, assassinations of Party officials, stonings, and beatings—

162

the peasants resisting by any means they could muster. But by far the most common method of resistance had been the peasants' slaughter of their own livestock in order to prevent collectivization by the State. And after the January announcement the number of livestock slaughtered increased astronomically.

The consequence was that in February and March of 1930 alone, some fourteen million head of cattle were destroyed, one-third of all pigs, one-quarter of all sheep and goats. During January and February, around ten million peasant households were forced to join the collective farms.[28] By 1934, the Seventeenth Party Congress announced that more than 40 percent of all cattle in the country had been lost, together with well in excess of 60 percent of all sheep and goats. Western estimates were even higher.[29]

Thought by the Party to be resistant to any real "rehabilitation," the kulaks were not to be admitted to the collective farms; instead, they were to be "liquidated as a class." This was to take the form of exile either to Central Asia or to the timber regions of Siberia, where they were used as forced labor in the most dire of circumstances. Many of those exiled died, either along the way or in the makeshift camps where they were dumped, with inadequate food, clothing, and housing.

During the crucial six months of October 1928 to March 1929—the period when Stalin was formulating his views on the kulak—neither Duranty, nor any of his colleagues, had been able to discern that it was Stalin's policy driving forward the collective farm movement.[30] Sporadically reported in the Soviet press, the drive toward collectivization appeared only as an uncoordinated effort in widely separated outposts, a sequence of cause and effect apparent only in retrospect. Indeed, Duranty's only incisive comments concerning this important period were written long after the fact.

In January 1929 Duranty did report that during the previous year Stalin had used the army, the secret service (now called the OGPU), the Communist Youth League, and other government organs to force the peasants to sell their grain to state collectors at state prices, preventing them from selling to private competition. Although grain production had increased, he wrote, it had not done so sufficiently for export, leaving the Soviet government with a bad trade imbalance. This fact in turn resulted in the use of "extraordinary measures."[31] But by the time Duranty and his colleagues had begun to discern the seri-

ousness of those "extraordinary measures," the drive in the countryside had already been redirected toward the kulaks. It was a case of too
little, too late.

Not until 1930, when on a trip into Central Asia, was Duranty to
see at first-hand any exiled kulaks. There had been a celebration in one
of the provinces he was visiting, a local festival of villagers dressed in
brightly colored clothing, when suddenly at a distance, he noticed "a
dark gray train on a siding, with foot-square windows heavily barred
and armed guards lounging beside it."

> At the windows haggard faces, men and women, or a mother holding
> her child, with hands outstretched for a crust of bread or a cigarette. It
> was only the end of April but the heat was torrid and the air that came
> from the narrow windows was foul and stifling; for they had been four-
> teen days en route, not knowing where they were going nor caring
> much. They were more like caged animals than human beings, not wild
> beasts but dumb cattle, patient with suffering eyes. Debris and jetsam,
> victims of the March to Progress.[32]

But Duranty quickly dismissed their suffering, saying he had "seen
worse debris than that, trains full of wounded from the Front in France
going back to be patched up for a fresh bout of slaughter.

"Patriotism and Progress are high-sounding words and noble as
Ideals," Duranty added rhetorically, "but are they *always* worth the
pain they cost?"[33]

As to the Soviets' "Progress," the lot of the peasants who had been
spared exile was, if anything, worse than it had been before collectivization. They were now entitled to less of what they grew than before
joining the State-supported farms.

> The typical kolkhoz was the old village, with the peasants—actually
> somewhat fewer peasants than before, as a result of migration and
> deportations, and considerably fewer draught animals—living in the
> same wooden huts and tilling the same village fields as they had done
> before. The main things that had changed in the village were its man-
> agement and its marketing procedures.[34]

In effect, the peasants had returned to the feudal serfdom that had
bound them to the land before 1861, when they had been emancipated

by the Czarist State. The tractors that had been promised from the industrial sector failed to materialize, and with the loss of the draught animals, the State farms fell into a state of decrepitude, with little actual tillage being initiated.

By the 2nd of March 1930, Stalin himself put the brakes on the drive to collectivize, admitting frankly that things had gotten out of hand. In an article entitled "Dizzy with Success," Stalin took the rank and file members of the Party to task for having, in their enthusiasm, exceeded their authority and the intentions of Party leaders. Except for the animals belonging to the kulaks, Stalin ordered the return of most of the collectivized livestock, in what appeared to be a complete reversal of the policies he had publicly initiated only a few months before. Apportioning blame to those whose excessive zeal had caused a state of chaos in the countryside, he held local authorities responsible, although, in truth, these Party workers had been carrying out, in both word and spirit, the orders they had been issued.

Within the Party there was much disillusionment at Stalin's apparent disaffection from the effort, but the retrenchment turned out to be only temporary because, within a short time, Party workers were again being encouraged to return to the countryside to coerce more peasants onto the State-supported farms.

The peasants, whose only course of action was to obey Party workers, would find themselves rewarded first by shortages in supplies, then by shortages in food, and finally by slow starvation. The initial secrecy of the collectivization drive, its inconsistent and haphazard application, the "on-again off-again" frenzy with which it was finally forced upon the peasants seemed an appropriate beginning for the age of "iron, and the machine, and the power of 'death'" foreseen by the despairing poet Esenin.

Despite tangible evidence of excess, Western enthusiasts continued to laud the achievements of the Five-Year Plan, citing events in the Ukraine and environs as worthy of emulation. The optimism was perpetuated in reports like that of Maurice Hindus, sympathizer to the cause, who in 1930 wrote in his book *Humanity Uprooted*, regarding collectivization, that "The movement is sweeping the land like a prairie fire on and on over fresh and ever increasing areas."[35] Although his assessment of the cost was high and he called the drive "a stupendous gamble," his evaluation of the Stalinist regime remained essentially favorable; the collectivization scheme, he said, "was not without economic merit."[36]

Like Duranty and others, he made much of the March to Progress, characterizing the Bolsheviks as millenarians who remained deaf to the outcries of the kulak. Their only concern, he wrote, was that the path to the Communist millennium was cleared.[37] A year later, making a second and perhaps more penetrating assessment, Hindus wrote that he had begun to see danger signs and he warned that the worst was still to come. In the main, however, Hindus still believed in the effort.[38]

Like Hindus, but without his commitment to the final outcome, Duranty had been among the first to identify the Bolsheviks as utopians. In an early dispatch, he compared their attitudes to those of religious enthusiasts, paralleling their beliefs with fundamentalist thinking. He had reported that they were at once "ruthless, narrow minded, and self-centered, but like the fanatics they are nevertheless without thought of self. In a country rotten with corruption," he wrote in 1921, "the communists are honest."[39] Nine years later, so far as Duranty could see, the Bolsheviks had not so much replaced religion as supplanted it, and he pointed to the Lenin corner that now stood in apartments and houses where the religious corner once dominated.[40]

To the Bolshevik mentality, Duranty wrote early on,

> ... communism is not atheism as the word is generally understood. In it human labor—man's endless struggle upward from the beast—takes the place of God, and the "millennium" on earth when peace shall reign and plenty and happiness, and man shall not oppress his neighbor or profit by his neighbor's weakness, is the ideal goal instead of a heaven after death.[41]

The means by which the millennium was to be achieved had only begun to make themselves felt when Duranty wrote these words. Now, at the end of the decade, during this period of cataclysmic upheaval, the lengths to which the Bolsheviks were prepared to go began to be revealed.

It was the old question of whether the means justifies the end writ new.

Meanwhile, in the industrial sector, the cult of iron and steel assumed heroic proportions, the workers overreaching themselves in a massive effort to achieve and, if possible, exceed the targets of the Five-Year Plan. Appropriately, the leader who carried them forward to victory became the focus for their inspiration, and the cult of personality shifted from Lenin to Stalin.

The first to isolate this phenomenon, Duranty is credited with coining the term "Stalinism."[42] "The dominant principle in Russia today," he wrote in 1931, was not Marxism or Leninism, but "Stalinism": it was "a tree" that grew from "the alien seed of Marxism planted in Russian soil, and whether Western communists like it or not it is a Russian tree."[43] Lenin had taken the basic principles of Marxism and tranformed them as he could to fit the Russian situation, but found it necessary to retreat into the New Economic Policy—although he always maintained that this was a temporary expedient and not a "basic change" in Marxist teachings.

> Stalin got rid of NEP as soon as he could, but instead of reverting to dogmatic Marxism, went forward to a collectivist system which the Russians. . .call socialism and which actually is not far removed from state capitalism. This is Stalinism as distinguished from Leninism.[44]

In Duranty's equation, "applied Stalinism" equaled the Five-Year Plan, and with typical logic, Duranty associated the popularity of the plan with the emerging cult of personality surrounding Stalin himself, identifying the plan as little more than a slogan around which the simple Russian people could rally their hopes and energies. Stalin, he said, was giving the Russian people what they wanted—"joint effort, communal effort; and communal life is as acceptable to them as it is repugnant to a Westerner." In the same sense, the attachment of the people first to Lenin, and then to Stalin, investing the two leaders with the characteristics of "semi-divines" was nothing more than the renewal of the concept of the Czar, which suited the Russians and "is as familiar, natural and right to the Russian mind as it is abominable and wrong to Western nations."[45]

All the more disquieting, then, was the manner in which Duranty had begun to portray Stalin for his Western readers as a wise and perceptive leader capable of great powers of understanding: "a quiet,

167

unobtrusive man named Stalin, who saw much but said little—[who] began to realize that the main job before them and their revolution was to train and discipline and give self-respect to a nation of liberated slaves. . . ."[46] Under him, Duranty wrote, the Bolsheviks' advance would "show in history."[47]

This tendency to portray Stalin in a favorable light was only just beginning, and Walter Duranty was far from being the only Western newsman to credit Stalin with a vast array of achievements. Duranty is frequently cited as being the first Western reporter to interview Stalin; it was not Duranty, however, but Eugene Lyons, the United Press correspondent, who was first given the opportunity to go to the Kremlin and meet the Soviet leader face to face in his office. No doubt chosen because of his Communist sympathies, Lyons was a "fellow traveller" who had formerly worked in the New York office of Tass and who found the Soviet Union "the culmination of his political and emotional loyalties."[48]

In November 1930, persistent rumors were circulating, mainly in Riga but reaching both the East and the West, that Stalin had been assassinated. Lyons—through "no merit of my own," as he put it later—was chosen from among the Western correspondents in Moscow to conduct a personal interview with Stalin, thus proving to the outside world that the reclusive dictator was unharmed and in good health.[49]

The story turned out to be a sorry piece of work, the heavy-handed propaganda of an obvious sycophant, so much so that in later years, after undergoing a political reversion, Lyons would find difficulty in living the story down. But for now, he presented Stalin as a burly but gentle leader—"the hardest man in the Soviet Union to get to," but once you got there, "the easiest to talk to."[50]

Lyons described the dictator as being in fine health, although his "eyes seem tired." His "dark face" showed no "sprightliness," but "he is entirely human, quick to smile and has a sharp but kindly sense of humor." Stalin also demonstrated the intellectual capability to assemble information in forms readily understandable to the common worker.

In referring to the rumors of his assassination emanating from Riga, Stalin told Lyons he felt sorry for the foreign correspondents who were forced to produce false reports in order to suit the political whims of their capitalist employers. But the decision to grant the interview was motivated by more important concerns than simply to demonstrate that the assassination rumors had been false. Stalin had a message for the West. In the absence of being able to strengthen political ties between his country and America, he hoped the United States would recognize the desire of the Soviet Union "at least ... to strengthen its economic ties." He maintained that America had suffered the least of any country for the Bolshevik repudiation of their debts, pointing out that when the Americans carried out their revolution, they had repudiated their debts to England. "And you did right, too," Stalin said.[51]

Before Lyons left, Stalin ordered tea and sandwiches for him and provided him with a room in which to type his dispatch. Faced with this kind of consideration, Lyons found it difficult "to see this man as being 'rude' as Lenin [had] said."[52]

Duranty had been abroad when the interview was granted to Lyons. Caught short, he returned to Moscow angry, protesting to the Soviet Press office that as the longest-serving Western correspondent in the country it was unfair not to give him an interview as well.[53] Surprisingly, the officials agreed. So, only one short week after Lyons's interview, Stalin again greeted a Western correspondent—this time Walter Duranty.

From the beginning, the tone of Duranty's interview was serious, taking up crucial issues. One was the vulnerability of the Socialist state, which, Stalin maintained, was now no longer at issue. There had been a time, Stalin admitted, when the capitalist countries could have crushed the U.S.S.R. "But they waited too long. It is now too late." There was nothing for the Americans to do but watch Socialism grow, he said triumphantly. It was a form of propaganda they could do nothing about.[54]

The interview also yielded new insight into the urgency with which Stalin was forcing the pace of modernization. He admitted to Duranty that he was motivated by the fear of a new war, one that, like World War I, would involve many countries and would inevitably draw in the Soviet Union. The basic nature of the capitalist system would be the cause. "When, where, and on what pretext it will begin I cannot tell," Stalin said, "but it is inevitable that the efforts of the stronger power to overcome the economic crisis will force them to crush their weaker rivals. That does not necessarily mean war—not for the time being—until a later day, when the giant powers must fight for markets among themselves."[55]

In his interview, Duranty had tapped a nerve of the dictator, anticipating what would soon become the avowed purpose of rapid industrialization in the Soviet Union. In perhaps Stalin's most famous speech, delivered just a little more than a year later, the threat of war, mentioned in Duranty's interview only briefly, would become his full justification for any excesses of the Five-Year Plan and the speed with which it was implemented.

> No, comrades, . . . the pace must not be slackened! On the contrary, we must quicken it as much as is within our powers and possibilities. . . .
>
> To slacken the pace would mean to lag behind; and those who lag behind are beaten. We do not want to be beaten. No, we don't want to. The history of old . . . Russia . . . she was ceaselessly beaten for her backwardness. She was beaten by the Mongol Khans, she was beaten by Turkish Beys, she was beaten by Swedish feudal lords, she was beaten by Polish-Lithuanian *Pans,* she was beaten by Anglo-French capitalists, she was beaten by Japanese barons, she was beaten by all— for her backwardness. For military backwardness, for cultural backwardness, for political backwardness, for industrial backwardness, for agricultural backwardness. . . .
>
> We are fifty or a hundred years behind the advanced countries. We must make good this lag in ten years. Either we do it or they crush us.[56]

In his interview with Stalin, Duranty had mirrored the Georgian dictator's value system, and if the piece seemed subdued in comparison to Duranty's usual style, he compensated for it a few weeks later in a profile of Stalin he produced for the *New York Times Magazine.* With customary flair, Duranty recalled the tale of an old Chinese Emperor who wore many masks, so that his appearance "struck awe and wonder in all the hearts of the beholders." Like that ancient ruler, Stalin also wore many masks. He knowingly cultivated the image of "the Recluse of the Kremlin," the "Man of Steel" who stood strongly behind government policy. Stalin had grown hard and cruel under the repression of the priests during his years as a novitiate in the Russian Orthodox Church, said Duranty. When he threw off the yoke of their control, Stalin demonstrated that he "would brook no master."

Unlike Trotsky, Duranty wrote, Stalin was not gifted with any great intelligence, but he had nevertheless outmaneuvered this brilliant member of the intelligentsia. And although he had a soft voice, there was about him a "crust of rough brutality and harsh words" which belied any gentleness he might display.[57]

Finally, in a typical burst of theatrical prose, Duranty concluded by declaring that Stalin was now indispensable to the survival of the Communist Party, for its members could not "remove him without a risk they dare not take," so integrated was he in the totality of power.

> Stalin has created a great Frankenstein monster, of which . . . he has become an integral part, made of comparatively insignificant and mediocre individuals, but whose mass desires, aims, and appetites have an enormous and irresistable power. I hope it is not true, and I devoutly hope so, but it haunts me unpleasantly. And perhaps haunts Stalin.[58]

With the publication of this highly dramatic character analysis, Duranty's career underwent a change. The interview marked the beginning of his true international celebrity, and he became one of the best known journalists in the world.

For Lyons, whose adoring interview of Stalin had been completely eclipsed, there would be a sense of ill-usage and injustice. The way most people would remember it, Walter Duranty was the first Western correspondent to interview the great Bolshevik dictator, and for decades to come Lyons would remain peeved at the unfairness of it all.

CHAPTER X

Dizzy with Success

William Seabrook, journalist of "the exotic" and long-time pal of Aleister Crowley, had not very long since returned from the interior of Africa, where, he had promised his editors, he would eat the flesh of a human being and write a book all about it. In the early 1930s, however, going native had already begun to take on a commercial aspect, and the African cannibals saw Seabrook coming. They wanted an exorbitant fee for the privilege of taking part in their tribal customs and eating the sacred flesh of their enemies. A stickler for authenticity, Seabrook paid the money and described for his readers in exacting detail the taste of human flesh (not unlike veal, a little "stringy," satisfying).[1]

It was almost the truth. The real story was that Seabrook suspected the natives were too civilized for the sort of thing he was after, and had literally palmed off the flesh of an ape on him. That being so, and Seabrook the determined sort, he returned to France, paid a hospital attendant to furnish him with "a chunk of human meat" from the victim of a fatal accident, boiled it up, and ate enough of it to satisfy his own sense of journalistic ethics that he had in fact eaten of human flesh.[2]

Seabrook had known "the Beast Crowley" in his Paris years, during the time of "the Paris workings," as well as in New York, and although he and Duranty probably knew one another in passing, they dated

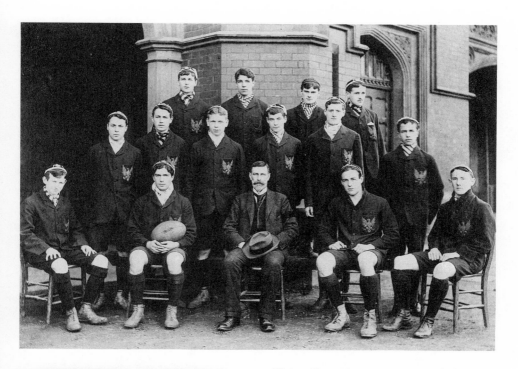

Walter Duranty as a member of his rugby team at Bedford School, Easter 1903 (standing on extreme right of middle row). Album of H.S. Morris in collection of A.D. Nightall, Bedford; reproduced by permission.

Close-up of Duranty in above.

Duranty (center) as Prometheus in a Bedford School production of a scene from Aristophanes' *The Birds*, July 1903. *The Ousel*, Bedford, 16 December 1903, p. 6.

Duranty (center) in part of a group photograph at Bedford School, Summer 1903. *The Ousel*, Bedford, 16 December 1903, p. 7.

Duranty's rowing cap at Emmanuel College, Cambridge, 1904. Collection of S.J. Taylor, given by Parker F. Enwright.

Walter Duranty as a war correspondent, 1917-1918.
Files of *New York Times*.

Opposite. Part of Duranty's dispatch on the death of Lenin. *New York Times*, 2 January 1924, p. 1.

LENIN DIES OF CEREBRAL HEMORRHAGE; MOSCOW THRONGS OVERCOME WITH GRIEF; TROTSKY DEPARTS ILL, RADEK IN DISFAVOR

SOVIET CONGRESS IN TEARS

Mass Hysteria Only Averted by a Leader's Brusque Intervention.

BODY WILL LIE IN STATE

Is to Be Taken to Moscow Today From Village Where Premier Passed Away.

KREMLIN WALL HIS TOMB

Washington Expects No Immediate Change in the Policy of the Russian Government.

By WALTER DURANTY.
Copyright, 1924, by The New York Times Company.
By Wireless to The New York Times.

MOSCOW, Jan. 22.—Nikolai Lenin died last night at 6:50 o'clock. The immediate cause of death was paralysis of the respiratory centres due to a cerebral hemorrhage.

For some time optimistic reports had been current as to the effects of a previous lesion gradually cleared up, but Lenin's nearest friends, realizing the progress of the relentless malady, tried vainly to hope against hope.

At 11:20 o'clock this morning President Kalinin briefly opened the session of the All-Russian Soviet Congress and requested every one to stand. He had not slept all night and tears were streaming down his haggard face. A sudden wave of emotion—not a sound, but a strange stir—passed over the audience, none of whom knew what had happened. The music started to play the Soviet funeral march, but was instantly hushed by Kalinin who murmured brokenly:

"I bring you terrible news about our dear comrade, Vladimir Ilyitch."

High up in the gallery a woman uttered a low, wailing cry that was followed by a burst of sobs.

Kalinin Breaks the News.

"Yesterday," faltered Kalinin, "yesterday, he suffered a further stroke of paralysis and—" There was a long pause as if the speaker were unable to nerve himself to pronounce the fatal word; then, with an effort which shook his whole body, it came—"died."

The emotional Slav temperament reacted immediately. From all over the huge opera house came sobs and wails, not loud nor shrill, but pitifully mournful, spreading and increasing. Kalinin could not speak. He tried vainly to motion for silence with his hands and for one appalling moment a dreadful outbreak of mass hysteria seemed certain. A tenth of a second later it could not have been averted, but Yunakidge, Secretary of the Russian Federal Union, thrust forward his powerful frame and with hand and voice demanded calm. Then Kalinin, stumbling, read out the official bulletin.

"Jan. 21 the condition of Vladimir Ilyitch suddenly underwent sharp aggravation. At 5:30 P. M. his breathing was interrupted and he lost conscious-

NIKOLAI LENIN (VLADIMIR ILYITCH ULIANOV), A sketch made from life for THE NEW YORK TIMES by Oscar Cesare in Moscow, November, 1922, and autographed by Lenin.

EXPERTS PROPOSE GERMAN GOLD BANK

It Would Be Absolutely Independent and Under International Control.

SCHACHT URGES MEASURE

Dawes Committee Will Go to Berlin on Monday to Discuss Proposal There.

Copyright, 1924, by The New York Times Company.
Special Cable to The New York Times.

PARIS, Jan. 22.—Its first decisive step toward accomplishing the task which has been set it of reorganizing German finance and showing a way of balancing the budget was taken today by the Expert Committee studying the problem under the Chairmanship of General Charles G. Dawes. In a communiqué issued this afternoon the committee announced that it had reached the opinion that an independent gold bank under international control was the first essential to any plan for securing the budget equilibrium and stable currency in Germany.

This opinion, it is emphasized, was a unanimous one, and though the French have been largely instrumental in forwarding the suggestion, they claim no more credit than any other delegate of the five nationalities represented on the committee.

BRITAIN ACCEPTS THE LIQUOR TREATY

Document Is Approved by All of the Dominions and Hughes Is Notified.

GEDDES MAY SIGN TODAY

Washington Makes Preliminary Proposals for Similar Compacts to Other Powers.

Copyright, 1924, by The New York Times Company.
Special Cable to The New York Times.

LONDON, Jan. 22.—The Anglo-American liquor running treaty is ready for the signatures. All the British Dominions have approved it and the British Ambassador at Washington has been asked to notify the United States State Department that Britain is prepared to sign. The treaty, of course, must be ratified by the British and Dominion Parliaments, but with the possible exception of Canada, where the King's Government is in a nominal minority, there is thought to be no likelihood of an upset of the verdicts already given. British governmental authorities are now satisfied also that the treaty, as revised, will not conflict in any way with the American Constitution. Apprehension had originally existed that the treaty's proposal to allow British ships to carry liquor stores within the three-mile limit might not square with the Eighteenth Amendment and whether he had

Captain of Tacoma and Two Radio Lose Their Lives in Vera C

Special to The New York Times.

WASHINGTON, Jan. 22.—Wireless messages from official sources tonight report that Captain Herbert G. Sparrow of the wrecked cruiser Tacoma and two radio operators have lost their lives in a severe hurricane outside Vera Cruz Harbor.

The State Department received this dispatch late tonight from Consul Wood at Vera Cruz by Navy wireless:

Vera Cruz, Jan. 22, 1924.
Secretary of State,
Washington.

I am profoundly distressed to announce the death of Captain of the U. S. S. Tacoma and also of two wireless operators through an accident on board her during a norther, while in the performance of duty. Particulars will follow.
WOOD, American Consul.

The first intimation that the Tacoma had figured in another tragedy reached Washington early in the evening, when Señor Alvarez del Castillo, diplomatic agent of the revolutionary faction, received this radio message from Adolfo de la Huerta:

"By orders of the supreme chief, in the midst of a furious hurricane, our small naval transports steamed out of

the port to go to the—
Our vessels daringly
tempest, regardless
own loss, and succee
remainder of the cre
which now comple
Offici.ls have been
from the Tacoma th
the cruiser Richmond
at Tampico. The dea
row and the radio
her failure to report

The news of the tr
in Washington with
Captain Sparrow wa
the seasoned naval
The Tacoma was
re-establish cable co
tried to make the b
Cruz at dawn one c
caug t by a 'north
Blanquilla reef.

Most of her men
beach at Vera Cruz
later by the Richmo
they are at Tampico
row, six officers an
remained on the Ta
Captain Sparrow
was appointed to t
in 1895. He had se
service at sea.

DECLARES ANDERSON FORCED HIM TO SPLIT PART OF HIS 'DRY' PAY

Chief Accuser of Anti-Saloon League Official Then Admits Trying to Sell Exposure.

DENIES HE TRIED BLACKMAIL

Defense Links Witness With Brewers and Wet Organization at Forgery Trial.

Light on the financial arrangements of the Anti-Saloon League of New York State was contributed by O. Bartsall Phillips, former collector for the league, who was the chief witness yesterday at the trial of William H. Anderson, State Superintendent of the league, on a charge of forgery, before Supreme Court Justice Tompkins and a jury. In turn, the defense launched an attack on the personal character of Phillips.

According to Phillips, he entered into a contract with Superintendent Anderson whereby he was get commissions on all money he collected for the dry propaganda of the league. This contract, according to the witness, stipulated that he was to get 20 per cent. on the first $25,000 he obtained yearly, and 10 per cent. on all money over that figure.

In the course of his direct examination by Chief Assistant District Attorney Pecora, Phillips charged that Anderson had forced him to split "fifty-fifty" on all collection commissions in excess of $10,000. As the witness told it, Anderson declared that his own salary was then only $10,000 a year and that no employee of the league was to get more than he.

Taking over the witness for cross-examination, former Governor Charles S. Whitman, leader of the defense, pounded away unmercifully at Phillips. He asked the witness if he had not "deserted" his wife and six children, and Phillips denying it, was forced to admit that his wife won a "technical" decree of divorce on the grounds of abandonment. He admitted that he had married again and that his wife taught school, but he refused to admit that she worked in order to support herself.

Denies He Tried Blackmail.

Mr. Whitman asked Phillips if he had not tried to "blackmail" the Anti-Saloon League leaders by threats of crim-

LABOR TAK FULFILLING BRITISH C

Macdonald Kiss Hand in Accep sion to Head

THREE PEERS

New Premier Office Also a His Policy

By EDWIN
Copyright, 1924, by The
Special Cable to Ti

LONDON, Jan. 22.
ting of Buckingham
the symbolism of l
more than a th
George today enth
workingmen the ch
ernment of the Brit

Events moved sw
ment when Premier
King this morning
nation of his Mi
night in the House
hands of the King
mended to the King
for James Ramsay
ministry Labor I'a
The King acted on
fere Mr. Baldwin
Mr. Macdonald had
Clynes and J. H. 7
Mr. Macdonald a
sion, kissed the K
to custom, and the
Government in the
once into being.

The New

The new Ministr
follows:

*Prime Minister,
Treasury and Secre
eign Affairs*—JAMES
Lord Privy Seal
House of Coun
CLYNES.
Lord President
PARMOOR.
Lord Chancellor
DANE.
Chancellor of th
SNOWDEN.
Secretary of Stat
ARTHUR HENDERSON
Secretary of Sta
J. H. THOMAS.
Secretary of Sta
WALSH.

Walter Duranty in Paris shortly
after losing his leg in a train accident, 1925.
Files of *New York Times*.

Opposite top. Duranty at a dinner party in his Moscow apartment, 1930s. Files of
Walter Duranty, Orlando, Florida. Reproduced by permission of Parker F. Enwright.

Opposite bottom. Duranty being served a drink by his servant, Grisha, in his Moscow
apartment, 1930s. Files of Walter Duranty, Orlando, Florida. Reproduced by permission
of Parker F. Enwright.

RED SQUARE: RUSS

Ancient and Modern, Ugly and Fantasti
Lenin's Tomb Is Found the Harmon

By WALTER DURANTY

"WHY call it Red Square," ask strangers, "when it isn't Red
and isn't Square, but oblong?"
The answer is, Russians don't call it Red Square, but Krasnaya Ploshchad instead.

Ploshchad doesn't mean Square but Place, like market-place or dwelling-
place,
and Krasnaya does mean Red but other things as well.
Krasnaya has the same root as Kraseevaya, which means Beautiful, as
this place is beautiful,
Because red is the color of beauty and life in Russia, where white is
death and cold.
Red is beauty and life and sun, but white is ice and snow.

SOME people think it's Red Square because red is the color of blood;
And well they might, since its cobbles have stunk and dripped with
blood.
More blood than that other place called Place of Concord,
Where women of Paris sat knitting and watched the guillotine.
Watched the triangle of steel slice necks of Aristos as they sliced
carrots
Watched heads fall in the basket and blood trickle down to the Seine.
No trickle of blood in Moscow's Place but a rushing stream,
when Peter slaughtered the Streltsi, thousands day after day.
Peter the Tsar sat high on the porch above Kremlin gate,
under the great clock tower, to see the Streltsi die.
while his chief executioner, a thick-set man named Tolstoy, which means
Strong or Husky,
(He founded that noble family, for Peter made him a Count)
hacked at the necks of rebels till his arms were red and tired.
Then Peter rose to his six foot nine and shouted, "Way for the Tsar,"
and ran down the stairs and pushed through the crowd and came to the
round stone scaffold,
which still stands blocking traffic, in memory of Imperial Mercy,
and took the sword and finished the job in competent royal fashion.
Which doubtless gave pleasure to his obedient subjects.

But the real reason why Red Square's so named
is that Red is the Russian version of what Rome called Purple:
the flaming dye which Tyrians made from shell-fish, honor-stripe of
Senators and Caesars.
Purple not at all but deep blood-crimson, heritage from Rome,
Caesar's Imperial Crimson, as Tsar is Russian heir to Caesar.

ONE side of this great Red Place, eightscore yards wide, twice ten-
score yards in length,
Is still as Peter saw it, the steep cliff Kremlin wall,
with two tower gates, and a tower between, save for one thing more.
Save just one thing, which is different and strange and new.
A small square block of reddish marble, built like a Maya temple,
Close to the Kremlin wall, perfect in line and color,
Fitted to match the middle tower, with rows of low stone seats on
either side.
This is the first true Thing of Beauty Revolution has created.
This is Lenin's tomb.
Lenin shattered Tsarism and brought death to Peter's heir,
yet it is not all difference between Lenin and Tsar Peter.
Both had unflinching confidence in Russia's Destiny,
and both were set to break her oriental apathy and spur her with
Western spurs.
"Learn from your enemies," said Lenin, and "Tractors plus Electric
Power spell victory."
While Peter worked in an alien shipyard, dreaming of sea-power
and ice-free ports.
And plugged a swamp with a myriad lives to build him "Russia's
Window on the West"
as he boldly termed St. Petersburg, named for his patron saint,

The Banners of the
Soviet Proletariat
Carried Below the Feudal
Walls of the Kremlin,
Where Russia's Tsars
Ruled.

Soyuzphoto

The Square That Is Oblong and More Than Red—A View From t

to serve until passage of time and Russia's weight and strength
should give his country Tsargrad, as Window to West and South,
Tsargrad, now Istanbul, which Constantine Caesar named
Constantinople, Constantine's city, Asia's gate, Byzantium.

BUT Lenin dreamt wider dreams than Peter, called the Great.
There was nothing small in Lenin, no degrees of race or rule,
nothing short of world dominion under one Red Flag
Red as Blood and the Rising Sun and Caesar's Tyrian Crimson,
Is the Red Flag of Soviet Russia which flaunts from the Kremlin
tower.
So every day come pilgrims to salute the corpse of Lenin,
embalmed like Egyptian Pharaoh, corruptless as Russian saint,
pilgrims in long slow lines, thousands come day by day,
wet or fine, sun or snow, silent in waiting lines,
reverent as other worshipers of other gods,
Which would surely annoy Lenin, if he saw it, because he was an
iconoclast,
and hated Worship and what Americans call Idealism, and every
kind of Fetish.

Yet this old side of the Square is right and true for Russia.
Peter's bloody old Russia and Lenin's new devoted Russia
They harmonize exactly, Kremlin tower and Lenin tomb.

Photo Courtesy Contempora, Inc.

The Shrine of the Iberian Virgin Destroyed to Make a Road

When Peter Slaughtere

"Red Square": Duranty's poem and its epic presentation.
New York Times, 18 September 1932, pp. 10-11.

SIA'S PULSING HEART
Here in the Shadows of Kremlin Tower and
y of the Old Russia and the New Faith

Photo Courtesy "USSR in Construction"

Art of Soviet Russia's Sanguinary and Historic "Centre of a New Faith."

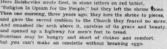

Marching Men in the
Square That Is Now the
Parade Ground of the
Military Forces in the
New Russia of the
Soviets.

Soyuzphoto.

From the Painting by V. I. Sourieov

e Streltsi in the Red Square.

Photo Courtesy Intourist.

Fantastic Domes and Cupolas of the Cathedral of St. Basil.

And nothing could be more appropriate to present conditions in the Soviet Union
Than the monstrous empty Department Store which fills all the opposite side.
New and vast, utilitarian, ugly, like the Soviet State.
Empty, that's what's wrong, no goods in windows, neither food nor clothes nor tools.
They talk about Socialist Achievement and put most of their effort into Means of Production,
but "When do we eat?" ask the workers, and "What shall we wear?" ask the peasants.
A Department Store may be ugly, but it must have goods to sell.
Lenin's tomb may be Mecca and Medina, but men must eat or die.

IF you doubt the Soviet future, if you think these shortages mean ruin,
Look again at Krasnaya Ploshchad; at the level granite paving, which replaced the ancient cobbles; at the sweeping open entrance, which replaced the ancient archway and the shrine of Iberian Virgin.
A small and lovely shrine by the gate to Krasnaya Ploshchad. . . .
No bigger than a newspaper kiosk on Paris boulevard, but sacred as Notre Dame,
the shrine of Iberian Virgin, who gave victory to Holy Russia.
Here Tsars came praying in hours of national despair. . . .

Here Bolsheviks wrote first, in stone letters on red tablet,
"Religion Is Opium for the People," but they left the shrine alone.
Then one morning, three years ago, they tore the shrine to pieces,
and gave the sacred emblem to the Church they feared no more,
And smashed the arch above it, careless of its grace and beauty,
and opened up a highway for men's feet to tread.
Russians may be hungry and short of clothes and comfort,
but you can't make an omelette without breaking eggs.

NOW turn and view both ends of the Krasnaya Ploshchad.
To the south a fantastic church, all cupolas and colored domes, older than Tsar Peter.
To the north a pseudo-gothic modern building that once housed the Bishop of Moscow.
According to popular legend the first was built by Ivan, well named the Terrible;
He wanted, he said, a church unique, stranger than Babylon or Hekatompylos . . . .
And to make sure it remained unique, he blinded the architect who built it,
and the church to this day is called Church of Basil the Blind.
It remains unique, incredible, beyond De Quincey's dream of Babylon or Hekatompylos . . . .
Untouched by Soviet iconoclasm, a subject for postcards, an attraction to tourists.
The Bishop's Palace is now a historical museum, and looks it.
That's the Red Square, Moscow's Red Square, Peter's Red Square, Lenin's Red Square.
Modern, utilitarian and ugly,
Lovely, fantastic and ancient,
And something more.
The Centre of a New Faith, perhaps of a New World,
And the parade-ground of the Red Army and the Red Proletariat.

TWICE a year, on the first of May and November seventh, anniversary of Soviet revolution,
A million trained soldiers and organized workers march through this square,
past Lenin's tomb, where their leaders stand on a narrow ledge,
past the Kremlin tower, where Peter sat, and the round scaffold, and Basil's church.
Nearly a million workers, women and youngsters and men,
Wide and flowing like a river, from the mountains to the sea.
Roaring like a mighty river, wave on wave from noon to dusk.
Before them come troops, not many, twenty or thirty thousand.
With tanks and guns and all the grim machines of modern war.
Moving together and disciplined, the way only good troops are disciplined,
to startle foreign military attachés, Japanese and Poles.
The square echoes the clatter of hoofs of Siberian ponies,
tough Siberian ponies, inured to Siberian Winters—Can the Japs stand cold?
And the Cossacks race through, whips flailing, those Cossack whips. . . .
Do the Poles remember Cossack whips in the Bad Old Days?
And the bomb-planes roar above, in squadrons twenty square,
One, two, three, five, ten, squadrons each twenty square.
And chasse-planes, flight after flight, like V-shaped geese on the wing,
Breaking their order to tumble and rise like pigeons.
Looping loop and falling leaf and Immelmann-roll,
All the manoeuvres of modern war above Moscow's Square.
To resume formation beyond and give place to the next.
USSR isn't defenseless, think the Poles; a tough nut to crack, say the Japs
A place of Power is the Red Square.

Malcolm Muggeridge (center right, bare-headed, standing behind Sonia Chamberlin) with other journalists visiting the Dnieper Dam in 1932. Reproduced by permission of Malcolm Muggeridge.

"Russian Ballet": Cartoon by David Low of Roosevelt and Litvinov preparing the U.S. recognition of the Soviet Union. First published in the London *Evening Standard*, 24 October 1933; reprinted in *Time*, 20 November 1933. Reproduced here by permission from the original drawing at the Centre for the Study of Cartoons and Caricatures, University of Kent at Canterbury.

Walter Duranty, *c.* 1935. Files of *New York Times*.

H.R. Knickerbocker at his desk. H.R. Knickerbocker Collection, Columbia University, New York.

"It was in Russia during the famine ..." *"The Arabs calmly kicked him to death"*

Duranty, left—"Once on the Yellow River ..." *Seabrook, right—"The strangest thing I've seen ..."*

Duranty with Willie Seabrook.
The American Magazine, July 1936, pp. 54–55.

Willie Seabrook on one of his African expeditions on the Ivory Coast. *Jungle Ways*, 1931, p. 285.

Duranty and Mary Loos in Hollywood, 1944–45.
Reproduced by permission of Mary Loos, Santa Monica, California.

John Gunther with his second wife, Jane, 1947.
Reproduced by permission of Mrs. John [Jane Perry] Gunther, New York.

Duranty's second wife, Anna Enwright, 1956–57. Reproduced by permission of Parker F. Enwright, Orlando, Florida.

Duranty within a year of his death, 1956–57. Reproduced by permission of Parker F. Enwright, Orlando, Florida.

their friendship from the time when they had "picked roses together in Emma Goldman's garden on the Riviera."[3] By then, Seabrook was living with Marjorie Worthington, a delectable brunette, who dressed like a Toulon market girl, in bright rag-like dresses, with plenty of silver and copper bracelets to please Seabrook, who had a bona fide fetish for women in chains—among other things.

Sometime in the spring of 1931, following Duranty's triumphant interview with Joseph Stalin, Willie Seabrook and Marjorie Worthington became the house guests of Walter and Jane Duranty in St. Tropez, where Duranty had come for a quiet holiday away from Moscow. Earlier, Duranty had run into George Seldes, who, having quit the newspaper business a short time before, was now working on one of the many books he would author during his long life.

Seldes had fallen in love. In Vienna, he made the acquaintance of "one of the prettiest girls I have ever met in my life," and proposed marriage to her. The girl, a lovely left-wing blonde, had accepted his proposal, and now the pair were traveling together in the south of France—when they came across Walter Duranty. Duranty invited them to join him and the Seabrooks for a weekend at his wife's villa.[4]

It was possible Jane Cheron Duranty knew nothing of her husband's invitations until the guests actually arrived on the scene, but she must have been long used to her husband's whims. For several years, they had lived apart, seeing one another either in Paris, or in St. Tropez, on the occasions when Duranty came "out." When he was in Moscow, Jane Duranty dutifully performed whatever errands her husband required from one of her European homes.

Earlier, she had written Knick in Berlin in her broken English to tell him she was sending a suit of clothes Duranty needed. She apologized for having to bother Knick, but "Walter gave me your address so short that I did not dare to risk the parcel." Would Knick please "to phone" the courier she had used because "Duranty tell me that one of his friend is going back to Moscow and ought to get it from you."[5]

It is likely that Jane and Walter Duranty had very little left in common. Many years later, there would be an oblique reference in his writings to a woman who gave up her addiction to opium for love: "My dear, you must choose. I can't have a wife like that, a dope fiend, a slave to this stuff." According to the story, the wife chose and freed herself.[6] But it was by no means clear that Jane Duranty herself managed to give up the drug, and she may well have been something of an embarrassment to Duranty, who was approaching the peak of his career.

At the villa that weekend, "there was a lot of drinking and basking in the sun, and eating delicious meals, and listening to the brilliant conversation, and reading the article on Stalin and congratulating Duranty."[7] And it seemed, to everyone present except Seldes and Jane Duranty, that Seldes's fiancée "Donna" and Duranty had become involved with one another. To Seldes's surprise, at the dinner table one evening Duranty asked the girl to go to Moscow with him when he went back.[8] A shocked and furious Jane Duranty grabbed a platter, and threw its contents, a large fish, across Duranty's face. Then, Seabrook's companion recalled, "Jeannot rose up in wrath, like Hecuba or another of the Trojan women, and ordered everyone from her house, especially Donna."[9]

Later, Duranty wrote a note to Seabrook asking him to look after the girl, whom he had taken to a nearby hotel for a few days and was now leaving behind. As Marjorie Worthington remembered the affair a few years later, the last she saw of George Seldes, he was sitting on a park bench, looking bemused. As Seldes recalled the event over half a century later, Duranty had offered his fiancée a job in Moscow for $50 a week. "I couldn't match *that*," Seldes protested.[10]

It was the last time anyone who knew Duranty ever made reference to his French wife Jane, or "Jeannot." Duranty himself spoke of her only when asked, with a bright reply. The reason they lived apart, he would say, was that his wife lived in a house at the top of a hill, and he had a wooden leg.[11]

Back home, Duranty remained "the unofficial social host of Moscow" for a steady influx of visitors—all of whom wanted to meet him personally so they could boast of it to their friends. To them he was "Mr. New York Times," "the dean of foreign correspondents."[12] Among the Western press corps, he was the object of envy: "there was more talk about him in Moscow than anyone else, certainly among foreigners."[13]

Not all of it was good. Long-time resident A. T. Cholerton, who reported first for the London *News Chronicle* and later for the *Daily Telegraph*, spoke of an early scrape Duranty had gotten himself into, something unpleasant that had been hushed up; but he never did say what. There were other insinuations, nothing concrete, just talk, probably motivated by jealousy.

By now, Duranty was "a well-groomed gnomelike person of about fifty winters, with a sparkling answer to any banal question hurled at him."[14] He was a frequenter of the bar at the Metropol Hotel, the "focal point of a glittering bourgeois society in a dull setting of Proletarianism."[15] It was little more than an alcove off the main dining room, yet sooner or later, practically every American who visited the Soviet Union made his way there. On the weekends, there was American jazz, Soviet-style, played by the band of Alexander Svartsman, who specialized in barely recognizable renditions of American favorites such as "Peanuts" and "Yes, We Have No Bananas."[16]

Duranty couldn't dance because of his wooden leg, but that didn't seem to slow him down any when it came to the opposite sex. His growing fame permitted him to indulge his taste for women who were sweet and dumb and young—in that recreational mold that appealed "to men like me, who earn their bread with their brains and are glad of relaxation. . . ."[17] He was like a magnet to attractive young college girls from the Eastern seaboard who were eager to have "an affair with Walter Duranty."[18] In male company, Duranty recounted these little episodes, miraculous for their frequency and variety, with calculated enthusiasm. It shocked Duranty's twenty-four-year-old assistant to think an old guy like Duranty had paired up with girls younger than he was.[19]

At a more prosaic level, Duranty was good friends with a number of men in the business world and diplomatic corps. One was the industrialist Armand Hammer, who remembered Duranty as "a close personal friend"; when the famous humorist from Oklahoma, Will Rogers, visited Moscow and wanted to meet Duranty, Hammer helped them to get together.[20] Another friend was the Greek ambassador, with whom Duranty played bridge whenever he could. Along with bridge, Duranty also harbored a great weakness for "whodunits," reading one or more a day when things were slow.

Duranty made frequent forays "out," more than the other correspondents, mostly to Berlin, where he was always having one or the other of his artificial legs adjusted. Knick was still located there, and they usually had a few drinks. The *Times* always picked up the tab. Less often, but on a regular basis, he went to Paris, where other Moscow correspondents also went whenever they got any leave. Louis Fischer, William Henry Chamberlin, Duranty: they all turned up sooner or later in the French capital.[21] The young William Shirer, who would become a well-known CBS correspondent during World War II and author of many highly respected books, was then working for the Chicago *Tribune,* alongside James Thurber. Shirer met all of the Moscow crowd, took a particular liking to the witty and bohemian Duranty. Years later, during the war, he would meet up with him again. And of course, Duranty always saw Gunther, who was to become one of Shirer's best friends as well. "The life of correspondents then," Shirer said, "was such that people retained their friendships. Being separated didn't affect them. They always took up where they left off when you last saw the friend. You kept in touch with a few letters."[22]

It was when Duranty was on one of his trips "out" that his Russian mistress Katya got something of the upper hand. Up until that time, Duranty had viewed her as a mistress in the French sense, a matter of convenience, tucked safely away, the best-known secret in town. He never took her out socially, nor did he make reference to her. This time, while he was away, International News Service correspondent Lindesay Parrott and his wife invited her to their home for a party. Katya turned out to be a popular guest. She brought along her guitar and sang Russian folk songs, winning the hearts of the Americans who didn't much take to the idea of a mistress anyway. When Duranty returned, he realized he could no longer hide Katya from society. Thereafter, "and with a sheepish air," he escorted her to parties and dinner engagements.[23]

A couple of years before, in 1930, Duranty and the household he had assembled around him—his chauffeur, a charlady, his cook, and mistress Katya—had moved out of his little house and into an apartment at 53 Bolshaya Ordinka, where he had a telephone installed. By Western standards, it was a rudimentary standard of living, but in Moscow in those days it was unwonted luxury. Set back from the street, the apartment was approached through a courtyard by a side alley. Inside, a foyer that was little more than a dark, narrow hallway led on the left to the kitchen, on the right to a bedroom and bath. Immediately ahead was the dining room, furnished with a birch table and usually covered with a tablecloth, which Duranty had purchased at one of the State-run Commission shops where foreigners could pick up amazing bargains for foreign currency, or "valuta" as it was called. Beyond the dining room was a sitting room, which Duranty used as his office. He had furnished it with a desk, armchairs, and a small sofa, brightly upholstered.

The apartment was located directly south of the Kremlin, the better part of a half-hour walk from the center of things. It would have been impossible for Duranty to walk back and forth, or even travel by tram, so he bought an automobile.

It was a Model A, five-passenger touring car, and his chauffeur's name was Grisha. Later, in 1932, he acquired a Buick sedan, which was shipped into Leningrad. Grisha took the train there, picked up the car, and drove it back to Moscow. He had several flat tires from the nails along the road. Duranty was furious when Grisha returned late, with far too many miles on the odometer, from Duranty's point of view. The Buick became a familiar sight on the streets of Moscow, driven "hell-for-leather" by the wild man Grisha, honking and tearing around corners at break-neck speeds.

Besides the chauffeur, Duranty had taken on a secretary, Beth Gilles, the daughter of an American engineer. He also took on a young man to do the leg work, which was becoming too taxing for him to do himself.

Robin Kinkead arrived in Moscow just before Christmas in 1929. He had just been graduated from Stanford University, a foreign language major, and he had been finding it hard going to get a job in post-Depression America. In a spirit of adventure, he and his brother worked their way over to Europe on an oil tanker, finally making it to Moscow. Kinkead figured anybody who could speak several languages would be able to find work there. In Germany, he was warned that food was being rationed in the Soviet capital, and without a ration card, he and his brother would soon starve to death.

It turned out otherwise. As soon as they arrived in Moscow, Kinkead made his way to the apartment of Alexander Wicksteed, whose book *Life Under the Soviets* he had read. Wicksteed, on his way out for the evening, invited the two young men to join him. He was going to Walter Duranty's flat for dinner. Out of the blue, about halfway through the evening, Duranty asked Kinkead if he wanted to become his assistant and do all his leg work in the capital. He offered him $15 a week. Kinkead immediately agreed, and Duranty told him to report for work at about noon the following day.

Kinkead arrived the next day on the dot, excited, but Duranty was still in bed. Soon enough, though, he appeared, unshaven, his hair unbrushed, and without his collar. He wore a rumpled tweed jacket which he had buttoned up to the very top to keep warm. Paying scant attention to the young man, he ate the breakfast Katya put before him. Kinkead would watch Duranty eat the same breakfast at the same hour every day for the next two years—two soft-boiled eggs, toast with marmalade, and coffee. Then Duranty sparked up and began rustling through the Soviet newspapers to see whether or not there was a story to write.

When Kinkead went to work for him, Duranty had just begun experimenting with dictation. Duranty was nurturing an ambition to become a novelist, he told the young man, and he thought he could speed up the process by learning to dictate. Kinkead had the impression Duranty liked dictating, not because he needed a typist, but because he wanted the company, somebody to talk to. Usually, Beth Gilles sat at the typewriter, waiting for him to dictate the day's story. But when she wasn't there, Kinkead did the typing. As he worked, Duranty continuously sipped Burgundy or Madeira, stopping from time to time to explain to Kinkead why he did what he did—in the same way Wythe Williams had explained it to him many years before. The dispatch, like the others to follow, was one and a half pages long, double-spaced, and written in cablese. Duranty was a fast reader and a fast writer, who went over his work cursorily, perhaps with only one quick check.

As soon as it was finished, Duranty would put on his dark brown coat lined with muskrat and his snap-brim hat and walk over to the Soviet Press Office, now headed by Constantine Oumansky, who later became the Soviet Ambassador to the United States. The other two censors were Podolsky and Mironov. These were the men who wielded all the power. Duranty would slap the dispatch down on the desk, and one of the censors would pick it up, read it, and then discuss anything they intended to cut. Over the two years he worked for Duranty, Kinkead rarely saw them cut Duranty's work. Duranty had been there long enough to know what would and would not pass, and he didn't waste time writing what wouldn't go out. Then the two men walked over to the Central Post Office on Tverskaya Street. The cable went via a Danish line from Moscow through London and into New York. The Moscow deadline was 2:00 a.m., just in time for the early edition of the *New York Times.*

Duranty usually carried on a rambling conversation with Kinkead, one in which he did most of the talking. He told Kinkead he was born on the Isle of Man, "where the cats have no tails." Inevitably, he boasted of his former addiction to opium, but his reason for quitting, he told Kinkead, was not the expense or the difficulty in getting the drug, but the fact it took away his sex drive—"an intolerable condition," Duranty said, his eyes glistening. As he talked, he chain-smoked Camels, whenever he could get them, Gertsagovina flores when he could not.

He gave the young man lessons in reporting, telling him the several things that made up a good story. "What most people are interested in," he said, "are sex and gold and blood, and if you get a story in which the lead combines all of those, you've got something."[24]

One anomaly in Duranty's personality was what Kinkead termed "a peculiar penuriousness." Kinkead found it hard to pry his weekly salary out of the hands of the Moscow correspondent. Duranty never offered him the money; Kinkead always had to ask for it. Then, there was the other thing. Duranty asked him at the beginning whether he wanted his money in dollars or in rubles. Kinkead said he would take it in rubles. It was sometime before the young man discovered Duranty was giving him an unfavorable rate of exchange. Eugene Lyons finally found out what Duranty was up to, and he told Kinkead to take his salary in dollars from then on and showed him how to exchange it on the black market.

For Kinkead, it amounted to a substantial raise in salary. For Lyons, it was simply further confirmation of Duranty's general depravity.[25]

Duranty's method of working was not unlike that of the other correspondents in the capital. They all had the same basic statistics to work from. After he took on Kinkead, however, he was able to supplement his stories with "local color" without troubling himself too much. In March of 1930, when Stalin made his famous "Dizzy with Success" speech, Duranty sent Kinkead down into the countryside to see how the peasants were reacting. Kinkead found that the local peasants had knocked over newspaper kiosks in their eagerness to get at the newspapers. After the announcement, they slacked off in joining the State-supported farms until another drive began, and they were again forced to join up.

A second example of how Duranty worked was the way he plotted out the rate of gold production in the Soviet Union, a figure which, for some reason, had been draped in secrecy by the Soviets. One day Duranty noticed something in the paper about gold production being up a certain percentage, but the story neglected to give what the production rate was. Duranty told Kinkead to go over to the Press Office and get back issues of all of the economic papers. Together, the two went through all the old newspapers, until, several years back, they found how many kilograms had been produced that year. Subsequent papers told the percentage of increase each year following. They calculated the sum, and came up with an annual production rate that put the Soviet Union second only to South Africa in the production of the precious metal.[26] From this particular calculation, Duranty was to benefit for many years to come, since diplomats and political figures in the United States were eager to seek his advice on the subject. Kinkead believed that many of the other correspondents thought Duranty had an inside source who fed him information like this.[27]

Others besides the inexperienced Kinkead were more cynical about reporting in the Soviet capital. Malcolm Muggeridge, who came to string for the Manchester *Guardian* in the autumn of 1932, found "being a newspaper correspondent in Moscow ... in itself, easy enough." Since the Soviet press was "the only source of news," all he had to do, he said, was leaf through the papers, "pick out any item that might be interesting to readers of the *Guardian*, dish it up in a suitable form," and after getting it past the censors, fire it home in a cable.

> One might, if in a conscientious mood, embellish the item a little with back references or some extra statistics, easily procured from the Commercial Attaché at the British Embassy, where also the Press was meticulously gone through and analysed. Or perhaps, fancifully, sow in a little local colour, usually unobjectionable to the censor. Blow it up a little, or render it down a little according to the new exigencies of the new situation. The original item was almost certainly untrue or grotesquely distorted. One's own deviations, therefore, seemed to matter little; only amounting to further falsifying what was already false. ... Soviet statistics have always been almost entirely fanciful, though not the less seriously regarded for that. ....[28]

In 1930, Duranty suffered a shock, one that would deprive him of the counsel of his best friend. At the start of summer, on the 2nd of June, William Bolitho died at the age of thirty-nine. He had gone through

Ypres and been spared, only to die of complications from a burst appendix. The way Duranty figured it, what killed Bolitho was getting what he wanted.

Bolitho had bought a little château near Avignon, called La Préfète "because it was said to have been built by Napoleon's Préfet de Police . . . for one of his mistresses." All around the small mansion was a complicated irrigation system with fences of "towering cypress trees eighty or a hundred feet high for shelter against the mistral." Bolitho began importing exotic plants, planning to landscape a garden "that would be the wonder of France." After the success of his book *Twelve Against the Gods*, he was able to put a good deal of money into the garden, determined to "make a place of wonder and beauty, no matter what it costs."

"Poor Bolitho!" Duranty wrote. "He did not know it would cost his life." The attack of appendicitis was wrongly diagnosed by the local country doctor, causing a delay in the operation. By the time the mistake was discovered, Bolitho had died on a surgeon's table in Avignon.[29]

Several years later, when Duranty was asked what was the unhappiest moment in his life, he would answer "very definitely" that it had been when he received news of Bolitho's death.[30] But Duranty believed the loss of William Bolitho was more than a personal one. His work was of the caliber of great writers, and Duranty believed the world was deprived of a man whose talent would perhaps have made him one of the major figures of the twentieth century. Duranty was not alone in this view. Noel Coward said Bolitho had "a mind that colours life with imagination based on necessarily bitter experience, a mind that has survived the squalor of small humiliations and the melancholy of great disillusions. . . ." A great loss to his generation, Coward continued, Bolitho belonged to a tradition "of literature to which no short cuts are possible, but which must be, when attained, well worth all the agony and bloody sweat which went into its achievement."[31]

Certainly, Bolitho had the talent for fiction Duranty lacked. In that sense if not in others, he was the man Duranty should have been.

There was another death that summer, one which seems to have affected Duranty less—the passing of his forty-five-year old sister, Frances Emmeline Duranty, on the 14th of August. She had died in

England, a spinster who earned her living in a hospital as a masseuse. If her death troubled Duranty, nobody knew it. Her home at 107 Hamilton Way in Golders Green, a suburb of London, was inherited by Duranty's father, his mother having died many years before. Duranty's father, now in his eighties, was weak and poor and living alone.

For all of his many junkets abroad, Duranty seldom turned up in England. The little island seemed to hold little interest for him.

In 1931, Knickerbocker, who was now back working for the New York *Evening Post* and the Philadelphia *Public Ledger*, won a Pulitzer Prize for his reporting from Germany. Duranty, still feeling guilty about the O. Henry Prize, lost no time in cabling his congratulations, saying he was "TERRIBLY GLAD ABOUT PULITZER PRIZE BECAUSE ALWAYS FELT BADLY ABOUT THAT OTHER BUSINESS AND THIS MUCH BETTER YOU SURE DESERVED IT STOP EXPECT ARRIVE BERLIN TWENTY EIGHTH PLEASE KEEP LUNCH AND LAURA IF POSSIBLE DURANTY."[32] Despite his professional success, Knick was having serious personal problems that would end with his divorcing his first wife and marrying a second. A short time later, Duranty would be sending his regards to Agnes instead of Laura.

But by then, Duranty himself would have won a Pulitzer Prize for the best news correspondence of 1932. The Pulitzer Committee cited especially "those [dispatches] dealing with the Five-Year Plan." The panel said the stories were "marked by scholarship, profundity, impartiality, sound judgment and exceptional clarity. . . ."[33] Indeed, the very dispatches criticized and condemned by Simeon Strunsky from inside the *Times* New York office were among the stories praised by the Pulitzer Committee. It was a time for "anti-Duranty-ites" on the staff to go underground, and for the time being, they did just that, though they remained in wait for the chance to jump again. They had been joined by Jimmy James, Duranty's old foe from the war days and just after. Predictably, James's star was also on the ascendant. He was soon to take over as the managing editor of the newspaper.

Duranty was in no mood to be worried by minor obstacles. The seriousness with which he viewed himself was obvious from the tone of his acceptance statement:

"I went to the Baltic states viciously anti-Bolshevik," Mr. Duranty said recently. "From the French standpoint the Bolsheviks had betrayed the allies to Germany, repudiated the debts, nationalized women and were enemies of the human race. I discovered that the Bolsheviks were sincere enthusiasts, trying to regenerate a people that had been shockingly misgoverned, and I decided to try to give them their fair break. I still believe they are doing the best for the Russian masses and I believe in Bolshevism—for Russia—but more and more I am convinced it is unsuitable for the United States and Western Europe. It won't spread westward unless a new war wrecks the established system."[34]

"[D]espite present imperfections," he continued, he had come to realize that there was something very good about the Soviets' "planned system of economy." And there was something more: Duranty had learned, he said, "to respect the Soviet leaders, especially Stalin, whom I consider to have grown into a really great statesman."[35]

A short time later, Duranty expanded upon his ideas in an interview with *Editor & Publisher,* the respected academic magazine for journalists. In it, he defended his decision to interpret news from the Soviet Union for his Western readers. "When you write about Russia, you're writing about a nation and a people whose customs and ideals are as strange to the Western mind as are those of the Chinese," Duranty said. This brought a barrier to "the sympathetic interpretation of Soviet news." What presented the most difficulty was the "clash of Asiatic thought with the accepted standards of the West."[36] It was a matter of a wholly different perspective which was difficult for Westerners to accept.

The Soviets' concept of news was different from America's in that the emphasis was on production quotas and industrial achievement. More important news was subject to strict censorship. The Bolsheviks nevertheless viewed their press as free, the Western press "as being fettered by capitalistic rule." Also, the press there was thought to function only as an educational tool for training "a very ignorant class of people," and, as such, it was "a fine thing for Russia," whereas the Western press had other functions, which included entertaining readers as well as informing them of the facts. All in all, Duranty concluded, the attempt "to replace the individual stimulus with a collective stimulus . . . [was] working remarkably well in Russia" although it would be inappropriate elsewhere.

You see, the Russians, except for those on top, never had any sort of freedom at all before the advent of Soviet rule. They never had the benefit of private capital. And so, what may seem to an American to be a state of abject slavery, is to the Russian a wonderfully new freedom.[37]

That Duranty saw himself as the judge of these matters was apparent from his somewhat patronizing tone, which came out sounding like a peculiarly personalized version of the White Man's Burden. "Russians," Duranty said, "take delight in knowing that they are being noticed. They have a certain childish naiveté about the matter."[38]

Duranty's method of working, he explained, was simply to put himself in the other person's shoes in order to understand his motivations, and when he did this, he was usually able to predict what would follow. The other principle he lived by was based on the advice of his best friend, the late William Bolitho: that if you departed from the view of the majority, you would be able to see things others could not.

Duranty had somehow moved into position as the Western representative of things Soviet, and the Pulitzer had given him the authority he needed to quell his critics. He now became a leading figure in the tug of war between pro- and anti-Soviets regarding the question of American diplomatic recognition of the U.S.S.R. Unlike the other European Allies, America had never officially recognized the Soviet State, and that action seemed long overdue.

The same year Duranty won the Pulitzer, Franklin Delano Roosevelt, then governor of New York, was campaigning for the presidency. If Roosevelt were elected, recognition would follow, so it was thought by those who favored the move. Duranty's growing importance on the world scene made it politically expedient for Roosevelt publicly to summon Duranty to the governor's mansion to talk over the Russian situation.[39] What Roosevelt wanted to discuss at the lunch to which he invited Duranty in late July of 1932 was Soviet gold production, and Walter Duranty was the expert. Roosevelt's main concern, Duranty said later, was whether or not the Soviets would be able to pay if they were given the trade concessions that usually go along with official recognition.[40]

If Duranty was now a man of the highest prestige, the fact was highlighted by a most amazing occurrence. His poetry, always remarkable for its mediocrity, was published in no less a vehicle than the *New*

York Times itself. In 1932, his poem "Red Square" appeared in a two-page spread accompanied by six photographs. The pictures included an aerial shot of Red Square, two of troops in the Red Army, one of the Shrine of the Iberian Virgin, which was later destroyed to widen an access street to the Square, and one of the famous painting of Czar Peter the Great, slaughtering the Streltsi. Amidst these dramatic depictions of Russian history and pageantry, Duranty's blank verse was particularly lame. Three stanzas might suffice:

> Lenin dreamt wider dreams than Peter, called the Great.
> There was nothing small in Lenin, no degrees of race or rule
> Nothing short of world domination under one red flag
> Red as blood and the Rising Sun and Caesar's Tyrian crimson. . . .
>
> Yet this old side of the Square is right and true for Russia. . . .
> Peter's bloody old Russia and Lenin's new devoted Russia. . . .
> They harmonize exactly, Kremlin tower and Lenin tomb.
>
> And nothing could be more appropriate to present conditions in the
>   Soviet Union,
> Than the monstrous empty Departmental store which fills the opposite
>   side.
> New and vast, utilitarian, ugly like the Soviet state.[41]

There was one thing worth noting, however. The poem contained a new idea that would appear again and again: first in Duranty's own work, then in that of historians and economists dealing with the Soviet Union, finally in the increasingly numerous attacks of Duranty's enemies.

> Russians may be hungry and short of clothes and comfort
>   But you can't make an omelette without breaking eggs.[42]

The statement would become the standard rationalization of Stalin's actions during the First Five-Year Plan, years that would cover the brutal process of collectivization, the "liquidation of the kulaks as a class"—and the devastating famine that followed.

In autumn of 1932 Duranty's friend Aleck Woollcott made a much publicized trip to Europe, with plans for a month's stay in Moscow. After Woollcott had arrived in Berlin, Duranty cabled the well-known

185

dramatist "that he had laid in a supply of whiskey and other rarities for the occasion of Aleck's visit."[43]

Once in Moscow, Woollcott was escorted around the city by Duranty who was delighted to act as his guide. Not surprisingly, Woollcott showed most interest in the Russian theater, "to the detriment of what he should have [seen] of the Communist experiment."[44] In this stark setting, Woollcott's sense of humor seemed at times vastly inappropriate, especially when he drew attention to the "embarrassing experience that all Russians, young and old, whom I pass on the street not only stare but halt in their tracks as though astounded and then grin from ear to ear." He was in fact referring to the "very disconcerting experiences of a fat man in the Soviet Union."[45]

Woollcott's only political statement about his experience in the Soviet Union was that "except for a few such men from Mars as Walter Duranty, all visitors might be roughly divided into two classes: those who come here hoping to see the communist scheme succeed and those who come here hoping to see it fail. . . ."[46] The jovial fat man made jokes about what he thought must be the major industry in the Soviet Union—"printing pictures of Stalin"—and he attended various social functions.

One of these was a literary evening held by the wife of the correspondent of the *Christian Science Monitor*, William Henry Chamberlin. It was attended by a young Englishman who took careful note of the New York dramatist when the conversation turned to the playwright Anton Chekhov.

> Woollcott . . . suddenly gave his attention to what was being said. He saw a splendid piece in this, whimsically reporting how, at such a dingy, unappetising gathering in Moscow, new vivid reminiscence of the famous Russian playwright had been recounted. . . . A dusty, muffled, stale old house, and these people part of the dust and the staleness themselves. Ideological waifs and strays—he liked that phrase. He was a well-covered man . . . with a wide expanse of face, gleaming spectacles, and a camel-hair coat and fur hat hanging in the hall ready for when he went out. Clearing his throat noisily to attract full attention, he enjoyed telling them how that morning, when he stood on the steps of the Metropol Hotel where he was staying, a passer-by had come up to him and just gently passed his hand over his camel-hair coat, following the curve of his ample stomach, by way of a salute to his *en-bon-*

point, his well-being, his affluence. The others laughed, but uneasily; they felt they were themselves rather in the position of the passer-by. They, too, metaphorically speaking, had been stroking Woollcott's stomach, so beautifully moulded, mounted and arrayed.[47]

The merciless portrait Malcolm Muggeridge drew of the New York dramatist was typically sardonic, and showed the contempt Muggeridge reserved for those he adjudged frivolous. His list included, of course, Walter Duranty, whom Muggeridge knew more than passing well.

In Duranty, Muggeridge found a subject he would caricature in the most unflattering of portraits, in a novel about the major figures in Moscow at the time, whom Muggeridge scarcely attempted to disguise. In *Winter in Moscow*, Duranty appears as Jefferson, to whom the young hero of the novel, presumably Muggeridge, is referred when he first arrives in the Soviet capital. A character tells him, "I always say to youngsters like yourself, a bit bewildered, a bit uncertain, take [Jefferson] for a guide and you won't make any serious mistakes."[48] Jefferson duly instructs the young man to consider the country as a whole—"the broad outline." In the scene, Jefferson is listening to a speech delivered by one of Stalin's chief lieutenants:

Jefferson sat in a corner by himself. He was an old hand and needed no translator. Sometimes he looked rather tired and wistful. So many fighting speeches since he'd been in Russia. So many leads and declarations and conferences. So many thousands and thousands of words typed and then telegraphed. He was half sick of visions, and at times thought of clearing out perhaps even taking Sonya with him; then settling down in New York on what he'd got saved in the bank, and trying to write stories. *Saturday Evening Post*. Once you got the trick it was easy enough. Easier even than sending messages from Moscow. Only there was no security. Not even money in the bank was security. Not even money in several banks and in several currencies. He loved New York; smart people; really smart people who weren't getting away with it but had got away with it; a little flat in a tall block, fitted with labour-saving devices, and a cocktail bar, and shaded lights, where he could bring a girl after a show, and lounge about, and make love in a straightforward American way. Here there's no comfort; no security, he thought bitterly. . . .[49]

Thus Duranty as conceived by one of his fellow countrymen: charming and at the top of his powers, and yet insecure and desperate in the fictional cameo. Without really trying, Duranty had accrued a number of enemies—some motivated by envy, some by contempt, some by plain suspicion. They all had one thing in common, though. They were watching and waiting for him to make a false step.

In the presidential election of 1932, one important issue was whether or not the United States should assume normal diplomatic relations with the Soviet Union. Not unexpectedly, Duranty sided with those who favored recognition. He pointed out that Catherine the Great had waited thirty-three years after the American Revolution to recognize the United States; an "unnatural delay," he called it, as was the current reluctance of the United States to recognize the Soviets. America and the Soviet Union were alike in several regards. They shared a similar climate and geographical advantage, including rich natural resources. Furthermore, the Soviets had now applied standardization to their industrial complexes, in imitation of the United States.[50] Any further delay, he believed, would be foolish.

With the election of Franklin Roosevelt to the presidency of the United States, the diplomatic recognition of the Soviet Union seemed assured, and negotiations were set in motion to bring about the momentous event. In November 1933 the Soviets were invited to send a representative to America, and Duranty, with his unerring sense of the newsworthy, asked permission of the *Times* to accompany Soviet Foreign Minister Maxim Litvinov on his historic journey across the Atlantic on the S.S. *Berengaria* to negotiate terms. Duranty thus cemented in the public's mind the idea that he himself was a central character in the international drama about to unfold.

In truth, the two men had little to say to one another. Duranty saw Litvinov only when Litvinov took his daily constitutional around the deck. Most of the time, the Soviet statesman stayed in his cabin working, avoiding others on the boat even during dinner. The only exchange between the pair came when Litvinov asked Duranty if he thought crossing the English Channel would be rough, and Duranty replied that it probably would not be, since they were on a large ship.[51] But to the outside world, Duranty gave the impression he was beating his competitors' heads off, even though his own lead said bluntly Litvinov wasn't talking. From "his own earlier experience in Moscow,"

Duranty blithely produced a thousand words telling Americans what to expect.[52] His agile human interest angles would fill dozens of inches in the *New York Times* in the days to come.

Litvinov's first request—to travel closer to the Statue of Liberty, which he admired "no less than the New York skyline looming like castle giants in the hazy morning"[53]—was dutifully recorded by his uninvited companion. Like Dr. Johnson's Boswell, Duranty shadowed the Russian representative, nothing too trivial for his pen. He "Americanized" the Soviet statesman during his first few days in the United States, recording with enthusiasm Litvinov's approval of Virginia ham and corn fritters.

"M. Litvinov remarked repeatedly," Duranty wrote, "on the multiplicity of power lines and the height of buildings in comparatively small towns."[54]

For nine days the American press filled thousands of column inches with copy about the impending normalization of diplomatic relations between the United States and the Soviet Union. In a context of romantic synecdoche, Franklin Roosevelt had been presented as the bridegroom who would, at last, make an honest country of the renegade Bolshevik state, and Maxim Litvinov, as his none-too-reluctant bride. The London *Evening Standard*'s cartoonist, David Low, aptly depicted the staginess of the affair, in the cartoon "Russian Ballet International Pas de Deux," which was reproduced in America's news magazine *Time*. Low pictured Roosevelt on full point, handsomely garbed in starred and striped tights, as he gallantly presented the blushing prima ballerina, Litvinov, with a bouquet of roses. The vulgarity of Roosevelt's masculinity was counterpointed by the curtsy of the spectacled, dog-faced ballerina, whose tutu was encircled by huge rolls of fat.[55] The unlikelihood of this exotic pairing was only slightly more absurd than the laudatory treatment it was receiving from the press.

On the 18th of November, Duranty published his account of President Franklin D. Roosevelt's quixotic press conference. Duranty had been among the 200 reporters ushered into the Oval Office, the number of papers represented indicating a genuine event. The newsmen's air of expectancy, as they crowded into the President's inner sanctum, was high. The big question: whether or not the President and Litvinov had been able to come to terms. In the front row stood Duranty, leaning on his cane, his eyes missing nothing of the unfolding scene.

It is typical of Duranty that, in reporting this fitting climax to what

189

he would term "the ten days that steadied the world,"[56] he made himself one of the most important of the dramatis personae in the President's *coup de théâtre*. He stood with those nearest the President's desk, waiting for the room to fill, as Roosevelt, at his blandest, smiled and puffed calmly on the cigarette in its yellow bone holder. After they were all in, the President said that the doors would remain closed until the conference ended, in the interests of fairness. Then, conversationally, he remarked he had received some rather good news from the iron and steel industries about the progress of the National Recovery Act, and he wanted to share it, along with other gratifying reports from the textile industry, with the press.

"[T]here was something like a gasp of suspense from his hearers," Duranty wrote in his story proclaiming the President's disarming prelude to the announcement of U.S. diplomatic recognition. "Reporters are supposed to be toughened by their profession against surprises, but speaking personally, at least, there was one of them who was startled. And the President knew it and got the full moment of that thrill."[57]

Duranty—the pivotal butt of Roosevelt's little joke, the intimate of presidents and dictators, the matchmaker for the marriage of convenience between two superpowers—this is how he viewed himself. And the public, finding his name printed dozens of times in the media hyperbole describing the event, tended to believe in the self-aggrandizing vision of the little man with the limp. Duranty had charted the meteoric rise of Stalin after Lenin's death, he had reported the growing strength of the Communist Party, and he had insisted upon the permanence of the fledgling state. At last, he was reaping his reward.

On the same day that the *Times* splashed the news of the happy outcome of the negotiations between Litvinov and Roosevelt, Duranty, in an unattributed story, spun out his prose to fill the gap created by time lag in Soviet response. He admitted that "Official comment is not available at this hour," but the feelings of the Soviet leaders must be something akin to "the same degree of elation felt by the 'ugly duckling' of Hans Christian Andersen when it was recognized as a beautiful swan. 'It hid its head under its wing,' said the old fairy tale, 'and felt too happy—but had no thought of pride.'"[58]

Duranty's bird metaphors caught the whimsy of *Time*, which reprinted a paragraph from his by-lined dispatch: "If one wants to estimate the 'horse-trade,' I should say M. Litvinov has got perhaps a shade the worst of it," Duranty wrote, "but on the other hand, to vary the metaphor, Mr. Litvinov is taking home a pretty fat turkey for Thanksgiving."[59]

Within two days, news began to trickle in from the Soviets of the official response to the high honors accorded them by the Americans. If the first public toast went inevitably to President Roosevelt, the second went to Walter Duranty, who according to one representative of the Soviet Foreign Office, helped "to facilitate America's discovery of the U.S.S.R."[60]

America had indeed discovered red. Greeted by footmen in red livery and by red roses on dinner tables,[61] Litvinov walked down the crimson carpet rolled out by America. But the highest honor, the enthusiasm of his peers, was reserved for Duranty alone.

Among the 1500 dignitaries attending the dinner given in Litvinov's honor at New York's Waldorf-Astoria, Duranty was the most popular. He mingled with representatives from the Pennsylvania Railroad, Baldwin Locomotives, General Motors, and Ford. Even the elder J.P. Morgan partners, who chose to eat their dinner elsewhere, sent an affiliate from their firm.[62] When toastmaster Colonel Hugh L. Cooper, who had built Russia's great Dnieperstori dam, introduced members of the distinguished audience, each was received with polite if unimpressive applause. But when Cooper introduced "one of the great foreign correspondents of modern times, serving a great newspaper of this city," and the small Englishman stood to acknowledge the introduction, the crowd "rose for the first time and cheered."[63]

Aleck Woollcott, who attended the dinner with his friend, would later write, "Indeed, one quite got the impression that America, in a spasm of discernment, was recognizing both Russia and Walter Duranty."[64] Certainly, those attending the Russian-American Chamber of Commerce dinner believed Duranty had carried the day.

When William C. Bullitt—the Philadelphia millionaire—traveled to the Soviet Union as the U. S. ambassador a few days later, Duranty returned with him. His presence, first at the side of the Soviet foreign minister, then at the side of the newly appointed American ambassador, had provided a convenient frame for the media etching of those "ten days that steadied the world."

It now seemed that Duranty was at the zenith of his career, the highest peak he could attain. But there was still more to come.

Four weeks after his return to Moscow, Duranty was dealt his final

trump. Stalin, at last breaking his silence on the United States diplomatic recognition of his country, called the *New York Times* correspondent to the Kremlin where the pair talked for an hour, secreted in
the northeast corner of "that medieval fortress," at a table covered
with red baize, Stalin seated midway between photographs of Lenin
and Marx.[65] Duranty's interview with Stalin rated full-page treatment
in *Time*, which ran Duranty's portrait and characterized him as "a
small, calm, wooden-legged Englishman from Moscow."[66]

It was Christmas Day, 1933, the last time Duranty was to see Stalin, and, in parting, the dictator said something that would find its way
into practically every book Duranty wrote ever afterwards:

> You have done a good job in your reporting the U.S.S.R., though
> you are not a Marxist, because you try to tell the truth about our coun-
> try and to understand it and to explain it to your readers. I might say
> that you bet on our horse to win when others thought it had no chance
> and I am sure you have not lost by it.[67]

Whether these words were Stalin's own or Duranty's version of
them, the sentiments were no doubt those of the Georgian dictator. By
putting his faith in the iron determination of the Bolsheviks to bend
the fate of the nation to their will, Duranty had come out a winner. He
was arguably the best-known foreign correspondent in the world, a
central figure in the new dialogue between East and West, the star of
the international social circuit. By putting his money on Stalin, he had
climbed from anonymity to celebrity, the recognized world authority
on Soviet Russia. You might say that Walter Duranty was "dizzy with
success."

CHAPTER XI

A Blanket of Silence

About a year before U. S. recognition of the Soviet Union—and Walter Duranty's rise to fame—in the spring of 1932, a young Canadian agricultural expert was just setting out on an extended trip across the grain-growing districts of southern Russia. Andrew Cairns, under the authority of the Empire Marketing Board, was to make an exhaustive first-hand appraisal of the process of collectivization, sending back typewritten letters dozens of pages long as well as a number of confidential telegrams summarizing what he observed during the spring and summer when the first real effects of collectivization were being felt. His unusually candid letters were addressed to the assistant secretary of the Board—"My Dear Lloyd," as Cairns called him.

Cairns traveled with Dr. Otto Schiller, an agricultural specialist attached to the German Embassy in Moscow, whose expertise perhaps outflanked Cairns's own, since he was fluent in both Russian and Ukrainian and had made a number of trips into the area earlier.

Cairns's letters were made available to the staff of the British Embassy in Moscow, and from there, to the British Foreign Office in London. Thus, on the 21st of June 1932, the British Ambassador in Moscow, Sir Esmond Ovey, informed the Foreign Secretary, Sir John Simon, that the initial report by Cairns represented

... a record of over-staffing, overplanning and complete incompetence at the centre; of human misery, starvation, death and disease among the peasantry. ... the only creatures who have any life at all in the districts visited are boars, pigs and other swine. Men, women, and children, horses and other workers are left to die in order that the Five Year Plan shall at least succeed on paper.[1]

Then, in a somewhat puzzling statement, Ovey wrote, "The pity of it is that this account cannot be broadcast to the world at large as an antidote to Soviet propaganda in general. ..."[2]

Begun as a brisk, unpretentious survey of the areas he visited, Cairns's report quickly subsided into a weary chronicle of systematized inequity, indignity, and hunger. At the Omsk Agricultural Research and Teaching Institute, he found zealous staff involved in inconsequential agricultural experiments that, in some cases, succeeded in actually retarding productivity. There, he attended a meeting in which one expert spoke for two hours on the expectation of a yield so high that Cairns regarded the prediction as downright irresponsible; he then watched with surprise as all those attending the meeting spoke one by one, condemning the original speaker for being too pessimistic. Carefully documenting these unrealistic statistics and requisition goals, Cairns believed they wholly misrepresented future crop yields.

In his tireless comparisons of conditions at various villages and cities, Cairns pointed to the shortages everywhere of draft animals, with no tractors to replace them. What machinery there was, he wrote to Lloyd, was "simply beyond belief." On the vastly overstaffed collective farms, he and Schiller all too often found inhabitants who sat idle and hungry, complaining bitterly of not having enough to eat even as volunteer Komsomol workers tried to hush them up.[3] The prices the State paid to the farms were, Cairns wrote, "next to nothing," while in the private bazaars and markets the prices of poor quality manufactured goods were astronomical and certainly well out of reach of the common laborers.

In the canteens, Cairns was surprised to find "classes of rationing or entitlements" according to the category the State assigned to the importance of a given job. Apologizing for introducing such an unpleasant subject into a letter, Cairns pointed out that the human

194

faeces that lay out in the open showed "even more fibrous material in [the workers'] diet than grain offal."[4]

In Slavgorod, Cairns and Schiller came upon their first case of actual starvation: "a small boy on the point of death" who was

> standing holding up his little shirt displaying thighs only about three or four inches thick. As Schiller took a photograph of him, two women with tears streaming down their face, said "that is what is going to happen to all of us. Will you give that picture to the newspapers in America, so that they will send us food?"[5]

In Kiev, Cairns witnessed "a horrible sight—a man dying on the street." He had apparently been driven mad from starvation "as he was going through all the motions of eating and rubbing his stomach with apparent satisfaction." A crowd gathered and threw kopecks to him, but the man remained unconscious of their presence and "soon stopped moving." Cairns turned to those left on the street and asked them why everything cost so much, and "seeing I did not understand a word of Ukrainian, they pulled in their cheeks, pretended to vomit, drew their fingers across their throat, and said, in Russian, 'Kushat nyet, nichevo nyet' (There is nothing to eat, nothing at all)."[6]

At the beginning of August, in two confidential telegrams to Lloyd, Cairns spoke of "DEFINITE PROOF FURTHER APPALLING LOSS ANIMAL DRAFT POWER," mentioning as well "WIDESPREAD RESISTANCE" of the farming population to collectivization. There had been, he wrote, "VERY HEAVY LOSSES OF ALL CLASSES OF LIVESTOCK," and insufficient fodder and hay to feed those animals that were left. Finally, he said he had witnessed in the Ukraine, Caucasus, Crimea, and Volga

> ACUTE WIDESPREAD HUNGER AND NOT INAPPRECIABLE AMOUNT ACTUAL STAR-VATION STOP PRACTICALLY UNANIMOUS BITTER HOSTILITY OF COLLECTIVE AND INDIVIDUAL PEASANTS ALIKE WILL SERIOUSLY INTERFERE WITH GOVERN-MENTS COLLECTION PLANS.[7]

It was the usual practice of the Empire Trading Board to publish the results of any agricultural studies it conducted, but in this case it failed to do so because of a complex series of events.

The British Foreign Office wanted to send Cairns back to the area the following spring, but because of the controversial nature of Cairns's first report they feared he would be refused a return visa if it were published. They therefore requested the Board to postpone publication. As it turned out, by the date Cairns should have returned to the Soviet Union, the Empire Trading Board had gone into liquidation, putting out of the question any possibility of publication. Cairns himself was appointed to the International Wheat Advisory Committee and no longer available for travel.[8]

Many years later, asked why he had not published the report on his own authority, Cairns would admit that he had been overtly discouraged, even threatened, from doing so by powerful political figures of the Left in Great Britain whom he believed at the time could do him great harm.[9] He named Beatrice Webb, specifically, who, with her husband Sidney, would praise the accomplishments of Stalin's Five-Year Plan in their massive, two-volume work *Soviet Communism: A New Civilization?* Among other things, the Webbs' survey implied that any misfortunes that had occurred in the process of collectivization had been brought about by the actions of the peasants themselves.

As was noted by the British Embassy in Moscow, Cairns's companion, Schiller, did succeed in returning to the area, and he published in Germany a devastating report about his trip. In consequence, he sustained a heavy attack from *Pravda*, who said his findings were little more than "a dirty 'erudite' libel on the agriculture of the Soviet Union." Schiller himself was only "a tool of fascist masters." The respected Dr. Schiller protested that his work had been conducted prior to the Nazi takeover in Germany, but it was all in vain. He was expelled from the Soviet Union immediately.[10]

In mid-November 1932, Walter Duranty paid a visit to William Strang, counsellor at the British Embassy in Moscow. By this time, the British Foreign Office was formulating a general assessment of Duranty's character that was less than flattering. Duranty was described as

a somewhat shady individual, who has been accused (though not on convincing evidence, as far as I can tell) of being in the pay of the Soviet Government. But [*sic*] But he is an able journalist, and—what is not always the same thing—a man of general intelligence.[11]

196

It was felt to be out of the question, however, that any of Duranty's opinions favoring the regime sprang "from genuine conviction," as was the case with other correspondents who held pro-Soviet views. Duranty seemed to be his own man, a fact that would call forth a number of cynical observations from embassy staff over the next twelve months.

On this occasion, Duranty made several assertions to Strang about the state of agriculture in the Soviet Union which eventually ended up on the desk of the foreign secretary, Sir John Simon. "His description of conditions," Strang wrote, "was not very different from what we have ourselves been reporting for the last six to nine months."

Duranty attributed what he called "the present breakdown in agriculture" to the shortage of labor and of draft power. The peasants' slaughter of livestock in 1930 and its continuation "by fits and starts" since then, plus a serious shortage of fodder, meant that the livestock population of the country had shrunk to "only about 40 percent of the population in 1929." Current grain collections, Duranty continued, were "going badly." Providing enough food for the workers was already a problem, even now, when fruit and vegetables were still available from the summer before, "but what of the late winter and early spring?"

Duranty believed there were several possible solutions, the first—a return to a modified form of NEP—having already been rejected by the Central Committee. A second possibility, he believed, was to bring in the grain reserve the government now had stored against the possibility of a war with the Japanese, whose aggressive policies had forced the Red Army onto alert along Far Eastern defense lines.

Duranty even considered the importation of grain, although this would be at odds with the current plan to use agricultural exports to finance heavy industry. "There are millions of people in Russia, peasants," he told Strang, "whom it is fairly safe to leave in want. But the industrial proletariat, about 10 percent of the population, must at all costs be fed if the revolution is to be safeguarded." Failing these two alternatives, Duranty asked, "What then? . . . Is there no limit to the people's endurance?"

In answer to his own question, Duranty told Strang that no evidence existed of any subversive elements or conspiratorial groups to challenge the regime. Within the Communist Party as well, Stalin seemed safe: there was no sign of a "palace revolution" among Party activists.[12]

Beyond Duranty's suggestions, Strang wrote, there was

> a still further alternative solution of the whole complex of Soviet difficulties ... recognition and a loan from America in return for a stronger anti-Japanese policy, heavy orders in the United States, and the handing over to United States interests for reconditioning or exploitation on a technical aid basis of part of the railway system, of the gold-producing industry, or even some of the Soviet giant industrial enterprises.[13]

Even at this late date, the assumption of Strang and Duranty was that the regime would attempt to avert what they both believed was about to become a human tragedy of incalculable dimensions.

Less than a month later, Duranty again visited the British Embassy, this time as a result of a dispatch he had written on the agricultural situation which paralleled his earlier conversation with Strang. It seemed the Soviets had viewed the report as being far too unfavorable, and shortly after its publication,

> Duranty was visited by emissaries from governing circles here (not from the Censorship Department or the People's Commissariat for Foreign Affairs but from higher spheres) who reproached him with his unfaithfulness. How could he, who had been so fair for ten years, choose this moment to stab them in the back and when the prospects of recognition by the U.S.A was [sic] brightening? What did he mean by it, and did he not realise that the consequences for himself might be serious. Let him take this warning.[14]

Duranty had planned a trip to Paris, but now postponed it, Strang wrote, worried that he wouldn't be allowed back into the country. "I am sure he knows that any such fate is almost out of the question," Strang commented drily, "but he says the authorities here are in such a state of nerves that there is no knowing what they may do."[15]

Other Western correspondents documented the methods of coercion exercised by Soviet authorities over foreign newsmen, whom, it was said, they managed to control "almost as rigorously as they did their own."[16] For the Western reporters, there was the ominous threat of losing their visas, which were "granted to foreigners for a maximum period of six months at a time; and the foreigner who leaves the country even for a short time must reapply for an entrance visa."[17]

A delay in granting the return visa was one way of indicating to a journalist that he was treading on thin ice and that his work was not regarded as sufficiently "objective." On occasion, as with the respected correspondent of the *Berliner Tageblatt*, Paul Sheffer, the visa was simply revoked when he left the country and re-entry denied.[18] In most cases, loss of the visa meant loss of the job.

The Sheffer incident had taken place in the late-Twenties, but it still served as a reminder to the Western press corps that journalists could be vulnerable to the whims of Moscow.

In Duranty's case at present, there was a new and unexpected sense of urgency in his need to be able to re-enter the country after an absence, something he neglected to mentioned to Strang. His Russian mistress Katya had become pregnant at the end of the summer and was expecting their child in late March or early April. From the point of view of Duranty, the timing couldn't have been worse. From the point of view of the Soviet authorities, it couldn't have been better—not even if they had planned it themselves.

At the end of December 1932, Soviet authorities introduced a system of internal passports for its populace, ostensibly for the purpose of purging kulaks and other "anti-social elements from the cities." There could be no doubt, however, that the action was motivated by other concerns. The first was an attempt to bring a halt to the restless movement of peasants from the countryside to the industrial centers, where living conditions were far better. There was also the haunting possibility that hunger was beginning to cause mass migration as the population in the stricken areas started out on a search for food.

Then, in early spring, a second law was put into effect, one that effactually created the "second serfdom" in Russia. Under this new law, it was no longer possible for a peasant to leave the collective farm where he was employed "without a contract from his future employers, ratified by the collective farm authorities."[19] A catchment to prevent further movement from country to city, the law also prevented from leaving those who were trapped on collectives where there was little or no food.

Duranty reported the event without even a hint at its underlying

199

purpose, saying only that the system was designed "to purge the city of undesirable elements." Reporting more than a million and a half passports had been issued since December, he praised the recently introduced system and the new law for preventing overcrowding in the cities.[20]

At about the same time, a curt announcement of the execution of thirty-five agricultural officials for "wrecking" appeared in the Moscow papers. Forty others had been given long prison sentences. Among those shot were a prominent member of the Tractor Department and a former Vice-Commissar of Agriculture.[21] Duranty was to attribute much of the mismanagement of collectivization to this "quite efficient conspiracy," persisting with a version of events that ignored all of the outward signs of a major catastrophe.

It was during the lead-up to the famine that Malcolm Muggeridge arrived in Moscow in September of 1932, accompanied by his wife Kitty, the niece of prominent socialist Beatrice Webb. Kitty was several months pregnant with their second child, their son having been left behind in England at school. Muggeridge had made arrangements for a time to string for the Manchester *Guardian* in order to support himself and his growing family, but this he viewed as only a temporary expedient. His real purpose in coming to the Soviet Union was to join in the great effort of "building Socialism," and he had every intention of relinquishing his British citizenship and becoming a citizen of the new Soviet state.

His first visit to the tomb that housed Lenin's body in Red Square was slightly deflating to these aims. There, viewing the "endless procession of people shuffling past the embalmed corpse under the watchful eye of gray, impassive sentries," it seemed to Muggeridge that there was a religious or mystical aspect to what he uncomfortably interpreted as the worship of power. "I didn't quite like it. The whole thing was tawdry," he later reported.[22]

A second doubt arose when he began to search for an apartment suitable for him and his wife. Unlike the other correspondents, Muggeridge intended to live like the common Muscovites since he planned to become one of them. All he could find, however, were rooms that "invariably turned out to be part of a room, with, at best, the possibility of hanging a blanket to curtain off the portion offered us, and the use of corporate cooking and washing facilities. . . . an impossible arrangement."²³

Falling back on the Western establishment, he opted for a dacha offered him free of charge by a German businessman, settled in quickly, and soon began making his way across the city, visiting places the other foreign correspondents usually avoided. In the course of his movement, he visited the Moscow markets and was suitably delighted by the ebb and flow of deals taking place. In his fictionalized account of the experience, *Winter in Moscow*, the visit of the character Pye [Muggeridge] to the marketplace is the turning point of his stay in the Soviet Union. Watching a piece of sausage change hands, he sees a bearded peasant stuff it "greedily into his mouth; then, as he gobbled, retched."

Something in his face as he gobbled and retched; something animal, desperate, fearful; appetite and disgust mingled in the two actions of gobbling and retching, brought a sudden doubt into Pye's mind. The man is starving, he thought. Were the others starving? Was there the same look in their eyes as in his? Were they, like him, pale and agonised with starvation? Was this market a kind of scavenging; like cats he had seen in the very early morning? . . . Were they famished animals fighting over refuse?

The doubt haunted him on his way back to his hotel. He saw hunger everywhere; in the faces that hurried past him, and in the patient queues, and in the empty shops, dimly lighted and decorated with red streamers, whose windows contained only busts of Marx and Lenin and Stalin. Stone busts exposed to ravenous eyes. Instead of bread, the law and the prophets offered as tasty morsels to a famished population. . . .

Pye thought things out over dinner. In the first place it was absurd to imagine that the Dictatorship of the Proletariat would serve such an excellent meal to him, a foreigner, if their own people were going short. . . . He must keep his head. Not get hysterical. The great English Liberal newspaper wanted facts, the truth, and not impressions of sudden emotional reactions.²⁴

The real Muggeridge put the idea out of his mind, at least for the time being. For one thing, his wife had become seriously ill, and it suddenly became necessary for him to devote all his time to caring for

201

her. For another, the idea, viewed in the cold light of day, seemed utterly preposterous.

A young Arthur Koestler, later to make a name for himself as a writer of philosophy and fiction, passed the winter of 1932–33 in Kharkov, then the capital of the Ukraine. It was a terrible time, he wrote later, that winter when the famine began to claim the lives of the children in the Ukrainian countryside. They looked to him like "embryos out of alcohol bottles." Traveling through the countryside by rail was "like running the gauntlet; the stations were lined with begging peasants with swollen hands and feet, the women holding up to the carriage-windows horrible infants with enormous wobbling heads, stick-like limbs, swollen, pointed bellies."[25] Soon after, Soviet authorities began to require that the shades of all windows be pulled down on trains traveling through the North Caucasus, the Ukraine, and the Volga basin.

To Koestler, it was most unreal to see the local newspapers full of reports of industrial progress and successful shock workers, but "not one word about the local famine, epidemics, the dying out of whole villages. . . . The enormous land was covered with a blanket of silence."[26]

Sometime just after the beginning of 1933, Natalya Petrovna Shiroshikh, translator and secretary to Eugene Lyons, spotted an account in the newspaper *Molot* of "a rampage" of the GPU that had taken place down in the Kuban. Lyons sent a cable to Rostov-on-Don, but otherwise did nothing about the report, except pass the word along to William Stoneman of the Chicago *Daily News* and Ralph Barnes of the New York *Herald Tribune*.[27] The two of them decided to go down and tour the area, managing to travel in the North Caucasus, the Ukraine, and the Kuban district by Rostov-on-Don, until they were arrested by the Soviet police and sent back to Moscow.[28] What they saw was famine, and both wrote stories describing the conditions they witnessed. Knowing these would be rejected by the censors in Moscow, they sent them out "by an obliging German Jewish fur buyer" who was returning to Berlin.

The publication of these reports in the United States so alarmed the officials in the Soviet Press Office that a ban on travel for journalists went into effect soon after Stoneman and Barnes returned to Moscow. As early as the beginning of March 1933, the British Embassy reported to the Foreign Office in London that travel into the afflicted area had now been suspended for all members of the foreign press.[29]

Then, on the 12th of March 1933, Linton Wells, Bureau Chief of the International News Service, broke the news of another important event, which would become the center of international controversy. Six Englishmen, along with several Russians, had been arrested and charged with industrial sabotage. They were to be tried publicly in what would come to be known as the Metro-Vickers trial, since the Englishmen were employees of that well-known British firm. Readers clamored for news of the fate of the British engineers who had been accused of sabotaging machinery they themselves had come to the Soviet Union to install and supervise.[30] The British would eventually be found guilty—and expelled from the country. For a time, the trial occupied the attention of newspapers around the world, while the famine faded into the background.

Inside the British Embassy, a great deal of attention was paid to the question of who would cover the trial for the British papers; there was much alarm among members of the diplomatic staff that Duranty might be asked to cover it for the London *Times* and the *Evening Standard*, a fear that turned out to be unfounded. A report reflecting badly on Duranty's reputation and character went out from the Embassy in Moscow to the Foreign Office in London from M.V. [S.M.K. Vyvyan], one of the secretaries in the Embassy. In his confidential profile of Walter Duranty's personality, Vyvyan speculated about a rumored split between Duranty, the well-established A. T. Cholerton, and the less experienced Malcolm Muggeridge. Either of the last two, Vyvyan gleefully reported, "would admittedly have welcomed an offer themselves from the 'Times'. . . ."[31]

As for Duranty, Vyvyan wrote, he had become "a celebrity and, in some people's views, a very pernicious one."[32] Vyvyan particularly objected to those dispatches by Duranty that claimed people in the Soviet Union were firmly behind Stalin. He went on to say:

Duranty is an avowed proponent of American recognition of the U.S.S.R. since he is aware that recognition would greatly enhance his reputation in the Soviet Union and give him a cheap triumph in the United States.[33]

Vyvyan concluded by alleging that Duranty had probably been bought by "the recognition racquet."

Soon afterward, a report was filed from the Moscow Chancery that concurred with Vyvyan's "estimate of Mr. Duranty's character." A. Dalker agreed that Duranty wanted U.S. recognition of the Soviet Union, "as such a recognition would, [Duranty] felt, have been in some sense an official tribute to his estimates of Soviet conditions, policy and prospects, and would at the same time have been of personal advantage to him—i.e. leading possibly to his appointment on the arrival of an American Embassy in Moscow to some such post as that of the Press Attaché."[34]

At about the same time these observations were being filed with the Foreign Office in London, there was a heated exchange between Duranty and Constantine Oumansky, the head of the Soviet Press Office, which immediately made the rounds of the Western community in Moscow. News had leaked that supplies of grain were being diverted into the areas believed afflicted by famine, the natural assumption being that they were intended for the peasants' relief. At the same time, Oumansky continued to insist that there was no famine.

"But why then," Duranty was reported to have asked, "are you sending corn there?"

"Ah, yes," was the reply, "but it is not for the peasants."[35]

Oumansky's cryptic comment would remain a source of speculation until Malcolm Muggeridge discovered its meaning later on.

Hard on the heels of the Stoneman and Barnes incursion into the famine-afflicted area, the increasingly disenchanted Muggeridge began to report events in the countryside with a new toughness. He wrote a penetrating article for the *Guardian* pointing to the major problems of collectivization. The most competent farmers, expected to produce the raw materials for export to finance planned industrial programs, were, he wrote, being "booted about." Vastly over-optimistic estimates for the spring harvest had given a completely false sense of expectation to the authorities, with the probable effect that food supplies for many areas were now under threat. Muggeridge concluded that "not enough grain has been collected to feed the towns properly."[36]

Six weeks after writing this clearly stated account of events, Muggeridge found an equally uncomplicated way of documenting them. Informing no one, he bought a train ticket and simply set off for Kiev and Rostov-on-Don.[37]

In a series of articles published in the *Guardian* at the end of March 1933, he confirmed the existence of widespread famine in his eyewitness account. The peasant population, he wrote, was starving:

> I mean starving in its absolute sense; not undernourished as, for instance, most Oriental peasants . . . and some unemployed workers in Europe, but having had for weeks next to nothing to eat.
> "We have nothing. They have taken everything away. . . ."[38]

"It was true," Muggeridge wrote. "The famine is an organized one." But, he continued, it was more than a famine: it was "a military occupation; worse, active war." In Kuban, well-fed troops were being used to control and coerce peasants who were in many cases starving to death. The supplies of grain sent into the area were being used to feed the troops who, along with Party activists, were still searching barns and cellars for hidden grain or hoarded food. Meanwhile, Muggeridge reported, there were "fields choked with weeds, cattle dead, people starving and dispirited, no horses for ploughing or for transport, not even adequate supplies of seed for the spring sowing." These facts, along with the ominously "deserted villages," led inescapably to the conclusion that "altogether in the qualitative sense, collectivisation was a failure."[39]

In Rostov-on-Don, Muggeridge found a populace "dressed in tatters" and slowed by "lethargy." Many of the peasants had bodies swollen from hunger, and there was an "all-pervading sight and smell of death." When he asked why they did not have enough to eat, the inevitable answer came that the food had been taken by the government. It was, Muggeridge wrote, an ironic ending to Stalin's optimistic words about collectivization.[40] He concluded that "To say that there is a famine in some of the most fertile parts of Russia is to say much less than the truth; there is not only famine but—in the case of the North Caucasus at least —a state of war, a military occupation."[41]

Muggeridge reported his findings privately to the British Embassy in Moscow and his conversation was duly repeated to Sir John Simon by Ambassador Ovey, who wrote at the end of March of "frequent cases of suicides and sometimes even of cannibalism. . . . the conditions would have been incredible to [Muggeridge] if he had not seen them with his own eyes."[42]

But the stories, smuggled out via a diplomatic bag,[43] seemed to Muggeridge to have been displayed in a less than prominent position by the *Guardian*—despite a continuing interest in the topic that showed up in the paper's Letters to the Editor columns. Later on, he would say they had been altered, or, in his own words, "mutilated" by his editors.[44] An embittered idealist, Muggeridge left the Soviet Union immediately, stopping off in Berlin, where he "watched the Nazis march along the *Unter den Linden* and realized, of course, they're Comsomols, the same people, the same faces. It's the same show."[45] As to the Soviets and the famine, he continued to believe it was "one of the most monstrous crimes in history, so terrible that people in the future will scarcely be able to believe it ever happened."[46]

In England, there was immediate skepticism about the truth of Muggeridge's reports. His wife's eminent "Aunt Bo," Beatrice Webb, called his coverage "a hysterical tirade," dismissing him publicly in a subdued but patronizing manner. Others weren't so subdued, and to his surprise, Muggeridge found himself subjected to vilification and slander.[47]

More than half a century later, Muggeridge was able to review the facts of the famine without rancor; above all, baffled that such a horror could have happened and then just fallen away, ignored by everyone. As to his own fate, he seemed more surprised than anything else. "Me?" he asked, querulous, still awed by the injustice of the thing. "What happened to *me*?"

Then he remembered. "Oh, yes. I couldn't get work."[48]

After Muggeridge's report, there was yet another published in the pages of the Manchester *Guardian*. A young man named Gareth Jones, who had taken a three-week walking trip through the stricken area, reported that he had seen mass starvation on a wide scale. He announced this first in a press conference in Berlin, then at a lecture at Chatham House in London, and at last in a story written for the *Guardian*, published only two days after Muggeridge's last dispatch on the subject, on the 30th of March 1933.[49] His statement was followed by a bizarre set of events, which were later divulged by Eugene Lyons.

According to Lyons, Jones's report, coming hard on the heels of Muggeridge's eyewitness account, put the Soviet Press Office into a terrible state of nerves. Knowing that the Western correspondents were desperate to cover the Metro-Vickers trial, which was at the time creating a divisive sense of competition among the newsmen, Oumansky indicated that the reporters would be denied credentials to cover the trial if Jones's report were not repudiated. Discussing the matter among themselves, they came to the conclusion that "compelling professional necessity" required them to go along with Oumansky's request. In a story that tended over the years to change in the retelling, Lyons claimed that the newsmen—including Duranty—then invited Oumansky to meet in a hotel room where they worked out the language that would undercut Jones.

> We admitted enough to soothe our consciences, but in roundabout phrases that damned Jones a liar. The filthy business having been disposed of, someone ordered vodka and *zakuski* (canapés), Oumansky joined the celebration, and the party did not break up until the morning hours.[50]

Whatever the facts of this alleged collusion, Duranty himself took the lead in disputing Jones's account, and on the 31st of March 1933, Duranty wrote an important dispatch, one that worked out his rationale for collectivization, with a maxim tried out briefly the autumn before in his poem "Red Square." Duranty agreed that it was "all too true that the novelty and mismanagement of collective farming," plus a conspiracy in the agricultural sector by "wreckers" and "spoilers," had "made a mess of Soviet food production."

> But—to put it brutally—you can't make an omelette without breaking eggs, and the Bolshevik leaders are just as indifferent to the casualties that may be involved in their drive toward socialism as any General during the World War who ordered a costly attack in order to show his superiors that he and his division possessed the proper soldierly spirit. In fact, the Bolsheviki are more indifferent because they are animated by fanatical conviction.[51]

He was ready to agree that there had been "serious food shortages"; there was no question of that. But on the question of starvation, he was adamant: "There is no actual starvation or deaths from starvation but there is widespread mortality from diseases due to malnutrition, especially in the Ukraine, North Caucasus, and Lower Volga." It was cutting semantic distinction pretty slim, and it remains the most outrageous equivocation of the period. Yet the statement seems to have pacified almost everyone.

As to Gareth Jones, who had found famine after spending a short three weeks in the Soviet Union, Duranty had little patience with him. It had frequently been predicted that the Soviet Union was "on the verge of a terrific smash," and Jones's story amounted to nothing more than a new twist to an old prediction.[52] In fact, said Duranty, there would be no smash, and the young Jones, like his earlier predecessors, was indulging himself in wishful thinking.

Jones didn't hesitate in striking back. A young Welshman who had received a first in Russian Studies at Cambridge, and who had at one time been secretary to the British Prime Minister, Lloyd George, Jones turned out to be a man who would not tolerate having his words twisted.

He wrote to the *New York Times* taking Duranty to task for making "the strange suggestion that I was forecasting the doom of the Soviet regime, a forecast I have never ventured."[53] He would stick by the facts, he said. He had visited some twenty villages where he saw incredible suffering, and those suffering were not only kulaks. He had talked personally with peasants and officials in the district who told him that indeed the peasantry was starving to death. And although he saw no bodies, he had every reason to believe that the catastrophe was worse than that suffered in the same region in 1921. Reiterating his statement that Soviet Russia was then in the throes of "a severe famine," he called attention to letters he had in his possession that documented his charges.

But Jones pitied the journalists who had been turned "into masters of euphemism and understatement." Hence, "they give 'famine' the polite name of 'food shortage,' and 'starving to death' is softened to read as 'wide-spread mortality from diseases due to malnutrition.'"[54] It was an uncompromising statement, one that showed integrity and courage, but Jones was up against an establishment larger than Duranty.

The home offices of the newspapers in the West were for the moment more interested in the Metro-Vickers trial than in any reports of famine, and the sorry conspiracy either of exquisite doubletalk or of total silence that greeted Jones continued. Eugene Lyons thought in retrospect that "Poor Gareth Jones must have been the most surprised human being alive when the facts he so painstakingly garnered from our mouths were snowed under by our denials."[55]

"Throwing down Jones" signaled one of the sorriest periods of reportage in the history of the free press, one in which Walter Duranty led the way—with others in the pack not all that far behind.

CHAPTER XII

The "Famine" Is Mostly Bunk

"The 'famine' is mostly bunk," Duranty wrote to Knickerbocker in late June of 1933, "except maybe in Kazakhstan and the Alti where they wouldn't let you go." In any case, he continued, the Soviet Foreign Office was becoming "rather crotchety about reporters traveling these days."[1]

The ban on travel for Western newsmen was now being strictly enforced and would continue, another correspondent later pointed out, "until a new crop had been harvested and the outward signs of the mass mortality had been largely eliminated."[2] As impossible as it might seem, this simple ban, plus continual and vehement denial of starvation, was extremely effective in discouraging reports on the subject in the Western press. The story was now several months old, and "[f]ew correspondents were inclined to risk difficulties with the censorship by sending the story of events which had occurred some months past."[3]

Although the ban lasted six months—from early spring through summer—it was not until late August that the *Christian Science Monitor*'s William Henry Chamberlin actually mentioned it in one of his dispatches back to America. This occurred only a short time before Soviet authorities allowed correspondents back into the area. Meantime, a number of requests from Western correspondents outside the

Soviet Union to go there had been refused, including those of journalists who were traveling only as tourists, one of them granted permission "only if he pledged not to leave the train en route."[4]

The fate of the kulaks and their methods of deportation had been
briefly covered by Duranty as an intellectual concept, one that demonstrated, as per usual in Duranty's work, the fanaticism of the Bolsheviks in their March to Progress. The year before, he had given a
glimpse of what it might be like to be in the shoes of a kulak. He would
be transported to Siberia, told he was not going to live well, not eat a
lot, and he would be ostracized as "an outsider, an enemy." If he did
not help in the gigantic effort to build Socialism, his reward would be
death.[5]

But somehow, Duranty's words fell short of the deed.

One of the few records kept of "the liquidation of the kulaks as a
class," a report from the Soviet secret police in the city of Smolensk,
tells us more clearly what occurred. Victims about to be deported were
stripped of their shoes, and their clothes were taken and given to lower
peasants as a bribe to ensure their cooperation. Kulak children were
left as beggars on the streets. The trains could hardly handle the heavy
loads assigned them, and railroad stations had improvised prisons
where the kulaks had to await their forced migration. These were the
"caged animals" Duranty had seen on his trip through Central Asia in
1930.

As panic seized the countryside, some couples tried to divorce in
order to disperse their belongings and thus escape deportation on legal
technicalities. Others tried to flee the country. When all else failed,
there were waves of suicides of families who preferred death to
separation.[6]

Those transported to Siberia faced insuperable hardship. If a village
existed, they were squeezed into it. Otherwise, they were simply abandoned without shelter in extreme cold and ordered to build dwellings.
Many managed to do so by working almost around the clock, without
sleep, in order that they and the others would not freeze to death.[7]
Those employed as forced labor in mining regions faced starvation
rations of one bowl of thin gruel a day and eight to ten ounces of bread.
They died in waves, their numbers replenished by the arrival of new
deportees.

As to the children left behind, a new generation of *bezprizornye* now roamed the countryside searching for food and shelter. Neighbors refused to take them in for fear of retaliation. The State found it necessary to found new orphanages for those unwillingly abandoned by their families. By a cruel twist of fate, many of these abused children would be recruited into the newly reorganized Soviet Secret Service, now called the NKVD, in time to serve for Stalin's purges.[8]

It has been estimated that, in all, some six to seven million "souls" were expropriated. Soviet sources admit to one million households, at least five million "souls." Soviet historian Roy A. Medvedev has indicated that there is "every reason to believe . . . that even [the] 'more exact' official statistics are understated."[9]

Ironically, the fate of those left behind was destined to be far worse than that of the kulaks. With their deportation, the amount of land under cultivation was reduced dramatically. Yet, enthusiastic estimates of crop yields continued, as Andrew Cairns had observed in his swing through southern Russia in 1932. A new method of estimating grain crop—which ignored harvesting losses and weather conditions—contributed to an exaggeration of more than 40 percent of the harvest for the year 1933. The State's share was estimated on that basis, leaving the balance to the peasant.[10] Reports remained frankly over-optimistic.

> The village soviet lied to the district, and the district lied to the province, and the province lied to Moscow. Everything was apparently in order, so Moscow assigned grain production and delivery quotas to the provinces, and the provinces then assigned them to the districts. And [the] village was given a quota that it couldn't have fulfilled in ten years! In the village soviet even those who weren't drinkers took to drink out of terror. It was clear that Moscow was basing its hopes on the Ukraine. And the upshot of it was that most of the subsequent anger was directed against the Ukraine. What they said was simple: you have failed to fulfill the plan, and that means that you yourself are an unliquidated kulak.[11]

The term "kulak," always defined with soft edges in Party jargon, originally included at maximum 3 to 5 percent of peasant households. The property that admitted peasants into the category was the possession of two or perhaps three cows, some few chickens, and twenty-five acres of land for an average family of seven members.[12]

When the plan for their elimination was sent from Moscow to the provincial soviet authorities, lists of names had to be compiled, and a troika—three people—made the final determination of exactly who would be included. A corrupt process in and of itself, "the elimination of the kulak" created a system receptive to further corruption.

> It was so easy to do a man in: you wrote a denunciation; you did not even have to sign it. All you had to say was that he had paid people to work for him as hired hands, or that he had owned three cows.[13]

The troika of bureaucrats who processed the lists of deportees could scarcely be relied upon, in an atmosphere of escalating fear and hatred, to carry out their duties with dispassion and integrity.

> There were bribes. Accounts were settled because of jealousy over some woman or because of ancient feuds and quarrels. And what kept on happening was that the poorest peasants kept getting listed as kulaks while those who were more prosperous managed to buy themselves off.[14]

And inevitably, such a process required dehumanization—if those charged with such onerous duties were not to lose hold of their senses by the very nature of the task. Thus ordinary people were threatened with guns, their children called names like "kulak bastards" or "bloodsuckers," and they grew to be considered by Party activists as "pariahs, untouchables, vermin." Their parents were viewed as parasites with no souls: "they stank; they all had venereal diseases; they were enemies of the people and exploited the labor of others."[15] There were documented cases of atrocities; starving mothers caught stealing potatoes were beaten to death, children shot, pregnant women publicly beaten. There were reports of drivers of death carts who took the dying as well as the dead to save an extra trip; reports of living children thrown on piles of corpses, still conscious and crying out for help.[16]

Outside the area, rumors circulated among Party activists "about the slaughter of livestock" and a "'scorched earth' resistance to forced collectivization." These were soon followed by stories that Communist officials had been murdered and that "recalcitrant peasants were being executed en masse." There was talk of heavy grain requisitions against meager stores, then of outright starvation. The appearance of beggars on the streets in many cities corroborated much of what had been said.[17]

When word of the famine reached Nikita Khrushchev, then a young Party activist, he had difficulty believing the rumors.

> I'd left the Ukraine in 1929, only three years before, when the Ukraine had pulled itself up to prewar living standards. Food had been plentiful and cheap. Yet now, we were told, people were starving. It was incredible.[18]

He would also recall a trip he made into the area. He and other Party officials made a short visit to a collective farm, "appalled by the conditions we found there. The farmers were starving to death."[19]

The symptoms of starvation are harrowing. There is a brooding for nourishment, a psychological obsession, which leads to involuntary movement of the jaws, as if chewing. A sucking movement occurs, saliva flows and must be swallowed down.[20] The gums turn white, the skin an unwholesome gray, suggesting "rather a consuming disease more like leprosy than appetite."[21]

There is an unnatural aging that causes even children to look old. As the body shrinks, the eyes become large and unfocused, bulging and immobile. Some who suffer from severe malnutrition shrink and become like skeletons, with skin stretched taut over the bones. More commonly and especially among children, the body swells; there is a huge, distended stomach. The need to urinate increases, finally becoming uncontrollable. Festering sores appear, and the diarrhea associated with starvation begins. As the body consumes itself, there are sometimes hallucinations and other symptoms of madness. In the final stage, the sufferer becomes semi-comatose for several days, until, at last, the heart stops beating.

One observer later likened the children who starved to death in southern Russia in 1933 to the faces of those incarcerated in the German concentration camps during World War II, their heads "like heavy balls on thin little necks"; "the entire skeleton . . . stretched over with skin that was like yellow gauze." Instead of human faces, they now had beaks, "or frog heads—thin, wide lips—and some of them resembled fish, mouths open."[22]

In the countryside, the peasants were "dazed and resigned," accepting death as part of "a natural calamity."[23] The men died first, then the children, finally the women. Eyewitness accounts documented the eating of dogs and even cannibalism: corpses in the streets became commonplace.[24] To make matters worse, at the peak of the famine, there was a typhus epidemic.[25] Everywhere in the stricken area were

> people dying in solitude by slow degrees, dying hideously, without the
> excuse of sacrifice for a cause. They had been trapped and left to starve,
> each in his home, by a political decision made in a far-off capital
> around conference and banquet tables. There was not even the conso-
> lation of inevitability to relieve the horror.... Everywhere [were]
> found men and women lying prone, their faces and bellies bloated,
> their eyes utterly expressionless.[26]

As if in official mockery, in shop windows everywhere, in Moscow, in the villages where the famine raged, were wooden cheeses and card-board cut-outs of succulent foods, luxuries that the Revolution prom-ised someday to bring to the people.

Duranty, for his part, stuck to his guns. Maybe there were "food short-ages," but that was all.

In the middle of May 1933, he reported that conditions around the Odessa region had been bad, with poor livestock and shortages of grain. But so far as he could determine, it was the "same story as in 1921." The people would say that they were okay in their village, but further along, others were starving. He admitted to typhus in the region, but according to resident foreigners in Odessa, it was not epidemic.[27]

Duranty himself, of course, did not set foot in Odessa. The ques-tion arises as to where he got his information.

One possibility is that it came from his assistant, Robin Kinkead—a man whose self-confessed "predilection for the bottle" was the sub-ject of comment at about this time by a staff member at the British Embassy.[28] Some fifty years later, when his memories of the famine were uncharacteristically hazy, Kinkead recalled having traveled into the region around Odessa—he could not remember whether it was 1933 or 1934—accompanied, he believed, by Lindesay Parrott of the International News Service. Together they could find no trace of the famine.[29] This, despite the fact that the Odessa province was one of the hardest hit, "usually with from 20 to 25 percent [mortality], though even higher in many villages."[30]

If in fact Duranty's source was Kinkead, then that meant the ban against travel was being enforced only intermittently, and others, including Duranty himself, could have entered the area. It also showed Duranty's willingness to leave a gravely important story in the hands of a colleague, who by his own admission, had ceased to be reliable. If, on the other hand, Duranty's source was not Kinkead, then it meant he was relying almost entirely upon Soviet press reports for his information. Either way, Duranty was at fault.

At the end of the following month, in June 1933, Duranty was obliged to comment on another report, this time emanating from Riga. Here it was alleged that the provincial Soviet press was carrying news items not being published in the major media outlets of the Soviet Union, and these facts showed the existence of a famine that was being covered up. In this instance, peasants had been said to be digging up seed potatoes. In other reports, the story maintained, corpses with swollen faces were continuing to turn up in Moscow.[31]

Predictably, Duranty put little stock in stories from Riga, remembering as always his own false dispatches from that Baltic capital over a decade before.

Nevertheless, he found himself coming under pressure from his editors back home to comment on the alleged famine, once the Metro-Vickers trial had ended.

Duranty remained unshaken. At the beginning of July, he wrote an answer to the charges of a U.S. agricultural expert who had claimed that collectivization would have proceeded better if the Soviets had gone more slowly. Duranty, beating his old thesis like a dead horse, pointed out yet once more that "in this Soviet revolution there is no pity." What Americans failed to realize, he said, was that the Bolsheviks knew their own country, that "they [were] fanatics and they [did] not care about the costs in blood and tears." Their attitude—that the old and the weak should be the first to go—was still reflected in the phrase which had been popular in Czarist Russia, "One life, one kopek." And he reiterated what was becoming a refrain in all his public utterances: "The Kremlin believes with fanatic fervor that hardships are worthwhile."[32]

Then, in late August, 1933, Ralph Barnes, who had so upset Soviet officials by going into the Ukraine with William Stoneman earlier in the year, returned home to the U.S. and published a report on the ban that had been in effect for several months. The only conclusion that could be drawn from this regulation, which prohibited travel in the Ukraine and North Caucasus, Barnes reasoned, was that there were

216

terrible conditions that the authorities were determined to keep under wraps. He estimated that there were "as many as one million now dead from diseases and outright hunger."[33] On the same day that Barnes's story appeared, an Associated Press release, probably written by Stanley Richardson, declared that Moscow was doubling the price of bread, and that William Henry Chamberlin had been denied the right to travel to the Ukraine to observe conditions there.[34]

Just returning from one of his many junkets abroad, Duranty churned out a rather hurried and uncertain dispatch, which, in its complete lack of direction, suggested that, although he was still sticking to his guns, it might be a result of the rigorous censorship his work was being subjected to. He began by saying that officials in Moscow scorned any "help" that the Nazis in Germany might want to offer to alleviate the effects of a famine. As to the famine itself, which was now being reported as worse "than that of 1921," he wished to point out that these stories had originated in "uncensored dispatches from Berlin"—whatever that statement was intended to imply. He then spoke of the "growing tendency" in recent months for Moscow "to try to cover up or minimize the difficulties—for foreign consumption."

> The censorship in particular seems unable to realize that the U.S. Department of Commerce, to take a single instance, has sufficient representatives in countries bordering the Soviet Union, who not only collect and carefully sift reports from people visiting Russia, but are able to read accurately between the lines of Soviet newspapers, which those representatives receive a day or two after publication.[35]

He made cryptic references to "heavy costs for the Russian people," saying "until this harvest the picture was dark enough."[36] But despite these tactics, the story came off as a pathetic attempt to sideline his earlier stubborn denial of the famine. It was the kind of thing that made it easy for Malcolm Muggeridge to lampoon Duranty.

> He'd been asked to write something about the food shortage, and was trying to put together a thousand words which, if the famine got worse and known outside Russia, would suggest that he'd foreseen and foretold it, but which, if it got better and wasn't known outside Russia, would suggest that all along he'd pooh-poohed the possibility of there being a famine.[37]

Three days later, Duranty gave it another try, but the results remained sadly inadequate. His story began with a statement of excellent grain forecasts for the coming harvest. The next sentence, however, spoke of "the food shortage which has affected almost the whole population in the last year, [causing] heavy loss of life." Computing the loss of life, he said, was now "pure guesswork." He was certain, however, that the deaths were not so much a result of "actual starvation as from manifold disease." Duranty then turned to what he would give as "certain approximations."

He ventured to suggest that the death rate in the North Caucasus, which was usually twenty to twenty-five per thousand, would be quadruple that rate; in the same sentence in which he made this pronouncement, he praised the ample bread rations now being dispensed by the authorities. As to the Ukraine and the lower Volga area, the normal death rate for forty million would be one million. "Lacking official figures," Duranty wrote, "it is conservative to suppose that this was at least trebled last year in those provinces and considerably increased for the Soviet Union as a whole." Thus, in a roundabout way, Duranty was giving his estimate of the number dead there at two million in addition to the million that would have died anyway from natural causes.[38]

In the meantime, his colleague on the *Times*, Frederick T. Birchall, who had left the position of assistant managing editor in New York and returned to Berlin, reported that the number of famine victims as estimated by the Germans was four million. According to sources there, Birchall wrote, four million was considered a conservative figure, and he made reference to repeated reports of cannibalism.[39]

Duranty was clearly unnerved by this new estimate, and he swiftly wrote a story calling attention to the Intourist Guide Books which said that collective farms, or "Soviet grain factories," as they were known in the propagandistic jargon of the time, were interesting tourist attractions. But what good was such an attraction, Duranty asked, if they cannot be visited? The reason must be that the Soviets bit off too big a chunk in the drive to collectivize.[40]

At the Soviet Press Office, Duranty confronted the head of the department, making a little scene, an account of which found its way into the report of the First Secretary of the British Embassy, Edmond Coote, to Sir John Simon in London. Duranty had addressed a letter to Maxim Litvinov protesting the travel prohibition for Western correspondents and "stating that he intended to tour in the grain districts of the Ukraine on a certain date in September, accompanied by a colleague." In due course, Coote wrote, "[Duranty] received orally from the Press Department an assurance that he might travel on a fixed date later in the month." Coote apparently found Duranty's part in this exchange typically self-serving, for he added that

> Duranty proffered to be much irritated by this action, which he felt had cut the ground from under his feet by obliging him to recognize a ban upon his movements which infringed the liberty of the press. Nevertheless, he and his colleague have set out happily enough, and I have no doubt that, as a totally unqualified agricultural observer, he will have no difficulty in obtaining sufficient quantitative experience in tour hours to enable him to say whatever he may wish to say on his return.[41]

At long last, in September 1933, Walter Duranty headed south to report the famine.

Duranty spent the first few days going around the towns and markets in the North Caucasus, interviewing heads of the central administration of their political departments and other officials. At the beginning, he and a colleague who traveled with him were limited to a radius of about twenty to thirty miles, but later they ventured further afield.[42]

His first three stories were datelined from Rostov-on-Don, the heart of the famine district. Consisting mostly of praise for the operating procedures used on the communal farms he visited, they merited headlines like "Soviet Is Winning Faith of Peasants" and "Members Enriched in Soviet Commune" and "Abundance Found in North Caucasus." He spoke of happy workers, plentiful harvests, congenial conditions. Any talk of famine, he said in his dispatch published on the 14th of September, was "a sheer absurdity." Characteristically, he took a swipe at Frederick Birchall, calling him the "credulous American correspondent in Berlin," who had been taken in by the false estimates of the Germans. Duranty now felt safe enough to take back his original estimate of two million victims, and his dispatch was smug and self-congratulatory.[43]

But he spoke too soon.

Once he reached Kharkov, new evidence forced him to change his tack dramatically. "Early last year, under the pressure of the war danger in the Far East," he reluctantly admitted, the authorities took too much grain from the Ukraine. Meanwhile, a large number of peasants thought they could change the Communist party's collectivization policy by refusing to cooperate. Those two circumstances together—the flight of some peasants and the passive resistance of others—produced a very poor harvest last year, and even part of that was never reaped. The situation in the winter was undoubtedly bad. Just as the writer considered that his death-rate figures for the North Caucasus were exaggerated, so he is inclined to believe that the estimate he made for the Ukraine was too low.[44]

That estimate had been three times the normal death rate, but since Duranty did not mention in his dispatch the number of inhabitants or what the death rate was, the actual figure remained unspecified. The only clue he offered to the devastation was a comparison of the famine to the Battle of Verdun.

By this, Duranty no doubt intended to indicate the extreme gravity of the famine. But his symbol of ultimate carnage fell short of the mark. As scholar Marco Carynnyk has pointed out, during World War I people were dying at the rate of 6,000 a day; in the Ukraine, peasants had died at the rate of *25,000 a day*.[45]

There was a moral to all this, Duranty concluded, a lesson well learned: "Those who do not work do not eat."[46]

By the end of his ten-day trip into the area, Duranty had returned to the original tone of reporting that marked his first three stories—statements of praise and support for the commune in general. The government, he believed, had youth on its side, and even those who had once been skeptical of the success of the communal way of farming had now been convinced.

But, he stressed, the workers on the farms were new to the area, and many had been there for only six months. As to where they had come from and why they were there, he offered only vague and unsatisfactory answers.

"The Kremlin," he wrote, quite accurately, "has won its battle."[47]

Within days of returning to Moscow, Duranty turned in a full spoken report of his trip to the British Embassy, painting a much grimmer picture of what he had seen than the one in his dispatches.

It was a chronicle of hardship and cruelty. Near Rostov-on-Don, the Party had found it necessary to send everyone on the farm into the fields, with the exception of the top two administrative officials. The fields there had been full of weeds (especially *spiroea* and *Barbarea vulgaris*). Some settlements had been completely deserted, and among those that were populated, the differences were enormous. He noted the low numbers of livestock everywhere and a complete absence of small cattle and poultry. In the place of draft animals, there had been the promise of tractors, but the tractors he had seen had been ill-cared for, allowed to deteriorate, in many cases not in working order at all. Manufactured goods were in short supply.

Despite the optimistic tone of his dispatches, he estimated that the population in the North Caucasus and Lower Volga had in the last year decreased by some three million people, whether by death or deportation or desertion, he didn't indicate—but this figure was at direct odds with what he had published. He said frankly that some officials talked openly about attacks that befell Communist officials in the years 1930 and 1931. "In some places Cossacks had gone into the hills, formed themselves into bands, and raided the inhabited points."[48]

In Kharkov, conditions were much worse, and his movements were constricted by close supervision. Throughout the difficult year, peasants had flooded into the city, dying off "like flies." There was mention of houses standing open and deserted, of corpses.

Summing up, Duranty said: "The Ukraine had been bled white. The population was exhausted, and if the peasants were 'double-crossed' by the Government again no one could say what would happen." Finally he thought it "quite possible that as many as 10 million people may have died directly or indirectly from lack of food in the Soviet Union during the past year."[49]

This estimate was the highest ventured of victims of the famine of 1932–33.[50]

Disquieting stories about Duranty began to make the rounds. At a dinner party given for Anne O'Hare McCormick, roving correspondent for the *New York Times*, Duranty described "a picture of ghastly horror" in the Ukraine, estimating that many millions had died from the famine of the year before.

"But Walter, you don't mean that literally?" Mrs. McCormick exclaimed.

"Hell I don't . . . I'm being conservative," he replied, and as if by way of consolation he added his famous truism: "But they're only Russians. . . ."[51]

Predictably, this version of events belonged to Eugene Lyons, who never explained that Duranty's comment—"But they're only Russians"—was the bitter punchline of a well-known Georgian joke, intended no doubt to be an ironic commentary, since Stalin was Georgian. Lyons later revealed that the figure of dead which Duranty gave at that dinner party was seven million, at odds with the written report filed in the British Foreign Office.

Muggeridge reported a similar scene with less rancor and probably more accuracy; this time with Duranty banging the side of the sofa he was seated on with his cane, saying "You can't make an omelette without breaking eggs. They'll win. . . . they're bound to win. If necessary, they'll harness the peasants to the ploughs, but I tell you they'll get the harvest in and feed the people that matter."[52]

Muggeridge's anecdote is characteristic too for having Duranty quoting yet again his favorite proposition—the maxim about omelettes and eggs.

In writing his trenchant satirical portrait of the Western correspondents in Moscow during the famine year, Malcolm Muggeridge wrote a scene in which one newsman justifies the terrors of forced labor to another on the basis of the maxim.[53]

In another scene, the character Jefferson (Duranty) explains the proper interpretation of events going on in the countryside at the time:

"Of course there's a shortage in some districts," Jefferson said in a tone of emphatic finality. "No one denies that. You might even call it in certain rare cases a famine. But, as I said in a piece I sent a few days ago, you can't make omelettes without cracking eggs."

"You sure can't," Stoope agreed enthusiastically. "I like that phrase. No omelettes without cracking eggs. Very illuminating. Thank you."[54]

The phrase did seem to take on a life of its own, turning up again and again in Duranty's work—and in the work of others. It was to become the historical rationale for the whole of the process of modernization as epitomized by the Five-Year Plan.

The economist Alec Nove has perhaps stated it best: he lamented the creation of a situation wherein "certain behavioural tendencies" that exist at all times in any given society are unleashed, and although undesired, become unavoidable. "The saying that 'you cannot make omelettes without breaking eggs' has been used so often as an excuse for excesses and crimes, that we sometimes forget that you really *cannot* make omelettes without breaking eggs. . . ."[55]

It was only a short time after he returned from the Ukraine, a matter of some few weeks, that Duranty was to make his well-publicized trip to the United States, crossing the Atlantic alongside Maxim Litvinov who was on his way to Washington, D.C., there to work out the last few remaining details still to be settled before the recognition of the Soviet Union by the United States. What awaited Duranty was that "cheap triumph" predicted by a staff member at the British Embassy in Moscow who had identified this as the underlying motivation for Duranty's pro-Soviet stance.

He found that moment of triumph at the celebratory dinner in New York in late November 1933, when the crowd went wild, cheering and applauding their approval of "the great Duranty."

He found it too in the exclusive interview granted to him a month later, on Christmas Day, by Stalin himself. The sentiments of the great dictator, recounted so often by Duranty as proof of his importance on the world stage, seem in retrospect to take on new and sinister meaning. Said Stalin: "I might say that you bet on our horse to win when others thought it had no chance—and I am sure you have not lost by it."[56]

CHAPTER XIII

The Masters of Euphemism

On the 30th of December 1974, syndicated columnist Joseph Alsop was bowing out. His last column, intended as a warning against the dangers of "the reporter's trade," turned into a character assassination of Walter Duranty—a man who had succumbed, Alsop said, to "that fatal hankering to be fashionable, which is one of the trade's occupational weaknesses today." Alsop's shot at Duranty was based on the famine cover-up, and he singled Duranty out as the one who threw a blanket over the fire. "Duranty . . . covered up the horrors and deluded an entire generation by prettifying Soviet realities. . . . He was given a Pulitzer Prize. He lived comfortably in Moscow, too, by courtesy of the KGB."[1]

In discussing Duranty privately, Alsop was even more adamant. Duranty had been "a fashionable prostitute" who received every kind of reward from the Soviets—a car, an apartment, a mistress—in return for reporting what he was told. Said Alsop, "Lying was his stock in trade."

As the main source of information for the leftists of the 1930s, Duranty told them what they wanted to hear, fanning the flames of Western Communism. Everybody quoted Duranty—Edmund Wilson, Beatrice Webb, the entire group of intellectuals who admired the Soviet experiment. But, Alsop said, they had been quoting "a lower class

Englishman who had a thing about girls, a shrivelled little man with a clubbed foot and a limp . . . not a man ladies leapt naturally into the bed of."[2]

Close quarters, a keen sense of competition, jealousy, and gratuitous ill-will: these were the realities beneath the surface among the Western press corps in Moscow during the 1930s. Young reporters were quickly initiated into the personal rivalries among factions, about which the Soviet Press Office knew a great deal, and as often as possible, exploited, in a policy of divide and conquer, which for the most part worked out better than even they themselves could have hoped.

There was the Cholerton-Duranty split, which, even though the two men remained on speaking terms, had tended to spill over into the memoranda of the British Embassy staff. Cholerton was a ragged man, of large bulk and shaggy appearance, whose brilliance was depleted by chronic illness and a chronic propensity to drink his days away in a kind of hateful indolence in some part caused by daily witness of a regime he despised. Every morning, he lined up the bottles of red Caucasian wine for the day's consumption.[3] Almost as long in Moscow as Duranty, Cholerton had reported mainly for English newspapers, the *News Chronicle* before taking up the post with the *Telegraph*. He gained instant fame among the press corps for his witticism about the Soviet legal system. Asked by ingenuous Western visitors whether or not the Soviets respected the principle of *habeas corpus*, Cholerton responded deadpan that it had been replaced by the concept of *habeas cadaver*. The story was so good it surfaced frequently in the writings of the Western newsmen, most of whom passed it off as their own.

The young Muggeridge fell immediately and by natural inclination into the pro-Cholerton, anti-Duranty camp, and Cholerton entertained him with allegations of Duranty's earlier crooked dealings, all of which remained unspecified.[4] The British Embassy told a different story—of competition between a young Duranty and a younger Cholerton which had taken place in early days, led by the eminent German correspondent Paul Sheffer. After Sheffer was refused his return visa into the Soviet Union, according to the Embassy version, Duranty and Cholerton fell into a state of permanent disenchantment with one another.[5]

There was still another version of the split—one that didn't make it into the records of the British Foreign Office and that Muggeridge wasn't informed of by Cholerton. Knick told John Gunther "a superb story" about Cholerton, which Gunther wrote in his diaries.

Sometime during the mid-Twenties in Paris, Walter Duranty found Cholerton "down and out, brilliantly ejected from Cambridge, like Walter himself many years before." Duranty believed Cholerton was just what he had been looking for—"an able young fellow who would do his work for him for almost nothing." At the time Knick was still working in Moscow, and Knick gave Cholerton a story "and showed him how to write it." The next day, Knick ran into Cholerton and asked him if the story went "off all right."

"No," said Cholerton, "I met Sheffer after I left you, and he told me your interpretation was incorrect, so I wrote it over." Knick looked at the new version, and seeing it was wrong, harangued Cholerton into changing it back to the original version.

> [Cholerton] has been in Moscow ever since, eight or ten years. Year by year he hates the regime more. He married a White [Russian] wife. He does not dare leave the country, because if he does the government will take out its hate for him on his wife's family.[6]

William Henry Chamberlin came into the Soviet capital at about the same time as Cholerton, and had been there long enough for most people to forget that his original sympathies had been with the Bolsheviks. It was only after a considerable period of attrition that he earned his reputation with the British Embassy as the most dependable of the Western reporters. Knick said that Chamberlin ate only two things: beefsteak and chocolate, and he liked telling the story that when Chamberlin came to Berlin, Knick took him out for "the thickest steak he could find in Berlin and an enormous chocolate soufflé. Chamberlin was as happy and grateful as a child."[7]

Among the Moscow crew Chamberlin was a figure of fun, described as "fat, and prissy when he walked."[8] Stories circulated, some of them intentionally demeaning, about his addiction to chocolate, which, it was said, "he chewed steadily, reckoning to consume his own weight annually." This was the reason, perhaps, why "he came increasingly to resemble a figure of the Buddha."[9] He had special permission from the Soviet authorities to import the chocolates, and there were stories about how he was rewarded for writing by his wife Sonia, who rationed out the candies in return for words written.[10]

As to Sonia Chamberlin, Malcolm Muggeridge took special delight in depressing any delusions of grandeur she might have entertained.

Sonia was a low-built solid little woman with clumsy features and the shades of the ghetto still about her. There was also a strong flavour of Brooklyn, topped up with cultural and social aspirations, which took the form of wanting to have a salon frequented by professors and writers and musicians; people she regarded as having intellectual or artistic distinction.

In Moscow she was well placed to assemble a creditable salon; though no Madame du Deffand, a warmed house and modest refreshments were a big draw, and she had no difficulty in attracting to her evening parties quite an impressive collection of the more old-fashioned sort of Russian intelligentsia who had somehow managed to survive into the Stalin era. . . ."[11]

Louis Fischer, who wrote for *The Nation* and the Baltimore *Sun*, began as a fellow traveller, sticking to his version of the truth until well after the purges. He consistently reported the more favorable side of the Soviet experiment, generally staying out of the venomous exchanges among his colleagues. After Fischer's change of heart, Duranty always referred to him as "the rat who left the sinking ship that didn't sink."[12] But there seemed to be nothing particularly complicated about Fischer's character; no underlying currents of envy or of hate.

The same could not be said of Eugene Lyons, whose relentless attacks on Walter Duranty contributed to a continuing over-simplification of his character, especially in the years after Duranty's death. Lyons had always been baffled by Duranty's psychological distance from what was happening in the Soviet Union. He himself had come in full of enthusiasm; an eager admirer of Stalin, the Five-Year Plan, and all things Soviet. Ever since Duranty upstaged him after his cloying interview with Stalin in 1930, Lyons had been gunning for Duranty, searching for signs of weakness. When visitors came to Lyons for help, he admitted that he sent them on to Walter Duranty, but always with the proviso that "you'd better not tell him I sent you. . . ."[13] Publicly, Lyons accused Duranty of juggling his phrases, of leaving "a fuzzy margin of uncertainty" in his work, even in pieces that stressed the accomplishments of the regime.[14] It was a charge which showed no particular power of perception.

More damning were Lyons's charges of Duranty's complicity with the KGB. Lyons said Duranty had been provided with an automobile, a particularly comfortable apartment, and a mistress by the KGB. The car apparently always rankled Lyons, and he said that the loss of a leg seemed a small price to pay for the convenience of having an automobile in crowded Moscow.[15]

Later, grasping at straws, Lyons claimed that "Mrs. Ivy Litvinov, wife of the Soviet Foreign Commissar, once told him 'that she walked in on a scene at the Paris Embassy when Duranty was receiving some cash.'" Although he admitted this was not proof of Duranty's ultimate corruption, Lyons was happy enough to offer it up as the next best thing.[16]

There was in all this crossfire of accusation and belittlement an unpleasant smell of fear. Beyond the normal professional frictions among competing reporters, the corruption and treachery of Stalin's regime does appear to have made itself felt in the tiny elite community of men whose duty it was to understand and report what was happening. In the aftermath of the famine and of the purges, when the true nature of the regime at last became widely recognized, they would turn one against the other as they searched for someone to carry the blame.

They were privileged characters, all of them. Living in "a hardship post," they enjoyed a level of consumption inconceivable to the ordinary citizens of the country and falling just short of that enjoyed by the highest echelons in the West. Although the privileges were virtually the same among the newsmen themselves, somehow they managed to squabble over minuscule differences or imagined favoritism. They shopped in special stores where there were fine wines, superior goods, and foods of high quality.[17] Whether or not they were permitted special import privileges, such as Chamberlin enjoyed for his chocolate, the foods made available to all the foreign correspondents were superior to those of the Russians in every way: butter, eggs, ham, beef, and pork were all on sale in the special shops. Despite this, there were still complaints over the monotony of having to eat the same foods at one another's dinner parties. It took hours to purchase these foods, but almost every foreign correspondent had a servant to do it for him.[18]

The servants were cheap—about nine dollars per month in hard currency.[19] Linton Wells, who took over as head of the International News Service in Moscow, recorded that he could easily afford to employ two cooks, a butler, a secretary-interpreter, and a chauffeur. He also cheerfully reported the bitter complaints his colleagues had lodged when he wangled a particularly good apartment. At first lodged in a terrible place, with overflowing toilets and restricted space, Wells quickly procured, by negotiating with the head of the Moscow soviet, a "spacious, brand new apartment, more elaborate than was occupied by my less fortunate colleagues. . . ." Wells's apartment had a living and a dining room, a bedroom, office, kitchen and bath, hallway, and balcony.[20]

Eugene Lyons's apartment, even nineteen years after he had left it, was described as "a showplace" by later correspondents.[21] Like Wells's apartment, it was also spacious—with living and dining rooms, two bedrooms, office, kitchen, and bath. What made it an especially enviable place to live in was its convenient location, an easy fifteen minutes' walk from the Kremlin.

Lyons obtained his apartment by advancing $2500 to a group of "Moscow literary figures" who were building a cooperative and who desperately needed trucks to haul construction materials; in return, they gave Lyons his apartment. It was to become a well-known landmark for the Western community in Moscow, remaining in the possession of United Press "for almost forty years, the only one owned by an American news-media organization in the Soviet Union."[22] During Lyons's tenure in the city, it was the location for the "large parties" he and his gregarious wife Billie regularly gave.[23]

Linton Wells furnished his apartment with fine Oriental carpets, icons, prints, and tapestries from the commission shops that the correspondents frequented, using "valuta," or hard currency, to pay. Lyons too was extremely fond of the things available in these shops; his wife earned a reputation for picking up the very best bargains, which, it was rumored, added up to a six-figure sum on the New York market after the couple returned to the United States permanently.

During the years Duranty reported from Moscow, he was one of the highest-paid correspondents in the world.[24] Rumors abounded as to what that salary was, but Duranty kept the figure tightly under wraps. It was generally thought to be somewhere in the neighborhood of $10,000 a year, plus expenses, and Duranty's expenses were very high indeed, with frequent trips to Paris, Berlin, and New York.[25]

The apartment he lived in was smaller than Lyons's, and although it amounted to luxurious quarters in Moscow, it was nothing special by Western standards. Today, it houses a small government office. Surrounded on all sides by similar block buildings, it seems hard to imagine that it contributed to the accusations of bribery leveled at Duranty. The apartment was located at Number 53 on Bolshaya Ordinka, a heavily trafficked but well-located thoroughfare, just south of the Kremlin. Nevertheless, it takes the better part of a thirty minutes' brisk walk to reach the center of the city. It would have been impossible for the crippled Duranty to walk the distance. For him, a chauffeur was a necessity, and the *New York Times* agreed to pay his chauffeur's salary, as well as for the Buick that so excited the envy of Lyons.[26]

Like the other correspondents, Duranty had picked up most of his furnishings from the commission shops in Moscow, but, unlike the others, Duranty was never very much interested in his surroundings. There were no icons or Oriental carpets or tapestries to decorate his flat: such things held little interest for the bohemian Duranty. Living comfortably by Soviet standards, as he did, Duranty's privileges went no further than the general standard of all the correspondents.[27]

Putting aside the trivial and misleading accusations of Alsop and Lyons about Duranty's car and apartment, what about those concerning Duranty's mistress Katya?

It is safe to assume that Katya was reporting regularly to the NKVD, and to the GPU before them, since shakedowns of the Russian servants, translators, and secretaries of foreign correspondents were a common occurrence in Moscow. The newsmen generally assumed that any Russian associates would be required to report on a regular basis, and most of them put it down to their employees and girlfriends doing what they had to in order to survive. If a newsman needed to talk privately, he usually went to a public place or took a long walk. In any event, the girls the correspondents slept with were assumed to be informers.[28]

There is no reason to assume otherwise regarding Katya. Although those who knew her described her as "a simple, nonpolitical woman," she no doubt informed on Duranty as a matter of routine, whether from conviction or necessity. We can assume that Duranty was not exempt from the subtle pressures that could be brought to bear on correspondents whose wives, lovers, or children were Russian. Adding to the pressure upon Duranty was the birth of his son, Michael, who was claimed as a Soviet citizen; and certainly the timing of the pregnancy was significant. The question of how seriously Duranty regarded that pressure remains open to speculation.

According to his friends, Duranty believed that a mistress was to be kept strictly in her place, and in this regard, his attitudes were positively Victorian. Duranty kept Katya well in the background, only acknowledging her existence after the incident at Lindesay Parrott's party, and then begrudgingly.

It was common knowledge of a private fact, however, that Duranty was against Katya's having any children, and when, in 1932, she chose to have her child, the decision was hers alone. It is unlikely, nevertheless, that Duranty could ever have been manipulated by the birth of his son. Although he grew to be fond of Michael, none of his friends ever saw evidence of the family man in Duranty, not in the traditional sense, although he accepted the responsibilities he couldn't easily get out of.

He also tossed them aside as quickly as possible. The last thing that could be said of Walter Duranty was that he devoted himself to his family's well being. His reputation as a womanizer didn't dim after the birth of Michael. So far as Alsop's statement that Duranty was not the sort of man "ladies leapt naturally into the bed of," all evidence points precisely to the opposite conclusion. For whatever reasons, and some say the answer could only be found in the pages of Krafft-Ebing,[29] the only thing in Duranty's life that never failed him was this intense attraction he held for women.

Duranty was a complicated man, "more than a simple crook," as Muggeridge put it; and his motivations are not easily divined.

But there is no shortage of theories.

Harrison Salisbury, who was the correspondent longest in the Soviet Union after Walter Duranty, made something of a study of his predecessor, whom he found an intriguing if dislikable man. Not for a minute did Salisbury believe that Duranty was playing the game of the regime. "Every kind of brick was thrown at Walter Duranty," Salisbury said, "when it was obvious he was *not* in the pay of the KGB or anybody except the *New York Times*. Duranty was simply incapable of reporting something that broke the pattern he had established."[30]

Salisbury believed Duranty's major failure—missing the famine—resulted from the fact that he had for a year been pushing all reports of a famine aside, dismissing the stories because his "superior" knowledge of Russia discounted the possibility. When he finally did go down, said Salisbury, he gave it only a quick going over, doing a less-than-satisfactory job in an effort at "protecting his behind," to use Salisbury's words.[31]

Other newsmen who knew Duranty personally found it a laughable

231

proposition that he would sell out to the KGB. "It would have been totally out of character," Robin Kinkead said, insisting that those who make such charges fall to the extreme right or left.[32]

Malcolm Muggeridge opined that the war had exercised a great influence on Duranty, and in considering what made Duranty tick, Muggeridge reckoned that it was during the war Duranty had developed

> his basic impression of the world [as a] place where men, in their unutterable folly, tore out each other's hearts and probed cruelly into each other's souls; but where an intelligent minority, standing apart, directing, controlling, orating, buying and selling, writing, was able, not merely to be immune from, but even to profit by, these disasters.[33]

Muggeridge believed that Duranty had "made up his mind that he must belong to this minority," this ruling class, wherein, Muggeridge mused, Duranty felt safe. Also in Muggeridge's assessment was a homing in on the elitism that formed the basis for Duranty's philosophy of life. Having earlier attached himself to the idea of an intellectual elite, as explained to him by his friend William Bolitho, Duranty believed that whatever flew into the face of conventional wisdom stood a better chance of being right than any belief that was widely held. The masses, Bolitho taught Duranty, were little better than sheep, and all his life, Duranty adhered, with almost fundamentalist literalism, to Bolitho's philosophy.

But just as there was a basic difference in character between the two men—Bolitho had fought as well as reported the World War and emerged from it with a burning sense of commitment to right over wrong—there was a major difference between Bolitho's philosophy and the one that Duranty evolved. Duranty consistently discarded "moral issues," believing them to be irrelevant to the job of a reporter. Indeed, such issues had never interested the unconventional Duranty, who affected an immunity from any kind of morality throughout his life. The deeply held moral convictions of other men served only to make Duranty uncomfortable, and he liked to believe he was better than they were because he was free from the bonds that tied their hands.

At times, he appeared to worry about his remarkable lack of interest in the outcome of human affairs, and felt obliged to make public apologies of a sort:

> I did not particularly ask myself whether [a course of action] was a right path or a wrong path; for some reason I have never been deeply concerned with that phase of the question. Right and wrong are evasive terms at best and I have never felt that it was my problem—or that of any other reporter—to sit in moral judgment. What I want to know is whether a policy or a political line or a regime will work or not, and I refuse to let myself be side-tracked by moral issues or by abstract questions as to whether the said policy or line or regime would be suited to a different country and different circumstances.[34]

Duranty did not believe he was less realistic about the Bolshevik regime because he "failed to stress casualties so hard as some of [his] colleagues"; any more than the fact that in his war reporting he had stressed victories more than the losses in human lives.

> I saw too much useless slaughter in the World War—for that matter I think the War itself was useless, unless you believe that Hitler in the Kaiser's place is a benefit to humanity—to allow my judgment of results to be biased by the losses or suffering involved. I'm a reporter, not a humanitarian, and if a reporter can't see the wood for trees he can't describe the wood. You may call that special pleading or call me callous, and perhaps it is true, but you can't blame me for it: you must blame the War, because that was where my mental skin got thickened.[35]

Those were the reasons Walter Duranty advanced as to the source of his failures, as a reporter, perhaps as a man. But what of the other members of the Moscow press corps? How much better had they fared?

Ralph Barnes and the young William Stoneman had indeed, early on, traveled into the famine-stricken area, with the result that a ban was imposed against further trips by journalists. The only person who had actually defied the ban was the implacable Malcolm Muggeridge, who broke a story he discovered most people didn't want to hear about—one which proved to be the signal event in his life.

As well as Muggeridge, William Henry Chamberlin, Duranty's keenest competitor, turned in impressive reports of what had happened. Oddly enough, Chamberlin's dispatches to the *Christian Sci-*

ence Monitor, sent directly from the stricken areas shortly after Duranty's in September 1933, were thin and watery, probably under the threat of the Soviet Press Office. They amounted to little more than four short rundowns which, like Duranty's, were more notable for what they did not reveal than for what they did.

On the 13th of September, with a dateline of Pavlovskaya, Kuban, Chamberlin echoed Duranty's most optimistic statement: "The whole North Caucasus," he said, "is now engaged in the task of getting in the richest harvest of years, and shows few outward signs of recent poor crops."[36] The other two stories were equally evasive, mentioning only briefly "a famine last winter."[37] Chamberlin, however, was leaving the Soviet Union permanently, totally disenchanted with the regime. Presumably, what he witnessed on his "Tour of Inquiry" into the Kuban and Ukraine contributed to that decision.

In the middle of the following month, in what were clearly uncensored stories, he published a series of five hard-hitting and thorough articles in the Manchester *Guardian*, describing in detail what he had seen in the Soviet countryside a month before. The area, he wrote, was now governed "with laws of action no less ruthless than those of war. Ordinary standards of legality and economics have gone completely by the board in the course of [this] inflexible drive. . . ."[38]

It was true that the harvest for autumn 1933 was a bumper crop, but, Chamberlin wrote, there had been hunger "in all three districts which [he] visited, Kropotkin, in the North Caucasus, and Poltava and Belaya Tserkov, in Ukrainia." Both the peasants and local officials "in unanimous testimony" had said unequivocally "that hunger accompanied by quite abnormal mortality, had prevailed with varying degrees of intensity from January until June, when the relief of the new harvest began to be felt."[39]

In what turned out to be a logical follow-up to Muggeridge's dispatches written seven months before, he said that the dogs of the regions had been "all eaten up or perished during the hunger," and he spoke of tall weeds, boarded-up houses, and dead inhabitants.[40]

On his return to Moscow from the famine area, Chamberlin, like Muggeridge and Duranty, had reported his findings to the British Embassy. His estimate to them was of four to five million dead, about half as many as Duranty had indicated. His breakdown was that two million had died in Kazakhstan, a half a million in the North Caucasus, and two million in the Ukraine.[41] Later, Chamberlin would revise his estimate upwards to seven million.

Like Muggeridge, Chamberlin would find the famine the turning point in his life, and he returned to the United States a hardline right-wing conservative. During the 1950s, he would become a staunch supporter of Senator Joe McCarthy, moving from one extreme to the other in a reactive attempt at halting the growth of a system he knew to be malignant.[42]

On the other hand, the leftist Louis Fischer never reported the famine at all, and in fact was on a lecture tour of the United States when Gareth Jones's revelations were published. Even from that great distance, Fischer was not content to let the matter lie. From Denver, he called into question Jones's estimate of a million dead:

Who counted them? How could anyone march through a country and count a million people? Of course people are hungry there—desperately hungry. Russia is turning over from agriculture to industrialism. It's like a man going into business on small capital.[43]

In a way Eugene Lyons's record on the famine was worse than Fischer's. He had been among the earliest to hear of it, suggested at first by the investigations of his own secretary and confirmed later by the findings of Barnes and Stoneman. But Lyons declined to go into the famine-stricken area, or, as Bill Stoneman later put it, he "never went down to view the performance."[44] The zealous Lyons fulminated about moral and ethical issues, but he had shown little inclination himself to interrupt what was an unusually successful social life in Moscow by documenting what he would later not hesitate to call "Stalin's wholesale destruction of human life."[45] So far as Louis Fischer could see, Lyons "limited his Russian experience to Moscow social circles, rather than studying villages or factories . . . ." and seemed, moreover, "resentful at not receiving special attention from the Soviet leaders as reward for his communist activities at home."[46]

Besides Fischer's remarks, there were other, even less complimentary versions of Lyons's motives. His story of collusion between the Western correspondents and the Soviet Press official Oumansky over the Gareth Jones affair is a case in point. As of 1977, he was unable to remember who was at the party in which it was agreed to "damn"

Jones as "a liar," saying only that "presumably" Walter Duranty had attended. Nor was it clear whether it was a "general meeting" of the press corps, or where it had taken place, or whether Oumansky had done more than "hint" at what he wanted reporters to say about Jones.[47]

Lyons also bitterly denounced Duranty for being given a ten-day lead on the others when the area was finally opened up—a falsehood that has found its way into otherwise scrupulous academic accounts of the concealment of the famine. But Duranty was actually accompanied by Stanley Richardson of the Associated Press, and William Henry Chamberlin's first dispatch from the area appeared no more than two days after Duranty's first.

Suffice it to say, Lyons learned quickly that it was easy enough to divert blame from himself and onto others, by protesting much, and often.

Considering the entire Moscow press corps—Muggeridge, Chamberlin, Fischer, Lyons, Duranty, and all the rest—and their editors back home; add in the reports carried in the newspapers of France and even of Canada, the whole lot. What kind of record did they make?

In the free and unfettered press of the West, fewer words were actually published on the subject of the famine than the number of men, women, and children who had perished. Even by the most conservative estimates of famine victims, the average must have been something like one word printed for every 140 deaths.

But if few newsmen put themselves on the line, what about the Western governments and their embassies, whose papers prove conclusively that they monitored events all along and knew exactly what was happening?

Engulfed by their own problems during the Great Depression, their leaders, in effect, disregarded news of distant hunger in a widening expanse of apathy. The rise of Fascist Germany and Imperialist Japan eclipsed fears of the Stalinist regime, which seemed to many at the time to be at least a potential ally and even to offer answers where democracy had failed.

The U. S. State Department, under instructions to bring about recognition between the United States and the Soviet Union, viewed reports of famine in southern Russia as "unhelpful," rebuffing entreaties to intervene. Official response to requests for help from relatives of the victims and other interested parties seemed nothing less than Kafkaesque in its strict adherence to the principles of bureaucratic expediency.[48]

As for the British Foreign Office—informed of the devastation by Muggeridge, by Chamberlin, by Walter Duranty himself, each of whom no doubt believed, to some extent at least, that his reports were reaching those in a position to intervene—the diplomatic staff remained content merely to fill their files with cynical observations on the failings of the Western press corps. They themselves did nothing at all.[49]

At the highest level, decisions *were* taken, and Britain blithely continued importing Soviet grain.[50]

For five years after its publication, Bill Stoneman retained in his files a copy of Joe Alsop's attack on Walter Duranty. When asked for his evaluation of Duranty's performance, Stoneman mailed out the scrap of paper, with the comment that the column, "by another former friend of his will serve to explain my reluctance."[51] Shortly before his death a few months later, Stoneman had a change of heart. He wrote a long letter to a friend, taking a stand on the career of Walter Duranty.

It was true, Stoneman wrote—as if in answer to Alsop's charges—that Stoneman and Ralph Barnes had gone to the North Caucasus and the Ukraine when the famine broke out, and Duranty had not. "But," Stoneman said, "nobody else among the Moscow colony seemed to be in any hurry to cover the story." The way Stoneman saw it, Walter Duranty was "simply amoral, without any deep convictions about the rights and wrongs of Communism." He added a note "that Walter, when Moscow correspondent of the NYTimes, was no more cooperative with the local regime than other NYTimes men were, during the same period in Paris, Madrid, Berlin and London, with the authorities in their countries."

To Stoneman, Duranty would always remain

the grand old man of Moscow correspondents to whom everybody was referred if and when he was assigned to cover Paradise. Walter Duranty was invariably kind and considerate and went out of his way to help stray characters like myself. In return a hell of a lot of them took pleasure in criticizing him as "a fellow traveller." I have tried to avoid doing so.[52]

Did Duranty, in retrospect, ever change his views?

In his autobiography of 1935, *I Write As I Please*, he managed to avoid the subject of the famine altogether. Elsewhere in the same year, however, in the context of a general political survey of Europe, he came up with the first of several facile explanations to account for the event: in *Europe—War or Peace?*, he put the famine down to Nazi propaganda. Hitler's Germany had been conspiring against Soviet Russia, its agents conducting intrigues with subversive Ukrainian nationalists. "As the [secret service] was not slow to discover," the Nazis "utilized the food shortages caused by the collectivization movement to develop a great 'famine-in-Russia' campaign supported by the alleged testimony of German stock."[53] Not altogether surprisingly, Duranty decided not to pursue this line.

By 1941, he would bring himself to admit that he had made an error about "the extent and gravity of the 'man-made famine' in Russia during the fight to collectivize the farms in 1930–1933."[54] He had earlier referred to a desperate situation at the end of 1932, but at that time he had not admitted that the famine was "man-made."[55] He now sought to correct that impression.

By 1944, however, Duranty had found a justification for the Soviet government's actions, one that proved he had been at least partially right all along. During the process of collectivization, the Japanese war machine had taken the Manchurian capital Mukden, and in the months following, extended its conquest to the whole of Manchuria, including the jointly owned Chinese-Eastern Railroad of the Russians and the Chinese. This action represented a threat to the U.S.S.R., and Stalin met the challenge by diverting sufficient food supplies to the Red Army in the East to support what he no doubt believed would evolve into a major war between his country and Japan.

Looking back, Duranty remembered that both gasoline and grain had been in short supply, not only in the countryside, but also in the city of Moscow. It had been difficult even for foreign correspondents to get petrol. He had not understood at the time, but now it was clear that both food and fuel were being diverted to an Eastern Front where Stalin expected a war with the Japanese. Duranty explained what had escaped him then but was now so painfully obvious:

> That was the dreadful truth of the so-called "man-made famine" of
> Russia's "Iron Age," when Stalin was accused of causing the deaths of

238

four or five million peasants to gratify his own brutal determination that they should be socialized . . . or else. What a misconception! Compare it with the truth, that Japan was poised to strike and the Red Army *must* have reserves of food and gasoline.[56]

It was important that the Japanese believe the Soviets "awaited their attack without anxiety." Thus Stalin allowed the food and fuel shortages to be attributed to difficulties accompanying the first Five-Year Plan. "It worked," wrote Duranty. "The Japanese moved south instead of north, and China bore the brunt of Japanese Imperialism."[57]

It was no secret, either in 1944 or at the time it was happening, that the Japanese represented a threat to the Soviets in the East. George Kennan, working as an under secretary to Ambassador William Bullitt, had noted the fact in his records,[58] and many others have pointed to the dangers inherent in Japanese aggression against Manchuria, which had indeed by 1932 "provoked a Far Eastern crisis."[59] It was common knowledge also that Stalin had replenished his "war chest" that spring in order to meet what could possibly develop into open warfare with the Japanese.[60]

But Duranty's new-found theory hardly justified the events that accompanied collectivization; rather, it was an unseemly attempt at exonerating himself for what he knew very well was bad reporting. Instead of convincing anyone of his innocence, he succeeded only in drawing attention to his own failure.

By 1949, Duranty would become desperate: "Whatever Stalin's apologists may say," he wrote, "1932 was a year of famine in Russia, with all the signs of peasant distress which I had seen in 1921; the mass migration of destitute peasants from the countryside to towns and cities; epidemics of typhus and other diseases of malnutrition; great influx of beggars into Moscow and Leningrad." Although he still found the peasants and their revolt against the government's requisitions partially to blame, he was now willing to put the chief blame on the government for not anticipating "the muddle and mess," and taking proper measures to correct it, before it affected "the lives of millions."[61]

Thus, "the great Duranty," wriggling on a spit of his own making.

The Ukrainian Famine of 1932–33 remains the greatest man-made disaster ever recorded, exceeding in scale even the Jewish Holocaust of the next decade. It was Walter Duranty's destiny to become, in effect, the symbol for the West's failure to recognize and understand it at the time.

When all is said and done, he alone, of all the witnesses to the terrible events, had sufficient prestige and prominence to exert an influence. Walter Duranty stood perhaps in a unique position in the history of journalism. There had been before him, and would be after, journalists who told their particular stories, took their chances, and let the chips fall where they might: men with a compelling regard for the truth. Had Duranty, a Pulitzer Prize-winner at the peak of his celebrity, spoken out loud and clear in the pages of the *New York Times*, the world could not have ignored him, as it did Muggeridge and Jones, and events might, just conceivably, have taken a different turn. If Duranty had taken a stand, he might now be accounted one of the century's great, uncompromising reporters. But he did not.

When it came to discretion and expediency, the Western establishment that fêted him, no less so than the Kremlin, had found their man.

CHAPTER XIV

Getting Away With It

Robin Kinkead, who had always come and gone as he pleased at Duranty's place, suddenly found his way barred.

"You can't come in," the maid said, barely cracking the door, "we're having a baby."

"*Who's* having a baby?" Kinkead asked, incredulous.

"Katya!" answered the maid, equally incredulous that Kinkead hadn't known.

Kinkead was stunned. He had been there every day for months and never noticed any change in Katya. Duranty hadn't uttered a word on the subject. But when Kinkead returned the following day, sure enough, there was Katya, sitting up, with a baby boy in her arms; she had expertly wrapped him in swaddling clothes, peasant-style, his legs and torso immobilized, only his little arms left free.[1]

Duranty, for his part, was petulant. There is a story that he went into the bedroom to see Katya right after Michael was born and said, "Well, let that be a lesson to you, Katya!" and then stomped down the hallway.[2]

Thus did the fifty-year-old Duranty face the responsibilities of fatherhood, taking on with utmost reluctance the domestic chores that went with the territory. At the beginning of June 1933 he wired Knick in Berlin, asking him to pick up "four summer caps for Mike,"[3] and before the month was up, he was asking for more. This time he wanted "six thin knitted shorts or undervests of silk or cotton for [three-month-old baby], but thin and light. I am sorry to bother you," he apologized, "but this business of parenthood is Hell in Moscow."[4]

Whatever fondness he had for the baby took on the tone of a kind of quizzical pride. He complained to Kinkead that "Mike crawls around under the refrigerator and growls at me."[5]

Among the Western establishment in Moscow, there was renewed talk about what was viewed as an extremely complicated relationship. Each new generation coming to the Soviet capital found it more difficult to fathom Duranty's outdated attitude toward his mistress. Even to his close friends, he seemed downright Victorian. His epic womanizing, a source of disapproval among the women and not a little envy among the men, was directly at odds with his new role as father. But nothing had changed much: Duranty had always left Katya at home whenever he could, and after Mike's birth that turned out to be more and more often.

The young Henry Shapiro always considered the pair husband and wife because, under Soviet law, they were legally married. As to Duranty's steady refusal to go through with the ceremony, there was a rumor that his French wife wouldn't give him a divorce. About such speculations, however, Duranty himself said nothing whatsoever and, to all intents and purposes, continued to act exactly as before.[6] He had in his own mind an idea of the way life should be lived, fast-moving and decadent in that 1930s mold, and that was the way he would live it.

If the birth of his son had little ostensible effect on Duranty, the death of his father had even less. The elder Duranty died at the age of eighty-six, attended only by a distant relative, little more than a week before his only grandson was born.

William Steel Duranty had continued living in the house in Golders Green after his daughter died in 1930. A year after his father's death, Duranty wound up the estate with the National Provincial Bank of England, instructing them to send the proceeds directly to him in Moscow.[7]

The house was modest, but owned outright, and it might have provided Walter Duranty with a convenient second home in London. It was located close enough to the station to be convenient for central London, far enough away to miss most of the disadvantages of city living. But Duranty sold the house as quickly as he could and pocketed the proceeds, showing no interest whatsoever in returning to live in England.

During that summer after the death of his father and the birth of his son—as the famine raged in the south of Russia—Duranty made an escape and traveled for a solitary holiday to one of the Greek Islands. On his way, he stopped off in Athens. He took a room in an unfamiliar but pleasant enough hotel, and in the evening, sat by the window in the sitting room near the balcony.

He had begun to read a mystery novel when, as he recalled a couple of years later, the smell of burning carrion reached his nose. He hadn't noticed it until, unthinkingly, he sniffed at his own sleeve and thought somehow the smell was coming from his own clothes. He suddenly fancied that the odor was that of the burning flesh of human corpses, and he took the strange notion that his hosts were getting rid of the bodies of their guests, whom they had robbed. When this thought entered his mind, he became wildly frightened, believing "they" were waiting to kill him like the others.

Duranty limped across the terrace, as fast as he was able, and hailed a passing taxi, leaving everything behind. He checked into another hotel, and the next morning, sent a cab over for his things.

"Is that or is that not an utterly silly story?" he would ask later, when recounting what had happened. The idea of his own cowardice seemed to amuse him, and he generalized the story to represent the absurd fears men conjure up for no apparent reason.

Still, he reflected, the burning smell at the hotel had reminded him of the summer of 1918, during the second battle of the Marne, when he had come upon a German battalion that had been blown all to pieces, "torn bodies of men and horses all sprawled anyhow where the shells had hit them and stinking to high heaven, because they had been there for several days and the weather was hot." He attributed his odd behavior to that moment when he had sniffed his own sleeve. He remembered having done the same thing that summer during the war, and that simple action seemed to bring it all back.

Duranty protested that he did not believe in presentiments, but

243

admitted, nevertheless, that "there are some things in life which are not easy to explain." He whimsically persisted in the belief that his quick action in leaving the hotel might very well have saved his life.[8]

Back in Moscow, where he tended to spend much of his time either at home or at the bar of the Metropol Hotel, Duranty continued to occupy the position of reigning social host. George Kennan, who had accompanied William C. Bullitt over to his post as the first U.S. Ambassador to the Soviet Union, met Duranty in Moscow, later remembering that Duranty and his "lady" had been extremely kind to him. They had taken him skating "in the Park of Culture and Rest with some of their Russian friends."[9] For the young Kennan, it was "a wonderful and exciting time. The extreme cold of the Moscow winter was healthy and exhilarating. One could exist on four or five hours of sleep." At that time, the great blocks of buildings between the National Hotel and the Kremlin had not yet been torn out, and the three-car trolleys jangled as they made their way across the busy city. The building of the Moscow Metro was under way, and volunteer workers in mud-splashed overalls often jumped onto the trams.

"Even the political atmosphere was relatively favorable," Kennan remembered. There were, among the journalists, "uproariously informal parties," which included a large number of Russians as well as Americans.[10]

For Moscow and the rest of the country, it was like a last breath of fresh air.

At the end of 1933, Henry Shapiro, who had come to the Soviet Union as an attorney but quickly fallen into the newspaper business, was just starting out as a cub reporter with the New York *Herald Tribune*. He would later become the Moscow Bureau Chief of the United Press, serving in that capacity for some forty years. But for now, he was a rank beginner, with a good deal of apprehension.

On his first assignment, Shapiro was sent to cover the World Congress of Physiologists, which was being held in Leningrad. The famed Pavlov was to chair the convention. After Shapiro boarded the train, he discovered there was only one other person in his compartment—a diminutive man with graying hair. Beside his feet were a cane and a brown paper bag. It was "the great Duranty," and he seemed friendly. Katya had fixed sandwiches for the trip, and Duranty offered to share them with the young Shapiro. After a while, Shapiro admitted to Duranty that this was his first big story, and the complexity of the subject matter worried him.

"Don't worry," Duranty said. "There will be enough for everybody." What Shapiro remembered most about the incident was Duranty's steady effort to instill confidence into him, but secretly Shapiro was still "rather awed" that Duranty would be his only competitor.

As it turned out, Shapiro ran into a former professor from Harvard, where he had studied law, who had come to Leningrad to attend the convention. He explained every aspect of the sessions to Shapiro in non-specialist terms that he could easily understand.

Duranty, in the meantime, took up his post by the bar, where he spent most of his time during the conference. Each day, when Shapiro came in, Duranty would ask, "What happened today?" and Shapiro would tell him. All of Duranty's dispatches came from these little sessions.

Later, Shapiro would say, "Of course, I kept the best for myself." But Duranty didn't seem to care one way or the other.[11]

Very early in what would turn out to be a watershed year, Duranty had come up with an idea, one that paid off handsomely for him. He wired his old friend Alexander Woollcott the following message: "WHAT NEWYORK PUBLISHER SUITABLEST INTERESTEDEST BOOK OF FIVEYEARPLAN PAST FUTURE BY WELLKNOWN SOVIET DEPARTMENT CHIEF READY ABOUT MAY BEST REGARDS."[12]

Woollcott gave the telegram to the Viking Press, and Viking confirmed its interest, writing to Duranty by return mail. Although they had a number of questions to ask about the proposed book and were "reluctant" to burden him, they would not apologize since "in a way, you have brought this on yourself."[13] Duranty had no intention of being burdened. He put the manuscript into the hands of an American college professor in New York who took care of all the editing responsibilities, including the selection of what was to be included, and who dealt with all the tiresome business details. It turned out to be an extensive compilation of columns Duranty had written in the first twelve years of his tenure in Moscow. Published in the United States under the name *Duranty Reports Russia*, the book sold a respectable 4,156 copies, and it was successfully reprinted in Britain, where it was widely read.[14]

For his part of the enterprise, Duranty was responsible for dashing off a two-paragraph preface, leaving everything else in the hands of Gustav Tuckerman—except the collection of royalties.

Duranty now achieved, if not the impossible, at least the improbable. In April of 1934, he managed to talk the *New York Times* into keeping him on a retainer basis as a special correspondent in Moscow, while employing someone else to hold down the bureau. The deal he wangled was remarkably good, so good it must have stuck in Managing Editor Jimmy James's craw. Duranty was to be paid $5000 to spend approximately three months of the year in Moscow; the rest of the time, he was free to follow his own pursuits.[15] Duranty had in mind getting into radio, and he still nursed the desire to try his hand, unimpeded, at fiction. For years now, he had desperately wanted out of Moscow. The gloomy, gray, chilly capital held no special attraction for him, despite the speculations of those who believed his life there was irresistibly cushy.[16]

In the announcement of Duranty's changed status, the *Times* hastened to explain Duranty's point of view, so that his admirers would not believe it was an attempt to oust the popular newsman. Duranty, they wrote, felt he was entitled "to a certain respite from his arduous and successful labor in Russia during the critical and changing conditions since the war." He would still be at the disposal of the *Times* at critical junctures. "His reputation as by all odds the most outstanding correspondent of an American newspaper during all the years of his faithful and brilliant work at Moscow will remain unimpaired in the slightest degree by the change now made," the *Times* reassured its readers.[17]

That was the public statement. Behind the scenes, James continued to be suspicious of Duranty. He was, in fact, looking for a way to unload him, although the time was far from being ripe for such a move. The gossip being passed from correspondent to correspondent showed that maneuverings were continuing behind Duranty's back, nevertheless. Frederick T. Birchall, still in Berlin, continued to smart from Duranty's wrist-slapping during the famine—when Duranty had called him in print "the credulous American correspondent in Berlin." Birchall's anger was justifiable since he had turned out to be more nearly correct than Duranty.

Birchall passed along the news in strictest confidence to John Gunther that "it was not at all sure Walter's contract would be renewed after the present (first) year of the new arrangement." Gunther swiftly drew a conclusion Birchall would have found irritating. "Old Birch," Gunther entered into his diary, "is jealous of Duranty."[18]

For now, Duranty satisfied himself with getting what he wanted from the *Times*. He was replaced by Harold Denny, a reporter described by colleagues in unflattering terms: "a police-beat reporter," they would call him, or more damning still, "a this-and-that reporter."[19] Denny would find himself embroiled in the same controversies as his predecessor; but without Duranty's broad political vision, his penchant for style, and, most importantly, his thick skin, Denny's position would be tenuous, his reportage over the next few years remaining mediocre at best.

Duranty stayed in Moscow only long enough to celebrate the first birthday of his son before embarking for the United States. On his way he stopped off at Toulon, in the south of France, where he served as best man for John Wiley at the American diplomat's wedding, which was conducted in a curious ceremony "under the law of the gypsies." Irena Wiley would later record the event in a book she wrote, remembering with amusement that Duranty was not allowed to use his own pen to sign the register for fear he would use invisible ink, thus vitiating the legality of the marriage.[20] He would remain close friends of the Wileys for many years, often enjoying a game of bridge with them and going out of his way to see them whenever he could.

Duranty arrived in New York on the 9th of May 1934, on what was intended to be a personal trip to visit old friends and to bask in the limelight of his own success. The *New York Times* announced his arrival as if he had been a visiting dignitary. Surprisingly, Duranty had few comments to make to the reporters waiting for him when his ship docked. He registered only a few sparse remarks about dancing, shaving, cleanliness, and the theater life of Moscow before darting away, out of the public eye.[21] He was becoming the kind of celebrity reporters chased, and, curiously enough, he didn't like the reversal in roles.

Later he would learn to deal with his celebrity in characteristic style: "Look here, you fellows," he once said to a group of newsmen who were hounding him, "you know I'm a reporter on a regular daily newspaper, like yourselves, and dog don't eat dog."[22]

During his stay in the United States, Duranty demonstrated a real flair for public speaking. Asked to address the James G. Blaine Republican Club in New York City, he startled his listeners with a prediction that another major war was "near and inevitable." A summary of his speech was run in the *Times* under the headline, "Duranty Predicts a Major War Soon."[23] Although he declined to predict when and where the war would start, Duranty named Germany and Japan as dangerous threats to world peace. He pointed out that the imports of these two countries—"nickel, nitrate and other things used in munitions"—demonstrated their intentions. The result of his announcement was that the question-and-answer period, which lasted a full hour, had to be called to a halt by a reluctant master of ceremonies, who himself became carried away by what Duranty was saying.[24] Duranty, always referred to by the younger members of the press corps as "the great Duranty," was beginning to take on the role of international pundit and oracle on world events.

Duranty now published, at the age of fifty-one, an autobiography entitled *I Write As I Please*. The book became an unexpectedly brilliant success, hitting the bestseller lists and bringing its writer even more fame than he had imagined. *I Write As I Please*, published in 1935, turned out to be an extremely readable book, written in the style of a comfortable, chatty monologue, and it remains perhaps the only record of Duranty's distinctive conversational style, capturing the considerable, if highly perishable, charm of his talk.

The book was widely and favorably reviewed, most notably by Alexander Woollcott, who gave it a grand send off on "The Cream of Wheat Broadcasts," a popular radio show in which the well-known dramatist and critic reviewed books each week, virtually ensuring their commercial success.[25] The *New York Times* hailed the autobiography as a "no fanfare . . . tell-it-like-it-is" record of the foreign correspondent and his problems.[26] The reviewer summed up his evaluation by saying that Duranty would "make every reporter proud of the reporter's trade." Duranty had made mistakes, and he admitted them.[27]

But there was one man who no doubt viewed the book as annoying at best. Duranty had used the opportunity presented by his autobiography to slip in a very nasty aside about his boss Jimmy James. In the text, Duranty put the insult in the mouth of his dead friend William Bolitho, but it was hardly the kind of comment Bolitho would have made. No, the style was distinctively Duranty. In the episode, Duranty and Bolitho are enjoying a leisurely chat about the fate of newspaper men and how few of them manage to parlay their work into something more substantial than mere reporting. The question arises as to who among their acquaintances will ever become executive types in the newspaper game. Bolitho says he can think of only two: one of them is Paul Scott Mowrer, "who takes life seriously." The other, Bolitho is purported to say, is "your friend Jimmy James, who is as hard as nails and has ambition in every strut of his cocky little body. . . ."[28]

Duranty believed he could get away with it. Indeed, he was beginning to believe he could get away with anything. The antagonism between him and his boss, James, erupted on occasions into the open, with Duranty as often as not going over James's head to the publishers of the paper. Nor were his relations with other colleagues on the *Times* always congenial. He and his full-time successor, Harold Denny, did not get along, and whenever he was in Moscow, there were squabbles over trivial matters. Although Duranty no longer wanted to do the leg-work, he big-footed Denny whenever there were hot stories to report. In the arguments with Denny, indeed with James himself, Duranty usually won the round. No doubt about it, Duranty had emerged as a "star."[29]

Though now generally revered by all the media, underneath it all, Duranty remained as harebrained as ever. In *I Write As I Please*, he came up with a solution to the Great Depression: a scheme of privately administered programs of "social insurance" for businessmen, indeed for anyone who had income or who owned property. He asserted that such a scheme would take care of the whole problem facing the West instead of adding to the gigantic bureaucracy.[30] What is notable about the idea was that Duranty now considered himself a world figure of sufficient importance to influence the outcome of major social and economic issues. But whatever the heights to which his fame had carried him, his solutions were as outlandish as his earlier project to sell Oscar Wilde's "nephew" as a great American boxer to a naive Rumanian populace.

Duranty wasn't the only one with crazy schemes, though. An old friend of his from the Paris days contacted him about this time concerning an idea he had come up with of giving the Bolsheviks "a substitute for the god they have spurned"; namely, himself. Aleister Crowley had not been idle over the years. He still believed himself to be the incarnation of Satan, and, since he last saw Duranty, he had accumu-

249

lated a growing number of followers, one of whom had approached Duranty in Berlin. It was strongly felt among the Crowley set that the time was ripe for him to make his entrance into Soviet Russia.

Duranty could not in good conscience agree. At present, he wrote to Crowley, the "spiritual" had been completely eliminated from Russian life.

> I don't say for a moment it has ceased to exist, or won't come back—perhaps all the stronger from repression—but for the time being, the Kremlin won't hear of it. And what the Kremlin won't hear of doesn't count.[31]

Stalin, he continued, had succeeded in "applying 100 percent Marxism" where Lenin had failed, but Crowley shouldn't just take his word for it. He should come and have a look for himself. No one, Duranty wrote Crowley, who hadn't been to the Soviet Union recently could hope to understand what was going on there. It was good advice, true enough; but, ironically, Duranty himself wasn't following it.

He was now in and out of Moscow at a hectic pace, turning more and more to writing special reports for the *New York Times*' Sunday Supplement—"think pieces" that allowed him to ruminate about a new trend or an old event. During the mid–1930s, his actual reporting dwindled to a handful of dispatches. In all this was a steady erosion of his expertise, as Denny was left to handle the routine, day-to-day work. Although in the columns of the *Times*, Duranty had become resident specialist on all things Soviet, and his name a symbol of the new rapprochement between East and West, the fact is that he was now out of Moscow so often and for such long periods that his grasp of events in the Soviet Union was becoming more and more tenuous.

In early December 1935, Duranty wrote his good friend John Gunther that his autobiography was selling surprisingly well, and the reviews had been excellent. He was keeping a sharp eye on the market: there seemed to be some hope "for the book-writing game once more." In the same letter, Duranty lamented the fact he had not stayed in London with Gunther instead of pushing on to Moscow, because he had fallen prey to a "foul sore-throat" in Anvers and was still unable to leave his hotel room. "It is very tiresome," he complained.[32]

Just after the turn of the year, he again wrote Gunther, this time from Berlin, sympathizing with him over the "horrors of proof-read-ing." Gunther, who had just brought out his British edition of *Inside Europe* with the publisher Hamish Hamilton, had apparently been required to make extensive changes. Duranty was sorry Gunther had been subjected to "all that fuss and the cuts for fear of libel." Duranty said he thought J. H. [Jamie Hamilton] was "a trifle over-sensitive on the subject—on the once bitten twice shy principle—but of course libel actions and blackmail are the English form of what is known as gangster activity in God's own country. Milder, and less interesting to read about, but sometimes equally poisonous."[33]

In the same letter he mentioned that he was sailing for New York the following Tuesday. John and Irena Wiley, he said, "will join the *Manhattan* at Havre on Wednesday or Thursday, so we are looking forward to a pleasant trip if the Atlantic isn't too stormy."[34]

When Duranty's ship docked in New York on January 23, 1936, he carried two messages to the American people: first, that the popularity of Stalin was increasing in the Soviet Union and second, that the Soviets were building up militarily.[35]

Although the troubles between the Soviets and the Japanese had been settled by a negotiated sale of the railway which had formerly brought the two countries to the brink of war, Stalin remained suspicious of Japanese aims. And by 1934 Russia had faced a new threat.

Hitler's non-aggression pact between Germany and Poland demonstrated that Hitler had no intention of honoring the Treaty of Rapallo, a diplomatic agreement between Germany and the Soviet Union signed in April of 1933, which was the source of a "most-favored-nation" trade agreement. As the militaristic Nazi regime rose in power, Russia embarked upon a policy of Collective Security, which led, in September of 1934, to her entry into the League of Nations. By May of 1935, she had signed the Franco-Soviet Pact, determined to present a united front against the rise of Fascism. As tensions built up in Europe and the Japanese continued to be perceived as a threat in the East, the Soviets tried to stave off involvement in war.

International tensions came to a crisis when, in 1936, civil war broke out in Spain. The Nationalists were backed by the European Fascist states, with advanced weaponry being supplied by Italy and Germany; this, plus the discipline of General Francisco Franco's well-trained soldiers, gave the Nationalist side an insuperable advantage. It became apparent that the hastily formed coalition of leftists, Socialists,

251

and Trotskyites that made up the Republican side would quickly fold without some sort of aid. The Soviets rushed into the breach, bearing the brunt alone. Other countries stayed out.

Factionalism among the ranks of the Republicans took a further toll, and even with the help of the U.S.S.R. it became increasingly apparent during the course of the war that, if the Soviets continued to send arms and other forms of aid to the leftist side, they were doing so at the risk of war with the Axis powers. The Soviets reluctantly withdrew, but with renewed bitterness toward the Allied powers, whom they were now convinced would be only too happy to let them fight the battle against Fascism alone. France and Great Britain, Stalin believed, could not be depended upon to halt Hitler.

During this period, Duranty briefly covered the war in Spain on a retainer basis for the North American Newspaper Alliance (N.A.N.A.), a news service associated with the *New York Times*. His reporting, from the Republican side, was undistinguished and rather sparse. His only memorable piece was a short story—"The Witch of Alcazar"—a tale of bizarre sects and mysticism, fabulous in its sheer exoticism. In the story, a young man is captured by a group of fanatical cultists and very nearly meets a hideous death by slow torture, as part of their sacrificial rites. Although at times the story invokes a sense of helplessness and futility, it remains light reading, demonstrating ultimately that Duranty was shooting for a popular audience.[36]

He was also working by this time on a novel; he finished the first draft on the 13th of March 1936. He wrote to Gunther, "I am completely exhausted but think the poor child is good in parts, and with a little more revision may be creditable enough." Nevertheless, for the time being he shelved the book, called *One Life, One Kopeck*. He proposed in the meantime "a big reunion" with Gunther in London in early April, when they would "drink hail to books and down with newspapers."[37] He was planning a holiday in England in the summer.

Although Knick and his wife Agnes had visited Moscow frequently and for as long as three weeks at a time, she had never met Katya or Michael. Duranty made it a point to meet the Knickerbockers at the Metropol or the International, "never at his digs." So it was something of a surprise to Knick's wife when Duranty brought Katya and his son to England, where he was joining the Knickerbockers for a holiday on the "Cornish Riviera," a term the couples bandied about.[38]

Katya, according to Knick's wife, had always longed to go abroad. She wanted silk stockings and makeup, and she was rarely able to have them unless Duranty remembered to bring them into Moscow for her. Sometime while they were all still in London, Agnes Knickerbocker took Katya along Piccadilly to show her the sights. It was high excitement for the young Russian woman who had never before been out of the Soviet Union. During the taxi ride, Katya turned pale and said, "Oh my God, if there were this many cars in Moscow, we'd be killing people all the time."

At Harrods, though, Katya seemed to Knick's wife to undergo a change—from a rather shy and frightened girl into a condescending foreigner. Conscious of the great discrepancy between living conditions in Great Britain and her own country, it became a matter of pride to her not to appear too impressed by what she was seeing. When they lunched in the department store, Katya ate with great appetite but didn't say much about the food. Yet when asked to try some wild strawberries, Katya's enthusiasm got the better of her.

"Oh, *wild* strawberries!" she replied, as Agnes Knickerbocker recalled, and proceeded "to stuff them down with great dispatch."

Knick and his wife stayed in the same hotel as Duranty and Katya, once they arrived on the southwest coast of England. Both Knick and Agnes got the impression that the relationship between Katya and Duranty was essentially sexual, at least as far as Duranty was concerned. He made no secret of the fact he viewed women primarily as a form of relaxation and tended to enjoy himself more, Agnes Knickerbocker believed, when he was in the company of men, talking about politics and world events. But Katya seemed genuinely to love Duranty and was extremely pleased that Duranty's son looked very much like his father. The young boy was rather shy, but he loved being in the water, where he spent most of his time during the brief vacation.[39]

The holiday had an unexpected ending, with Katya complaining of being unhappy. She said that she didn't like being in the West and missed her friends back home. Duranty was forced to take her back to Russia early.[40] This would turn out to be the opportunity lost, and forever, for Duranty to bring his family to the West. His serene belief that things could go on as they were, that he could have his cake and eat it too, persisted, and Duranty played through the summer of his success, as was his way, without considering the future.

Wherever Duranty traveled, he carried his typewriter with him and worked, even during vacations. Besides his attempts at fiction and his new line in lectures, he carried on writing his armchair political analyses. In June of 1936 he reminded the American public that he was completely out of patience with politicians who said people had to choose between Washington and Moscow. Duranty sputtered out his frustration: "What I am trying to do, and have been trying for the last eighteen years to do, is to tell you people over here what Russia is like, not to say whether it's good or bad—that isn't my business either—but what it's like."[41]

He admitted in his letters to Gunther that he was more interested in "the newspaper" game than he often led people to believe. He could never bear wholly to desert it for "the fleshpots of fiction." But he issued Gunther a warning: he advised him not to allow himself to be driven by success into working harder than he ever had before. It had happened to Duranty, and he did not recommend it to his friend. Paradoxically, in the same letter that contained this sage advice, Duranty told Gunther that Simon and Schuster in New York and Jamie Hamilton in London wanted him to write a semi-autobiographical piece. It was obvious that, despite his counsel to Gunther, Duranty was going to accept the offer.

He knew Gunther would agree that "a novel is dearer to its author's mind" than the most successful non-fiction piece, but Duranty was intrigued by the idea that "one could write something in the third person saying a lot of things that none but the most shameless would dare say in the first person."[42]

Search for a Key did nothing of the kind. When the book finally appeared seven years later, it was a watered-down, washed-out version of *I Write As I Please*. There, Duranty's personality had emerged, giving the book a sense of authenticity. In *Search for a Key*, the fictional element of the book negated any impression of honesty, and any revelations it contained remained highly dubious. Characteristically, he shielded his private life from the curiosity of the public, totally omitting, for instance, any mention of his French wife or any accurate depiction of his childhood years. Historians who took this book at face value would publish embarrassing versions of Duranty's childhood, looking for deep psychological significance from episodes that never happened.[43] The only deep significance in Duranty's ramblings about his youth must finally be ascribed to his obsessive desire for secrecy about those years. If Duranty was a man prone not to talk about his private life, he was similarly prone not to write about it.

Instead, he had turned to a kind of trivial and oversimplified conversational style, which patronized the reader, possibly a result in part of his insistence on dictating much of this work. He was on the lookout for shortcuts, never a particularly good formula for quality.

Accompanying the *Times* review of the earlier autobiography, *I Write As I Please*, had been two casual snapshots of Duranty. They were taken by H. R. Knickerbocker's son, Hubert Conrad Knickerbocker, probably during the holiday the two families had taken together in the south of England. Looking surprisingly old, Duranty is seated in a wooden lawn chair on a terrace. Behind him is a cloudy sky and the ocean. Before him on the table is an empty glass and the remains of a meal. His book was lively and vibrant, but Duranty was tiring.

A short cameo of Duranty was published a year later, in 1936, in the *Saturday Review of Literature*, and yet another photograph of him appeared. By then, his hair had begun to thin and was turning gray. In the picture, he is wearing a vested suit with a tie as he sits upon a sofa looking extremely intelligent, keen—and old. A portion of a soda bottle appears in the foreground on the coffee table, signifying once again that there had been drinking. Duranty's eyes, described by friends as always "glittering," "shining," or "glinting," look weary and unfocused.[44]

Hitherto a moderate drinker by the standards of most journalists, Duranty had started to hit the bottle more than was normal, sufficiently so for friends to notice. Whether it was all that he had seen, or simply that he had overreached himself, the going was getting rougher.

The end of 1936 found an aging Duranty in New York.[45] He had made it to the city he idolized, taking his place as a celebrity among the very people he had admired all his life. He was the best-known newsman in the world, a man who could set his own terms. Duranty was "getting away with it," all right. But at the precise moment when his fame and success were at their height, he had begun to slip.

CHAPTER XV

Hypocritical Psychologists

Willie Seabrook had cooked up one of his schemes, and Walter Duranty immediately agreed to go along with it. Duranty would take time out for a weekend visit to Dutchess County, New York, where Seabrook had bought a farm, and the two "famous globe-trotting reporters" would interview one another, swapping "thrilling yarns," for publication in *The American Magazine*.

During the years Duranty covered Moscow, Seabrook's travels had carried him to Haiti, to Arabia, and to Timbuktu, where he had had the kinds of "adventures" that pleased his editors and made Seabrook himself an enormously rich man. He had lived in Greenwich Village, among the intellectuals of his generation, and in the south of France, among the trendsetters of the age—people who, it was said, would try anything for a few moments' diversion.

Since his earlier trip into the jungles of Africa to seek out the cannibals, Seabrook and his first wife had amicably divorced, and he had married his frequent companion Marjorie Worthington, herself a writer, who had been present when Jane Cheron Duranty flung a fish into the face of her husband.

But Seabrook had made another trip as well, into the dark interior of his own mind, and there was some question whether he would ever be the same after the visit. In his book *Jungle Ways*, in one of those statements that turn out to be hideously prophetic, Seabrook had ventured to express the hope that ordinary people would not view the sometimes "crazy extremes" of his behavior in such a light as to "consider it necessary to take steps toward having me locked up in jail or put in a lunatic asylum."[1]

Unfortunately, they had.

The "cannibal journalist," who entertained more than a fleeting interest in bondage and sado-masochism, was known for his outlandish antics, and to the jaded group of opium addicts, deviates, and pleasure seekers who had been his habitual companions in Toulon, these seemed part of a boyish pose which Seabrook could drop whenever he liked. But as his behavior became increasingly distorted by a growing dependency on alcohol, the clinically diagnosed sado-masochistic streak in his personality seemed much less an affectation than a real need to do serious harm to others and to himself. Just before his commitment, he and Worthington had returned to New York, and he began having penthouse parties that were monitored by a trained nurse "to see no one got really hurt."[2] Thus it was that with the utmost reluctance, Marjorie Worthington, along with one of Seabrook's doctors, succeeded "in the winter of 1933—just before Christmas, in having [him] committed, through the New York courts . . . to one of the oldest and largest insane asylums in the East."[3]

Publicly, Seabrook admitted only to the problem of "acute alcoholism," managing to get a readable, if rather self-effacing book out of the experience, one that made his addiction to alcohol seem regrettable but not unreasonable. But the Seabrook who greeted Duranty in Dutchess County sometime during the spring of 1936 was overweight, ill-kempt, and clearly disturbed; his seedy appearance reflected his continuing fight for his sanity. It was a fight that, despite his release from the sanatorium, was far from over.

For his part, Duranty contributed only a brisk three paragraphs to the article for *The American Magazine*, putting a brave face on Seabrook's misfortunes:

And when Seabrook returned from the dark places of the earth, he set out upon a stranger trek than he had ever known—through the dark continent of the mind. A victim of alcoholism, he entered a sanatorium to be cured. And his report of his life there among the insane is one of the most sane and illuminating documents of recent years.[4]

257

As for the rest of the interview, Duranty sat back and permitted Seabrook to carry the weight of it himself. As the more prominent personality, Duranty could afford to be offhand about his contribution, and he seemed to trouble himself very little, only to answer whatever he was asked, and pretty much enjoy the performance.

The four photographs accompanying the interview show Duranty, looking spruce and self-important as he sips a drink and gestures with his cigarette, while a sagging Seabrook struggles to stay alert. The way it turned out, the interview seemed a kind of exercise in schizophrenia wherein Seabrook would ask Duranty a question about his career; then, ask himself the same question, and then, answer it. A stenographer was there to keep track of Duranty's answers and Seabrook's doublegangers.

"If you ask a newspaperman to name the world's greatest reporter," Seabrook began, "he will probably say Walter Duranty. . . . Really, he is a citizen of the world."[5] Even as Seabrook was writing the article, he said, Duranty was packing his bags to return to Moscow, where he had made his name by reporting "bloodshed, famine, [and] political earthquakes." Duranty was the man who, more than anyone else, had been credited with accomplishing diplomatic recognition of the U.S.S.R. by the United States.

It was a moment Duranty relished, and he recounted to Seabrook an episode that continued to give him "great, real satisfaction." It had occurred when Duranty stood among the reporters in President Roosevelt's office, just after the President announced recognition of Soviet Russia.

> As everybody was walking out, he held me back for a moment and said cordially, "Well, don't you think it's a good job?" I felt proud and pleased, because for seven or eight years I had been trying, had been doing, all I could toward bringing about a Russian-American *rapprochement* and understanding. I felt I had some small, definite share in it. I suppose it was the greatest satisfaction I have ever had.[6]

This was the first time Duranty had ever referred publicly to a personal relationship with Franklin D. Roosevelt and to the enormous prestige he had accrued during that period of time he had dubbed "the ten days that steadied the world." Realistically, it is doubtful that Duranty had made any special effort on behalf of recognition, except as a temporary maneuver, adopted after he saw which way the wind was blowing. Certainly, it had not been an aim of his for any period of years, despite any protestations to the contrary. Such a sustained effort toward a desired political end would have been far beyond Duranty's capabilities. More likely, he had been dealt a particularly good hand, and he had simply played the cards—an opportunist who had no intention of missing the best opportunity that had come his way.

Ironically, when Seabrook asked Duranty what the most pathetic thing he had ever seen was, Duranty cited the famine—the 1921 famine. There had been two little boys, he remembered, "one about twelve and the other seven, sitting in the dirty courtyard of a house that had once been a fine mansion." The day had been a hot, dusty one, and all around the courtyard were children lying unattended, "dying at the rate of about 100 a day." Duranty noticed these particular boys "because they wore the remnants of two tiny uniforms, the sort which only sons of the nobility wore in the very expensive, smart Russian schools." He offered one of the boys a chocolate biscuit, but the child was far past being able to accept nourishment. He simply sat there, listlessly ignoring what Duranty offered. "Of course, they were dying. And nothing could be done about it, you see," he told Seabrook. This, in the final instance, was what made a thing "pathetic," that you could do nothing to help: that was the way Duranty saw it. As to the famine of 1932–33, which by his own estimate had killed many millions, Duranty made no mention.

Seabrook moved swiftly on to other questions, about the cruelest thing he had ever seen, and Duranty remembered an incident he had witnessed in 1919 in the bull ring in Madrid, when picadors, preparing the bull for a novice matador, "kept forcing the bull to rip open the bellies of blindfolded horses to tire it out, and to weaken it from the loss of its own blood, jabbing their lances into it as it killed the horses."[7]

Perhaps it was this incident in particular, among these various tales of cruelty and death, that caught the eye of Ernest Hemingway, who mentioned his liking the article to an editor friend.[8] Both Seabrook and Duranty, like Hemingway, had been part of the elite group of expatriates in Paris just after the war, men of letters who gathered at the sidewalk cafés as each made his bid for fame and success. Duranty was now a permanent fixture among the intellectual elite of the age, and as for Seabrook, despite his present disarray, he would always belong to it, admired rather than pitied for the extremes of his nature.

When Seabrook's turn came to recount the most remarkable moments of his life, his disclosures were very much more terrible than those of Duranty. His illness seemed to have left him no defenses, and the reader entered into his perceptions of reality with the same vulnerability that Seabrook himself must have felt. There was that awful sense of viewing events through the eyes of a madman. Seabrook dwelt obsessively on his "worst periods," saying they had been, if Duranty could forgive the term, "psychological."

> My blackest depressions, despairing, tragic, almost suicidal, have been when I've tried to write and couldn't. I think my worst moment came after I had signed a contract to write my first book. . . . I thought I could never write anything good, and wished I were dead.[9]

Duranty blandly agreed that to feel like that had to be "pretty bad," but it was, in the last instance, something he himself had never experienced. To Duranty's way of thinking, any moments of "profound discouragement" were nearly always related to "something physical— metabolism, indigestion, or something of the sort, if not actual pain." He could never remember a time he had "wallowed in despond except from causes of a physical character." There had been so many high-points in his life, times when he felt satisfied with himself and with life; periods of reward and enjoyment. He couldn't for a moment understand what Willie Seabrook was complaining about.

For his part, Seabrook said he envied Duranty his balance and peace of mind. It was true he had experienced moments of happiness, but

> real satisfaction is something that I've never earned or felt. I've never been satisfied with anything I've ever done. I'm afraid I could even shorten that sentence: I've never been satisfied with anything.[10]

Then too, he couldn't forget the horrible insight he had once had "in a drunken flash" that his alcoholism was "destroying Marjorie, my wife. . . ."

260

Duranty ended his three-paragraph blurb on Seabrook with typical media hype about Seabrook's condition: "He is cured now," he wrote, "of everything except his brave and boyish thirst for adventure."

Despite this upbeat version of events, Seabrook was far from cured. A diagnosed neurasthenic, he would, in the following few years take up an interest in witchcraft, dabble in the mysteries of the black arts,[11] and finally attach himself to a thorough-going sadist, who would find for him more horrific cures than could be thought of in a sanatorium.[12]

The only thing that could cure Willie Seabrook, as he himself well knew, was death. And in 1945 he took his life with an overdose of sleeping pills.[13]

But for the more fortunate Duranty, for now at least, there was something akin to a normal home life, during those brief periods of time when he actually was at home—in Moscow, with Katya and Mike.

He had developed a kind of fatherly pride in his son, and wrote to John Gunther that Mike was a chip off the old block, at least in matters concerning the fairer sex. At "the age of 3.8," Mike had found a girl-friend, an older woman of nine. Whenever she had to go to school instead of staying there to play with him, Mike yelled his head off, giving Katya occasion to make "flip remarks about heredity."[14] Gunther had apparently been sent an advance copy of Duranty's new novel, *One Life, One Kopeck*, and had complained that one of the characters in the book, a four-year-old Siberian boy, talked too much. Duranty fired back a letter asking Gunther, "and what do you know about being the father of Russian kids age three? Mike is still three months short of four, and even before I left Moscow in August, he talked quite as volubly as that creature in Siberia."[15]

Gunther apparently had a second complaint about Duranty's novel. This concerned the love scene in which Duranty's Russian hero at last consummated his love for a sturdy and faithful peasant woman. Duranty railed at Gunther's suggestion that the scene might have ended improperly. He had intended it to be of "the most tender and most romantic Romeo-Juliet character—although if I remember rightly those naughty brats did find out what made the nightingale sing. . . ."[16]

Duranty had pulled the typescript *One Life, One Kopeck* off the shelf where he had left it some two or three years before, and it had been largely due to the persuasions of Knick and Gunther that he had decided to publish the novel at all. But for the first time, Duranty received unfavorable reviews, and the book quickly flopped. Fletcher Pratt, who reviewed the book for the *Saturday Review*, complained that it was too fast and mechanical; it constituted a *reportage* instead of a novel.[17]

Indeed Duranty's novel was written in an unfortunate style—something between Soviet Realism and the King James version of the Bible. In it, a heroic Communist Party battles against the forces of injustice. It is filled with platitudes that tell the reader that a good Party member never fears death; he does what he is told "like a soldier."[18] Enter a prostitute who was "what life had made her, as Marx said."[19] She sells information concerning the whereabouts of the hero of the tale, nearly bringing about his death.

The romantic subplot is equally artificial, and distinguished by excruciating moments of embarrassment: "She called Ivan 'little brother,' but did she kiss him like a sister?"[20] In the end the hero is killed as he carries out his orders, dying so that his child can build a better communal future. The novel is highly propagandistic. The problem is that the propaganda is unconvincing, probably because Duranty did not believe it himself. All told, Duranty was ill-advised to bring this work out of the closet.

During the same year, 1937, Duranty brought out, at his own expense, in a special limited edition, a slim volume that contained one poem—*Solomons Cat*. Duranty liked to think of it as being in the style of e. e. cummings, one of his favorite poets. Improbably, the poem was an attempt to interweave events Duranty had witnessed in Moscow with the story of the Queen of Sheba's love affair with King Solomon. Graced with drawings of nude women in Solomon's harem, the poem offered insight into a certain preoccupation Duranty had with cats, which seemed in his mind to symbolize in some way or another the sexual relations between men and women. In a typical line, which defies poetic scan, Duranty asks the rhetorical question, "did you ever see such a thing in your life/as three white cats on leashes in Soviet Moscow in December 1921?"[21] These cats are kept on leashes because they "gallivant" away from home far too often. On the other hand, Duranty explains, in something of a non sequitur, some cats can perform miracles—like settling an argument in the harem.

All this aside, *Solomons Cat* is primarily a love poem about the

Queen of Sheba, a shrewd, no-nonsense woman, who loses her head
entirely when she falls in love with King Solomon.

> girls are like that you know be they prima donnas or phi beta kappas
> they can ride a man ragged with disdain and intellectual superiority
> until they begin to love him love his voice his eyes and his body
> then its the same with all of them and the most sophisticated fall hardest
> who start thinking they know all about it
> and that men are just a means
> for one spermatozoon amongst millions
> they know what they think and say what they think until they fall in love
> and love a man the way other girls do
> the same foolish antics
> and thrilling delights and mixture of awe and affection. . . .[22]

It is one of the more intriguing imponderables that this poem must
reflect, to some extent, that sensibility which had attracted so many
women to Duranty. It must also provide insight into the kind of sexual
fantasies he seemed to thrive on.

Along with this steady output of sleazy pap during 1937, Duranty
produced, somewhat surprisingly, a collection of not half-bad short
stories. A man who had made something of a fetish of his mistrust of
human emotions, Duranty did his best work when he made use of
irony as a literary tool. Although his collected short stories appeared
under cheap, slick, pasteboard cover, with garish colors to attract cus-
tomers, they were, after all, carefully crafted work reflecting a cynic's
sensibilities. Since they dealt mainly with the trials and tribulations of
the Russian peasantry, they did not go over particularly well with their
American audience, however. Duranty, the amoral, non-emotional
intellectual, who prided himself on his detached drawing room wit,
wrote in the tradition of de Maupassant, and when he was not trying
to chronicle highly romantic or emotional events, he could be both
provocative and entertaining.

John Gunther, on the other hand, during that year, was just finishing up another of his many revisions of *Inside Europe*, which had
become an international bestseller. It seemed obvious that Gunther's
work would soon outpace that of Duranty. To his credit, Duranty bore
Gunther no ill will; he predicted, somewhat sardonically, the book
would "outlast the wretched continent from which it took its name."[23]

A compliment to Gunther, the remark also indicated Duranty's belief, shared by most of the correspondents, that Europe would very soon plunge into war. In Moscow the Russians were arming themselves in anticipation of the expected fight, Duranty wrote to Gunther.[24]

But there had been other troubling events inside the Soviet Union, events which had been passed over by Duranty because of his sporadic movement in and out of the country. Professionally, he had chosen to ignore what had happened, leaving the day-to-day reporting to Denny. Personally, he had been very little touched, and except for one seemingly insignificant episode, uninvolved. But, in a way, that episode foreshadowed the terrible series of events that would follow.

Duranty's chauffeur Grisha was known throughout the Moscow colony for his wild and irresponsible driving. He delighted in plowing through the crowded streets at high speeds, laying on the horn and scaring the daylights out of anyone who was sitting in the backseat with Duranty. Linton Wells remembered that the horn on the car sounded something like the one used by the NKVD.

One day Grisha was as usual sounding his horn loudly when he pulled up at the address of a Russian friend of Wells and Duranty. The two men got out of the car and rang the bell. Although they were expected, nobody came to the door. It was the kind of stillness, Wells would later remember, that "could be felt." At last, a woman came, saw them and nearly "fainted from relief." The two men entered the apartment to find men, women, children "almost paralyzed with fear." They had been trying to conceal everything that could be interpreted as subversive, thinking it was the Soviet secret police. Wells recalled he had almost laughed, the incident seemed so humorous, but caught himself just in time.[25]

The increase of tension among the inhabitants of the country stemmed from an incident that had taken place in Leningrad at the end of 1934. A prominent member of the Politburo, Sergei Kirov, had been assassinated by a lone gunman, who was later identified as a member of the Left Opposition. He, along with about a hundred others who were allegedly involved in the crime, were summarily shot, and the matter was thought to be at an end. Almost immediately afterwards, though, there began a sweeping away of Party officials in a ruthless and unanticipated purge, which climaxed, in August of 1936, in the first of the so-called "show trials." To the consternation of most observers, Grigory Zinoviev and Leo Kamenev, survivors of the Old Bolshevik group from the decade before, along with other important figures, publicly confessed their complicity in the murder of Sergei Kirov as well as their participation in a far-reaching conspiracy designed to overthrow the government of the Soviet Union.

In the months leading up to the first of the show trials, and just after, the country was plunged into a new and stifling atmosphere of repression that marked a change from what had seemed, since the unhappy days of collectivization, a steady progression toward a new openness between Russia and the West. Duranty now found that his closest Russian friends, "men of unimpeachable standing," most of whom he had known for years, stayed as far away from him as they could, pretending only a slight acquaintanceship. In the most serious cases, they simply dropped from sight, unacknowledged.[26] "Things got so bad that if you telephoned to some office asking for someone who as it happened had been purged, they'd often reply that they'd never heard of him, that no such citizen had ever been employed there at all."[27] Into this highly charged atmosphere Duranty was about to be drawn, and the year 1937 would find his name once more thrown into a maelstrom of controversy.

On the 23rd of January 1937, what the scholar Robert Conquest has termed "another gruesome little pageant,"[28] the second of the show trials, began its relentless course toward a preordained conclusion. Sixteen prominent officials—including Karl Radek, the outstanding Soviet journalist; Grigory Piatakov, former assistant commissar for heavy industry; and Grigory Sokolnikov, former vice-commissar for foreign affairs and ambassador to Great Britain—were accused of attempting to destroy the Soviet government by plotting with Germany and Japan. The exiled Trotsky was implicated in the proceedings, charged *in absentia* with cooperating with the Nazi regime in order to regain his former position of importance. According to the bill of indictment, Trotsky had master-minded the plan to assassinate Stalin and other high officials in the Soviet Union, enlisting the accused in his nefarious plotting. He had sent messages to them written in invisible ink and he had smuggled in funds, helping to arrange for the false passports and papers that were to be provided for the actual assassins. Roughly sketched, the scenario was for Germany to get the Ukraine and Japan to get Sakhalin and part of the Pacific littoral of Siberia.

Predictably, Western response to this second trial was one of confusion, and there was a half-willing reluctance to believe in the guilt of the accused. If the confessions were true, the reasoning went, it demonstrated that conditions within the country were so bad that avowed and dedicated Party members would conspire with Fascists to overthrow their own government. If untrue, the trials were an indictment of the entire system in the Soviet Union.[29]

Among the Western establishment stationed in Moscow, the disarray among both correspondents and diplomatic staff was not unprecedented. A whole new generation of reporters had entered the capital since Duranty had struck his deal with the *Times*, and few of them had sufficient experience to do more than make educated and occasionally shrewd guesses. There was Henry Shapiro of the United Press, who by now was considered to be something of an old hand, and Harold Denny, who had taken over from Duranty the day-to-day operation for the *New York Times*. Others included Joe Barnes and Joe Phillips of the New York *Herald Tribune*, Charles Nutter and Dick Massock of the Associated Press, Normal Deuel, like Shapiro, an employee of UP, Jim Brown of the International News Service, and Spencer Williams, of the Manchester *Guardian*. On those few occasions when Duranty was in the city, he joined this group for a drink or two and a bit of conversation in order to catch up on what was happening.

Joseph E. Davies had replaced William C. Bullitt as the U. S. Ambassador, and in light of recent events he now initiated discussion sessions with the correspondents which took place each night at the Embassy after the proceedings of the day.[30] Davies offered perhaps the foremost record of the absolute confusion they all experienced in the face of the show trials. From the beginning, Davies himself believed that the trials showed "the threads of a conspiracy to overthrow the Soviet regime,"[31] and he was later to write that the general consensus of opinion among the newsmen at his late-night gatherings was that "the truth at least in part" was emerging.[32]

Sometime during the trial, Duranty handed Davies a cable from a group of prominent journalists in the West which was marked "Strictly Confidential." It was a request for clemency for one of the defendants, a former editor of *Izvestia*. The telegram sought to verify Vladimir

Romm's loyalty to the Soviet Union and to credit him to a wide extent with the popularization of the Stalinist regime in the United States. Using Duranty as a go-between, these opinion leaders in America were asking that the cable be certified to the judges of the trial by Ambassador Davies. Davies concluded, however, for reasons of his own, that it would be improper for him to intervene, and he wrote a letter to that effect to Arthur Krock of the *New York Times*: "The poor devil," Davies said, "did not leave himself a leg to stand on."[33]

Davies was far from being the only Westerner to be taken in. There was a tendency to accept at face value the confessions so freely given during the course of the trial, a steady disbelief that these could be staged. In his book describing Moscow as he found it in 1937, the respected German novelist Lion Feuchtwanger—who had earlier condemned the trials of Zinoviev and Kamenev as "utterly incredible" and a "frightful artistry"[34]—found, once he was inside the Soviet Union and could actually observe day-to-day developments in the second trial, that his doubt "melted away as naturally as salt dissolves in water."[35]

That Duranty had in 1936 seen nothing sufficiently remarkable in the trial of Zinoviev and Kamenev to justify comment did not in any way discourage him from giving out a new and fanciful thesis regarding the current proceedings.

He reported to *The New Republic* that this latest trial had inevitably led him "to the conviction that the confessions are true." If Westerners found them incredible, Duranty continued, then they did not understand the peculiar Russian temperament. Inviting skeptics to read Dostoyevsky, he spoke darkly of "the Russian soul," implying that there was in the very nature of the Russian psyche a willingness to assume guilt that other nationalities might find fantastic.[36] He was referring to a school of thought, sometimes referred to as the Dostoyevskian dilemma, that only through a ruthless callousness toward individual human beings could the great mass of mankind be spared from suffering. As a result, there was a special dignity in the assumption of guilt that went along with the carrying out of certain unpleasant tasks, in order that others might be spared these tasks and remain free from guilt. There was even considered to be a certain superior virtue in sacrificing oneself to the employment of "evil means for worthy ends."[37] Presumably, those now making public confession of their guilt fell within the bounds of this philosophical concept.

Within a week of Duranty's unveiling of his latest theory on the Soviets, Trotsky, now living in exile in Mexico City, publicly attacked Walter Duranty and any like him "who tried to explain the confessions of the accused in the Moscow trials by references to the 'Russian soul.' . . ." Trotsky had planned to deliver a telephone speech to a waiting audience of nearly 7000 of his followers in New York City, but he was prevented from doing so because, somewhere south of Monterrey, the wire was cut. The frantic Trotsky had raced all over the city from telephone to telephone, trying to get his speech through, to no avail. At last, his prepared speech was reluctantly read out by one of his adherents in New York City.

In the text, Trotsky called Stalinist Russia a "madhouse," and he then assailed Walter Duranty specifically, for spinning out a nonsensical theory concerning "the Russian soul."

"No, the Messieurs Duranty tell us, it is not a madhouse, but the 'Russian soul.' You lie gentlemen about the Russian soul. You lie about the human soul in general," Trotsky said. In times like these, he continued, to concern oneself "with psychological divinations" was criminal and absurd. He condemned the Stalinist regime "for betraying Socialism and dishonoring the revolution," picturing the leadership in Moscow as being "dominated by a clique which holds the people in subjection by oppression and terror." The trial, Trotsky continued, was a "frame-up," that lacked "objectivity and impartiality," and he volunteered to go before an international commission to prove his innocence.[38] Finally, he called Duranty and all those who agreed with him "hypocritical psychologists," who tried to explain away the terrors of the regime with glib and facile phrases.[39]

Trotsky's direct attack on Duranty would prove to be of inestimable value to Duranty in keeping his name before the public. His publishers were privately so impressed over the Trotsky controversy that they wanted Duranty to write a special answer to the charges which they would then publish. But, Duranty wrote to Gunther, he didn't "propose to engage in controversy with Trotsky or anyone else on this matter," although he had, he admitted, rewritten a chapter about Trotsky in a book he was working on, changing fairly standard stuff to materials "of a somewhat polemic character."[40]

In the meantime, his theory touched off a new round of controversy in the editorial pages of *The New Republic*, with American intellectuals lining up to debate the merits of the case against the defendants. *The New Republic* carried letter after letter, first one subscribing to Duranty's thesis, then another condemning the Stalinist regime and siding with Trotsky.[41] The blizzard of mail that descended upon *The New Republic* offices was so contradictory in character that, at last, the editors decided to call a moratorium upon all letters on the subject unless they revealed new information.[42]

But if his theory on "the Russian soul" had not pleased Trotsky, neither had it pleased Stalin, as Duranty was soon to discover, for suddenly the censors in Moscow refused to pass any of Duranty's dispatches on the topic, excising all reference to the idea that appeared in his work.[43]

Most improbably, Duranty would find his theory denounced from an unexpected platform some two years later. In 1938, during the last and greatest of the show trials—that of Nikolai Bukharin and Alexei Rykov, former members of the Politburo and by far the most prominent men to be publicly prosecuted during the purges of the 1930s— Bukharin himself would condemn Duranty's theory from the dock. In his lengthy confession of complicity in the widespread plot to overthrow the government, Bukharin stressed that he and others who had been on trial had retained their "clarity of mind," dismissing as absurd any hypothesis that would explain the confessions as somehow emanating from a mysterious "Slavic Soul."[44] As a sophisticated intellectual fully conversant with Western ideals, he denied that any archaic or superstitious influence held sway over his actions, fully discrediting the concept of the *âme slave*.[45]

In a piece that was first published in *The New Republic* in 1937 and later as a preface to a revised edition of *I Write As I Please*, Duranty revealed the pages "of a somewhat polemic nature" he had written about Trotsky.

In them, he delineated three phases of development in the Soviet Union. The first phase was one of "Open Controversy," when Lenin was alive and ruling, and free-ranging debate was allowed in policy decisions made in the Politburo. The second he termed a period of "Reconciliation," which lasted from 1928 to 1934, when former Trotsky supporters recanted their sins, paying abject lip service to the now-powerful Stalin. The third phase was one of "Secret Conspiracy," which lasted from November of 1934 to the present. By now Japan and Germany had infiltrated the ranks of the Soviet leadership, while Trotsky, like an exiled monarch, had become the center of a conspiracy to overthrow Stalin.

The three phases outlined by Duranty amounted to an almost total vindication of the findings of the show trials. In effect, Duranty was taking at face value the government's contention of actual wide-spread conspiracy which involved many men in the highest echelons of government. But now, Duranty wrote, "their Trojan horse was broken, and its occupants destroyed."[46]

The article laid the foundation for what would become his "Fifth Column" thesis, one which is still advanced today by Stalinists to rationalize the necessity for the purges of the 1930s. Unlike the French and Belgians, the theory went, who were riddled by saboteurs and traitors from within, the Soviets had managed to eliminate subversive elements who might have contributed to their defeat in the war.

In 1941 Duranty published his book *The Kremlin and the People*, and in it the "Fifth Column" thesis emerged full blown. To understand the trials, he wrote, one first had to understand the Soviet judicial system, which was very different from the Western concept of justice. Conducted when the Soviets were on the verge of war, the trials more nearly resembled court martial proceedings than a Western trial court. It was the rule in Soviet treason cases, he reminded his readers, not to bring a case to trial unless the defendant had already confessed his guilt. In fact, the entire purpose of the trial was to demonstrate to the populace what had already been decided *in camera*.[47] The "masochistic eagerness of the accused" to admit their guilt could be understood only if one had insight into the propensity of the Russian to paint a gray complicity in the blackest of terms.[48]

If Russia was to enter the war devoid of saboteurs, the trials and accompanying purges had been a necessary evil. The actual conduct of the purges, he admitted, had been carried out with unnecessary brutality. Duranty ascribed the blame, however, not to Stalin, whom he insisted was not the prime instigator, but to "the sadist lunatic, Yezhov," who was the chief of the NKVD during its worse excesses.[49] Stalin himself was guilty only of becoming so dissociated from actual day-to-day events that other, lesser men were given free rein to wreak havoc by indulging their sadistic impulses on the Soviet populace.

As to Stalin, Duranty believed implicitly that history would ultimately vindicate him.[50]

In 1949, Duranty would develop a second tier to his "Fifth Column" thesis. During those years when the world concentrated its attention on the Great Purge, he would write, the mass of the Soviet populace was enjoying a level of prosperity never before attained in the country. To a large extent unaffected by the political upheaval going on around them, these ordinary citizens remained grateful and loyal to the government who had so bettered their standard of living.[51]

As for the number of resulting casualties from the Great Purge, Duranty's estimates, which encompassed the years from 1936 to 1939, fell considerably short of other sources, a fact he himself admitted. Whereas the number of Party members arrested is usually put at just above one million, Duranty's own estimate was half this figure, and he neglected to mention that of those exiled into the forced labor camps of the GULAG, only a small percentage ever regained their freedom, as few as 50,000 by some estimates. As to those actually executed, reliable sources range from some 600,000 to one million, while Duranty maintained that only about 30,000 to 40,000 had been killed.[52]

As to how and why such a thing could have occurred, Duranty fell back on an old technique—the fable—in this case, an old Russian folk tale, which he now put forward as offering the vital clue to the events of the late Thirties. There was once a magic mill, he wrote, that ground out salt whenever it was needed. One day, the mill was stolen by a villain who found he did not know how to turn off the magical machine. It made hills of salt, mountains of salt, threatening to cover all the land. Then, the thief hit upon an idea: he would drop the mill into the middle of the ocean to solve his dilemma. And that is why, Duranty wrote, the sea is made of salt. Without belaboring the point further, what Duranty intended to say was simply that things had gotten out of hand.[53]

It was true, Duranty admitted, that many had suffered during the purges; many too had died unnecessarily, perhaps weakening the Soviet Union in crucial ways just before the war. But Duranty retained the right to view the matter for himself and in his own way. He would not follow the herd and join in what had become, during the intervening years, a general condemnation of such methods. Instead, he would follow Bolitho's credo, and think out the matter for himself.

Earlier, Duranty had explained his personal goals in life as wanting "to see and hear new things . . . not for any profound purpose, good, bad, or indifferent, but for my own interest, entertainment, and in lat-

ter years, amusement." Now, nearly fifteen years after writing this dis-
tillation of his own philosophy, he restated his position. It had changed
very little, but it showed the logical outcome of a life lived on the
peripheries, without moral commitment to his fellow beings.

> But while you are living you live, and I think that life is fun. I think it
> is fun to search and to try to find things out. And to match my guess
> against others, to think that I am right, not they. Which is why I have
> written so much about the Treason Trials.[54]

CHAPTER XVI

A Citizen of the World

William Shirer, born in Chicago, raised in Cedar Rapids, streetwise and country-boy shrewd, was one of a new breed who had turned up in Paris in the mid–1920s to take their chances. On the surface, he seemed a mild-mannered, ineffectual type who wore thick spectacles and puffed away blandly on his pipe, giving an appearance completely at odds with his complicated temperament and awesome intelligence. By the time he was thirty, he had worked his way up to the position of chief of the Central European bureau of the Chicago *Tribune*. In the following few years, he would report from practically every major capital on the Continent, as well as locations as far flung as India and Afghanistan. Quite simply, Bill Shirer knew everybody in the newspaper business in Europe.

On the same day his wire service gave him notice that his position had been cut back, Shirer received a telegram from Edward R. Murrow of Columbia Broadcasting suggesting the two of them have a talk over dinner. Until then, radio had been viewed mainly in terms of its entertainment potential, with an emphasis on oompah concerts and "You-Are-There" travelogues. Now, Murrow told Shirer, the medium was about to change its role dramatically. He and a handful of other men were trying to put together a series of linkages between the major capitals of Europe in a hurry; in time, they hoped, to cover a war that was rapidly approaching. With the built-in prejudices of any hard-boiled newspaper man, Shirer might not even have taken the trouble to listen to Murrow's spiel if he hadn't been out of a job.[1]

That was in August 1937. By December, Shirer had become an old hand at arranging broadcasts out of Berlin, and sometimes Vienna.

Shirer had known Walter Duranty for years, an acquaintanceship that grew into friendship through their mutual regard for John Gunther. Shirer was also close to John and Irena Wiley, Duranty's frequent companions and traveling partners. Then too there was the Knickerbocker connection. As a wire-service man stationed in Berlin, Shirer had worked side by side with Knick, bumping into Duranty frequently at bars and restaurants.

Now deeply involved in what would become a legendary team of war-time broadcasters, Shirer was shuttling between cities, learning everything he could about transmitters, time zones, and telephone lines, taking on stringers, and generally familiarizing himself with the bumpy ride of transatlantic broadcasting.

Christmas of 1937 found him in Vienna, at the Wileys' house for the traditional feast. John Wiley was serving a term there as the U. S. Chargé d'Affaires, and Duranty, "as always," was also present. Many years later Shirer seemed to have the hazy recollection, maybe it was only something overheard, of a lengthy discussion regarding Walter Duranty's Russian son. Duranty was apparently trying to get his boy out of Russia, and the Wileys had agreed to help, maybe even to adopt Michael, to try to facilitate the matter. But there had been resistance from unexpected quarters, Shirer remembered. The boy's mother didn't want to leave the Soviet Union, and she was resisting letting her son go without her.[2] Michael was turning out to be extraordinarily bright, and maybe that was why Duranty had begun to think about his future. The boy, not quite four years old, had already begun reading in Russian, and had picked up some English along the way.[3] Otherwise, after dinner, Shirer and Duranty holed up for a time to discuss the political situation in Moscow.

Duranty was staying in Vienna for a couple of months, and only a few weeks before, at Shirer's request, he had done his first radio broadcast. There had been some worry in New York that Duranty's voice was too high for transmission, and wouldn't carry well. But on the day of the broadcast, Shirer received a telegram from a friend of his in Chicago, saying his "clear, bell-like voice" had come through just fine.

Shirer was surprised that anybody could mistake Duranty's clipped British accent for his own, especially a close friend who should have known better.[4]

True to form, the *New York Times* carried a short piece on Duranty's first broadcast under the headline: "Duranty Discusses Situation in Russia," giving a rerun of what he had said. The U.S.S.R. was frightened of Germany to the west, of Japan to the east, and was looking at China with renewed apprehension. There was a pervasive feeling of isolation, of facing hostile forces alone; that was his gist.[5] Duranty, Shirer remembered later, was working for N.A.N.A. on a regular basis, as well as doing his normal three-month-a-year stint in Moscow for the *Times,* and over the next year or so, Shirer would run into him often, asking him to broadcast on a number of occasions.[6]

This first time though, Duranty had seemed unusually subdued, probably because he was still recovering from an operation, described only as an "abdominal ailment." Caught short on one of his trips to the United States, Duranty had been in Maryland when the illness hit, and he had entered Johns Hopkins University Hospital at the end of July 1937. Doctors had at first described his condition as "good," predicting he would be able to return to work after only a week. But Duranty wrote Gunther from his hospital bed that "this operation was rather more of a job than they seemed to think ... and will require about three weeks in bed or anyway three weeks at the hospital here." He felt okay, he said, if one discounted the fact it seemed like "an elephant had been treading on my stomach."[7] In any event, he planned to leave the hospital as soon as he could, and sail back to Europe almost immediately. Characteristically, Duranty kept to his schedule, and was back in the saddle before he should have been, taking it for granted he would mend quickly.

By autumn, he was back having drinks at the Metropol, chatting with Henry Shapiro, whom he now met on a regular basis. For the new generation of reporters, Duranty's family had moved into the background, and people almost forgot they existed. Shapiro was one of the few people who ever saw Katya and Michael. They had moved from their old flat on Bolshaya Ordinka to another of the apartments in the same building, and Shapiro dropped in from time to time for coffee, talking with Katya and playing with Mike. The kind of man who has a good word for everybody, Shapiro seemed determined to remember Duranty as a dedicated family man.[8]

275

Duranty didn't measure up to Shapiro's assessment. He still had an eye for the ladies, and was off, at a moment's notice, on one of his frequent tours for N.A.N.A., criss-crossing the Continent, and settling in for months at a time at locations distant from his family, in order to write unimpeded and without interruption.

In Moscow, Ambassador Davies had begun to give his frequent off-the-record press conferences which encompassed everyone in the American press corps, including Duranty, whenever he was in town. The talks tended to center on the actions of Germany, which, everyone agreed, would soon force Europe into war. In March 1938, Hitler had been welcomed as a conquering hero into his native Austria, annexing it to Germany without so much as firing a shot. With Hitler's eye falling next on the Sudetenland —the strip of land in Czechoslovakia bordering Germany and inhabited by a German-speaking population— events continued to take their downward course. "Duranty," Davies recorded in his diary, "was very pessimistic. From what he knew of recent developments in Czechoslovakia and the Balkans, he was of the definite opinion that Hitler's war was approaching very rapidly."[9]

By August of 1938, Duranty was fussy, irritable, under strain to deliver 80,000 words to a publisher while sweating through "the hottest summer Moscow has ever known." It didn't make things any better that the *Times* had asked him to stay put for about five weeks while Harold Denny went out on vacation, he complained in a letter to Gunther. The truth was, Duranty felt he was above filling in for Denny, resented being asked to do it, forgetting entirely that the *Times* was entitled to something for the considerable sum they were paying him. Other things were getting on his nerves. His secretary had been ill, and he complained to Gunther that "it makes life more difficult when one has trained oneself to dictate and gotten used to someone taking care of letters, accounts and business details." He was "snowed under with work" and "harassed by heat."[10]

Gunther had agreed to go onto the U. S. lecture circuit and signed up for a lucrative tour arranged by the agent W. Colston Leigh, who was offering Duranty a similar deal. With a guarantee of $1000 per week "or more," plus all expenses, Duranty admitted he was beginning to feel the temptation. He kept thinking of all that money, he wrote to Knick, held directly "under my nose, which begins to twitch like a rabbit's in response."[11] He outlined Colston Leigh's offer in detail to

Knick, saying he thought maybe he would agree to a month from mid-November, unless things broke in the Far East or in Czechoslovakia.

By late September, however, the crisis had finally arrived, by way of the Munich Conference. Chamberlain, Mussolini, and Daladier agreed to Hitler's plan to annex the Sudetenland, in a continuing policy of appeasement that astounded almost everyone, not least the Czechs themselves, who had hoped for backing from the Western powers. The Soviets viewed the agreement with anger and suspicion. They had been openly committed to the defense of Czechoslovakia, but, in what they considered a glaring omission, they had not been invited to attend the conference at Munich, forced to stand by as an outsider, watching the betrayal of Prague to the Nazis. Stalin's sense of isolation increased as it became clear that all his attempts at collective security with Great Britain and France had failed.

Instead of signing up with Colston Leigh, Duranty agreed to a tour for N.A.N.A. from Paris to Bucharest and ending up at Warsaw, with various points in between. At his last stop in mid-November, he ran into William Shirer once again, and the pair made plans to meet for dinner.

The events that had taken place in Europe since Shirer last saw Duranty had been brought home to him by his partner Ed Murrow. In Vienna during the *Anschluss*, the young and inexperienced broadcaster had witnessed the wave of anti-Semitic violence that followed the Nazi takeover. He was unfamiliar, until then, with Nazi methods at first-hand. There was looting, breaking of shop windows, acts of brutality against Austrian citizens, indiscriminate killings of anyone on the streets thought to look Jewish, a rash of suicides. One night Murrow had been having a drink when a gang burst suddenly through the doors and threw a victim across the floor of the bar, kicking and beating him. With the cheers of the crowd ringing in his ears, Murrow had paid up and left in a hurry, nearly overcome by sickness before he could get out of the place.[12] Shirer, who had been in London at the time, was dependent upon Murrow to look after his wife and the newborn baby which had nearly cost her her life.

Confronted by events like these, even a hardened newsman like Shirer was feeling more and more depressed. November 11 had been particularly trying, although Shirer had managed to keep a sense of humor about the whole thing. He had spent the day attempting to set

277

up a broadcast, but found himself befuddled by technical problems. They had finally got the broadcast out, but it had been a tangled, inept mixup because the engineers had not been able to provide hookups at the right moments. The evening he spent with Duranty was more of the same.

Duranty was crazy, wild, out of control. He was having, as Shirer put it, one of his "Russian nights," and insisted on going to a little Russian place he knew about. Caught in the middle of a blizzard, Duranty nevertheless delayed the pair by insisting on giving the droshky driver all of his directions in Russian. The café, he kept assuring Shirer, was fabulous, worth all the trouble. In the meantime, Shirer recalled later, "the wind from Duranty's Russian steppes was whipping the snow in our faces, and after what seemed an age the driver finally pulled his dying nag up before a decrepit old building."

"Café Rusky?" Duranty had shouted, jumping from the carriage and making his way up the steps—only to discover that the driver had carried them to a Polish brothel. Back in the carriage and through a "curtain of snow," Duranty and the driver fell into a bitter argument, with Shirer growing increasingly restive as "the snow piled up on us." Finally, sometime after midnight, they made it to Duranty's café, where they were greeted by the smell of good food, the sound of balalaikas playing, and plump, cheerful waitresses who "would warm their backs against a great porcelain stove...."[13]

Years later, Shirer would still remember the evening with pleasure, and in seeking the right word to describe Duranty, he finally settled on "Bohemian."[14] To Shirer, Duranty was a likeable companion who knew the value of comic relief against a background of terror and hardship.

Duranty continued with his frenzied movement from place to place, without digging in anywhere. By now, he was approaching sixty, he had had his first real bout with illness since losing his leg, and his expertise on the Soviets was on the wane. Moscow seemed unbearable to him; he no longer really belonged, resented the time he had to spend there. Nevertheless, he remained confident his success with *I Write As I Please* would repeat itself with another work he had in the pipeline—if only he could manage the time to work on it.

By the end of 1938, John Wiley had been appointed Minister to

Latvia and Estonia, and Duranty decided to spend a week in Tallin and then join the Wileys in Riga for a month or so. He checked into the Hotel de Rome, but quickly fell into a foul mood. His work on the semi-autobiography, *Search for a Key*, had turned into a slog, he wrote Gunther, and he now found himself "paying the penalty for having wasted eighteen months in trying to write a book which I hoped would be the distilled essence of all my ways and wisdom, but find instead that it isn't even good enough to poison mice with. . . ."¹⁵

Duranty's down mood led him to seek the counsel of John and Irina Wiley, and what eventually transpired was the decision to cold-storage the book, at least for the time being. Back in Moscow, he again wrote to Gunther, full of excuses for what he had done, but insisting he really did expect to finish it by August "at the latest, in nice time for Fall publication." He was confident that if he could make it back to Riga for the spring, he would be able to finish it off.¹⁶ As it turned out, Duranty would not complete the book until nearly four years later.

He was also still feeling the effects of the controversy over his "Russian soul" thesis, which continued to be attacked from a variety of fronts. He made an oblique reference to the matter to Gunther, saying, "Unless I'm mistaken, the current news from Moscow does not tell people what they want to know, but I think it may be done through magazine articles, doubtless with certain risks and perils, but those I am prepared to take."¹⁷ This statement was probably more bravado than anything else, as Duranty faced a personal situation that was growing more serious.

He was nowadays relying more upon the magazine format to air his views on Moscow because he and James were continuing to argue, and with the *Times* at last showing reluctance to feature some of Duranty's more fanciful theories, James was beginning to win the battle. Duranty had admitted privately to an old friend, who also had no love for James, that of eight articles he had submitted to the *New York Times*, James had seen fit to publish only two. Duranty saw it as a form of suppression, a personal thing. "The *Times* never suppressed my stuff," Duranty complained to George Seldes. "*James* suppressed my stuff." James apparently had a ready answer for anyone who accused him of killing stories of particular writers. He pointed out that the *New York Times* published 150,000 words every day but that they received over 400,000 words. It was impossible, therefore, to accuse the *Times* of suppressing anything, simply because they were obliged to leave out 250,000 words daily.[18]

As for his other projects, Duranty had put off Colston Leigh to take up another quick tour for N.A.N.A., but he was seriously reconsidering Colston Leigh's offer. He hoped to be in New York by April, and maybe he would make a quick round on the circuit then, just to give it a try. But spring found Duranty still in Moscow, where things seemed to him to be in a state of flux, portending important events. He was angry that the *Herald Tribune* had chosen this precise moment to pull out Joe Barnes, "who knows more about it than anyone and was the best friend I had here, and lived quite near me."[19] Now Duranty fell back more heavily upon the person who was virtually his only close friend left in the city, Henry Shapiro.

Shapiro had noticed a change in Duranty, however, one that had at first been practically undetectable, but was beginning to emerge as a full-fledged problem. Duranty's increasing dependence upon the bottle, which no doubt carried him through the here-and-there lifestyle he insisted upon, had grown more pronounced. Shapiro saw Duranty drunk frequently. Whenever he finished a piece of work, Duranty drank. He preferred Scotch, but at parties, he imbibed "rather too freely," as Shapiro put it, of whatever was going, champagne if it was available, ordinary wine if it wasn't.

Then too, he would turn up at Shapiro's flat, which was also the UP office, usually in the afternoon, asking Shapiro if he had a drink. Shapiro would take a bottle of Scotch out of his drawer and sit with Duranty for a few minutes before going back to his work. When Shapiro returned later, he often had to call Duranty's chauffeur to take him home. What amazed Shapiro was that the next morning Duranty would call him, "clear as a bell," talking excitedly about what he was going to write that day.[20]

Meanwhile, the events that Duranty had believed were in the air materialized in a surprise announcement that caught everybody up short, including the most experienced correspondents in Moscow. On May 3, 1939, Litvinov was replaced as the Minister of Foreign Affairs by Vyacheslav Molotov. Shapiro had been sitting in his office with Harold Denny and Norman Deuel, relaxing a little before they listened to the main news of the day—the 4:00 p.m. broadcast. When the announcement that Litvinov had been relieved of his duties came over the air waves, the three men looked at one another in disbelief. They jumped into a car and drove straight down to the Foreign Ministry where they found the chief of the Soviet Press Office looking very worried. He had apparently been given no information about the new appointment. At the time, none of the correspondents believed him, chalking his protestations down as one more trick by the Soviets to try to prevent them from getting the full story.

There ensued a comedy of errors. The correspondents all jumped back into the car and rushed over to Denny's apartment, which, like Shapiro's flat, also served as his office. "Everybody," Shapiro recalled later, "phoned back sensational stories to their papers." Denny, according to Shapiro's euphemistic version of events, was "suffering from a cold," and he had been drinking steadily throughout the day, with the result that he was in no condition to phone back a story.

"You have a long time," Shapiro said to Denny. "Why don't you put your telephone call off?" Then Shapiro came up with an idea. He telephoned Duranty, who happened to be in town. He explained that Denny was in no condition to write this story, and he asked Duranty if he would write it for him.

"I'll do nothing of the kind," Duranty told Shapiro. "I'm going to write my own story. I have my own point of view. I wouldn't touch Denny's story."

In something approaching despair, Shapiro and Denny's wife hatched out a scheme: that Shapiro himself would write Denny's story and cable it in for him. The little comedy reached its climax the next day when a puzzled Denny, who remembered little of the previous day's happenings, received a telegram from Jimmy James, who was, Shapiro reported later, absolutely furious. In future, the telegram said, when both Denny and Duranty were in town, they were instructed to send only one story on a topic. The *Times* office had no use for two stories on the same subject—*especially* when they contradicted each other so much.[21]

Duranty had attributed the removal of Litvinov to ill health, dismissing any speculation that it might indicate a major change in Russia's foreign policy. But this sanguine interpretation would soon be proved incorrect. Since the Munich Conference, the efforts of the Soviet Union to achieve collective security with France and Great Britain against Germany had been frustrated. The dismissal of Litvinov and appointment of Molotov to the position of Minister of Foreign Affairs was a signal to the Germans that the Soviets were ready to deal seriously. Molotov, as Chairman of the Council of People's Commissars as well as an important member of the Politburo, was not directly associated with the policy of collective security, as Litvinov had been. There was also the glaring fact that Litvinov was Jewish. In fact, secret talks between the Germans and Russians had been going on since April.

Although negotiations among the Soviet Union, Britain, and France continued throughout the long summer months, the Western powers failed to come to terms with the Soviets, their attitude one of continuing confidence in the policy of appeasement. They were shocked out of their complacency on the 23rd of August, when, to the surprise of the entire world, a German-Russian agreement of strict neutrality was signed in Moscow. Within days, Hitler attacked Poland, and Great Britain and France were compelled at last to declare war on Germany.

Duranty, like most pundits on Soviet affairs, did not believe the Russo-German pact would last. In a lead article for the *Atlantic Monthly* published in the early spring of 1940, he suggested that, although Russia and Germany were "to all intents and purposes allies," the natural animosity between the two countries, and indeed their rival systems of government, dictated that such an alliance could not last. Duranty himself was "reluctant to believe it, if only for the reason that it is the view which the German Propaganda Bureau has been so eager to advance."[22] It was, he wrote, an alliance built upon "a temporary community of interests and a joint dislike of others, which is surely a slender foundation on which to build a permanent edifice."[23] As such, the question was not, would it last? but how long *could* it last?

To Shapiro, Duranty admitted that he had more faith in the pact than he had written in his *Atlantic* article. The two men, who saw one another practically every day whenever Duranty was in town, got into a good-natured argument one afternoon, as they sat in Shapiro's office. The question of how long the pact would last came up, and Shapiro said categorically, "Within a year, the Soviet Union and Germany will be at war with one another. This pact is a shotgun marriage."

As Shapiro remembered it, Duranty became irate, pounding his cane against the floor for emphasis. "Henry," he said, "you're crazy! Do you think Hitler is insane enough to attack this country?"

"Yes, I'm willing to bet you, Walter."

Duranty not only agreed to the wager, but offered odds of ten to one. Shapiro countered by offering odds of a hundred to one.

"It's going to be a shame," Duranty said, "taking money from a child."

Musing over the incident many years later, Shapiro tilted his head to the side and shrugged.

"Unfortunately, I won."[24]

For the time being the Soviets' pact with the Germans ostracized them from the Allies, and a series of moves by the Red Army increased their unpopularity in the West. The Soviets had occupied parts of eastern Poland, and they now signed "mutual assistance pacts" with the Baltic states of Estonia, Latvia, and Lithuania, agreements that would eventually lead to the occupation of those countries by Soviet troops. The Red Army turned next toward Finland, demanding that the Finns move their boundary some twenty miles farther away from Leningrad in exchange for Soviet territory elsewhere, so that the Soviets could build defense bases. When the Finnish government rejected the deal in late autumn of 1939, the Red Army invaded. Surprisingly, they met with fierce resistance from the Finns, leading to early reverses. This in turn led to the widespread belief that, if the Soviets ever did engage in warfare with Germany, they wouldn't last long.

The invasion of Finland was considered to be even more serious a breach than the Russo-German pact, and major Western news organizations began pulling their men out of Moscow as a kind of protest against the action. They had other reasons as well for withdrawing the newsmen, one of the most serious the growing severity of the censorship.

Sometime before these events, Harold Denny had encountered difficulty in his dealings with the Soviet Press Office, which threatened on at least one occasion not to allow him back into the country after a leave of absence. As early as 1937, Duranty had received warning from the *Times* that, were Denny not permitted to return, he too would be expected to vacate the country instantly.[25] There was nothing singular in the Soviets' dislike of Denny; to a large degree, they were unhappy with all the Western correspondents then reporting out of Moscow.

Eventually, Denny was reassigned elsewhere, and a somewhat dour Englishman, G. D. Gedye—described by one colleague as "vain and testy"²⁶—was sent in to take his place. Predictably, Duranty didn't get along with Gedye any better than he had with Denny, but Gedye, with his authoritative personality, was less easily pocketed by the older man.

At the end of January 1940, Jimmy James sent a cable to Duranty outlining the "extraordinary difficulties" Gedye had been experiencing under a new censorship that, since the purges of the 1930s, had stiffened to an almost intolerable degree. James asked Duranty's opinion about keeping a correspondent in Moscow under these conditions. Duranty quickly wired back a short answer, the gist of which was that, although present conditions seemed to preclude worthwhile coverage, things were bound to improve as the new censors learned from experience. In his opinion, the *Times* should keep a correspondent in Moscow because possible future developments required it.

Duranty followed up his short telegram with a lengthy Press Wireless letter in which he outlined in detail the current difficulties in dealing with the Press Office. The new men, he said, were not especially accomplished at English—let alone cablese. Their cuts were frequently illogical and inconsistent, and at times, they would take something out in one paragraph that they overlooked in another. Overall, they seemed very much aware of their responsibilities, and since the purges, extremely nervous, frightened of the effects a mistake might have in terms of their own survival. Duranty agreed that the new restrictions were "calculated to fill conscientious correspondents with despair," but he insisted that what could happen later might compensate for any frustrations suffered now.

Duranty's assessment, based upon more than twenty-five years of experience under one censorship system or another, was considered essentially correct by a later correspondent for the *Times*, Harrison Salisbury, who would cover the Soviet Union during the years of the Cold War, under conditions even more harrowing than those faced by Gedye. According to Salisbury, Duranty's advice was "an extremely sound analysis of the Moscow situation (completely fair to Geyde and to all parties)."²⁷

Jimmy James would choose not to take it.

As for Duranty, he was in a fair way toward fulfilling his fantasy of becoming "a citizen of the world," the role Willie Seabrook had obligingly assigned him in his interview a few years earlier. But the world had changed drastically since Seabrook wrote his lines. Europe was involved in a war that threatened once more to engulf the world, and a new crop of newsmen had appeared to cover it. Here and there, Duranty turned up, making the acquaintance of the youngsters who would change the rules of the game, writing in a plain-talking style Duranty little understood. He was seen at the Café Royale in London, matching drinks with the handsome young broadcaster who had hired Bill Shirer. As the others poured in, he met them as well.

One of them, a cub reporter for the *Times*, met Duranty just after he disembarked in France, sometime in early 1940. Drew Middleton noticed that "the great Duranty" could be argumentative with his contemporaries, but, with the young newsmen just making their start, he was unusually considerate. One of the questions he asked Middleton was what he had written about in his first story.

"I wrote about the trip over, the troops and officers," Middleton replied.

"Well," Duranty said, "that was probably a lot better than heavy think pieces about when and where the war will start."[28]

Middleton had no way of knowing, of course, that Duranty was referring to his own first war story for the *Times*, a think-piece that led, "Questions as to when the enemy will attack or where the blow will fall have given place to another—why doesn't he attack?" The story had won Duranty his first by-line and assured him a place on page one. Now, times had changed, and Duranty must have known it.

For his part, Middleton saw in Duranty a tremendous generosity, despite his gruff and sometimes irascible manner. He was at his best, Middleton remembered, when he was "entertaining the troops." At the various watering spots close to where they were stationed, the young British pilots liked to gather around Duranty to listen to his lively banter and amusing anecdotes. "They *loved* him," Middleton said later.

One night, near Rheims, at a spot called the Lion D'Or, not long before the fall of France, Duranty sat in the center of a large group of officers, buying them round after round of the local "bougie rouge," at pretty stiff prices.

"Walter," Middleton said, after they all had left, "you've been very generous here tonight."

"I ought to be," Duranty replied. "Those kids have about an even chance of living through the next six months."

Nearly forty years later, Middleton, military correspondent for the

New York Times, known himself for his generosity to newcomers, sat at Sardi's, close by the *Times* New York office, remembering Walter Duranty amidst the clatter of an army of waiters as they moved in and around the crowded tables.

"And he was right," Middleton said. "The Battle of Britain began on August 8, 1940, and few of the young pilots who had been drinking with Duranty and me that night survived it."[29]

Another reporter, a young English woman who had fallen into the profession somewhat by accident but who was already known for her tough dispatches under combat conditions, was Clare Hollingworth. She had just left the London *Daily Telegraph* to join the staff of the *Daily Express* when she ran into Walter Duranty for the first time in the lobby of the Athenee Hotel in Bucharest.

Bucharest, in these last days before it was overrun by the Germans, was something of a center for British espionage. Here, British secret agents could rub elbows with the Germans, Italians, and other enemies of the Allied war effort, and arrange espionage networks, which would pay off when Rumania became an occupied country. It was also a kind of listening station for the Western press corps, who, like Hollingworth, flocked in to learn whatever they could. Every day before lunch, a group of correspondents used to meet in the lobby of the Athenee to talk over the day's events.

Among these reporters, Duranty enjoyed a position of high status. Alternately referred to as "the dean of newspapermen" or "the great Duranty," he took over center stage with his usual flair, and perhaps something more. There were stock stories about him that made the rounds regularly. One of them, Hollingworth recalled, she heard more than once. According to the anecdote,

> Walter went to the border of Russia, and the man at the border said, "Where is your visa?" and Duranty said, "I haven't got a visa, I don't need a visa." And then he held up his attaché case and showed, pasted to the back of it, a letter from Stalin, saying "Comrade Duranty is welcome back whenever he wants to come."[30]

The story, obviously apocryphal, does serve to demonstrate the kind of legendary importance Duranty had assumed among newcomers to the profession.

Duranty was doing a stint for N.A.N.A. in Bucharest, and he struck Hollingworth as being very much a character. She remembered his gesturing widely with his cane, from side to side, as he climbed stairs or moved across the slick marble floors of the hotel. "'Get out of my way!' he would say," and Hollingworth swept an imaginary cane back and forth forcefully in imitation of Duranty as he had appeared to her more than forty years before.

In particular, there had been a young American writer whom Duranty was fairly tough on. "*You*," Duranty would say, "You don't know your ass from a hole in the ground." He was very authoritative, very much aware of his position as senior man, said Hollingworth.[31]

Other correspondents stationed in Bucharest could hardly overlook the flamboyant Duranty. Cyrus Sulzberger, who was there for the *New York Times*, recalled that Duranty "made a gallant figure hobbling around in his straw hat and his wooden leg."[32] He became a familiar fixture, sitting in "a soft leather chair, deep and comfortable, facing the door of the Athenee bar," yet another reporter would write later.[33]

Indeed, Duranty seemed to spend a good deal of his time in and around the bar, and as a special correspondent he did not have to meet the same deadlines as the other reporters. There was no little envy among the men, along with the general belief that he worked the least of anyone there.[34]

Duranty always got up rather late, probably after having his breakfast in bed. He would then have the "rum" (German) newspapers read to him by his secretary, before joining the throng before lunch. There was about him this tendency, grown quite pronounced, to tell everyone what was happening, almost showing off. Sometimes it could be irritating, as Hollingworth remembered it.

> He would get up from his chair and say, "I'm off to lunch with King Carol," and nobody would believe him, but it would be true. They would think, "It's Duranty showing off again," but he wasn't showing off at all. I went to the palace only a couple of times, but Duranty went there frequently.[35]

Despite such antics, Duranty still inspired respect. Hollingworth said she had a high regard for Duranty because of his work, if not for the way he conducted himself. "He was a respected, privileged senior correspondent, and as far as I knew, he was writing two or three pieces a week for the *New York Times*."

Hollingworth owned a car, and because of it, she became somewhat better acquainted with Duranty than some of the others, since it was pretty much incumbent upon her to give Duranty a ride, if he couldn't arrange for a taxi. "Whenever he got into the car," she said, "he would say to whoever was going, 'You sit here, you sit there, I'll sit here.' As the senior man, he could afford to be somewhat bossy."

One day, the pair traveled out alone to the oil country of Rumania, and they were together for quite some time. In strictest confidence, Duranty told Hollingworth the best known secret of his life: that he had taken to smoking opium when he lost his leg and that he still smoked the odd pipe from time to time. The way he did it, he explained, was to go off alcohol for two days, then smoke a pipe, then not drink for about two days afterwards. A widely traveled woman with a realistic view of the world, Hollingworth nevertheless found Duranty to be "a slightly shocking man," a fact that, had he known it, would no doubt have given him considerable amusement. Hollingworth found his language slightly shocking and his predilection for opium slightly shocking. He had a taste for young women, with whom he was seen in fairly large numbers and "for whom I presume he paid," Hollingworth said.[36]

Cy Sulzberger also remembered talk about Duranty's "great success with the ladies."[37] In particular, a rumor made the rounds that Duranty was involved with a countess or a duchess.[38] Although the woman was never identified, it was noted that he was very friendly with the daughter of H. H. Asquith, former Prime Minister of Britain, who had married the writer and diplomat Prince Antoine Bibesco. Princess Elizabeth was a popular figure in Bucharest, who, because her marriage was not a particularly happy one, evoked sympathy from the press corps. Duranty was extremely attentive to her, but whether she was the figure with whom he was said to be having an affair never became known. Duranty himself would only say that he was involved with a countess, and, with uncharacteristic tact, he remained unusually secretive as to her identity.[39]

As for his other women, Duranty seemed to delight in pulling off outrageous incidents, which he broadcast to the men in the press corps with obvious relish. Robert St. John, then reporting for the Associated

Press, ran into him early one morning at the Athenee, Duranty looking in very bad shape. If St. John would buy him a Scotch, Duranty said, he would tell him what had happened. Duranty had decided to go out and investigate the red light district of the city, quickly finding "a sweet enough looking young Rumanian girl," who took him to her room. But, Duranty told St. John, "when she saw his wooden leg, she howled with glee and ran down the hall." She soon returned with several of the girls who worked in the brothel with her.

"And so," Duranty said wearily, "I spent the whole damn night doing nothing—but putting on and taking off my wooden leg for the amusement of—well, it seemed like hundreds of lovely Rumanian girls!"[40]

Despite his propensity to make jokes about it, his leg had, during his sojourn in Bucharest, begun to bother him again, perhaps because he refused to stay off it. It became very sore, and at one point, when he could no longer walk, he had to call in a nurse to put a dressing on it. A friend who watched the whole thing described the stump where it had been cut off as "very nasty," because a mound of flesh had been left there which was a constant source of irritation against his artificial leg, causing at the best of times a good deal of discomfort. Doctors had always wanted to operate and clean it up, Duranty said, but he would never allow it.[41]

While Duranty was in Bucharest, a small piece of land, Bessarabia, became a bone of contention between Rumania and Russia. Russia had occupied the area for more than a century, until 1918 when the Allies had awarded it to Rumania as part of the Treaty of Versailles. Fred Hibbard, a frequent companion of Duranty's and the First Secretary of the American Embassy, had received the news early that Molotov had given an ultimatum to the Rumanian ambassador that he had twenty-four hours to agree to cede Bessarabia and some other territory to the U.S.S.R.

Soon after finding out, Hibbard saw Duranty and Spencer Williams, who had reported in Moscow for the Manchester *Guardian*, in the lobby of the Athenee Hotel. Hibbard asked the two men, both reputed experts on Soviet affairs, if they thought the Soviet Union would do such a thing as issue an ultimatum over Bessarabia. Both answered that it could not happen; such a suggestion was pure "poppycock." Later that evening, Hibbard, in front of the entire American colony, including Williams and Duranty, told his audience that when he had asked "the two experts" their opinion, he had had a copy of the ultimatum in his back pocket.

It was an embarrassing moment for both Duranty and Williams, but in the main, the incident was laughed off as a good joke. Everyone seemed to enjoy seeing "the great Russian experts" upstaged.[42]

Not long after this incident, the Rumanian government, acting no doubt at the behest of the Germans, expelled twenty-five British oil men and a number of staff members of the British Council. A British attaché, Lord Forbes, "finally left after counting more than 100 bullet holes in his apartment."[43]

On the 25th of September 1940, the Rumanian Foreign Office issued a statement that Walter Duranty's permit would not be renewed. To protests put forward by the U.S. Legation over Duranty's expulsion, the Rumanians answered that there were already too many foreigners in Rumania, and it was necessary to eliminate some of them "irrespective of occupation or nationality."

As per usual, Duranty seemed delighted over the controversy, saying with obvious amusement that there had been an "unwarranted suggestion . . . in certain quarters that I am regarded as a British agent!"[44]

Along with most of the other correspondents, Duranty left Bucharest and proceeded to Sofia, Bulgaria, planning to continue what had become something of a gay time for him. There was awaiting him in Bulgaria, however, an unexpected and unwelcome surprise. The *Times* had acceded to the wishes of Gedye and withdrawn him from Moscow, closing down the bureau. It was a decision which would cause consternation among *Times* men for some time to come.[45] The outcome of the decision was that, when the Germans invaded Russia, the *Times* found itself with no one there to cover it.

But for now, the closing of the Moscow bureau had an unanticipated effect upon Duranty himself. In a letter dated 30 September, James wrote to Duranty, outlining the reasons why, as of the end of the year, the *New York Times* would no longer be in need of his services. The ostensible cause was the large cost of the war and the newspaper's need "to tighten up a bit on expenses." But underneath it, there was the suggestion of "a very small return," that is, that the *Times* had actually been getting very little for the money it paid to Duranty, a statement that was true enough. As to the matter of the unspoken competition that had existed between the two men for over twenty years, James protested that he got "no delight out of writing" the letter, which, all said and done, was only one page long.[46] It amounted, nevertheless, to a curt dismissal of a prominent employee who had been on the payroll for nearly three decades.

Duranty cabled back a distressed response, one that reflected no little sense of being ill-used. He complained about "THIS SUDDEN RUPTURE OF WHAT HAD BEEN NO SMALL PART OF MY LIFE FOR TWENTY-FIVE YEARS." There was also a rather petulant aside that he had "THOUGHT YOU AND SULZBERGER WERE FRIENDS OF MINE AS WELLS BOSSES."

Several months later, James at last answered Duranty's wire, after Duranty had returned to Moscow for what would turn out to be the last time. James re-emphasized that Duranty's arrangment with the *Times* had ended on January lst, but he considered the matter still open for discussion, once Duranty arrived in New York.[47] Duranty quickly countered with a pathetic "thanks," saying he was greatly relieved because he had misunderstood James's letter regarding its finality.

It was probably the last time in their lives the two men ever communicated with one another.

It was now up to Duranty to put together a living as best he could, without the backing of the *Times*. Although there had been the impression that he was making a lot of money from his writing, the plain fact was that Duranty had always been a man who spent every penny of his income, and sometimes more besides, supporting a remarkably extravagant lifestyle. With his semi-autobiography on the shelf, and nothing else in the works, Duranty was caught short. He managed to make up some of the difference by taking on more wire service work. In late spring of 1941, Duranty, working for N.A.N.A., submitted his first dispatch from Japan, with a Tokyo dateline.

He reported that the German and Russian armies had been "jockeying" back and forth and that many viewed their moves as indication of an impending showdown between the two countries. In particular, he cited the American and British belief that the Soviets and Nazis would soon be at war. This was only "wishful thinking," wrote Duranty. He continued: "The question involved is not the possibility of a clash, as London would fain believe, but of closer collaboration and the price to be paid therefore."[48] Citing a recent report in *Pravda* that there were now some 12,000 German troops assembled in Finnish territory, Duranty called this grouping "a counter-bluff of German propaganda." He still believed that Hitler would be insane to invade Russia, as he had earlier told Shapiro.

In a second dispatch from Tokyo, Duranty was equivocal about whether or not the Russians would join the Axis lines.[49] By the time he wrote his third piece, however, he was ready to take a stand.

The duel between Stalin and Hitler was causing some to predict that an attack was imminent and that Russia would go fast. But Duranty didn't think so. He looked "for several more months or perhaps a year of collaboration between the U.S.S.R. and Germany." True, the relationship between the two countries was only a "marriage of convenience," and certainly, Stalin did have reason to fear Germany, because Hitler had his eye on the Ukraine and the Northern Caucasus. But when Duranty had last seen Stalin at the All-Union Soviet Congress, war appeared to be the last thing on his mind. Duranty then ran through one of the historical parallels that distinguished his writing: Stalin was like Alexander I, and Hitler was like Napoleon.[50]

In his last story for N.A.N.A., Duranty catalogued all the sources that now believed that war between Germany and the U.S.S.R. was imminent. He even included the section of a letter from an inside source in Moscow which said categorically that the two countries would soon be at war. The source, said Duranty, was unimpeachable, but the whole thing sounded "improbable . . . to me." He went on record as saying, "In short, it looks as though there was some rift in the lute, but I shall be surprised if the clash occurs now."[51] The date of Duranty's dispatch was 17 June 1941.

Five days later, on the 22nd of June, Operation Barbarossa began, in a blitzkrieg campaign along a 2000-mile front of Russian territory that included, in all, 162 divisions of ground troops—some three million German soldiers—the most massive and most ruthlessly sustained offensive in the history of warfare.

CHAPTER XVII

Hollywood

Duranty had already heard about the split-up, even before Marjorie Worthington wrote to tell him, and he shot back a letter, posthaste, commiserating.

> Of course I'm terribly sorry because I think you know how dear you both are to me. On the other hand, it isn't as if there was only the personal relation between you. You have your work to think of ...[1]

It had been a dreadful time for Worthington, divorcing Willie Seabrook, with no friend at her side, "a nightmare through which I walked like an automaton ... a major operation with no anesthetic."[2]

She had gone to live with her sister in the New England countryside, involved herself in volunteer work for the Civil Defense—checking to be sure blackouts were being properly observed and listening for air-raid signals. In between times, she wrote. The stories came "rushing in to fill the vacuum," and with amazing speed, she began to sell, and to sell well, first to the "quality" magazines, then, at prices that seemed fantastic to her, to the "slicks." Once outside Seabrook's thrice-woven circle, Marjorie Worthington began at last to flourish as a writer, even though, as a woman, she felt as though she had died.[3]

Duranty was back in New York, staying at the Hotel Elysée, after a pretty tough time himself. As he put it,

> I got myself stuck in the Balkans last summer and had a lousy time and was sick as well. And there was some hitch about my Russian visa until I thought I never could get back here. But finally did it about three weeks ago via Japan and then that good kind Mr. Hitler goes and gets me and the Russians out of the dog house (here) by taking a crack at them. Which did me no evil turn and I am busy as a bird dog in consequence.[4]

Whatever else he might have been, Duranty was not slow on the uptake, and he now suggested that the two of them arrange a date, not out in the country where Marjorie was, but in town. He was longing for a really good meal, "after all the foul food I ate last summer and winter," and suggested they meet at someplace like "21" or Voisin. If she could manage to get down to town, he would love to see her. "Yes, do that Marjorie darling," he wrote. "It's such a short journey and the change will do you good."[5]

For her part, Worthington thought an affair couldn't hurt and decided to make a stab at "trying to fall in love." With part of the earnings from her writing, she went out and bought herself a new wardrobe, not the "full gingham skirts" and gold chains that had pleased Seabrook[6] but clothes that she herself liked. About this time, she let it be known, she began to receive orchids twice a week from "a secret admirer," and it wasn't very long before she and Duranty were identified as a hot item in Manhattan, Worthington taking an apartment overlooking the East River and the pair of them cutting quite a figure at various night spots.

By now, Marjorie Worthington, always described as "majestic" by her ex-husband Willie Seabrook, had put on sufficient weight to be called "ample" by loyal friends; by others, "enormous." She had a soft, quiet, melodious voice, which had at times soothed the savage beast in Seabrook, but now seemed strangely at odds with her overwhelming presence. Duranty, on the other hand, was a little guy, who never stayed still or stopped talking even for a minute. The truth of it was, they were truly fond of one another, made no apologies for it, and managed to muster enough style to stay on the bandwagon for one more ride. As Worthington herself put it, "All my good friends were happy because I was so successful."[7]

Balmy weather and plenty of sunshine, a new book contract, and a lecture or two: that was all it took to persuade Duranty to settle down for a while in Beverly Hills.

In mid-September 1941, he wrote a letter to Worthington, telling her he had "taken a nice little cottage for six months, complete with car and an excellent colored couple." In a town full of transients, it was what everyone did, even the most stylish—rent a bungalow and see what would happen next.

Duranty had been "most frantically busy," he told Worthington, but planned nevertheless to pump out the book for Reynal and Hitchcock with all due speed. He had sold "a heavy political piece" for a hefty price and looked forward to seeing her the first week in October, when he was planning to fly back east.

Meanwhile, he had bumped into a mutual friend of theirs, "Aldous Huxley the other night, and Maria chez Anita Loos."

> He looked very well and was more bright and cheerful than I'd ever seen him, and equally excited about a book on the Pere Joseph, which he has just finished, and a fruit ranch he has just bought in central California.[8]

Huxley had been in Hollywood, off and on, since 1938, and once the war began, the British colony banded together into something of a clique, a group already popular among the movieland natives, now made more so for "patriotic" reasons.[9] Some of the stars, like Vivien Leigh, Laurence Olivier, and Leslie Howard, had managed, although it hadn't been easy, to get back home, refusing to be deterred by advice from the British War Office.

Others, however, followed suggestions that they should stay in Hollywood—like director Alexander Korda, who went home only to be sent right back, instructed by no less a personage than Winston Churchill, so went the story, that he might be of more use to the war effort making propaganda films than ducking air raids in London.[10] Alfred Hitchcock had stayed on, silencing critics with his film *Foreign Correspondent*, one of the first and best anti-Fascist propaganda films, based very loosely on the autobiography of Duranty's old pal Vincent Sheean, who had sold the film rights earlier for an unspecified sum.[11]

Perhaps it was this atmosphere as well as anything else that had prompted Duranty to remember that he himself was British. He

295

slipped in easily, expecting to work his way eventually into some studio, as so many other writers had done. To Worthington, he avowed he was avoiding parties in order to work on the book. But after the first few weeks, he realized "the picture people begin work so early that parties don't last at night as a rule,"[12] and he began to join in with his customary relish.

The guests were people like Greta Garbo, Paulette Goddard, Dorothy Parker, and Aldous Huxley. Mervin LeRoy sometimes dropped in, along with Robert Benchley or Eddy Duchin. Unbeknownst to Marjorie Worthington, Duranty set about making himself the center of attention, and in this he succeeded very well. His exhibitionist antics were crowd pleasers, and he became instantly popular. One night, he told the fortune of a well-known cover girl who was all the rage. A crowd gathered round to hear his witty rendition of the beauty's rosy future. As he traced out the lines in her palm with lingering fingertips, it became apparent that he had kept his eyes shut the whole time. At another gathering, he became so angry that he took off his wooden leg and threw it across the room. Before he could leave, he had to ask someone to go and get it for him. Everyone thought his little tantrum totally charming.[13]

Duranty was now an energetic, balding man who always had a cigarette going. His face had lost any of the roundness it once had, and appeared somewhat elongated. The sparkle had come back into his eyes, perhaps a reflection of his glittering surroundings.

About this time, the parties began to include the new influx of German émigrés, heavy intellectuals like Thomas Mann, and his brother Heinrich, and Lion Feuchtwanger—who attended somewhat reluctantly and mainly to lend their continuing presence as encouragement to the well-heeled groups that had sprung up to sponsor their fellow countrymen. Some of these had made harrowing escapes through occupied territory, arriving with no money, no English, and no prospects. Others seemed born for the part.

The handsome and suave Erich Maria Remarque, whose celebrated *All Quiet on the Western Front* had been made into a successful film some years previously, had left Germany before the war, an early victim of Nazi persecution. By now, he was a major-league celebrity, sometime companion of Marlene Dietrich, and a gallant escort to Greta Garbo ("I accompanied her frequently and enjoyed doing so").[14] Garbo in turn was close friends with John Gunther, in a relationship that would span decades—yet another connection for Duranty.

For all his success, Remarque had already, by the time Duranty arrived, found the hollow glitter of Hollywood unnerving. Like the other Germans, he inclined more toward weighty intellectual intercourse. At first taking rooms in the Beverly Wilshire Hotel, the German émigrés made this a sort of unofficial headquarters. Duranty met Remarque there, and they became instant friends.

Remarque and some of the other Germans were not allowed out after curfew because for a time they were considered by the government "dangerous aliens." Duranty, of course, was not subject to the curfew, but, like others, he sometimes got caught in the lobby of the Beverly Wilshire, where discussions became so involved that the 9:00 p.m. curfew passed without anyone's noticing. Duranty, realizing the others could *not* leave, often stayed up all night talking because he was ashamed to slink home since they had to stay. If perchance they got caught in a restaurant, the manager kept the place open all night.[15]

A few of the studios set up a stipend for the Germans, which amounted to a kind of charity whereby they paid the arrivés $100 per week for services rendered; in actual fact, these remained largely insignificant since many could not speak English or, like the seventy-year-old Heinrich Mann, would not, if there was any way he could avoid it. Extremely helpful were writers like Anita Loos, who was known for her lightweight but popular screenplays, like *Gentlemen Prefer Blondes,* and for her Sunday brunches, which took on the character of a salon. Loos along with others worked hard "on a personal level, using their best efforts to get distinguished émigrés work in the studios, signing affidavits to assist their immigration, and so on."[16]

Behind all the glamor, which was extremely pleasing to him, and the promise of easy money that might come his way, there was the more pressing need for Duranty to earn his keep. In a letter to Gunther, he admitted to feeling "overworked and mentally tattered." He had rolled out a 5000-word article, scheduled in a few lectures, and now he was "rushing this book."[17]

Perhaps it was this behind-the-scenes desperation that contributed to the miserable failure of *The Kremlin and the People.* Duranty managed to finish off the short book in record time, and it was published just before the end of 1941. In it, he introduced his ill-conceived Fifth Column thesis relating to the Soviet show trials and purges, probably, as much as anything, a trial-balloon to see if he could pass off those events as optimistic counterparts to the recent fall of France. It was clear that Duranty had invented his facile thesis, at least in part, to

297

cash in on the fact that Soviet Russia was now an ally, one that seemed to need shoring up with a little favorable propaganda. No doubt Duranty believed he was reading public opinion correctly, but *The Kremlin and the People* demonstrated exactly how out of touch he had become—with the Soviet Union, with the American public, perhaps with reality itself.

There were in the book patronizing words and phrases, actual baby-talk, designed perhaps to appeal to what he thought was the mentality of his readers. A phrase was making the rounds at the time ("General Mud") that purported to explain how the Russians would in the long run defeat the Germans. Duranty picked it up, but added to it "General Slush" and "General Cootie," along with a host of other great "military experts," who would, he predicted, eventually lead the Red Army to victory against the Germans.[18] Somehow, in his attempt to sound *au courant* with the catchphrases of the day, Duranty managed only to trivialize the war effort.

The book was reviewed in the *Saturday Review of Literature* by Duranty's old colleague from Moscow, Louis Fischer, who by this time, had switched sides from pro- to anti-Communist, reversing more than a decade of dedicated work on behalf of the Soviet regime. Regardless of his own about-face, Fischer's refutation of Duranty's "Song of Praise" for Stalin was hard-hitting and on target. Attacking Duranty's Fifth Column thesis, he pointed to the lack of evidence for such a fanciful construction. According to Duranty's logic, Fischer wrote, execution equaled "proof of guilt," with confessions a kind of optional extra in the proceedings. Most damning were Duranty's own words, which Fischer used to hang him: "It is unthinkable that Stalin . . . and the court martial could have sentenced their friends to death unless the proof of their guilt were overwhelming." Said Fischer, "How naive of the cynic!"[19]

Duranty sustained another attack in 1941, this time from Eugene Lyons in his book *The Red Decade*. Like Fischer, Lyons had also changed his political allegiance, but, unlike Fischer, his reversal was characterized by a mounting hysteria. As if Duranty's very real excesses weren't enough, Lyons now carried on the campaign of distortion against him which he had begun in his earlier book *Assignment in Utopia*. He said that Duranty never considered the Russians to be quite human, and based his opinion of them upon the thesis that they could "only be managed with whips, bayonets, and execution squads . . . ."[20]

As for Duranty's "Russian Soul" thesis, Lyons said he could "readily imagine the twinkle in his eye and the bulge in his cheek as he offered this consolation . . . to the faithful abroad."[21] Lyons's unchecked fury and the wildness of his accusations reflected a growing lack of balance, which in turn would lead to excesses at least as extreme as those of Duranty. Lyons had found his own Fifth Column, deeply rooted inside American society, which he believed had been "penetrated by a foreign nation and a foreign ideology."

> Stalin's Fifth Column in America, as in all other nations, has only one set of "principles": blind allegiance to the will of Moscow. It has only one "ideal": allegiance to a foreign dictator.[22]

In Lyons's estimate, the Red Decade of the 1930s would result eventually in the infiltration of "youth, Negro, consumer, women's liberation, anti-pollution and other current movements."[23] It was the kind of thinking that would usher in the McCarthy era and its peculiarly American version of purgation and self-mutilation.

In Hollywood at the time, however, such arcane attacks as those waged by Fischer and Lyons cut little ice, especially since being pink still gave an aura of social chic, and Duranty continued to have the necessary requisites for inclusion in the smart set of Beverly Hills— celebrity and the sheen of success.

He picked up his old unfinished semi-autobiography, *Search for a Key*, and with renewed vigor, began reworking the text, meantime speaking frequently on radio and stepping up his lecturing engagements. Once, when John Gunther saw Duranty and found out he was doing a series of political talks, Gunther asked him what kind of people came to hear him. "The kind who think that Prague is a ham," Duranty snapped back.[24] On the lecture tours, there were always admiring women to sweeten what was otherwise the toughest way to pick up quick cash. In particular, he met a flashy redhead in Cincinnati, with whom he was seen more than once and by more than one friend. Duranty apparently became, what was for him, fairly serious over the woman, whose identity was never disclosed, speaking of her often to close friends.[25] Meanwhile, he divided his time between California and New York City.

In New York, it was Marjorie Worthington, "21," and orchids, which had never ceased arriving at the rate of two per week since Duranty and Worthington had renewed their friendship. During Duranty's frequent and lengthy absences, Worthington's work had, if anything, improved, and she was considered quite a success in the literary world. Over the last few months, however, she had come to realize that Walter Duranty was, after all, only a close friend.

The truth of the matter was that she never really got over Willie Seabrook, whom she continued to see from time to time, on polite but distant terms agreed to tacitly between them. Seabrook had married again, sealing his relationship with a partner able to indulge him in ways Worthington could and would not, and he now had an infant son. Predictably, the marriage wasn't going well. Old, flabby, desperate, he dropped by Worthington's apartment whenever he was in town, and the two would have lunch together, usually something easily digested, like cottage cheese.

Seabrook, who had received the Croix de Guerre for bravery in World War I, now decided to go back to war reporting. He signed up with his old outfit, King Features Syndicate, inviting Marjorie to go with him to Brooks to pick up a uniform, then out to dinner at "21." The evening, she would later remember, reminded her of their early relationship, before the hard times —a night she recognized in retrospect as a farewell.

Seabrook left, not to cover the war, as he had planned, but for Rockland State Hospital to receive further psychiatric treatment. In 1945, after he was discharged, he took his own life.[26]

Worthington remained devoted to Seabrook, and after his death, to his memory. Although he was quickly forgotten by the public, she continued to believe for the rest of her life that he would eventually be rediscovered and live forever through his work.

About this time, Duranty received a reminder of his past, from a man who had become one of the great heroes of World War II. British General Harold Rupert Alexander, who as a young officer in Riga had become friends with Duranty during Duranty's short stay there in 1919, played a signal role in the evacuation of British troops from Dunkirk. On the final night of the evacuation he had personally toured the beaches to be certain no English soldier remained, before he himself made his escape. His courage under these most difficult circumstances made him a popular figure.

Alex had not forgotten his old friend, and in early spring of 1943, during the middle of the Tunisian campaign, Duranty received a telegram from Alex "asking why he wasn't there."[27] By the 13th of May 1943, victory in North Africa would be assured, becoming the prototype of future joint operations by the Allies.

Duranty was in no state to share the victories of old friends. Only a few weeks before the Allied victory in North Africa, his new book *Search for a Key* had been released, and Duranty faced, for the second time in his life, the hostility of the critics. In the *Saturday Review of Literature*, Maxwell Struthers Burt took note of the "curious atmosphere" that invaded Duranty's fictionalized account of his life. There was a sense "of evasion, of haste, as if this mind were a trifle weary and overloaded." But the book's real fault, Burt believed, lay "in Walter Duranty's openly expressed fear and distrust of emotion; he says, 'I have always been shy of feelings, as false beacons that lead men astray.'" Anyone who wished to become an artist, said Burt, simply could not afford that kind of detachment.[28]

Somewhat stung by this and other unflattering assessments of his more creative efforts, Duranty turned back to what he considered his own special turf—political analysis. He began work for Lippincott on a new political assessment of the U.S.S.R., spending the summer of 1943 on that book exclusively. Late July found him with no small share of trouble on the section dealing with the period before the Bolshevik Revolution, about which he described himself as being "all too fuzzy." He had moved temporarily to New York and was apartment sitting for Worthington, who had gone to the country to be with her sister.

He wrote to her to report that everything was in order in the apartment. It had been unbearably hot, but the weather was now letting up, so he would not go to Long Island as he had earlier planned. In the meantime, he hastened to assure her, he had been on the wagon, and "since the day when I had a touch of your red wine at the Veau d'Or, there has been no compromise with the demon rum." Practically every letter Duranty wrote to Worthington contained some reassurance of this kind—that he was in control of his drinking. Apparently, it was something she had spoken about with concern, knowing he had gone through difficult bouts with the bottle and of course remembering Seabrook's terrible addiction.

But he had to occupy his time somehow, he wrote, and he had

begun to play gin rummy, a game he had always detested. There was another first for Duranty: he started going to the theater. "One must, I mean, do something in the evening, because I defy anyone to sit and gossip cheerily for two hours or more with iced tea and coca-cola," he said. He had been to see *Arsenic and Old Lace*, and to his surprise, enjoyed it.[29] He predicted the "next such outing will, I think, be the Circus, which may or may not indicate a return to second childhood, milk and circuses instead of Scotch and nightclubs."[30]

In August he got a crack at doing a broadcast for CBS, for what he hoped would turn into something more permanent than one short stint. It didn't, but Duranty thought it went extremely well and remained optimistic about his chances to make a late entrance into the broacasting field. Worthington was returning from her summer in the country at the same time Duranty was coming back from a short trip from Washington, D.C.; he suggested they celebrate his broadcast by going out that night to "21."[31]

Worthington's success and Duranty's celebrity made them a highly sought-after couple at "21." All the literary people stopped by their table to chat a few minutes before moving on.

Behind the enviable façade, Worthington was worried. When Duranty had money, he spent it. When he didn't have money, which was more often the case nowadays, he still spent it. Somehow, the two of them, operating as a kind of team, began to share expenses, Duranty at first taking small loans just to tide him over. Worthington didn't mind, but she did notice that the orchids continued to arrive, even though Duranty could not afford them.[32]

With the onset of autumn, Duranty made his way to Chicago, one of his stops on a new lecture tour. He wrote to Worthington that it had been a long, lonely five-and-a-half-hour ride on the bus from his last engagement to the windy city, and he was cheered, upon checking into his hotel, to find a letter from her waiting for him. On the way, he had picked up a popular magazine and found one of her stories in it. It showed, he said, that she had "tenderness and comprehension" as well as a good sense of "clarity and drama," all characteristics of a fine writer.[33]

Maybe it was the ride that had tired Duranty—by now, he was almost sixty years old—or perhaps the sweeping winds off Lake Michigan had affected him. Whatever the case, only a few days after writing to Worthington, the *New York Times* announced that Walter Duranty had collapsed in Milwaukee just before he was to have delivered to the Council for Lasting Peace a lecture entitled "Can America Work with Russia?" He had been rushed to Columbia Hospital, where physicians reported that Duranty was "a very sick man."[34]

John Gunther saw the *Times* announcement in New York and got off a telegram the same day. "Just heard of your illness. Our hearts are with you old man. Profound wishes for a speedy and gallant recovery, ever best."[35]

Duranty had contracted pneumonia, an illness he described as "a dark deep wood," and he was genuinely shaken for the first time since losing his leg. He considered himself lucky to be alive, and in a frightened letter to Worthington he swore he would never again take any "foolish and unnecessary risks."[36] A couple of days later he seemed more himself, and he sent her a note that reflected his customary optimism. He had stopped running a temperature, he reported, and the pain was gone. Some of his strength was beginning to return. Meantime, he had been visited by friends who lived in Milwaukee, and they had asked him to stay at their home to recuperate, an invitation he gratefully accepted.

During the time Duranty was in the hospital, his room was deluged with people who wanted to meet him—"semi-strangers" and others whom he didn't know at all, admirers who had followed his writing for years. Finally, he had to make a special request that the hospital officials keep them out.[37]

By the end of the month, Duranty was back on the lecture circuit, this time in San Francisco, and able to deliver four lectures without dangerous after-effects. Of course, he wrote back to Worthington, he had to be careful to get nine hours of sleep every night, and he sidestepped all invitations for drinks. But in the main, he was now able to get through one of his hour-and-a-half talks without feeling completely drained.

The illness brought condolences from well-wishers and old friends whom Duranty hadn't heard from for years. One of them was Walter Kerr, an editor of the Paris *Herald Tribune*, who had known Duranty in Europe. No longer content to cover the war from the sidelines, Kerr mentioned in his letter that he planned to enlist.

Duranty wrote back immediately, complaining that he still felt bad, but not bad enough to prevent him from taking issue with Kerr about his plans. It was, Duranty wrote, "an argument [he] had in the last great war, and which I shall continue while breath remains to me."

> I feel strongly that there are millions of excellent soldiers in this country, but all too few topnotch newspapermen. . . . What I mean is that personal preference should be submerged by the idea of where and how the most useful job can be done. You and John Whitaker, who thinks exactly as you do and underwent two most painful operations to get himself accepted by the Marines, may fight with glory and success; but there are damn few people who can write about it the way you both do. And after all, the Home Front is hardly less important than the battle line.[38]

Duranty admitted, however, that he knew he was wasting his breath, and wished them both luck, predicting they would teach their comrades a lot about poker, "the poor suckers."

His letter to Kerr included an aside, a swipe at the war correspondent Ernie Pyle, who had become well known for writing about the ordinary enlisted man—"top sergeants, buck privates and an occasional lieutenant," as Duranty put it to Kerr. Pyle had gone into the foxholes alongside the men who were actually doing the fighting and written up their individual stories. His work signaled a change in emphasis which had been gradually taking place in war reporting—a departure from the grandiose in favor of the particular, from the generals to the GIs. Duranty didn't like it and said so to Kerr. It was not, "I assure you, Sir, my idea of war corresponding, with all deference to Comrade Pyle."[39]

Duranty was right: it wasn't his "idea of war corresponding." He would never be able to understand the new preoccupation with the average GI or the public's concern for real people; their hopes, their failures—their suffering. That would always be beyond him, the ability to imagine what others were feeling. Anything that came that close made him feel squeamish and uncomfortable. His distrust of emotion, never a handicap so long as reporting emphasized the epic and the heroic, now placed him outside the mainstream of his profession; just as it had, for so many years, protected him from an intimacy he simply couldn't endure.

At last, the book he had been writing for Lippincott appeared, and it showed that Duranty was still able to churn out armchair observations about the Soviet Union, this time from a historical perspective that hid the fact he was no longer up to date on what was actually happening there. However, his new angle could hardly hide the fact that Duranty was simply rehashing his old theses, although certainly, *USSR* was a much better book, more balanced, more sensible, and less wildly irresponsible than *The Kremlin and the People*, which had appeared three years earlier. He had come up with a new version of his old pronouncements on the strengths of the Soviet system, and it sounded better than it ever had.

He claimed that Russia had emerged from a semi-colonial state only because of the choice made by Stalin to industrialize rapidly. He re-emphasized the popularity of Stalin, looking at the widespread benefits the Bolsheviks had brought to the common people in terms of education, medical care, and even holidays from work. He discussed how the Soviet media dwelt on the achievements of the workers, bringing them the possibility of instant fame through the pages of *Pravda* and *Izvestia*. Via these outlets, a common laborer could be turned overnight into a national hero, by becoming a "shock worker."[40]

He also raised a valid question, that of bias in the reporting of the Western newspapers, which showed a tendency, he said, to acquire and publish only what was being suppressed in the countries they were reporting. Duranty now recorded what he believed to be the real achievements of the Soviet Union, regardless of the misfortunes that had befallen it:

> In a bare quarter-century the U.S.S.R. has accomplished ages of growth. The most ignorant and backward of all the white nations has moved into the forefront of social, economic, and political consciousness. Its obsolete agricultural system has been modernized and mechanized; its small and artificial industry has become gigantic and self-supporting; its illiterate masses have been educated and disciplined to appreciate and enjoy the benefits of collective effort.[41]

This would remain perhaps the best and clearest statement of Duranty's philosophy concerning the Soviet Union. Although full of factual errors that showed Duranty was now out of touch, *USSR* was nevertheless one of his better efforts; it was as if Duranty had managed, for the purposes of re-establishing himself in the public eye, to pull it all together just one more time.

The book came and went, without anyone taking very much notice.

After his illness, Duranty returned to Hollywood, where he hoped the climate would speed his recovery. He checked into the Hollywood Roosevelt Hotel until he could locate an apartment, a more modest place than the bungalow he lived in before, one that matched his ability to pay. As earlier, during his bohemian years in New York and Paris, when he was in his twenties, Duranty made no attempt to fix it up; he was "just living in walls," as one friend described it.[42]

During his earlier sojourn in Hollywood, Duranty was active in helping to establish relief funds for refugees from the war, speaking frequently at the celebrity dinners given to raise money. Anita Loos, who remembered Duranty's help, continued to include him in her Sunday brunches. These were held in her opulent home located on that stretch of the ocean front in Santa Monica called "the Gold Coast." It was at one of these gatherings that Duranty had another of his strokes of good fortune, this time in the shape of a young, good-looking brunette.

There was something special about Mary Loos, the niece of the famous screen writer. In a setting where pretense and guile tended to dominate, Loos was open—and likeable, in that frank way of someone who expects the best of people, and often gets it for just that reason. She had a dreamy look in her eyes and a complete sincerity of expression that seemed to symbolize the hopes and ideals of youth. Along with these characteristics, she was full of enthusiasm and a boundless energy just waiting to be harnessed.

Mary Loos met Walter Duranty one Sunday afternoon at her aunt's house. Several years before, in 1937, she had made a tour of Europe as a college girl, and departed from it, going around Russia totally on her own, out of curiosity. It was exciting for her actually to be talking to the man who was so great an authority on the U.S.S.R. At this initial meeting, Loos, like so many before her, became captivated by Duranty's charming conversation. He told her dreadful stories, in graphic detail, about the horrors of the purges. He was certain, he said, that he had unknowingly brought grief, and perhaps even death, to many of his Russian friends, just because he was acquainted with them.

For her part, Loos admitted that she had always wanted to become a writer, encouraged by having some of her poetry published when she was a school girl. She had come up with an idea for a story, the first she had ever attempted, which had been inspired by her visit to Russia. Duranty encouraged her, telling her he would give her a hand, and to her delight, Loos found that she and Duranty were, in her words, "immediate compañeros."[43]

Later, Duranty read over the story Loos had written and edited it. It sold immediately—her first sale. The upshot was that they decided to collaborate, using the same method that had proved successful.

Loos would write furiously during the mornings, then drive by Duranty's place on the days when she could get the gasoline, which was in short supply during the war. The two of them would head to Romanoff's, where they would have lunch and talk over the story. He took it home, rewriting and editing in the afternoon until he was satisfied. Duranty "didn't believe in wandering around in 'the glories of fiction,'" Loos remembered later, and he did a lot of cutting. When she had new material the next day, yesterday's story would be ready to be retyped and mailed off. It was a quickie operation, and the "slicks" picked up the stories as fast as the two of them could crank them out.

Duranty's entrance to Romanoff's, Loos remembered, was impressive. He would parade slowly past the bar, stopping along the way to chat with friends, making witty comments, before continuing out to the garden, where the pair always ate. They were a familiar, if strange-looking, couple at the famous restaurant. Loos was tall and young; Duranty was short and sitting just on top of sixty—"a little pistol," to use Loos's words.

She called the way he dressed "a riot," and at lunch one day, she finally came out with it: "Walter," she remembered saying, "that jacket is a little heavy for summer." She was referring to a tweed jacket with leather lapels and patches on the elbows that Duranty wore practically every day. "It must be ten years old," she said. "Why don't you get something new?"

"There is absolutely nothing wrong with this jacket," he answered. "I got it in Bulgaria ten years ago, and they don't make them anymore."

But then, when Duranty did dress up, as he had for some publicity photographs the pair had made, he looked strangely out of place and overly conscious of his appearance, not unlike a clown sporting new duds. By now, he was bald, so much so that it looked as if a swimming cap had been stretched across the top of his head. His sad sack face appeared distinctly unreal in the California sunshine, the wrinkles across his forehead so deep they looked as if they might have been stencilled in. His nose was large and prominent. His eyes, like dark half moons painted into his face and pointing slightly downwards at the sides, added to the appearance of self-parody. With a slightly pathetic expression on his face—half hoping, half expecting the worst—he seemed a caricature of the man he once was.

Duranty frankly needed the money from his collaboration with Loos, more than she suspected. He had tried peddling his talents to the studios, but without any luck. As one of his acquaintances reported, beneath the surface, Duranty had become increasingly bitter. He seemed "unable to understand why so many jerks can make fortunes in Hollywood while his genius goes unrecognized. . . ."[44] Things were bad: he had been forced to borrow from several of his friends, who eventually began to fall away, perhaps as a result. Yet he had one source that never seemed to give out.

John Gunther had become one of the top writers in the United States, a best-selling author whose books had been translated into many languages and whose work was known practically everywhere. A gregarious and good-hearted man, generous to a fault, John Gunther served as best friend to an amazing number of well-known writers, Duranty included. He lent Duranty whatever he asked for, in his careless way forgetting about it immediately thereafter. It was Duranty who felt guilty, never failing to mention in his letters that he remembered exactly how much he owed Gunther and that he would be paying up "soon." Gunther always said more or less the same thing: Duranty was not to worry about it unless he should find himself "to be very rich."[45]

On the 5th of January 1945, Duranty told Gunther he had good news. The next day, he would begin the first of a small series of lectures in California that would help him pay his rent and other incidentals that had been worrying him. Although Colston Leigh had been able to arrange "a very fat and profitable tour" for him in the East, Duranty was not able to take up the agency's offer because of bad health. He would nevertheless manage to send Gunther a check by the middle of the month. Most promising of all, Duranty and Loos were producing a book that was to come out in early February.[46] The novel, *Return to the Vineyard*, was slow getting started, Duranty wrote Gunther, "but it gets better as it goes on."[47]

Duranty's observation turned out to be fairly accurate. The novel *was* slow getting started, but it picked up as the plot unfolded. Mary Loos researched the book, and together, she and Duranty wrote the scenario, then abridged it, in this case both of them taking their turns at editing. Loos had created the imaginary setting, a location somewhere in Eastern Europe.

Return to the Vineyard is the story of people working together, rebuilding their village after its destruction during the war, and rediscovering religion. Some thirty-one refugees return to their home after World War II. Faced with the prospect of having to go to work in a factory, they mutiny against the new capitalist industrializers who have invaded their province, and return to the vineyards. Although the young hero of the novel originally plans to manipulate the villagers and become a prosperous capitalist himself, he learns, by the last pages of the book, to work with the others in selfless harmony.[48]

Loos—young, trusting, full of enthusiasm for her work—put her heart and soul into the book. Duranty gave rather less.

She was shocked that he showed no interest in her research. She wanted her novel to have "the feel of fact," and she studied carefully in order to be sure the wine-making process she described was accurate. Duranty chided her for her idealism, saying, "It doesn't make any difference. This is fiction."

Many years after her collaboration with Duranty, Loos remembered their argument almost as if it were a scene from one of the many screenplays she would later write for the Hollywood studios. In her rendition, she got the good lines.

"*What?*" Loos asked Duranty. "How can you say such a thing? It's like lying and cheating!"

Loos carried on with the work, but was deeply disillusioned, watching Duranty reserve his more serious effort for his magazine articles and political analyses. For his part, having long since been forced to relinquish any hopes of writing a great piece of fiction, Duranty now tended to discredit it, putting it down—somewhat to Loos's irritation. Characteristically, Duranty was contemptuous of something at which he himself could not excel. As Duranty continued publicly to denigrate literature and to elevate journalism, Loos began to wonder whether or not to continue working with him.

The book made something of a commercial hit, selling well over the counters, and the Navy bought 9000 copies for its libraries at sea.[49] It nevertheless met with unenthusiastic critical response, and Duranty wrote to Gunther that a "former" friend of his, Lewis Gannett, had pasted him badly, calling Duranty one of the "able correspondents" who insisted on trying to write novels for "psychopathic reasons." Furious, Duranty said that the book he had written with Mary Loos was good fiction, or, if it wasn't, Duranty told Gunther he told Gannett, he "would eat his hat or mine."[50] Gunther commiserated with Duranty, reminding him that he too had come in for his share from the critics, "but what the hell? They are all cretins, as we all know."[51]

Despite his angry reaction, Duranty suspected his time was up, and he had been trying to get a visa into the Soviet Union. Mary Loos, on holiday in Mexico City, had made it a point to go by and visit the former Soviet Press Office censor, Constantine Oumansky, who had become Soviet ambassador to Mexico, to see whether it could be arranged. Oumansky seemed friendly enough, giving Duranty several "go" signs. Not long afterwards, the Soviet diplomat was killed in a plane crash, somewhat ironically, since he had been the only one of Duranty's original censors to have survived the purges. Duranty's comment upon Oumansky's death was that it was too bad, because Oumansky could have "greased my wheels no little."[52]

There was in the aging Duranty, Loos noticed more and more often, a tendency to live in the past, no matter how much he appeared to enjoy the present. Mary Loos's aunt, Anita, no doubt observing how much Duranty had changed, predicted that her niece would probably end up taking care of Duranty for the rest of his life.

One afternoon at lunch Duranty suggested that the two of them go down to Mexico where they could live more cheaply. He asked her, "Would you consider living with me?"

"Frankly, Walter," Loos remembered replying, "It never entered my mind. But thanks for asking."

"All I can say is, you might be surprised."[53]

In the end, it was Duranty who was surprised, because Loos called a halt to the collaboration, striking out on her own.

Duranty, in the meantime, no longer as popular as he had been, found himself excluded from the social gatherings where he had once starred. Long since he had come to be viewed by the West Coast people as an

eccentric, or worse, "a has-been." Among the inhabitants of Hollywood, anyone on his way out has always been "feared and avoided,
like some kind of *memento mori*."⁵⁴ For Duranty, the party in California was over. He moved on to New York, to see if he could still
squeeze something out there.

There was a time in his life when Duranty vacated his relationships, swiftly and without looking back. He had rid himself of Aleister
Crowley, when "the Great Beast" had become a potential hindrance to
his career, and certainly when his ex-wife Jane Cheron Duranty made
heavy scenes in front of his friends, he had walked out, conveniently
forgetting she ever existed.

Now he had to face something entirely new, something he hadn't
anticipated: Duranty himself was becoming the embarrassment.

CHAPTER XVIII

I Write As You *Please*

Ed Murrow had bought a place in upstate New York, about seventy-five miles out of the city, not far from Pawling. After Drew Middleton returned from Moscow, where he had just put in a tour of duty as the *Times* correspondent, Murrow asked him up to the farm for a few days to unwind. The Cold War was in high gear.

Murrow told Middleton that Walter Duranty and Knickerbocker had thrown in together on the lecture circuit and were now doing a public debate on Duranty's old topic—"Can We Trust the Russians?" Backstage one evening after catching their act, Murrow was asked by the pair for his professional opinion of how he thought they could improve their performance.

"I told them they ought to liven it up . . . ought to change it into a vaudeville routine like Willie and Eugene Howard. Knick should come out in a dinner jacket and a straw hat as the heartless capitalist and Duranty should be dressed as a tramp. They should beat each other over the head with bladders or canes . . . none of this 'one life, one kopeck' stuff," said Murrow.

"How did this go?" Middleton asked.

"They didn't think it was very funny, Drew."[1]

In Moscow, Middleton had made it a point to go by Duranty's old apartment on Bolshaya Ordinka, to look up Katya. By then, Katya's blonde hair was going white, and she was no longer the beautiful peasant woman he had heard described so many times. But Middleton believed he could still see through the years to the handsome woman she once had been. She had high cheekbones and good carriage, and her hands had no calluses from rough work. When Katya heard Middleton was with the *Times*, she burst into a flood of Russian, none of which Middleton understood. Eventually, though, in English that came back to her gradually, Katya told him "how much Walter had valued his connection with the *Times*" and "how much she missed him now."

Katya had managed to hold onto the apartment by letting rooms to a major in the U.S. armed services, a fact that had struck Middleton as being somewhat out of the ordinary, given the conditions in the Soviet Union at the time. No Soviet citizen dared to consort with foreigners, except at terrible risk, and Middleton was left with an inevitable conclusion: Katya was reporting to the KGB.[2]

From the time his collaboration with Mary Loos dried up until Duranty teamed up with Knick, his life had been a desperate fight to stay afloat financially. Occasionally, one of the stories he had written with Loos would pay off, and Duranty would send Gunther "another snippet on that debt, which then meant so much to me and so little to you."[3]

And then there was the problem of his ill health, which continued to plague him. At the conference in San Francisco that convened to draw up the charter for the new United Nations Organization, Duranty met his old assistant from Moscow, Robin Kinkead, for lunch at the Olympic Club. Kinkead was shocked by Duranty's declaration that he would "like to have something to drink," but that his system couldn't take it. Finally, after some dithering, Duranty decided on an ale.[4] That was in late April 1945.

By June, he was feeling more like his old self. He had returned to Los Angeles, living more or less out of his suitcase, to give a few lectures. John Gunther turned up and the two had lunch together. Duranty was in one of his talkative moods and ruminated on the current state of affairs in the aftermath of the German surrender, which had taken place in May.

Soviet Russia could not be considered a nation of slaves, he told Gunther, countering one of the theories of the time. "You can make slaves work or even fight," said Duranty, "but you can't drive slaves to *victory*." He also emphasized the conservative streak in the basic character of the Soviets. In some ways—mainly other than civil rights—Soviet society was more conservative than New Zealand's. "Indeed," Gunther wrote in his diaries, backing up Duranty's thesis, "I can hear W. [H.] Chamberlin . . . that U.S.S.R. is less pink!" As to whether or not the Soviets were likely to attack the West—one of the basic assumptions that underpinned the Cold War ethos—Duranty said no. There were plenty of reasons why Stalin would want to stay out of a fight, but the most convincing was that he couldn't *afford* it.[5]

At dinner a couple of days later, Gunther told Duranty he had heard that the U. S. government was refining uranium. There was rumored to be a city in Tennessee, said Gunther, where the government had employees totaling 17,000, or more, and was thought to be spending millions in order to produce about two pounds of the stuff, which would then be used "to split the atom."[6]

About a month later, the first atom bomb was tested in New Mexico, and on the 6th of August 1945, the bomb was dropped on Hiroshima. Duranty wrote Gunther the same day, saying he was "vastly excited about this story about the atomic bomb. I heard it on the noon broadcast, which for some reason didn't play it up much. . . ." It was "far the most startling event in the war," and he was gratified when the "CBS Roundup" featured the story prominently in the afternoon broadcast. "I wonder what Uncle Joe thinks about it," Duranty said.[7]

The Pacific Surrender, considered a distant prospect until the atomic bomb was dropped on Japan, now became a reality. After the second bomb destroyed Nagasaki, the Japanese at last signaled their willingness to give up the fight, and on the 2nd of September 1945, they surrendered. For Duranty, these were distant events, and his life went on within a less significant context.

He and Gunther had placed a wager on the British elections, which were held immediately after the war ended. Gunther and Lester Markel, then Sunday editor of the *New York Times*, banked on the continuing popularity of Winston Churchill and believed the British would stay with the Tories; Duranty bet that Labour would win. The Labour landslide of 1945 amounted to one of the great election upsets of all time, ushering in the managed economy and welfare state of Clement Attlee, the dark horse in the race.

Both losers immediately put their checks into the mail, Markel writing Duranty "a funny note," saying he ought to be liable to "an excess prophet tax." On the other hand, Duranty found it "quixotic" that Gunther had paid up promptly, since Duranty still owed him money: "You perhaps thought that bets were something apart and that I deserved the satisfaction, which is indeed great, of winning from such experts as you and Lester Markel. . . . [or] that I could use the money, which is true enough. . . ."[8]

It *was* true enough; he *could* use the money. These days, his life was a treadmill of bus and train travel, of irregular speaking engagements in distant cities, of trouble with his health, and a thousand little worries he had never had to face before. In November, he traveled to Chicago to give a lecture, only to find that the hotel had lost his reservation. There was a convention in the city, and, to his dismay, he couldn't find a room. Then he discovered he had left his cane in the taxi that carried him from the train to the hotel.[9]

He worried a good deal about catching cold, which could instantly deprive him of much needed income, and about making laundry connections, a topic that became important enough to speak about at length with sympathetic friends.[10]

Some three weeks after the Chicago fiasco, after traveling from there to Milwaukee, then down to San Antonio, he had awakened in the city to find it "delightfully sunny and warm (80 at noon today) with lots of trees and shady gardens." He had caught a cold from the rough overnight ride to Dallas, and awakened with a temperature of 99.5°. He used it as an excuse to cancel his lecture in distant Detroit, and simply stayed in San Antonio for a few days' rest, avoiding what the doctor had told him was "the simplest form of suicide"—traveling with a fever.[11]

Duranty was now sixty-one years of age, and it was an old sixty-one. His handwriting had undergone a change in the past few months, from the vigorous and bold strokes that had always characterized it, to the shaky jumps and starts of an old man, the words looking as if he had trouble holding the pen to the page. The restless movement he had always loved now became a race against time, a breathless roaming from one set of strangers to another, in a lengthening list of one-night stands and overnight stays. The travel itself was growing more difficult, with "about a hundred thousand veterans, and their friends and relatives and babes,. . . . cluttering the railway stations and airports . . . ."[12] How much longer could he hold on?

More than a decade before, Malcolm Muggeridge had predicted a desperate ending for the celebrated newsman, putting worries into the head of his fictional Duranty, which now seemed to show an uncanny prescience:

> Golden youths and maids all must, like chimney sweepers, come to dust. Though you got away with it all your life, and always kept on the side of those who were getting away with it, there came an end. Something got away with you at last ... How would he finish? Cadging drinks in Paris cafés from patronising ashamed friends. Overgrown senility.... A home or an asylum or a charitable institution. There's no security nowadays, he fretted....[13]

Duranty became desperate, hatching a scheme he thought surely would provide him with the solution to his problems, bring in a little easy money, and put him back in the public eye.

In the spring of 1946, he made a public announcement that he was going into the business of giving advice. For $1 a month, Duranty would offer a newsletter, in which he proposed to discuss any topic requested by subscribers—from affairs in the Soviet Union to advice to the lovelorn. It was a bizarre enough proposition to be noticed by *Time*, which picked up the story, describing Duranty as "sixty-one and ailing." He had won a Pulitzer Prize some years earlier, the magazine said, and lately had written "some undistinguished fiction." Now, "the gay and worldly-wise little man" was willing to give up his own personal style of writing, and "write as *you* please."[14]

His bad luck continuing, Duranty kicked around, seeking a way out of his financial situation. Somewhere along the line, as he made his way from one speaking engagement to the next, Duranty ran into Knick, who was also stuck on the circuit and no happier about it than Duranty. A few drinks later, Knick—willing to try anything once—agreed to give it a go with Duranty. They approached Colston Leigh, and he immediately agreed, optimistic that "two old hams" like Knickerbocker and Duranty could make a success.

The pair created an overnight sensation, easily knocking back as much as $750 or even $1000 for each performance, plus expenses. Cashing in on the background provided by the Cold War, the debate took on a sense of immediacy, with Duranty and Knick striking exactly the right tone to give the whole thing verisimilitude and the appearance of red-hot controversy.[15] Friends came up with different versions of who took which side during the debate. One story was that Duranty and Knick flipped for it, leaving it to chance who would assume the "pro-Soviet" stance. Others believed Duranty always argued in favor of the Reds. One thing everyone agreed upon: neither of the two men really believed in what they were debating—it was pretty much a sham, designed mainly to please the Women's Clubs.[16]

William Shirer, who had returned from Europe to the United States, was doing a bit of lecturing himself. Knick had a house in Texas at the time, and on his way to one of his engagements, Shirer spent the night there, Knick and his wife Agnes telling Shirer all about "the show." Duranty and Knick would practically come to fisticuffs on stage; then they would go out and have a drink together.[17]

Both quickly became bored with the routine of non-stop shadow-boxing. Like actors on stage, they deviated from their scripts, played jokes on one another—anything to keep it fresh and spontaneous—and to keep the cash coming in. Then, too, life on the road hadn't gotten any easier, as anyone on the circuit knew only too well. One of them, Robert St. John, who had covered Bucharest for the Associated Press at the same time Duranty was there for N.A.N.A., advocated friendship with the Soviets, and as a result, he had been picketed by anti-Soviet leagues across the country, as well as by all kinds of extremists. Even the American Legion had shown up one night, much to St. John's chagrin.[18]

As for Duranty and Knick, together much of the time and under circumstances that were less than ideal, they were bound to argue, and it wasn't always part of the act. Duranty complained to Gunther that Knick had lost his temper at one of the debates, giving Duranty an edge, which he naturally took. Later, over drinks, Knick jumped him for it.[19] Knick was having tax troubles, Duranty told Gunther in strictest confidence, and was particularly hard to live with just then.

Regardless of the tiff and others like it, the two became almost inseparable. Duranty made New York his headquarters, and Knick showed up there with increasing frequency. They were often joined by their old friend Jimmy Sheean, who had met Duranty in the late-Twenties in Moscow when he had had his tragic love affair with Rayna

Prohme. Well-known at "21," the triumvirate, "friends and enemies all the time," argued endlessly about current affairs. For Duranty, it was back to success and the flashy New York high life he loved.

It was also back to the bottle, and in a big way. Jimmy Sheean drank more than anybody, and was known for his mammoth bouts, but Knick and Duranty weren't far behind. The club kept on hand a supply of Guinness Stout at room temperature especially for Duranty, who liked his beer as the British drink it. Although Colston Leigh did not smoke or drink and made it a practice never to become close friends of the men whose acts he managed, he met the three of them occasionally for lunch, and was sometimes struck by the amount of alcohol they put away.[20]

John Gunther remembered a typical episode at "21," when he had arranged to meet Duranty late at night. Not far from midnight, he found him asleep at the corner table. When Gunther woke him, Duranty "revived, brilliant," as Gunther put it. "He's gay, wise, a scamp, and he loves me."

Then Duranty left to telephone one of his many ladies, this one "with a broken leg!" and confirmed a date he had made earlier with her. He returned to Gunther's table, complaining that he had to buy a bottle of Scotch because the girl had only soda at her place, but when he tried to get it at the bar, he was refused. Jimmy Sheean approached and calmed Duranty, who was starting to create a scene, explaining the nightclub would lose its license if it sold Duranty whiskey by the bottle. "So," Gunther reported in his diaries, "I took him home with me, gave him half a bottle of Cutty Sark. Then put him in a taxi. He had the Scotch in his breast pocket. Stuck out like a tipsy gnome."[21]

Away from his drinking buddies, at his social club, Duranty was a model of comportment. There, he went out of his way to behave himself. He belonged to the Coffee House, which occupied two brownstones in midtown Manhattan, not far from the *Times* office. The club had 300 or 400 members, many of them distinguished—men like Humphrey Bogart and Basil Rathbone, J. P. Marquand, and Alec Waugh. Nelson Doubleday was a member, as were P. G. Wodehouse and Philip Barry, who visited the club whenever they were in town. Others included Ed Murrow and Fairfield Osborne.

The Coffee House had a library, which adjoined the dining room, where four large oak tables were placed in a row for the evening meal. In the living room, a large fireplace was flanked by two Windsor chairs with a large sofa facing the flames. In winter, the idea was to arrive early enough to get one of the seats by the fireplace. The living room was the heart of the club, which had evolved originally to facilitate conversation.

Richard Edes Harrison, a successful cartographer who belonged to the Coffee House, remembered Duranty as particularly free and easy, a little man who seemed to exude confidence. Since much of the conversation dealt with the "news of the day," Duranty stood out for his brilliant commentary. If someone happened to ask "who had said or done a thing, and everyone was stumped," said Harrison, "it was Duranty who came up with the answer."

To Harrison, as to many others before him, Duranty seemed an apolitical man, with no axe to grind. "He was aware of the fact he was a *reporter*, not a philosopher," said Harrison.

Someone once said to him, "Walter, I don't see your by-line in the *Times* much anymore."

"Well," Duranty said, "that's easy to explain. When we are 'at outs' with the Russians, I get no assignments. But when things are easier, I'm sent off to do stories." He said it was a foolish policy on the part of the *Times* because he would as soon report the seamier side of Soviet affairs as not.[22] It was slightly pathetic, Duranty's still passing himself off as a *Times* man. In his world, appearance was everything; his only value, he seemed to understand, was that attached to him by others.

Henry Shapiro came home, with his law degree, able to pick up a position lecturing at a university. He had planned to stay in the United States, but his wife, who was Russian, was not allowed to leave the Soviet Union with him. Neither was his daughter, who was claimed as a Soviet citizen. Marooned in New York, without any family or close friends, Shapiro rang up Duranty, suggesting they go out for a bite to eat and to talk over old times. That wouldn't do for Duranty. He took Shapiro to "21," along with Marjorie Worthington, ordering champagne and caviar—to Shapiro's horror. Duranty, he realized, was still living in the grand style that had typified his existence when he was top man at the *Times*. Shapiro believed no good could come of it.[23]

Not long out of the Soviet Union, Shapiro couldn't help noticing the contrast, how easy things were in New York, how difficult they had been back in Moscow. There, he had sometimes heard from Katya, who called him up, asking "about Duranty's health." Duranty in turn

319

sent money. In fact, a network of correspondents each took a turn delivering packets of cash to Duranty's former mistress, who depended upon these and renting out the rooms of the apartment to eke out an existence for her and their son.[24]

Duranty's attitude toward the family he left behind was, predictably, ambivalent. Although Shapiro remained stubbornly convinced throughout his life that the relationship between Katya and Duranty was not dissimilar to the one between him and his wife, other friends gave reports that did not tally with Shapiro's rose-colored view. Duranty had seemed to Mary Loos to be genuinely fond of his son, referring to Michael frequently and always describing him as bright and lively, with obvious pride. But whenever Katya's name came up, Duranty fell silent. In her direct way, Loos asked Duranty outright whether he felt bad about leaving her behind, and Duranty had responded, "Russians are like cats. They jump any which way."[25]

Even Shapiro, in retrospect, could not understand why, during these difficult years when anyone who had been associated with foreigners was deported to the camps, Katya had not been arrested. "But then," said Shapiro, thinking the matter over, "neither was my wife."[26] In the end, after a brief respite, Shapiro was forced to return to his old job in Moscow with United Press, unable to get his family out until after Stalin's death, and unwilling to remain in the States without them.

For Duranty, in some small way, Marjorie Worthington had taken over the role of Katya—minus the drudgery. His letters to her reflected a relationship not unlike that of husband and wife: there was affectionate concern, warm gratitude for kindnesses extended, the sharing of minor irritations and moments of triumph. He demonstrated a steady refusal to show her that side of his personality that was most flamboyant, most reminiscent of the excesses she might associate with her relationship with Seabrook.

Each summer Worthington went to stay with her sister, Della Hoffman, who had a summer home just outside the small town of Ashby, Massachusetts, not far from the New Hampshire line. It was quite a way from New York City, where the heat, reflected off the buildings and onto the pavement, would often become unbearable. The Hoffman house was on ninety acres, at the top of a high hill, where it caught the breezes from the surrounding countryside. There, Worthington could write without interruption, or take long walks to think things over. In that setting, she drew into herself, wrote her stories, and worked out the plots for her novels.

Sometime in the summer of 1947, Duranty came up for a weekend visit, flying into a nearby city, where the family drove to pick him up. During his stay Duranty underwent one of his chameleon changes, becoming the perfect house guest, charming Hoffman and her family with his wonderful talk.

As he was getting out of the car, Hoffman's grandson asked Duranty, "Why do you walk like that?" Duranty immediately lifted up his pants leg and showed him his wooden leg. The boy was fascinated, badgering him for the rest of the visit with questions of how it had happened and how he took it off and put it on. Usually, to pass the evenings, the family would play gin rummy or bridge. But the weekend Duranty stayed with them, everyone preferred to listen to him hold forth.

Marjorie Worthington had been asked to write a section for the *Encyclopaedia Britannica*—a high honor for a writer. Her pay was $35 and a certificate.[27] Duranty had also written for the *Encyclopaedia Britannica*, in fact, for two separate editions—in a clipped scholarly style unlike any of his other work.[28] But he made short shrift of the honor entailed, saying briskly, "You can't eat the glory of God or of *Britannica.*"[29]

About six months after Duranty's visit to the Hoffman house, where he and Worthington had talked about writing for the prestigious reference book, Duranty sustained an unexpected attack in *New Times*, the official English-language outlet for the Communist Party in Moscow. The basis for the attack was one of the articles he had written for the *Encyclopaedia Britannica*. Duranty's account of Allied Intervention was criticized heavily for his failure to mention "Churchill as the organizer" of that event. He was also attacked for failing to mention that "the British agent Lockhart organized a villainous attempt on the life of Lenin." By the same token, the article said, Duranty had tried to cover the fact that American troops had been involved in Intervention.[30]

The attack on Duranty was a signal that he was, after all was said and done, *persona non grata* in the Soviet state. Duranty always nurtured hopes of getting back in; he had been offered a chance at employment in Moscow by Western news organizations if only he could secure a visa. But the Russians had no further use for him, and although he continued to try, he had no luck.

John Gunther believed it was a great irony the Soviets were now rejecting "this man [who] did more for U.S.S.R. than any other living Anglo-Saxon." He had his own theories as to why Duranty couldn't get a visa: "The Russians don't want anybody who knew them *well* in older days. Walter could spot *anything* from 5 minutes' observation . . . ."[31]

Now, as old age began to claw into him, Duranty became greedy to soak up whatever he could get, his natural inclinations escalating—as sometimes occurs with the passage of time. In Duranty's case, there was this desperate attempt to recapture that wild, free-wheeling sense of endless pleasure that had carried him from the back alleys of Paris to the high life of New York.

It was Gunther who was the mainstay of Duranty's New York social life, and Duranty passed many evenings at Gunther's apartment, in a wild pastiche of drunken scenes, which Gunther tolerated with good humor.

One night, the broadcaster and columnist Edgar Mowrer was there, along with Knick and Duranty. Duranty had covered World War I alongside Edgar's brother, Paul Scott Mowrer, and perhaps he was envious of Mowrer, who had inherited Duranty's role as "dean of correspondents." With his dependable manner and deliberate style of talk, Mowrer had gained the respect of a wide-ranging audience. Whenever Mowrer tried to speak at dinner that evening, Duranty "shouted [him] down, . . . called him a prude or prig or puritan."

Well-oiled with liquor, Duranty proposed that the four of them kidnap an American millionaire, whose name was then frequently in the news, and "get close, like a dog sniffing, to [his] money." What they should do, said Duranty, was to force the rich industrialist to buy them a Greek island, "go there with him, teach him how to live, we to be his instructors, friends, allies—showing him the inner enjoyment of life."

As Duranty talked, Knickerbocker sat silently at the table, looking less than amused. Duranty glanced over at him, took his measure, and then denounced him violently for not taking his proposal seriously. To this attack, "Knick responded grandly: 'I am already thinking of how, after we get Pearson to the island, we are going to murder him.'"[32]

> Duranty then asked him if he would commit murder for $250,000.
> Knick answered, "Of course."
> "Would you murder your own child for $250,000?"
> Back came Knick's answer. "For nothing."[33]

It was a "guess-you-had-to-be-there" style of humor, inspired by drink and recorded faithfully by Gunther in his voluminous diaries.

Another night, Gunther described "a wonderful gag sequence here" involving John Whitaker, the journalist Duranty had mentioned earlier in his letter to Walter Kerr. Whitaker, who had returned from the war heavily decorated, had just finished a book he had been working on. He had dropped by Gunther's apartment for drinks, and the subject turned to Walter Duranty. "Whit," as he was called by Gunther, said he was down on Duranty because of a dinner he had given, where Duranty behaved "disgracefully." During the course of the evening, Duranty got drunk "insulted the other guests, . . . got sick, and even fell asleep at the table."

Unexpectedly, the bell rang and it turned out to be Duranty himself, who had come by unannounced, just dropping in to have a late afternoon drink with Gunther.

> Then, reminiscing idly, *Walter* told how he had never liked Red Lewis, since a time in Moscow when he, *Lewis*, had arrived at a dinner Walter had given for him, and was utterly, disgracefully drunk, insulting the other guests, getting sick, and even falling asleep at the table.
> It was bad manners, inconsiderate, and disgusting, W.D. said.[34]

"I did not say a word," Gunther wrote in his diary.

During the days Duranty spent partaking of New York's chic café society, the popular John Gunther remained at the center, including his friend whenever possible, tolerant of his wild antics. But the bachelor-party atmosphere of Gunther's social life was, to a large extent, a form of escapism; Duranty's antics, in some small part perhaps, a diversionary tactic.

323

In spring of 1946, Gunther had received news that his sixteen-year-old son was seriously ill. Gunther and his wife had agreed to a divorce several years before, in as amicable a parting as exists in the civilized world; that is, the couple agreed to bury their anger and disappointment and behave toward one another like the close friends they once were. Frances Gunther had been with John all through his climb to stardom, which had not been without its moments of sadness. When Gunther was twenty-six and working in Moscow, Frances was pregnant with their first child, a girl, who died as an infant of crib death. The birth of a son in 1930 had gone a long way toward putting back together a marriage strained by grief.

Now, the marriage finally dissolved, Johnny Gunther's parents reasonably parceled out his time between them, with the boy seeing "more of us together than a child usually sees of divorced parents." A student at Deerfield Academy, Johnny spent most of his winter and spring holidays with his father in New York City, most of his summer with his mother in Connecticut. Gunther's work took him to the far corners of the world, but he "specifically arranged almost every job and itinerary so as to be with him during his holidays."[35]

In March of 1946, Johnny Gunther suffered from eye strain but, after taking a few prescribed exercises, he seemed to recover. He also complained of a stiff neck, but since he had just finished his examinations there seemed no reason to assign any particular importance to the fact. About the third week in April, Gunther had received a wire from Deerfield that Johnny was in the infirmary, his neck pain having grown suddenly worse.

Then on 25 April, at about three in the afternoon, Gunther was apprised of the fact his son had a brain tumor.

There followed one of those scenes wherein people try to reach one another, organize things, talk to specialists, and make vital connections. Finally, with a well-known surgeon at his side, Gunther drove up to Deerfield, stopping along the way in New Haven to pick up Frances, who had made her way there to save time. "Five minutes after I got there," Gunther wrote later, "I knew Johnny was going to die."[36]

Gunther was working on the long and detailed *Inside U.S.A.*, with a cruel deadline, upon which depended the success of the book. At first tempted to put off writing it, he came quickly to understand that Johnny's medical expenses would be astronomical, and his entire situation depended upon the completion of the book on schedule. There were huge medical bills to be considered, the support payments to his wife—who maintained a house in Connecticut and a small apartment in New York City—and in the midst of all this, endless research as Gunther began reading everything he could lay his hands on in an attempt to find out for himself whether the boy could be saved.

Frances Gunther sprang into action as well, trying to locate the best specialists in the world, who might be able to help. The two worked as a team, following every lead. Then, as the answers came up negative, they began grasping at straws, Frances Gunther even searching for mustard gas, which they had heard could help retard the growth of the malignant tumor.

During the first operation, the doctor reported removing a tumor "the size of an orange" but regretted having to leave behind nearly as much malignant matter. With few complaints, Johnny suffered through X-ray treatments, gas treatments, vomiting, and periods of amnesia.

Gunther and his ex-wife were given to understand, in an oblique way, that the boy would eventually go blind. A nurse described to Gunther "that in tumors of this type the patient gradually lost all functions, even that of control of his own secretions, and died in the end like a kind of vegetable."[37]

The broadcaster Raymond Gram Swing put Gunther in touch with a physician named Gerson, who had developed a controversial treatment for cancer through diet. During the months Johnny continued to languish, moving closer to death, Swing kept insisting Gunther should try the diet. At last, Frances and John Gunther reluctantly put their son on Gerson's regimen, a saltless and fatless diet that permitted no protein.[38]

Through all of this, Gunther's confidant was his mentor and friend, Walter Duranty. On the 18th of October, some time after Johnny had gone onto the Gerson diet, Gunther dined with Duranty, telling him that his son was "much better!" He remembered the rest of the conversation as a "wild, confident talk with Walter, describing the diet and what it has done."[39]

Early in October, Gunther couldn't meet his expenses and had to ask his publisher for another $10,000 "advance."[40] Meanwhile, he began receiving the massive medical bills that would cause him at one point to say he had "never been so broke."

To stay afloat, he borrowed money from his ex-wife, who had saved her alimony and now turned it back to him. Meanwhile, he was racing to finish *Inside U.S.A.*, mopping it up by sections, often staying up half the night before making the trip to the hospital to spend the day beside his son.

By the middle of April 1947, Gunther had to borrow yet another $10,000 from his publisher.[41] "It's terrible, practically all the money I have in the world is gone," he wrote at the end of the same month. "And I still owe thousands in doctors' bills."[42]

But he had managed to finish the book a month before, and it had been chosen as a selection by the Book of the Month Club, a virtual guarantee of commercial success.

In May, there was a second operation ("I got two handfuls"), but the doctor held out no hope whatever. The tumor was growing at an unprecedented rate, and the surgeon later said "he had never penetrated to healthy brain tissue at all."[43]

On the 25th of May, Gunther received a surprise telephone call from the adviser at Deerfield, informing him, that along with the make-up work his son had been able to do while he was ill, they had discovered some extra credits taken in his freshman year, and that, unexpectedly, he was eligible for graduation.

Gunther and his ex-wife drove up to Deerfield, "and Johnny graduated on the 4th of June, though he had not been to school for fourteen months." Half-blind, unable to use his left arm, his head wrapped in a turban of bandages, Johnny Gunther walked across the stage, "slowly, so very slowly" to receive his diploma, as the applause from the audience thundered around him.

"Everything that Johnny suffered was in a sense repaid by the few heroic moments of that walk down the center aisle of that church," John Gunther later wrote. "This was his triumph and indomitable summation."[44]

A little over a week later, Gunther had lunch with Duranty, describing the boy's graduation, and listening in turn to Duranty's jokes: "What would you do if you were blackmailed? Say, 'Listen, you guys, we're newspaper men, we know how to get people like you killed, and for free, too!'"[45] Then there was talk about current affairs, predictions of the Soviets taking over much of Europe: "Not so much a question of the U.S.S.R. spreading out aggressively, but simply going into a place where nothing opposes her."[46]

Such talk helped Gunther stay above water, and he was grateful. A short sentence written into Gunther's diary summed up his feelings: "Persons whom I more and more like and admire: W. Duranty (full asleep) . . . ."[47]

On the 19th of June, after a day fraught with worries, Gunther had dinner at Voisin with Duranty and Walter Kerr, who had, like Whitaker, survived the war and become, as Gunther put it, "very smart, and some of his rough edges now smoothed off." The men discussed Russian topics, their opinions of Molotov and Vyshinsky, "one of the brightest guys who ever lived," Gunther wrote.[48]

Gunther's son had always loved being around adults, speaking as an equal, and sometimes, a group of them "drifted in" to talk to the boy. Johnny, still recovering from his last operation, "was marvelously amused . . . ."

> Walter Duranty, bless him, dropped in for two long afternoons, and enchanted Johnny with his conversation, making him laugh almost until he cried with anecdotes of his own school days at Harrow and how that he had played hookey to see the Grand Prix in Paris, and with questions like "Well, my boy, and what do you think of women?"[49]

A few days later, when Duranty met Gunther for lunch at the Alrae, Gunther confided to his old friend that his son was doing very badly since the operation. He seemed to be going downhill, even since Duranty had seen him a few days before.

For his part, Duranty had something to ask. The upshot of this request was that Gunther lent Duranty $500, after a good deal of confusion as to whether or not an English check Duranty held could be cashed in order to cover his most pressing expenses.[50]

The matter settled, the two men ordered their coffee. But before it could come, Gunther was called to the telephone and informed by Frances that Johnny had a headache, and she thought he had better come. It was the 30th of June 1947, and Gunther's son died that night "at 11:02 p.m."[51]

Duranty had no way of knowing, of course. But that couldn't alter the fact that he had actually put the touch on the beleaguered John Gunther the same day his son had died.

CHAPTER XIX

Midnight Minus One Minute

The night John Gunther introduced his fiancée Jane Vandercook to Walter Duranty—drinks, dinner, and the young woman herself "enchanted with him"—Duranty insisted on dragging the couple, late at night, to a party on the West Side. Marjorie Worthington would be there, he said, and he wanted Vandercook to meet her. The three of them took a taxi to the address, went "up dark stairs . . ." and, as Gunther remembered, saw "no sign of life." Finally, a door creaked open, and the "presumptive host" protested that he was sick; there was no party there. Undeterred, Duranty went up another flight, knocking loudly and disturbing a couple who were "obviously in the hay."

"Retreat," John Gunther wrote later, "To '21"—where Duranty tried unsuccessfully to reach Worthington, whose phone did not answer.[1]

John Gunther was perhaps the most eligible bachelor in New York, and he had at last been irresistibly smitten by the radiant Jane Vandercook, whose marriage to broadcaster Jack Vandercook had faltered many years before. Separated from her husband, Jane Vandercook now wanted a quick divorce in order to marry Gunther. The plan was for her to go to the Virgin Islands, where a divorce could be made final in a matter of weeks. But even before Duranty met Jane Vandercook, and unbeknownst to her, he had toyed with the idea of going along himself, as a kind of traveling companion, while she put in her time.[2] In August, the matter was settled.

Over drinks, with Duranty imbibing far too much, he met with the couple for "a noisy and disconcerting session," as Gunther put it. Duranty had brought along "his Florida girl," one of the many admiring women whom he had met on the lecture circuit, this time on a swing through the South. For a small-town girl from Orlando, the scene must have been irresistible: drinks in glamorous New York with two renowned journalists, along with Jane Vandercook, an East Coast sophisticate. Perhaps for his lady's benefit or maybe just from habit, Duranty made a spectacle of himself, insisting that he *would* go with Vandercook to the Virgin Islands. He met with unexpected opposition; from his girlfriend, certainly, possibly from Vandercook herself, who kept her own counsel. Later, Gunther would remember that "W.D. [was] not so good," and his fiancée had been "shocked, bitterly disillusioned." The outcome of Duranty's unpleasant little tantrum was, nevertheless, that Gunther lent Duranty $500 yet again, and "he will go on the same plane Jane does."[3]

A few days later, a disconcerted Gunther met the group at the Colony for one last drink before the departure. Gunther went to La Guardia with them, describing the scene that ensued as "terrible" and "crazy" as Duranty's girlfriend tried "to snatch Walter off the plane."[4] For the "Florida girl," what had begun as an amusing hi-jinx ended with her beau's airplane disappearing into the clouds, despite all her objections. "I behaved horribly," was all Gunther had to say.[5]

Once in the Virgin Islands, Duranty stayed at a place owned by friends of his, Bluebeard's Castle, while Jane Vandercook had lodgings elsewhere. Each day, one of them would pick up the other in a taxi and they would go out to the beach together. They usually carried a picnic lunch, and sat around eating and drinking and basking in the sun. Vandercook admitted to being "rather undone" the first time Duranty took off his leg to go into the water, but after that, she grew accustomed to it. He was completely unself-conscious about his leg, she remembered later. Despite his outrageous behavior back in New York, Vandercook now admitted that Duranty was awfully good company, and her earlier revulsion soon melted away. He loved the pelicans on the beach, and when he talked about them, they seemed to become a golden subject; such were the skills of his conversation.

One night, she sat watching Duranty drink an "enormous number of rums," and later, when he was leaving to go back to his inn, he had to walk down a long flight of steps. Vandercook helped him down the stairs to the main street. Someplace in the middle, with her arms around him as support, he made what she would describe many years later as "a mild advance." He stopped, and said to her expectantly, "I love kissin'." Somehow, Vandercook managed to get him safely into a taxi and sent him back to his hotel.[6]

Duranty returned to New York after two weeks, Vandercook remaining the requisite six. When she did get back, it was only natural that she and Gunther would want to be alone, but Duranty gave them a ring, "and of course we dined together." He brought along Marjorie Worthington, and the four of them fell into a discussion of what they thought constituted genius, Worthington insisting it could be defined only in terms of Willie Seabrook. As for Duranty, he was back up to his usual level of brilliance, Gunther recalling later that his "talk would be worth $100 an inch, transcribed on a wire recorder . . . ."[7] In actual fact, Gunther was paying not much less than that for the pleasure of listening to it.

Duranty was still managing to get by. He had signed a contract to do a new book on the Politburo for William Sloane and Associates, another armchair analysis about which Sloane seemed agreeably enthusiastic. As the Cold War escalated, it seemed like a sure thing.

But almost immediately after striking the agreement, Duranty pulled a boner, an embarrassing lapse in taste that nearly quashed the whole deal. Somewhere along the line, in his several chats with Sloane, the topic of another book came up—one that Duranty had much admired in his youth. It was the Weininger book, and he recommended that Bill Sloane read *Sex and Character*, perhaps to consider for a revival. Unfortunately for Duranty, Sloane did.

He sent back an immediate response, and even Duranty could sense the disaster. Beating a quick retreat, with the necessary breast-beating and *mea culpa*, Duranty wrote, by way of apology, "I read the W. book hastily last night and am quite horrified to have wasted your time with it."

> It is all the things you say and hopelessly dated to boot. Nevertheless, it did have a great vogue around the turn of the century and it was also

the fact that I was only 20 or thereabouts when I read it myself but even so I was astonished to think I could ever have admired the book, and what's more, that enough other people admired it in those days. To me, now, it seems a silly mess of Schopenhauer and pro-fascism, the sort of book that Hitler might have written at that time.[8]

Pacified, Sloane wrote back that he guessed "we think more nearly alike about the Weininger book than I was willing to presume when I wrote you my somewhat guarded letter."[9]

The sixty-four-year-old Duranty, as Mary Loos had noted earlier, was living more and more in the past, and he seemed unaware of the fact that, since the Jewish Holocaust, anti-Semitism, or anything that could remotely be construed as such, had lost any semblance of respectability, especially in the circles in which Duranty moved.

In his work and conversation, Duranty had always made much of a physical gesture, one that Bolitho had pointed out to him many years before. "To the Jew," Bolitho had told Duranty, "his nose is a badge of Race. Race is still the strongest factor in human affairs. When the Jew rubs his nose he is unconsciously appealing to the accumulated strength that has maintained Jewry intact throughout twenty centuries of persecution."[10] Duranty took to the notion, and made frequent use of it in his work.

The manuscript he submitted to Sloane showed Duranty's stubborn persistence in pushing an idea that continued to appeal to him. In it, he described any of the men he was writing about who were known to be Jews as "rubbing their nose in a Jewish gesture," even though, in many cases, he had never set eyes on them. The editor cut these badges of incipient bigotry from the text, causing Duranty to complain bitterly.[11]

There was never any sign of Duranty's understanding in the least of why it had been done.

Another sticky problem emerged. Duranty, it seemed, had received a sizable advance for a second book to follow *USSR* from the publishers J.B. Lippincott, who paid the money in expectation that Duranty would gain entry into the Soviet Union; indeed, it was a stipulation of the contract that he do so if the book were to go ahead. Now that he had contracted with Sloane to write a book on virtually the same subject, Lippincott expected Duranty to repay his advance. A number of letters crossed and recrossed, with Bill Sloane acting as middleman. With some exasperation, he wrote to Duranty: "Before proceeding further, may I make it entirely clear that I feel you are wholly free to write this book for us?"[12] By the following month, his attitude had somewhat changed, and he said the whole affair was "none of my damn business." If Duranty himself would work out the arrangements for repaying the advance, "it would probably save a good deal of postage."[13]

In the meantime, Duranty wrote to Jamie Hamilton, his old publisher in London, and explained he was finishing up a book for Sloane. He asked if Hamilton were interested in publishing the British version.[14] It was a natural enough thing to do, since he was a personal friend and had every expectation Hamilton would pick up the option. To his surprise, and somewhat to Sloane's, Hamilton did not. After this second ruffling of the waters, Sloane and Duranty agreed that it would be best if Sloane took over arranging any ancillary sales of the book.

At about the same time, Duranty came up with a new scheme to raise money, and he tried to talk Lincoln Schuster of Simon and Schuster, the original publisher of his autobiography, into bringing out a paperback version of *I Write As I Please* to sell at twenty-five cents a copy. Schuster rejected the idea, again to Duranty's surprise.[15]

As for the lecture circuit, he and Knick had come to a decision: they were big enough as a team, they believed, no longer to need Colston Leigh; so neither of them signed up, intending to "carry on that duet job on our own."[16] Why should they cut Colston Leigh into a percentage if they were perfectly capable of setting up their own engagements?

Then, in February of 1948, for the first time in many years, Duranty received a letter from Katya, carried into the United States by an army major and his wife who had rented Duranty's old apartment in Moscow. On the surface, it was only an introduction to the couple, intended as much for their eyes as for Duranty's, and as such, slightly constrained and formal. Beneath the surface was the suggestion of a great deal more, "things I keep in my heart all these years." Katya had received some money Duranty sent, thanked him for it, and said she wished she could write him "a long, long letter" to explain what she felt. A number of their friends had died: "the terrible news," she wrote, "absolutely killed me." She had seen Shapiro, talked to him, and "felt a little better."

The letter was signed "Yours, as ever Kit," Duranty's nickname for her. Then appeared the giveaway postscript—a seemingly innocuous line tacked to the bottom of her one-page letter, one that revealed more than perhaps she intended. She had heard, she said, about "your new book," and she hoped "it would not disappoint us very much."[17]

It was, of course, a coded message on behalf of the authorities Katya reported to—her first line of loyalty, whether voluntary or forced. It demonstrated the endless coaxing and subtle pressures that might still be brought to bear on men like Duranty, who had people they cared about in Moscow.

Duranty continued to send Katya money, as Shapiro indicated, through the network of correspondents who came and went to the Soviet capital; what Shapiro did not know was that much of it was borrowed from the correspondents themselves. Once the messengers took Duranty's measure, they were very eager to pass the onerous responsibility of delivering funds to Katya to the next man along the line. One of them complained to Duranty rather testily that $100 of the money he had given Katya had come out of his own pocket, and would Duranty be so kind as to repay the money right away, as he needed it himself.[18]

At the end of the summer the same year, 1948, Katya again managed to contact Duranty, but this letter, which was not open to the inspection of strangers, was marked by a different tone. Katya was sure he must have known "that I had to let three rooms to the Americans, and work for them." She had received the money he sent all right, but she couldn't accept the fact that "if you send money to us, you decline all the responsibility for life and education of Mike."

> I don't believe it is possible to forget, that here, in Moscow growing up your only the son, that we lived together nearly for twenty years, that I gave you the best years of my life, though I know, you hate when I say so, but it is true. . . . Could not you write to me something, or if you don't want to do that, for God knows what reason, you must send a letter to Mike. He is already 15 years old, he is not a child any longer and understands things very well. He wants to know and must know where his father is, why his father keeps silence for such a long time. For myself it is insoluble mystery, what happened to you, and why, when I ask your friends about you, all of them suggest me to write to you, but no one wants to give me your address, seems nobody knows your address, what I don't believe, of course.[19]

333

She questioned "what you think to do in further [*sic*]: Will I get the money from you or not." She had sent other letters, which he had not answered, which she wasn't even sure he had received. Under these circumstances, she wouldn't have bothered him now, only she wanted to inform him she had received the money he sent. Then, at last, she beseeched Duranty "not to leave me without any help."

By the time Duranty received Katya's letter, the *New York Times* had decided to send a new man to Moscow, and not long after he got his assignment, Harrison Salisbury received a phone call from Walter Duranty, who suggested they have lunch. The two men met at the Algonquin, where Duranty told Salisbury he had not been back to Russia for many years, saying he would be interested in going back if he had more freedom of movement. At last, he got to his point. Duranty wanted information about Katya, not about her so much—"She had been 'a bad girl' for not keeping in touch"—but about the boy. The impression Salisbury received was that Duranty was interested in news of his son Michael, and that was the real reason behind the lunch.

When he arrived in Moscow, Salisbury carried out Duranty's request, going by the apartment on Bolshaya Ordinka to see if he could find Katya and get news of Michael. At the time, relations between the U.S. and the U.S.S.R. had gone from bad to worse, and the American Embassy was trying to get all U. S. personnel stationed in Moscow out of the apartments owned by private citizens or by the government. At Duranty's old apartment, Salisbury found living there an American sergeant, a mechanic at the Embassy garage. The sergeant told Salisbury that there was no "Katya" at the address, but there was a "Russian witch" who lived in a room by herself at the back.

"That was Katya," Salisbury remembered many years later, and to Salisbury, she looked like a "kitchen slut." She showed no interest at all in talking to him, and even less in Duranty. Her son, she told him reluctantly, was eighteen and serving in the Soviet military service, and Salisbury wrote that back to Duranty. Soon after, the Embassy pulled all of its personnel out of the flats, and Salisbury assumed that Katya lost the apartment.

When he returned to the United States, a year or so later, Salisbury rang Duranty and invited him to lunch, where he gave him a full account of everything that had happened. At the first meeting and again at the second, Salisbury found Duranty a dislikeable character, not at all to his taste. At the same time, he was fascinated, even riveted by his personality. Struck by his own contradictory responses to the man, he made one of his many mental notes to keep track of what happened to him, as was usual with Salisbury.[20]

Despite what seemed like a steady stream of hard luck and the complicated situation concerning Katya, Duranty continued to live it up.

For a short time in the autumn of 1948, he went to Orlando, no doubt to deliver a few lectures. But there was another attraction to the small Southern city—"his Florida girl." Presumably, she had forgiven him for his little trip to the Virgin Islands the year before, and they were back on good terms.

Returning to New York and oblivious of the cost, he took up residence in fashionable hotels, like the Bedford or the Algonquin, running up gigantic bills he paid with the proceeds of his lectures. It was the old bohemian habit of living out of a suitcase, but the hotels he stayed in were posh, comfortable, well-situated. He was a frequent dinner guest at the apartment of John Gunther, who married Jane Vandercook that year, and he was often seen with Marjorie Worthington at "21," where they continued to enjoy the attentions of the literary world.

Worthington now hit what her sister would later describe as "a dry spell," one that became more and more pronounced. For a lengthening period of time, her stories ceased to sell at the rate they had, and her financial situation became uncertain, even precarious. Worthington was at pains to keep this information inside the family, however, and in this she succeeded.[21] No one suspected even for a moment that she was in trouble.

From someplace or another, Jane Gunther had got the mistaken notion that Worthington, whose girth by now was remarkable, had allowed her ex-husband Willie Seabrook to whip her while she was bound up and helpless. "The vision of her in chains being whipped by the cannibalistic Seabrook," Harrison Salisbury would later write, "sent John and Jane Gunther into paroxysms of laughter."[22]

During 1948, two incidents, one very minor, the other more serious, brought to light Duranty's political attitudes, which, after all, had undergone very little change since he had left the Soviet Union more than a decade before.

Cass Canfield, Gunther's publisher at Harper and Brothers, asked

Duranty to read and assess a novel that had been submitted to him, written by the wife of Louis Fischer—a dramatic chronicle of Russian aristocrats before the Revolution. Needless to say, it was not exactly to Duranty's liking. He believed the book romanticized unnecessarily the fate of the upper classes at the hands of the Bolsheviks. In writing his review for Canfield, he took the opportunity to reassert his thesis concerning the purges, blaming them again on the "lunatic, Yezhov," and tacitly absolving Stalin from blame. Duranty knew, he wrote to Canfield, that "many innocent people suffered unjustly, but the fact remains that Russia was swept clean of Fifth Columnists, enemy agents and a whole raft of other dubious elements."[23]

A second, more important event showed just how far Duranty was willing to go in excusing the actions of the Soviets. In March of 1948, Soviet expansionism brought about a crisis that underlined the seriousness of the break in relations between East and West. It had begun with a stepping up of the harassment of American and British personnel seeking access to Berlin from West Germany. A little over two months later, the Soviet walk-out from the four-power military commission in the city presaged dire consequences. Soon thereafter, all railway and automobile traffic between Berlin and the West was halted by Soviet occupation forces, thus isolating the German city from its vital supply line to the West. With less than a month's food supply for some two million inhabitants, the Western Allied military command put out an order to mobilize all aircraft. Thus, the Berlin airlift began, running on a split-second schedule under desperate conditions, a situation that threatened to escalate into full-fledged war.

In response to the event, Duranty wrote an article saying that the Berlin incident was a good example of the absurd state of misunderstanding to which the Soviets and the Americans had come by a series of missteps. He charged that "our relations with the U.S.S.R. have been perverted by error and exaggeration" to the current crisis mentality. The "unfortunate destruction of a British civilian plane by a Russian military pilot . . . might have been the spark to fire the powder magazine . . . if there had been a powder magazine," said Duranty. From his viewpoint, Soviet actions in Berlin were merely a "face-saving" action, and if only the West would realize it, the Berlin crisis actually offered the opportunity to bring about peace between the two countries, although he did not explain how this might be accomplished. The whole thing, he summed up, amounted to "a lot of sound, fury and exaggeration signifying nothing much."[24]

His manuscript went unpublished.

The article did demonstrate something incontrovertible in Duranty's character, however; that he remained incapable of seeing any event in a light other than that dictated by the pattern he himself had created over the years. His stubborn adherence to his own pronouncements made him a slave to his former convictions. It was impossible for the stagnating Duranty to re-evaluate and come up with new conclusions, or a fresh point of view.

By the end of the year, Sloane was able to pass along some good news to Duranty, the first after what must have seemed like a battalion of troubles and minor annoyances. In London, Secker and Warburg had agreed to publish his book on the Politburo, which had now been given the working title *Stalin & Co.* In his letter to Sloane, Fred Warburg had said "what a pleasure it [was] to read the book of an the author who keeps his head about the so-called Russian menace, and gives the reader the opportunity of judging for himself. . . ." But along with this gratifying signal from England came the daunting news that the Book of the Month Club had decided not to take the book as a selection, and would merely recommend it to their members.[25]

Duranty meanwhile holed up in his hotel room to finish writing the book, using issues of *Pravda* and *Izvestia* to update his final draft. An old friend, author Albert Rhys Williams, had given him a number of personal observations from a recent tour in Moscow in order to bring him up to date on the current issues and personalities in the Soviet capital.[26]

Another old friend, however, was less conciliatory. The long-lost A. T. Cholerton, who had befriended the young Muggeridge in the 1930s in Moscow and who had worked alongside Duranty there for over a decade, suddenly sent Duranty a terse note: "My Dear Walter," he began, "You still owe me at least five hundred dollars. I need them right now and in New York. . . . After that we will call it a day." If he wrote to Duranty only in regard to money, Cholerton said frankly, it was because he needed it.

Then, almost as an aside, he dropped in what he must have known Duranty was eager to hear—that Mike had gone into the Military

337

Academy: "(various faux frères, who mentioned it to me were proph-
esying woe). But I feel there is a good chance of his coming through
alright [sic]." As to the current state of affairs in the Soviet Union, "We
two know more about that show than all the rest put together."[27]
   Alas, it was no longer true—in Duranty's case at least.

Despite the fact he would soon be sixty-five, Duranty had been planning to take up a tour for N.A.N.A., probably initiated at the same
time as the Lippincott deal. Knowing he needed to get into the Soviet
Union for the book, he no doubt intended to get his expenses covered
by N.A.N.A. while he made the attempt. The idea was to go to Iran,
and from that vantage point, try to obtain a visa into the U.S.S.R. It
would involve hard traveling, brutal persistence, and a good deal of
energy. Despite this, it was as good a time as any, probably better, for
Duranty to make a quick exit. He owed money to practically everyone
he knew, and his welcome in New York City was wearing thin.
Besides, Knick had never ceased traveling for the press associations,
keeping his credentials up-to-date—a wise move viewed in retrospect.
Duranty had resisted until now, knowing it was a difficult life, but it
had become imperative that he take himself "off the shelf," if he were
to maintain any credibility at all. N.A.N.A. gave Duranty only one
directive if he did manage to get in: to find out "whether Russia
intends to start a war."[28]
   In carrying out these instructions, Duranty ran head-on into an
obstacle. There was one creditor who wouldn't take no for an answer—
the Internal Revenue Service. Since Duranty was not a United States
citizen, he was not permitted to leave the country until all his tax
arrears were paid. Duranty's accountant in California had given him
detailed instructions on how to facilitate his exit from the United
States—if he managed to get the money to pay.[29] Yet by April of 1949,
Duranty had not even signed and filed his 1948 return, intending to
wait until he got the money to pay.[30] He was still waiting in June.
Undismayed as always, he explained to his accountant that it was
impossible for him to to into Iran until the early fall, because of "the
unbearable heat."[31] He was certain something would turn up before
then.
   At the end of June, Duranty received his authorization from

N.A.N.A. to travel and within a week, all the credentials he needed to set out.[32] It was a trip he never made.

On the 13th of July 1949, a plane went down in India, and all aboard were killed. On the plane had been a group of American correspondents, among them Duranty's close friend Knickerbocker. Word of the accident hit journalists in the United States hard. The loss at one time of so many friends affected the entire network of professional correspondents. For Duranty, there followed a period of blank confusion, a peculiar period of passivity, of drink and days lost, a black hole in which time ceased to exist. The weeks quietly drained away, unnoticed.

What ruined Duranty, his friends would speculate decades after his death, was when he lost his visa into Soviet Russia, or when he started hitting the bottle too hard, or when he hit that period of sterility and stagnation. What *really* ruined Duranty, they would say, was that journalist's hand-to mouth mentality, that inability to plan for the future . . . that crazy bohemianism. What ruined him, they said categorically, was when Knick was killed in that plane crash.

It all added up to one thing: Duranty's luck had run out.

On the 21st of August 1949, from his hotel room, Duranty wrote a letter across town to John Gunther. He was "utterly in the soup, so deep that I dont know what to do and have no pride left." His finances were in tatters, he himself was shattered, he didn't know how to proceed.

Duranty had saved enough money, he told Gunther, to pay his back taxes, but there had been "a crazy delay" between himself and his accountant in Los Angeles. In the meantime, his living expenses had set him just below the amount of money he needed to pay the I.R.S. There was money still due him from work he had already completed, but instead of asking for it, he sat around "in reality doing nothing," while his cash reserves melted away on day-to-day living. "So Im good and stuck, because any hopes from Marjorie, on which Id counted since shes never had so long a period without selling something, seem to be quite vain."

Duranty took stock. He had a project going on some science fiction stories that he hoped to get published in an anthology. And of course, he had the N.A.N.A. job—which he was unable to get to because of the tax snafu. He couldn't go to Colston Leigh because he and Knick had refused to sign up with him the previous year.[33] Now Gunther knew all, and Duranty, plaintive in his closing lines, made this final request:

> O John, I hate to bother you, but there's noone else I can turn to, and I really refuse to believe that I cant earn money or am fit for euthanasia. Please help me, at least with advice, and dont dislike or despise me for this letter.[34]

Characteristically, Gunther was in touch with Duranty within hours of getting the letter, suggesting a number of alternatives and promising solid support. By the next afternoon, Duranty was seemingly back on his feet. Again from his hotel room, he wrote a second letter to Gunther asking him to intercede on his behalf—which was "really much easier than asking for oneself"—with a number of people who might give him work.[35]

Meantime, he would go on the wagon. And he would move to a less expensive location, where he could work on his fiction and where his dollars would stretch further.

Anna Enwright's grandfather had been the State's Attorney of Florida, known in those days simply as "the Judge," and at the age of twenty-one, her husband had actually become a judge—the youngest in the history of the state, the city judge of Orlando, a town his family had helped to found. Among the women of her generation, Enwright was unusually well educated, with a bachelor's degree from Florida State College for Women and a master's degree from Hood College in Maryland. Her distinguished background made Enwright one of the more socially prominent women in Orlando, which at that time was a small Southern city with a strict sense of propriety and social protocol.

But when Anna Enwright's husband was only twenty-four years old, he had died, only three years after their marriage, leaving his wife to raise their infant son alone. A strikingly beautiful woman in the tradition of the Southern belle, Enwright had no shortage of suitors.[36] Unexpectedly, she proved to be an extremely discriminating woman, with a singularly high level of expectation; and through the years, she continued to save herself—until the right man should come along.

That man was Walter Duranty.

All in a panic, Duranty now flew south to the woman John Gunther had earlier referred to as "his Florida girl," the one who had so vehemently objected to his trip to the Virgin Islands with Gunther's pretty fiancée. There were the explanations, the understandings; the sealing of a relationship.

It quickly became known in the city that the two formed a pair, and there was for Duranty an unexpected windfall, the sort of social splash he found most gratifying, the opportunity to be at the center of things once more. With his own penchant for scintillating conversation and the beautiful Anna Enwright at his side, he took over the role of big fish in a little pond as the couple made easy conquest of Orlando's most exclusive social clubs, the Sorosis and Rosalind Clubs—to which Enwright belonged.[37]

In great demand, the couple filled up their social calendar with dinner and cocktail engagements. At the Country and University Clubs, Duranty was occasionally asked to speak, much to the continuing gratification of Anna Enwright, whom he squired around with astounding agility. Enwright, always known as a paragon of quiet good taste, dressed in muted colors; blues, grays, and greens, accentuating her dark good looks with just a touch of bright color in a carefully chosen accessory.

A photograph of Anna Enwright, taken when she was well past fifty, shows a woman with intelligent eyes and character. She is wearing a simple scooped-neck, dotted Swiss dress, and her elegant hands are caught in a graceful gesture of amusement. Her figure is slim, and even at her mature age, she is beautiful.

As for Duranty, he soon became known throughout the city for his *bons mots*. At one official social gathering, the wife of an Egyptian ambassador talked incessantly about "what bastards the British were," and how pleased she was that Egypt had gained its independence from Great Britain. Said Duranty, "I'm awfully glad Egypt got its independence, and I'm awfully glad the British taught you what it was."[38]

There were other, less ostentatious triumphs for the couple, which served to affirm nevertheless their social ascendancy. Duranty quickly became friends with Marjorie Rawlings, author of *The Yearling*, whom Enwright had known for many years. It was not unusual on a Saturday for the two of them to drive out to Rawlings farm to spend the day.

Duranty had at first taken lodgings in a well-known hotel in the city, but he found it necessary to move temporarily to "a sort of little apartment with a private entrance, very nice, and at a really minimal rate."[39] Orlando didn't know it at the moment, but their new-found celebrity was strapped for funds, although he was certain his luck would change for the better at any time.

In the midst of this new lease on life, Duranty's book *Stalin & Co.* appeared to generally favorable reviews, and he was praised for refraining from passing moral judgments on the men whose lives he chronicled.[40]

But Duranty complained privately that Sloane had butchered his book. Whole sections had been deleted, he said, especially those that were the hallmark of his style of writing. Indeed, Sloane's editors had carefully removed all references to characteristics Duranty continually identified as being "Jewish." Slashed also was a discussion of the American Relief Administration's operation during the famine of 1921—a rehash that Duranty had served up far too many times already. Also deleted were any references to fairy tales or classical allusions or epic historical events; and most particularly, those expressions of candor that seemed most trivial and self-indulgent and that threatened to ruin the tone of the book.[41] Although Duranty complained bitterly about the cuts, with the petulance of the prima donna he still considered himself to be, the critical success of the book probably rested, in no small part, upon the excellent editing the book had been taken through.

Duranty, burning but hungry, wrote to Bill Sloane, asking what had become of his British royalties, and all that was due him. Sloane wrote back quickly and quite cordially, reminding Duranty that he had already had an extra advance against the book. Since they agreed "to pool all the earnings of the book against that additional advance," there was still a deficit in the arrangement. "I'm sorry about this," Sloane said, "but there it is."[42]

There were other rejections to be absorbed. Gunther had come up with very little in the way of a job, although he had touched base with practically everyone in the business.

It got worse. One of his "background pieces" sent to London had made the rounds there, where he expected his pro-Soviet views would find a friendlier audience, but it had been rejected by a variety of publications that once would have jumped at the chance to have his name appear on their pages. The *Sunday Times* rejected Duranty's latest effort; then the *Spectator* turned it down. No newspaper nowadays, he was told, could handle more than 1000 words, and in any case, background pieces were no longer in demand. The friend of Duranty's who sent the piece around suggested, next time, he go through an agent.[43] In the meantime, Gunther had returned an analysis Duranty had done on the relationship between Stalin and Mao, which he had been "unable to place."[44]

Duranty now depended almost entirely upon the lecture circuit for his support. Without Knick, the fees he could expect had shrunk significantly; without Colston Leigh, the jobs were hard to come by. In the spring of 1950, he managed to get himself booked in Tampa for a speech or two, and, via his friends who lived there, a few in Milwaukee. He had also been "plugging away at fiction and gotten nowhere, just dont seem to have any worthwhile stories and have known that while I was writing them." He still believed his fiction would eventually pay off, although he frankly admitted his "mind felt like a squirrel in a cage."[45]

As for his tax arrears, Duranty made steady if slow progress on liquidating the debt, and in 1950, his income was so small he owed the I.R.S. nothing at all. Belatedly, he received permission from the Treasury Department to depart the country.

His Milwaukee tour worked out well; he pleased the audience, and it led to further engagements. He returned to Orlando talking excitedly about Senator Joseph McCarthy, who was not very popular among the intellectuals in his home state, and who would inevitably, they had all told Duranty, be "coming a cropper."[46]

The involvement with current affairs and a renewed sense of success evidently gave Duranty a new wind, and he hatched out a scheme he was sure would work. He and John Gunther should become a radio team, with Gunther securing "a pitch on the air" and Duranty chiming in as Gunther's "Man Friday." They would explicate the problems of the Korean war, making a reputation for themselves into the bargain.

The newspapers were currently awash with the recent victories of General Douglas MacArthur, who had been named Commander in Chief of the United Nations Command in Korea. By the 26th of September 1950, and despite all odds, MacArthur had effected the miraculous Inchon landing, which had resulted in the liberation of Seoul from the North Korean Army, and, as it seemed at the time, essentially crushed the Communist attempt to take over South Korea. Although Communist China had threatened intervention if the 38th parallel were crossed, MacArthur did not heed the warnings, and his troops were penetrating beyond that demarcation line.

Duranty wrote to Gunther a political explication of these developments as they occurred, in an attempt to overwhelm him with his superior grasp of current events. He deprecated President Truman's announcement of "the smashing victory in Korea the very day not even your Tokyo friends could hide any longer, from themselves or others, that China was in."

> I suppose they think, still in Washington and Lake Success, that "our smashing diplomatic victory in the U.N. is a great step toward peace," as I heard one dope say on the air. Maybe Nero made better music.
> Don't they know it's midnight minus one minute? . . .
> China moved up troops, slowly of course but plenty, while we yipped about victory and fooled around with the U.N. Now comes winter, cold in North Korea, but likely to be hot in IndoChina, and China has men to burn for both, by the millions, with enough arms and modern methods to make numerical superiority count.[47]

Duranty called for reinforcement of the British in Burma and the French in Indochina "above Hanoi," and predicted that Indochina would be the one to go first, although "Korea is the worst at present." Unless the French and British could be "brought to realize the necessity to send quick reinforcement to their areas, the more distant outlook seems to me little better than the prospect—not too remote I fear—of a considerable war with China now in Korea-Manchuria."[48]

What was needed, Duranty said, not only in Korea and Indochina, but also in Malaya and Persia and Egypt, was

> plenty of food and manufactured goods and machines and public works . . . things, things, things. Things they need and seed and cattle and machines and medicine and doctors and rugs, not elections and talk about democracy or why our freedom is better than someone else's.[49]

344

With the French defeat at Dienbienphu less than four years away, if Duranty wished to demonstrate he could still understand the global effects of a limited engagement, he succeeded.

It was a thesis that demonstrated considerable prescience, and, what was unusual for Duranty, uncommon sensitivity as to the causes of disruption in what would come to be called the Third World. Walter Duranty, off the bottle at long last, clear-headed and feeling that old sense of confidence, still had the ability "to see through a brick wall," as he had so often put it.

In the next few days, Duranty would shoot off another letter to Gunther, urgently pushing his Far East thesis. It was a hell of a story, he said, which Gunther must get through to the American public. He would have written it himself "if I thought anyone would print it. If you write it they will print it. You can then give me a cut."[50]

He took on his old toplofty attitude, and along with it, a patronizing tone: "Why don't you talk yourself to some of the top soldiers in Washington [who] will soon clear things up for you."[51]

A short time later, after the devastating counteroffensive of the Chinese Communists, when 180,000 Reds ripped through MacArthur's troops, Duranty again wrote Gunther, this time shifting to the hard sell:

> Well, John, do you still think Im a doting alarmist or a pale and fearful Cassandra? It looks like the two weeks grace is ended now and the hour of decision near striking. But there may be time for you to swing that radio job, if you hurry.[52]

John Gunther had been hard at work on a book about MacArthur, and at the same time, he was revising *Inside U.S.A.* for a new edition. These were the reasons, he assured his old friend after a silence of several weeks, that he had been "very late in answering both your good letters."

He and Jane thought of Duranty often, missed him terribly, "and wish you were here all the time." They went out a good deal, "far too much, and never seem to have a moment free." He wished he could get away from the work piled up on his desk, come down to Florida, take a long rest. In the meantime, Jane sent her love, and they both hoped he had "an amiable Christmas." Someplace along the line, he briefly mentioned Duranty's proposal, saying he wished he could work with Duranty as part of a team, but "there aren't any radio jobs any more, at least for such as me."[53]

The rejection was sandwiched in between so many pleasantries and expressions of good will that it seemed as if Gunther had not rejected the scheme at all.

CHAPTER XX

Death Is the End

It was strange to discover, in these declining years, that everything seemed to militate against him, and Duranty was frustrated in even the smallest matters. His fiction was foundering, his articles were no longer considered relevant; even a piece he had written on bridge had been rejected as being too specialized.[1] Everything he had given to Gunther to place had been reluctantly returned, with apologies.

To Gunther, who remained his only close friend, Duranty now wrote a squeamish letter, full of obsequious passages and embarrassing words of praise, which he insisted upon sending, "even at the risk of shocking your modesty."

> Of all the successful people Ive come across, you, my dear John, are the most utterly and sincerely modest, and I suppose that even now at the height of your career you havent a tenth of the idea how much people really admire you. . . .
>
> For me, John, you stand so high above anyone I have known, you yourself as a person, not in relation to me, that I brought my troubles to you with complete confidence that henceforth it would be all right, that I could rely upon you. And of course you didnt disappoint me. You helped me not only with money but with encouragement that I needed equally, and I felt safe in your friendship. Perhaps I felt too safe, too sheltered and secure in the knowledge that I could count on you

always. Thats what worries me now, that you might think I would presume on that feeling of safety and take things for granted, almost as a matter of convenience. Perhaps in a way I did, but never in that way.

However gratuitous this kind of appeal must have seemed to Gunther, he hung on, remaining loyal to Duranty in his discreet way.[2]

The small town of Orlando, infatuated with Duranty at the beginning, began to close its doors against him. It had been thought, when Duranty was introduced by Enwright to the townspeople, that the couple would soon marry. Duranty resisted. In the same way he had avoided marrying Katya, for reasons never made clear, he now resisted marrying Anna Enwright, for reasons never made clear. Word soon got around that he was virtually penniless, and it did not go unnoticed that he maintained a transient lifestyle, moving from one small apartment to another, giving each up when he got a lecture tour that lasted for more than a few weeks, in order to save a bit of money. Significantly, a letter addressed to him at the *New York Times* was returned to the sender, marked "Address Unknown."[3]

Duranty's provocative manner and political views had always been strong medicine, even when he mixed with the most sophisticated people in the world. In Moscow, even in Paris and New York, he had taken a kind of perverse delight in outraging the more conventional thinkers. Standing in the shadows had always been a number of silent observers who disliked him or disapproved of his lifestyle. In Orlando as well, Duranty had taken little care to respect the prejudices of the small town, political or otherwise.

People would sometimes approach him and say, "Isn't this Communist situation terrible?"

"No," Duranty would reply. "They are better off than they've ever been. Half a loaf is better than none."

One night, he and Enwright returned from a dinner party, complaining about the couple they had just visited. Enwright said that they were "simply *petty*."

Duranty responded, "Petty is just the word—petty minds and petty lives—even their immoralities are petty. They're the kind of people who think they're living dangerously when they put a copy of D. H. Lawrence on the coffee table."[4]

Perhaps if Duranty had been able to maintain his role as one of the city's leading citizens, such responses might have been tolerated. But it was quickly recognized that he was down on his luck, and there was nothing to be gained by patronizing him. He "was literally living from hand to mouth . . . he was living from one little check to the next."⁵ If Hollywood hated "a has-been," deliberately avoiding anyone suspected of the offense, so much more a small town like Orlando.

Enwright's friends believed Duranty was freeloading off her, was taking advantage of her. Word quickly made its way back, by way of a warning.

In the spring of 1951, Duranty wrote to Marjorie Worthington, who had been ill. He sent his condolences, mentioning at the same time that he had heard John Gunther had contracted pneumonia, and he was concerned.

The doctor told Worthington she could no longer drink alcohol, but Duranty said it was unimportant. "I've cut my own alcoholic intake pretty nearly to zero," he wrote, "and it scarcely seems to matter." He recounted the story of an Englishman who got rich after World War I and moved to a château in Burgundy to enjoy the best food and drink in the world. But he was was smitten with gout and told that, if he wished to live, his diet must henceforth be "lentils and water, or something to that effect."⁶

Despite her illness, Worthington's fortunes had undergone a welcome reversal, and her stories began to sell again. In fact, she was working on the book that would become her biggest commercial success, a biography of Louisa May Alcott. The Gunthers tended to believe that Worthington and Duranty belonged together, but, as Jane Gunther put it, "Poor old Marjorie hadn't enough to keep him 'at the end.'"⁷

Meanwhile, from his isolation in Orlando, Duranty wrote that he wished the two of them could "get over to France for the June elections—that's only a tentative date I believe—and the Grand Prix. Well, perhaps. . . ."⁸

Gunther recovered from his illness, and the following autumn wrote to Duranty, saying "It worries us that we haven't heard from you for so very long. Lots of people ask about you, and I do not even know where you are for sure . . . Please drop us a line."⁹

Duranty wrote back, saying, "I don't flourish, but am well and happy enough." He had found a little garage apartment that suited him perfectly. In the meantime, he had come up with an idea. He wondered "whether I couldnt do some ghosting for you."

> I mean that youd suggest a story youd do for someone and then tell me what was wanted, the length and general treatment, and Id shoot it along in a nine-tenths finished state, only needing a touch of your polish and fixing to round it to final shape.
>
> I could easily do one or two a week and it would not only help me in a manner I could use but would also gradually pay back some of the money I owe you. Id take any percentage you thought fair and as you probably know I can write smooth enough and well enough on almost any subject you choose.[10]

He said he had been "quite vegetative" for a long time, but "a change is now due." He intended to get to Europe, but not until the weather changed, "tho my mind is now set on Tobago first."

Gunther immediately wrote back, full of enthusiasm "from knowing that you are in good shape and all." He also liked the "idea of our working together, but I don't see how we can do anything just now."[11] But he did give him some welcome news, that in addition to some of the other trips he was planning, there was the possibility that he and Jane would be coming to Florida, and they would want to see Duranty.

Duranty wanted to see him too, he wrote back, "without any other people, except of course Jane. . . ."[12]

In 1952, John and Jane Gunther made their trip to the South, staying in a small town near Orlando. While they were there Duranty came to their motel by taxi and, as Jane Gunther later recalled, he was "enchanting, in his very best form." The two of them stayed up practically all night, at least until 4:00 in the morning, listening to him. He was terribly funny, and "very very wicked." After he left, John turned to Jane Gunther and said, "Walter is just a *scamp!*"[13]

The reason Duranty wanted to see them alone soon became apparent. Duranty believed that his work was being rejected because he was being blacklisted for his pro-Soviet views. The McCarthy hearings were in full swing, and Duranty had at last made a connection between his relentless rejections and the events going on in Washington. He asked Gunther privately to see if he could find out whether this was, in fact, true.

It was one of the busiest periods of John Gunther's life, but even so, Gunther somehow found the time to do "a considerable amount of scouting around." He talked personally about Duranty's desire to return to work to five of the top men in journalism, checking out Washington as well as New York, and he reported back that they were willing to employ him if he would go into China (almost an impossibility at the time), or into Latin America, or even Eastern Europe.

But as for Duranty's specific request to be sent to Paris, none seemed particularly interested. It was a shame he could not find Duranty exactly what he wanted, Gunther wrote, "but it should at least relieve your mind of the thought that you were being black-listed."[14]

In fact, the Federal Bureau of Investigation, which had been compiling information on Duranty for well over fifteen years, would have found little to quibble about in the conclusions reached by Gunther. The fifty-nine-page file included a complete assessment of Duranty's reporting career, as well as a number of his more controversial articles, and summaries of his other works. It was clear that friends and acquaintances had, since the early Thirties, been reporting to the Bureau on Duranty's activities and beliefs. But there was no concrete evidence that Duranty was a member of the Communist Party, or a propaganda agent, or working on the behalf of the Soviets since he had been inside the United States, although these possibilities had all been suggested or hinted at, either in reports that catalogued his associations, or by unnamed informants. Even during these years of extreme paranoia, when "the Red Scare" was reaching its peak, the F.B.I. made the decision not to investigate Walter Duranty. Except for the inclusion of book reviews and a few of his articles, Duranty had ceased to be of interest to the Bureau after January, 1951.[15]

For his part, Duranty never thought it would come to this. As he told Gunther, he had always maintained the belief that "success was permanent, once grasped to flow on forever."[16] Now, isolated and ostracized, he recognized his mistake. He took it hard; drew into himself, becoming what the newspapers would later call "a recluse." After all, what were his choices?

Anna Enwright rejected her friends' advice, and did not desert the failing Duranty. The couple drew a curtain around themselves, withdrawing into a world of their own making. They went regularly to the public library, pulling books indiscriminately from the shelves, reading whatever they laid their hands on. Duranty often stayed behind, to read the *New York Times* and the London *Times*, which he called "the two best newspapers in the world."

He continued to live apart from Enwright. Typically, he made no attempt to fix up his efficiency, which was practically empty except for a few sticks of furniture. He filled his days sitting at a table in the center of the room, amidst the clutter of papers and books, where he beavered away, an old man, hard at work on something he was preparing for publication, when the day came.

In the evenings, Enwright prepared dinner, laid the table with a white tablecloth. On festive occasions, they took wine with their meal. If the weather was fine, she would put up a card table, and the couple would move to the back porch. There, they could catch the breeze through the trees and look out into the backyard where there was a pleasant garden of azaleas and camellias, orange and lemon trees, and a high bay laurel hedge that separated Enwright's yard from those beside it.[17]

Duranty came out of his retirement only once, in March 1953, when the great Soviet dictator he had so much admired during his lifetime died and the Orlando *Morning Sentinel* asked him to comment. Then, again, for one last time, "Walter Duranty, Famed *New York Times* Correspondent" wrote the lead story for page one, which appeared, along with a thumbnail photograph of the writer, above the paper's banner: a fifty-six-inch story that chronicled the life of "the red tyrant" and told "How To Defeat [the] Heirs of Stalin."

Characterizing Stalin as "a violent and crafty rebel," Duranty once more trotted out his "Man of Steel" thesis and outlined the history of "Stalin's creation, his life-work, the robot system of flesh and blood, which he . . . forged among his followers to lift himself and them to such heights of strength and influence as few mortals have ever known."

Then, as if exhausted by the effort, Duranty fell back and the article, in trying to predict what might happen to Stalin's successors, receded into hackwork, the words losing their power as Duranty lost the thread of his thesis.[18]

It was as if, with Stalin's death, Walter Duranty had nothing left to say.

The Gunthers heard from Duranty again in 1955, when he sent them a box of Temple oranges. There had been "a touch of frost —which the oranges need," he wrote, explaining that they were particularly good that season.[19] Gunther wrote back thanking him, and Duranty again asked for work, this time reading manuscripts. Obediently, Gunther put him in touch with a scholar at the University of Miami, who was looking for someone to read Russian manuscripts.[20]

Duranty's circumstances became desperate. He had agreed with Enwright to split the grocery bill, but he found himself unable to meet even this minor obligation, which was in truth more a matter of pride than of necessity. At his lowest point, his checking account showed a balance of just over five dollars.

But by 1957, when he was at last offered a writing job by the son of Ann Watkins, who had taken over his mother's literary agency in New York, Duranty found it necessary to decline. He wrote, by way of explanation:

> I am not anxious to do any original copy as my brain is soggy. Ten years of sunny Lassida have been charming and gay, but not conducive to work.[21]

He welcomed Watkins's idea, however, for a reissue of his old short stories, suggesting they be published under the pseudonym "Cawtney Rudge, which," Duranty explained, "is scholarly without gawdiness."[22]

On the 5th of September 1957, Duranty wrote to his old employer at the *New York Times*, Arthur Hays Sulzberger—in what has been described "as a really pathetic letter"[23]—asking for a pension of $155 per month. Sulzberger responded by writing him a personal check for $2500.[24]

Besides a few papers which he kept in an accordian file, Walter Duranty left a sterling silver cup which he had used as a child and his old rowing cap from Emmanuel College, both of which were wrapped carefully in tissue paper and stored, along with his file, in two suitcases—one alligator, the other pasteboard.[25] Among the papers was a clipping he saved from a speech Knick had given at Martha's Vineyard on July 16, 1948. In one envelope there were some canceled railway tickets,

353

the photograph of an unidentified young girl, and a social note from
Alexander Woollcott.

On September 8, 1957, three days after writing to Sulzberger, Duranty
checked into Orange Memorial Hospital in Orlando, feeling weak and
tired. He had an ulcer which had, of late, been troubling him more
than usual.

On the 26th of September, he and Anna Enwright were married in
a short ceremony conducted beside his hospital bed. One week later,
on the 3rd of October, at 1:49 in the afternoon, Duranty died from an
internal hemorrhage complicated by pulmonary emphysema. He was
seventy-three years old.

For Duranty, "the bitterness of death [was] past, or, if not past,
discounted."

> To human beings death is the End. One may think one believes in a
> life after death, but it is generally a vague sort of belief, rather a hope
> than a belief, and death is the End. If you come very near to death and
> get familiar so to speak with death, you begin to feel that you have
> reached ultimate issues and that you don't give a damn.[26]

The funeral ceremony for Walter Duranty was closed, with only
four friends, who had been invited, in attendance. Anna Enwright,
described by a close relative as "terribly overwrought and terribly mad
at the time," said she did not wish to include anyone from Orlando. A
friend turned away at the door of the funeral home said later, "I never
fully realized how much she must have loved him all those years."[27]

Duranty's death was recorded in the *New York Times*, the London
Times, *The Overseas Press Bulletin*, *Time*, *Newsweek*, and a great
many other publications, usually with substantial obituaries outlining
his career and achievements.

In a column devoted to chronicling his life, Walter Winchell wrote,
"Walter Duranty, who was one of the titans among foreign correspondents, has passed."

> He gained world renown while covering Russia and was crowned with
> a Pulitzer Prize. . . . When months of good weather helped Russia's
> Five-Year Plan, he sardonically quipped: "God seems to be on the side
> of the atheists."

He had a superior reporter's ability to spot significant details as well as a poet's eloquence.[28]

In a later testimonial, the journalist Walter Kerr, who, like Gunther, remained loyal to Duranty, had this to say about his controversial coverage of Russia:

> Others brought with them their own prejudices. They viewed everything with alarm. Duranty viewed it with alarm, but he always placed the horrors into the main picture. . . . he always saw more to Russia than just that. He saw a vitality, a strength, that most outsiders could not see.[29]

Other newsmen would be less generous. They would remember Walter Duranty as the correspondent who compromised the ideals of his profession, who concealed the truth to further his own aims. They would remember him as he was portrayed in the obituary in *Time*. By that estimation, he would remain "the No. 1 Russian apologist in the West."[30]

Duranty's remains were cremated and placed in Fairfield Crematorium in Orlando, Florida. Anna Enwright lived on for another fourteen years. In January 1971, following the instructions she left behind, her son, Parker F. Enwright, removed Duranty's ashes from the crematorium and placed them inside her casket for burial.[31]

There is no further record of Katya beyond Harrison Salisbury's remembrance of a withered hag, hovering in the backroom of the apartment she once inhabited with Duranty. As for Duranty's abandoned son Michael, who several years before, had wanted "to know and must know where his father is," there would be no answers, only a continuation of the silence his father kept "for such a long time."[32]

Notes

CHAPTER I. *Liars Go to Hell*

1. Harrison E. Salisbury, *Without Fear or Favor: The New York Times and Its Times* (New York: Times Books, 1980), 458.
2. Howard Channon, *Portrait of Liverpool* (London: Robert Hale, 1970), 74.
3. William Dunlap, *The Life of George Frederick Cooke*, 2 vols. (London: printed for Henry Colburn, 1813), II: 360–61.
4. Information about Duranty's family is taken from Gore's *Liverpool Directory*; from census records in the Land Registry Office, London; and from records of births, marriages, and deaths, wills and other probate documents in various branches of the Public Record Office in London and in the public archives of Liverpool. Checks have also been made in the records of Companies House, London, although it appears that the Duranty family's company was not registered as a limited liability company, and thus no business records survive in public archives.
5. Peter Howell Williams, *Liverpolitana* (Liverpool: Merseyside Civic Society, 1971), 10.
6. George Chandler, *Liverpool* (London: Batsford, 1957), 309.
7. Williams, *Liverpolitana*, 10.
8. George Chandler, *Victorian and Edwardian Liverpool and the North West from Old Photographs* (London: Batsford, 1972), "Introduction," n.p.
9. The Last Will and Testament of Alexander Duranty, dated 1 Feb. 1873, proved 19 June 1876 (Somerset House, London).
10. Channon, *Portrait*, 77.
11. Ibid., 88.
12. "Weather," *The Times* (London), 26 May 1884, p. 6.
13. "The Late Crisis on the New York Stock Exchange," *The Times* (London), 24 May 1884, p. 9.

14. "The North of England Iron Trade," *The Times* (London), 26 May 1884, p. 5.
15. Walter Phelps Hall and Robert Greenhalgh Albion, *A History of England and the British Empire*, 3rd ed. (New York: Ginn, 1953), 295.
16. "State of Trade," *The Times* (London), 24 May 1884, p. 13.
17. Walter Duranty to Parker F. Enwright, 18 Oct. 1953, Personal Files of Parker F. Enwright, Orlando, Florida.
18. Parker F. Enwright to SJT, in an interview 8 Feb. 1979.
19. Walter Duranty, *I Write As I Please* (New York: Simon and Schuster, 1935), 154.
20. Channon, *Portrait*, 75.
21. Ibid., 74–75.
22. Williams, *Liverpolitana*, 11.
23. Hall and Albion, *A History of England*, 802.
24. Duranty, *I Write*, 3–4.
25. Ibid., 5.
26. Ibid., 11.
27. Harrison E. Salisbury to SJT, 28 Sept. 1979, p. 2. A number of others share Salisbury's skepticism.
28. J. H. Simpson, *Schoolmaster's Harvest: Some Findings of Fifty Years, 1894–1944* (London: Faber and Faber, 1954), 18.
29. Parker F. Enwright to SJT, in an interview 8 Feb. 1979.
30. George Seldes to SJT, in an interview 6 June 1979.
31. Simpson, *Schoolmaster's Harvest*, 19.
32. Walter Duranty, *Search for a Key* (New York: Simon and Schuster, 1943), 7.
33. Simpson, *Schoolmaster's Harvest*, 57–58.
34. Ibid., 61.
35. George Seldes to SJT, in an interview 6 June 1979.
36. Bedford Grammar School *Register* for 1899.
37. *The Ousel: Journal of Bedford Grammar School*, Vol. VII, No. 219, 27 May 1903, p. 55.
38. *Ousel*, 25 March 1903, p. 34.
39. *Ousel*, 1 April 1903, p. 35–36.
40. Murray Park to SJT, in an interview 17 Dec. 1987.
41. *Ousel*, 7 March 1903, p. 22.
42. *Ousel*, 23 July 1903, p. 88.
43. Ibid., 89.
44. William Shirer, *Berlin Diary: The Journal of a Foreign Correspondent* (New York: Knopf, 1942), 89.
45. *Ousel*, 23 July 1903, p. 89.
46. Christopher Hassall, *Rupert Brooke: A Biography* (London: Faber and Faber, 1964), 99–100.
47. Ibid., 100.
48. Miss E. S. Leedham-Green to SJT, 5 Jan. 1979.
49. P. Hunter Blair to SJT, 2 Feb. 1979.
50. Frank Stubbings, *Emmanuel College: An Historical Guide* (Cambridge: The Masters and Fellows of Emmanuel College Cambridge, 1983), 2. See also E. S. Shuckburgh, *Emmanuel College* (London: F. E. Robinson, 1904), 17–26.
51. Stubbings, *Emmanuel College*, 22.

Notes

52. Ibid., 4.
53. *Emmanuel College Magazine*, Michaelmas Term, 1903, p. 68.
54. Walter Duranty, "I Write As I Please," Orlando *Morning Sentinel*, 24 Jan. 1947.
55. Walter Duranty, "I Write As I Please," Orlando *Morning Sentinel*, 27 Jan. 1947.
56. Duranty, *I Write*, 309.

CHAPTER II. *Maggots Upon an Apple*

1. John Symonds, *The Great Beast: The Life and Magick of Aleister Crowley* (London: MacDonald, 1971), 9–10.
2. Ibid., 10.
3. Ibid., 11.
4. Ibid., 13.
5. Ibid., 12.
6. Aleister Crowley, *The Magical Record of the Beast 666: The Diaries of Aleister Crowley 1914–1920.* Ed. by John Symonds and Kenneth Grant. (London: Duckworth, 1972), 4.
7. Alexander Woolcott, "A Personal Note on Walter Duranty," in *Duranty Reports Russia,* by Walter Duranty (New York: Viking, 1934), vii.
8. Parker F. Enwright to SJT, in an interview, 10 Feb. 1979.
9. Symonds, *The Great Beast*, 229.
10. Aleister Crowley, *The Diary of a Drug Fiend* (London: Collins, 1922), 65.
11. Crowley's own annotated copy of *The Diary of a Drug Fiend* which gives the names of real persons represented by the fictional characters, is preserved in the G. J. Yorke Collection at the Warburg Institute in London.
12. Crowley, *Diary*, 65.
13. Ibid., 69.
14. Ibid., 71.
15. Ibid., 70–71.
16. Crowley, *The Magical Record*, 240.
17. Robin Kinkead to SJT, in an interview 12 April 1979.
18. Harrison E. Salisbury, *Without Fear or Favor: The New York Times and Its Times* (New York: Times Books, 1980), 460.
19. Robin Kinkead to SJT, in an interview 20 April 1979.
20. Salisbury, *Without Fear*, 460.
21. Discretion dictates that both women remain unidentified.
22. Walter Duranty to William Sloane, n.d., Personal Files of Walter Duranty, Orlando, Florida.
23. Otto Weininger, *Sex and Character* (London: Heinemann, 1906), 89.
24. Woollcott, "A Personal Note," vi.
25. Ibid., vii-viii.
26. Wythe Williams, *Dusk of Empire* (New York: Scribner's, 1937), 30–31.
27. [Walter Duranty and Wythe Williams], "Flies Upside Down Quarter of a Mile; Experts Say Pegoud's Feat Is Epoch-Making Experiment in Aeronautics," *New York Times*, 2 Sept. 1913, pp. 1–2.
28. Williams, *Dusk*, 30.

29. Salisbury, *Without Fear*, 458.
30. Symonds, *The Great Beast*, 157.
31. Ibid., 187 n. 1. The Latin verses by Crowley and Duranty used to invoke Roman deities were collected under the title "The Holy Hymns to the High Gods of Heaven." They are published, with a translation, together with the diary of the Paris workings themselves, in Martin Starr, *Sex & Religion* (Nashville, 1981), esp. pp. 225–28.
32. Ibid., quoting Crowley, 167.
33. Ibid., 187; see also Salisbury, *Without Fear*, 459.
34. Williams, *Dusk*, 31–32.
35. Ibid., 35.
36. Samuel Hopkins Adams, *A. Woollcott: His Life and His World* (New York: Reynal and Hitchcock, 1945), 65.
37. Ibid., 305.
38. Emmet Crozier, *American Reporters on the Western Front 1914 - 1918* (New York: Oxford University Press, 1959), 4.
39. Ibid., 3–4.
40. Wythe Williams, *Passed by the Censor* (New York: Dutton, 1916), 3.
41. Ibid., 5.
42. Crozier, *American Reporters*, 5.
43. Williams, *Passed by the Censor*, 13.
44. Ibid., 15.
45. Ibid., 16.
46. Ibid., 264.
47. Ibid., 18.
48. Williams, *Dusk*, 50.
49. John Hohenberg, *Foreign Correspondence: The Great Reporters and Their Times* (New York: Columbia University Press, 1964), 212.
50. Walter Duranty, *I Write As I Please* (New York: Simon and Schuster, 1935), 232.
51. Crozier, *American Reporters*, 23.
52. A. J. P. Taylor, *The First World War: An Illustrated History* (Harmondsworth, Eng.: Penguin Books, 1986), 21.
53. Williams, *Passed by the Censor*, 56–58.
54. Taylor, *The First World War*, 34.
55. Crozier, *American Reporters*, 56.
56. Ibid., 57.
57. Ibid., 56.
58. Phillip Knightley, *The First Casualty: The War Correspondent as Hero, Propagandist, and Myth Maker from the Crimea to Vietnam* (London: Deutsch, 1975), 83.
59. Taylor, *The First World War*, 57.
60. Williams, *Dusk*, 53.
61. *Emmanuel College Magazine*, Vol. XL, 1957–58, *obit.* n.p.
62. Walter Duranty, *Search for a Key* (New York: Simon and Schuster, 1943), 64.
63. Hohenberg, *Foreign Correspondence*, 215.
64. Williams, "Foreword," *Passed by the Censor*, n.p.
65. Williams, *Dusk*, 129.
66. "Obituary," *Editor and Publisher*, 12 Oct. 1957, p. 44.

67. "London Surgeons Say Bombs from Zeppelins Were Impregnated with Disease Germs; Mortality of Victims from Gangrene High," *New York Times*, 19 Nov. 1915, p. 3.
68. [Walter Duranty], "New Zeppelin Raid on Paris Fails; 24 Dead, 30 Injured in Saturday's Raid; Majority Are Women and Children," *New York Times*, 31 Jan. 1916, pp. 1–2.
69. Ibid., 2.
70. Duranty, *I Write*, 304.

CHAPTER III. *For You But Not for Me*

1. John Symonds, *The Great Beast: The Life and Magick of Aleister Crowley* (London: MacDonald, 1971), 229.
2. George Seldes to SJT, in an interview 6 June 1979.
3. Symonds, *The Great Beast*, 229.
4. Ibid., 172.
5. Edwin P. Hoyt, *Alexander Woollcott: The Man Who Came to Dinner* (New York: Abelard-Schuman, 1968), 85.
6. Samuel Hopkins Adams, *A. Woollcott: His Life and His World* (New York: Reynal and Hitchcock, 1945), 90.
7. Hoyt, *Alexander Woollcott*, 85.
8. Ibid., 95.
9. Ibid.
10. Alexander Woollcott, *The Letters of Alexander Woollcott*. Ed. by Beatrice Kaufman and Joseph Hennessey (New York: Viking Press, 1944), 67–68.
11. Walter Duranty, *I Write As I Please* (New York: Simon and Schuster, 1935), 90.
12. George Seldes to SJT, in an interview 6 June 1979.
13. Duranty, *I Write*, 96.
14. Ibid., 95.
15. Ibid., 90–92.
16. John Hohenberg, *Foreign Correspondence: The Great Reporters and Their Times* (New York: Columbia University Press, 1964), 221. Joffre's figures have been revised downwards by historians to just under one million casualties on both sides, or somewhat fewer, depending upon the date the counting ends.
17. A. J. P. Taylor, *The First World War: An Illustrated History* (Harmondsworth, Eng.: Penguin Books, 1966), 136.
18. Ibid., 140.
19. Ibid., p. 53.
20. Joseph J. Mathews, quoting Frederick Palmer, in *Reporting the Wars* (Minneapolis: University of Minnesota Press, 1957), 157.
21. Phillip Knightley, *The First Casualty: The War Correspondent as Hero, Propagandist, and Myth Maker from the Crimea to Vietnam*, (London: Deutsch, 1975), 115.
22. Hohenberg, *Foreign Correspondence*, 213.
23. Knightley, *The First Casualty*, 115–16.
24. Hohenberg, *Foreign Correspondence*, 223.
25. Knightley, *The First Casualty*, 125.
26. Ibid.

27. Ibid., 95.
28. Ibid., quoting Sir Philip Gibbs, p. 97.
29. Ibid., 124.
30. Hohenberg, *Foreign Correspondence*, 218.
31. Knightley, *The First Casualty*, 114.
32. Emmet Crozier, *American Reporters on the Western Front 1914–1918* (New York: Oxford University Press, 1959), 192–93.
33. Hohenberg, *Foreign Correspondence*, 238.
34. Paul Scott Mowrer, *The House of Europe* (Boston: Houghton Mifflin, 1945), 284.
35. Ibid., 283.
36. Frederick Palmer, *With the New Army on the Somme* (London: John Murray, 1917), 197.
37. Ibid., 197.
38. Knightley, *The First Casualty*, 96.
39. Philip Gibbs, *Realities of War* (London: Heinemann, 1920), p. 19.
40. Ibid., 18.
41. Knightley, *The First Casualty*, quoting Sir Philip Gibbs, p. 109.
42. Palmer, *With the New Army*, 197.
43. Duranty, *I Write*, 8.
44. Gibbs, *Realities of War*, 3–5.
45. "Daily Express," Community Song Book No. 3, *Songs That Won the War* (London: Lane Publications, [1930]), 94.
46. C. E. Montague, *Disenchantment* (London: Chatto and Windus, 1922), 96–97.
47. Hohenberg, *Foreign Correspondence*, 216.
48. Ibid., quoting Palmer, p. 216.
49. Duranty, *I Write*, 7.

CHAPTER IV. *A Sea of Blood*

1. The descriptions here and elsewhere of conditions in France during 1918 are partially drawn from *The Annales de la Guerre*, No. 76, 1914–1918, part of the Official Documents of the Cinematographic Section of the French Army, made available to the author at the Imperial War Museum in London.
2. Paul Scott Mowrer, *The House of Europe* (Boston: Houghton Mifflin, 1945), 285.
3. Philip Gibbs, "Germans' Vast Superiority in Guns Is Backed by Fifty Divisions," *New York Times*, 24 March 1918, p. 1.
4. Ibid.
5. Ibid.
6. "French Capital under Fire," *New York Times*, 24 March 1918, p. 1.
7. "Cables Pershing for News of Drive," *New York Times*, 24 March 1918, p. 1.
8. "Commentary," *New York Times*, 29 March 1918, p. 1.
9. John Hohenberg, *Foreign Correspondence: The Great Reporters and Their Times* (New York: Columbia University Press, 1964), 238.
10. Ibid., quoting Clemenceau, p. 239.
11. Walter Duranty, "Shaken German Army Still Delays; Demoralized by Allied Air Raids, Dissention at Home, and Lack of Men," *New York Times*, 24 May 1918, p. 1.

12. Walter Duranty, "German Guns Pound British Lines, But Allies Wait in Confidence; Our First Warplanes Now in Use," *New York Times*, 27 May 1918, p. 1.

13. Walter Duranty, "Battle Factors that Favor Allies," *New York Times*, 31 May 1918, p. 2.

14. Walter Duranty, "Germans Outrun Their Artillery," *New York Times*, 1 June 1918, p. 3.

15. Walter Duranty, "Allies Standing Firmly at Bay," *New York Times*, 3 June 1918, p. 1.

16. Emmet Crozier, *American Reporters on the Western Front, 1914–1918* (New York: Oxford University Press, 1959), 222.

17. John Gunther, Personal Diaries, Personal Files of John Gunther, New York, made available by Mrs. John [Jane Perry] Gunther, widow of the late John Gunther, n.p.

18. Hohenberg, *Foreign Correspondence*, 239.

19. Gunther, Personal Diaries, n.p.

20. Crozier, *American Reporters*, 233.

21. Ibid., 235.

22. Walter Duranty, *I Write As I Please* (New York: Simon and Schuster, 1935), 7–8.

23. Ibid., 8–9.

24. Walter Duranty, "The Turning Point of the Battle," *Current History Magazine*, July 1918, p. 28.

25. Walter Duranty, "Germans Paying Appalling Toll," *New York Times*, 12 June 1918, p. 1.

26. Ibid.

27. Ibid., 2.

28. Duranty, *I Write*, 6.

29. Edwin L. James, "Germans Lose 1,500 Prisoners and Make No Progress on Our Front," *New York Times*, 17 July 1918, p. 1.

30. Walter Duranty, "Germans Paid Dearly at the River," *New York Times*, 17 July 1918, p. 1.

31. *Annales de la Guerre*, No. 76, 1914–18.

32. Walter Duranty, "How They Go to the Front," *New York Times*, 21 July 1918, p. 2.

33. Ibid.

34. Ibid.

35. Walter Duranty, "Can Overcome Gas by Being Cautious," *New York Times*, 5 July 1918, p. 3.

36. Ibid.

37. Walter Duranty, "U-Boat Officers' Orgies at Bruges," *New York Times*, 29 Oct. 1918, p. 11.

38. Walter Duranty, "American's Banner First in Bruges," *New York Times*, 30 Oct. 1918, p. 3.

39. Walter Duranty, "Held Till They Died on Plemont Hill," *New York Times*, 23 June 1918, p. 2.

40. Walter Duranty, "Germans in Full Retreat from the Marne; Seek Safety as Allied Guns Pound Salient," *New York Times*, 28 July 1918, p. 1.

41. Walter Duranty, "Foe's Fight Stiffens in Narrowed Salient," *New York Times*, 31 July 1918, p. 2.

42. *Annales de la Guerre*, No. 76, 1914–18.

43. Walter Duranty, "Germans Copied French Tactics But Gouraud Outwitted Them," *New York Times*, 27 Sept. 1918, p. 1.

44. Walter Duranty, "Final Atrocity of Foe at Roulers," *New York Times*, 21 Oct. 1918, p. 13.

CHAPTER V. *A Mad Hatter's Tea Party*

1. Harrison E. Salisbury, quoting Charles A. Selden, from records in the *New York Times*' files, to SJT, 9 June 1979.
2. Harrison E. Salisbury, *Without Fear or Favor: The New York Times and Its Times* (New York: Times Books, 1980), 461.
3. Walter Duranty, "Brilliant Opening Scene; Troops Pay Military Honors as Plenipotentiaries Arrive," *New York Times*, 19 Jan. 1919, p. 1.
4. Walter Duranty, "Signing Provides Brilliant Pageant," *New York Times*, 29 June 1919, p. 2. *See also* Charles A. Selden, "Three Tense Minutes as Germans Signed," *New York Times*, 29 June 1919, p. 2.
5. Walter Duranty, *I Write As I Please* (New York: Simon and Schuster, 1935), 101.
6. Ibid., 7.
7. Ibid., 101.
8. Ibid., 101–2.
9. Ibid., 10.
10. Ibid., 15.
11. Walter Duranty, "Finland Held Out for Guarantees," *New York Times*, 15 Nov. 1919, p. 4.
12. Walter Duranty, "Bolsheviki Agree to Free Prisoners," *New York Times*, 21 Nov. 1919, p. 17.
13. Duranty, *I Write*, 23.
14. Walter Duranty, "Reds Seek to Hide Truth About Russia," *New York Times*, 22 Nov. 1919, p. 15.
15. Duranty, *I Write*, 18.
16. Walter Duranty, "Germans Still Busy in Baltic States," *New York Times*, 19 Dec. 1919, p. 4.
17. Duranty, *I Write*, 34.
18. Walter Duranty, "Germans in Letvia [*sic*] Steal, Burn, Slay As They Retreat," *New York Times*, 24 Nov. 1919, p. 1.
19. Duranty, *I Write*, 47.
20. William G. F. Jackson, *Alexander of Tunis as Military Commander* (London: Batsford, 1971), 59.
21. Walter Duranty, "Reds No Match for Fighting Letts," *New York Times*, 6 Dec. 1919, p. 4.
22. Walter Duranty, "Baltic Landwehr Outfought Reds," *New York Times*, 16 Feb. 1920, p. 3.
23. John Gunther, *Procession* (New York: Harper and Row, 1965), 235.
24. Duranty, *I Write*, 74.
25. Walter Duranty, "Seize Red Courier on His Way Here," *New York Times*, 25 Dec. 1919, p. 1.
26. Walter Duranty, "Red Courier Tells Conflicting Story," *New York Times*, 31 Dec. 1919, p. 2.
27. Peter G. Filene, *Americans and the Soviet Experiment, 1917–1933* (Cambridge, Mass.: Harvard University Press, 1967), 62.
28. Duranty, *I Write*, 77–78.

29. Ibid., 41.
30. Ibid., 95. The play, which Duranty identifies as *Prelude*, was actually produced under the title *Overture*.
31. Duranty, *I Write*, 96.
32. Walter Duranty, "Bolshevist Menace Disturbs Paris," *New York Times*, 9 Jan. 1919, p. 2.
33. Duranty, "Seize," 1.
34. Walter Duranty, "Communist Terror Holds Red Armies," *New York Times*, 16 Jan. 1920, p. 2.
35. Duranty, *I Write*, p. 97.
36. Walter Duranty, "Peace Offensive Launched by Reds," *New York Times*, 2 March 1920, p. 4.
37. *See* Walter Duranty, "Soviets' Weakness Becoming Clearer," *New York Times*, 28 April 1920, p. 17 and "Says Soviets Cannot Last Six Months," 27 May, 1920, p. 17.
38. Walter Duranty, *USSR: The Story of Soviet Russia* (New York: Lippincott, 1944), 88.
39. Charles Merz and Walter Lippmann, "A Test of the News," *A Supplement to The New Republic*, 4 Aug. 1920, p. 10.
40. Ibid., 11.
41. Salisbury, *Without Fear*, 461.

CHAPTER VI *"Luck Broke My Way"*

1. Walter Duranty, *I Write As I Please* (New York: Simon and Schuster, 1935), 103.
2. George Seldes to SJT, in an interview 6 June 1979.
3. Duranty, *I Write*, 105.
4. Walter Duranty, "Lenin Abandons State Ownership as Soviet Policy," *New York Times*, 13 Aug. 1921, p. 1.
5. George Seldes, *Tell the Truth and Run* (New York: Greenberg, 1953), 126.
6. George Seldes to SJT, in an interview 6 June 1979.
7. Duranty, *I Write*, 107–8.
8. George Seldes, *The Truth Behind the News, 1918–1928* (London: Faber and Gwyer, 1929), 107.
9. Duranty, *I Write*, 122.
10. Ibid., 122; the full account of Gibbons's famine scoop is found on pp. 122–24.
11. Floyd Gibbons, "Waiting for Death in Russian Village," *New York Times*, 1 Sept. 1921, p. 2.
12. Floyd Gibbons, "1,000,000 Russians Are Dying Docilely," *New York Times*, 3 Sept. 1921, p. 3.
13. Floyd Gibbons, "Stricken Russia, Patient Under Famine; Pen Pictures from Two Correspondents of Her Deep Suffering and Fortitude," *New York Times*, 6 Sept. 1921, p. 2.
14. Gibbons, "1,000,000 Russians," 3.
15. Gibbons, "Stricken Russia," 2.
16. Walter Duranty, "Russia's Children Left to Their Fate," *New York Times*, 5 Sept. 1921, p. 1.
17. Duranty, "Russia's Children," 2.

18. Walter Duranty, "Famine Is Driving Russia to Revolt; Myriads of Victims Move on Cities; Peasant Vanguard Routs Red Troops," *New York Times*, 2 Aug. 1921, p. 1.

19. Duranty, *I Write*, 131–32.

20. Ibid., 128.

21. Walter Duranty, "Kazan Gets First of Our Food Relief," *New York Times*, 24 Sept. 1921, p. 11.

22. Walter Duranty, "Money Still Buys Luxury in Russia," *New York Times*, 1 Oct. 1921, p. 15.

23. Walter Duranty, "Bootleggers Busy in Soviet Moscow," *New York Times*, 3 Oct. 1921, p. 15.

24. Duranty, *I Write*, 111.

25. Floyd Gibbons, "Famine Not Visible in Dingy Moscow, But Poverty Plain," *New York Times*, 24 Aug. 1921, p. 2.

26. Duranty, *I Write*, 113.

27. Walter Duranty, "Russians' New Life as Lived in Moscow," *New York Times*, 14 Sept. 1921, p. 21.

28. Walter Duranty, *Duranty Reports Russia*. Ed. by Gustav Tuckerman, Jr. (New York: Viking Press, 1934), 329.

29. George Seldes, *You Can't Print That! The Truth Behind the News, 1918–1928*. (New York: Payson & Clark, 1929), 161.

30. John Hohenberg, *Foreign Correspondence: The Great Reporters and Their Times* (New York: Columbia University Press, 1964), 317.

31. George Seldes to SJT, in an interview on 6 June 1979.

32. Seldes, *You Can't Print*, 155.

33. Paul Sheffer, *Seven Years in Soviet Russia*, (New York: Macmillan, 1932), x.

34. William Henry Chamberlin, "Under Lenin and Stalin," in "The Moscow Correspondent—A Symposium," *Survey, A Journal of Soviet and East European Studies*, 68 (July 1968), 126.

35. Robin Kinkead to SJT, in an interview 11 April 1979.

36. Walter Duranty, "Soviet Still Bars Freedom of Speech," *New York Times*, 13 Sept. 1923, p. 10.

37. Walter Duranty, "Utters Defiance to Soviet Court," *New York Times*, 26 March 1923, p. 3.

38. Duranty, *I Write*, 206.

39. Ibid., 178.

40. Seldes, *Tell the Truth*, 146.

41. Walter Duranty, "Five Men Directing Destiny of Russia," *New York Times*, 18 Jan. 1923, p. 3.

42. Duranty, *I Write*, 181.

43. Ibid., 198.

44. Walter Duranty, "Lenin Places Hope in His New Policy," *New York Times*, 8 Sept. 1921, p. 2.

45. Walter Duranty, "Lenin Confesses Economic Defeat," *New York Times*, 22 Oct. 1921, p. 7.

46. Walter Duranty, *USSR: The Story of Soviet Russia* (New York: Lippincott, 1944), 72.

47. Ibid., 86–87.

48. Ibid., 86.

Notes

49. Walter Duranty, "Soviet Needs Money To Prevent Crisis," *New York Times*, 18 Nov. 1923, II: p. 1.
50. Duranty, *I Write*, 144–45.
51. Duranty, *I Write*, 145.
52. Duranty, *I Write*, 145–46.
53. Sheila Fitzpatrick, *The Russian Revolution, 1917–1932* (New York: Oxford University Press, 1984), 78.

CHAPTER VII. *A Roman Saturnalia*

1. Walter Duranty, *I Write As I Please* (New York: Simon and Schuster, 1935), 140.
2. George Seldes to SJT, in an interview 6 June 1979.
3. Jane Gunther to SJT, in an interview 21 Feb. 1979.
4. Duranty, *I Write*, 189.
5. Robin Kinkead to SJT, in an interview 20 April 1979.
6. Duranty, *I Write*, 169–170.
7. Ibid., 170.
8. Emma Goldman, *Living My Life*, Vol. 2 (London: Duckworth, 1932), 728–29.
9. Walter Duranty, "Bootleggers Busy in Soviet Moscow," *New York Times*, 3 Oct. 1921, p. 15.
10. Walter Duranty, "People in Moscow Spend More Money," *New York Times*, 15 Oct. 1921, p. 1.
11. George Seldes to SJT, in an interview on 6 June 1979.
12. William Bolitho, *Twelve Against the Gods* (London: Heinemann, 1930), 350.
13. Sheila Fitzpatrick, *The Russian Revolution, 1917–1932* (New York: Oxford University Press, 1984), 77–78.
14. Isadora Duncan, *My Life* (London: Gollancz, 1928), 374.
15. Gordon McVay, quoting Duncan, in *Isadora and Esenin* (London: Macmillan, 1980), 11.
16. Ibid., 17.
17. Bolitho, *Twelve*, 351.
18. McVay, *Isadora*, 41.
19. Duranty, *I Write*, 239.
20. Barbara Evans Clements, *Bolshevik Feminist: The Life of Aleksandra Kollontai* (Bloomington: Indiana University Press, 1979), 226–27.
21. Fitzpatrick, *The Russian Revolusion*, 79.
22. Cathy Porter, *Alexandra Kollontai: The Lonely Struggle of the Woman Who Defied Lenin* (New York: Dial Press, 1980), 446.
23. Walter Duranty, "Moscow Throng Sees a Babe Dedicated as a Communist," *New York Times*, 28 Nov. 1923, p. 4.
24. Duranty, *I Write*, 240.
25. Duranty, "Moscow Throng Sees a Babe," p. 4.
26. Bolitho, *Twelve*, 349–350.
27. McVay, *Isadora*, quoting D. I. Leshkov, p. 265 n. 64.
28. Harrison E. Salisbury to SJT, 28 March 1988.
29. Duranty, *I Write*, 242.

30. Ibid., 333.
31. The stories discussed above are all included in the collection *Babies Without Tails* by Walter Duranty (New York: Modern Age Books, 1937).
32. Edwin P. Hoyt, *Alexander Woollcott: The Man Who Came to Dinner* (New York: Abelard-Schuman, 1968), 127.
33. Irving Berlin's musical *The Cocoanuts* ran at the Lyric Theater from December 1925 to July 1926. Harpo Marx, *Harpo Speaks* (London: Gollancz, 1961), 191. *See also* Howard Teichmann, *George S. Kaufman: An Intimate Portrait* (London: Argus and Robertson, 1973), 91.
34. Hoyt, *Alexander Woollcott*, 127.
35. William Seabrook and Walter Duranty, "You're Telling Me!" *The American Magazine*, July 1936, pp. 105–6.
36. Duranty, *I Write*, 27.
37. Ibid., 246.
38. Richard E. Harrison to SJT, in an interview 17 Jan. 1979.
39. Duranty, *I Write*, 247.
40. Parker F. Enwright to SJT, in an interview 8 Feb. 1979.
41. Robin Kinkead to SJT, in an interview 11 April 1979.
42. Duranty, *I Write*, 36.
43. Ibid., 248.
44. Walter Duranty, *Search for a Key* (New York: Simon and Schuster, 1943), 141–42.
45. Walter Duranty, "Opium Smoking," *Atlantic Monthly*, Feb. 1943, p. 109.
46. Parker F. Enwright to SJT, in an interview 8 Feb. 1979.
47. Duranty, *I Write*, 253.
48. Ibid., 256.

CHAPTER VIII. *The Mysterous Fatalism of the Slav*

1. Walter Duranty, *I Write As I Please* (New York: Simon and Schuster, 1935), 219.
2. Walter Duranty, "Lenin Dies of Cerebral Hemorrhage; Moscow Throngs Overcome with Grief; Trotsky Departs Ill; Radek in Disfavor," *New York Times*, 23 Jan. 1924, p. 1.
3. Walter Duranty, "Enormous Crowds View Lenin's Body As He Lies in State," *New York Times*, 24 Jan. 1924, p. 1.
4. Ibid., 1, 4.
5. Walter Duranty, "Lenin's Body Lies in a Marble Tomb by Kremlin Wall," *New York Times*, 28 Jan. 1924, p. 1.
6. Ibid., 4.
7. William Henry Chamberlin, "Soviet Russia's First Steps Toward Democracy," *Current History Magazine*, April 1924, p. 34.
8. Duranty, *I Write*, 259–60.
9. Walter Duranty, "Stalin, Red 'Boss,' Outwits His Foes," *New York Times*, 31 July 1926, p. 4.
10. Walter Duranty, "Trotsky Admits Defeat, Bows to Stalin Group As the Real Red Chiefs," *New York Times*, 18 Oct. 1926, p. 1.
11. George F. Kennan, *Soviet Foreign Policy, 1917–1941* (Princeton: Van Nostrand, 1960), 35–36.

Notes

12. W. Averell Harriman and Elie Abel, *Special Envoy to Churchill and Stalin, 1941–1946* (New York: Random House, 1975), 48–49.
13. W. Averell Harriman to SJT, in an interview April 11, 1979.
14. Peter G. Filene, *Americans and the Soviet Experiment, 1917–1933* (Cambridge: Harvard University Press, 1967), 66.
15. H. R. Knickerbocker to Edwin G. Rich, 14 Nov. 1927, H. R. Knickerbocker Papers, Columbia University, New York.
16. Walter Duranty to H. R. Knickerbocker, 1 April 1927, Knickerbocker Papers.
17. Walter Duranty to H. R. Knickerbocker, 27 June 1927, Knickerbocker Papers.
18. The story appears in Duranty's collection *Babies Without Tales* (New York: Modern Age Books, 1937), 45–56.
19. William Seabrook and Walter Duranty, "You're Telling Me!" *The American Magazine*, July 1936, p. 106.
20. Ibid., 106.
21. Walter Duranty to H. R. Knickerbocker, 27 June 1927, Knickerbocker Papers.
22. Vincent Sheean, *In Search of History* (London: Hamish Hamilton, 1935), 243. (All Sheean entries in this chapter are from the British edition. The American title is *Personal History*.)
23. Ibid., 295.
24. Louis Fischer, *Men and Politics: An Autobiography* (New York: Duell, Sloan and Pearce, 1941), 154.
25. The story was reprinted in Duranty's collection *Babies Without Tales*, 144–68.
26. Walter Duranty to H. R. Knickerbocker, 4 Nov. 1927, Knickerbocker Papers.
27. H. R. Knickerbocker to Walter Duranty, 14 Nov. 1927, Knickerbocker Papers.
28. Ibid.
29. Dorothy Thompson, *The New Russia* (New York: Henry Holt, 1928), 97.
30. Fischer, *Men and Politics*, 154.
31. Sheean, *In Search of History*, 238.
32. Ibid., 239.
33. Ibid., 241.
34. Ibid., 274.
35. Ibid., 328–29.
36. Ibid., 331.
37. Harrison E. Salisbury to SJT, 28 Sept. 1979.
38. Walter Duranty to H. R. Knickerbocker, 9 Dec. 1927, Knickerbocker Papers.
39. Walter Duranty to H. R. Knickerbocker, 23 Jan. 1928, Knickerbocker Papers.
40. Duranty, *I Write*, 269.
41. Isaac Deutscher, *The Prophet Unarmed, Trotsky: 1921–1929*(London: Oxford University Press, 1959), 395.
42. Duranty, *I Write*, 269.
43. Walter Duranty, "The Greatest Theatrical Performance I Ever Attended," in *A Treasury of Great Reporting*. Ed. by Louis L. Snyder and Richard B. Morris (New York: Simon and Schuster, 1949), 421.
44. Walter Duranty, "Grim Soviet Court Opens Trial of 52," *New York Times*, 19 May 1928, p. 1.
45. Ibid., 2.
46. John Gunther, Chapter VIII, Personal Diaries, Personal Files of John Gunther, New York, p. 9.

47. John Gunther to Frances Gunther, 6 July 1928, Personal Files of John Gunther.
48. Walter Duranty, "Don Engineers Hear Fate Undismayed," *New York Times*, 7 July 1928, p. 30.
49. Roy A. Medvedev, *Let History Judge: The Origins and Consequences of Stalinism* (New York: Vintage Books, 1973), 112.
50. Duranty, "Don Engineers," 30.
51. Duranty, *I Write*, 269.
52. Walter Duranty to H. R. Knickerbocker, 14 Dec. 1928, Knickerbocker Papers.
53. Walter Duranty to H. R. Knickerbocker, 11 June 1930, Knickerbocker Papers.

CHAPTER IX. *Applied Stalinism*

1. Walter Duranty, *Duranty Reports Russia* (New York: Viking Press, 1934), 362.
2. Walter Duranty to H. R. Knickerbocker on 22 Nov. 1929, H. R. Knickerbocker Papers, Columbia University.
3. Walter Duranty, "In Russia's Giant Crucible," *New York Times*, 30 Nov. 1930, V: p. 1.
4. Duranty, *Duranty Reports*, 203.
5. James Abbe, *I Photograph Russia* (New York: Robert McBride, 1934), 271.
6. Peter G. Filene, *Americans and the Soviet Experiment, 1917–1933* (Cambridge, Mass.: Harvard University Press, 1967), 241.
7. Ibid., 189.
8. Ibid., 255.
9. M. Ilin [Ilia Y. Marshak], *New Russia's Primer: The Story of the Five-Year Plan*, translated by George S. Counts and Nucia P. Lodge (Boston: Houghtin Mifflin, 1931), 119.
10. Filene, *Americans and the Soviet Experiment*, 202.
11. Ibid., 194.
12. Ibid., 191–92.
13. Ibid., 199.
14. Robin Kinkead to SJT, in an interview 12 April 1979.
15. Walter Duranty to John Gunther, 8 Jan. 1930, Personal Files of John Gunther, New York.
16. Walter Duranty, "'Militant' Policies Revived by Russia," *New York Times*, 7 Jan. 1930, p. 10.
17. Harrison E. Salisbury to SJT, 9 June 1979.
18. Harrison E. Salisbury, *Without Fear or Favor: The New York Times and Its Times* (Times Books: New York, 1980), 463.
19. "Criticizes Mr. Duranty" (letter), *New York Times*, 5 Oct. 1930, III: p. 2.
20. "Events in Russia" (letter), *New York Times*, 8 Oct. 1930, p. 24.
21. "Russia's Five Year Plan" (letter), *New York Times*, 5 Dec. 1930, p. 24.
22. Thomas M. Turner, "News from Russia Contains a Lesson," *New York Times*, 28 June 1931, III: p. 2.
23. A. W. Kliefeth in a memorandum to the Secretary of State, Washington, D. C., 4 June 1931, among U. S. State Department Papers. I am grateful to James E. Mace for this reference.

24. Martin Kriesberg, "Soviet News in the 'New York Times,'" *Public Opinion Quarterly* 10 (Winter 1946–47): 540–64.
25. Walter Duranty to H. R. Knickerbocker, 9 Dec. 1927, H. R. Knickerbocker Papers.
26. Robert Conquest, *The Harvest of Sorrow: Soviet Collectivization and the Terror-Famine* (London: Hutchinson, 1986), 90.
27. Ibid., 94–95.
28. Roy A. Medvedev, *Let History Judge: The Origins and Consequences of Stalinism* (New York: Vintage Books, 1973), 87.
29. Conquest, *Harvest of Sorrow*, 159.
30. Michael Charles Emery, "The American Mass Media and the Coverage of Five Major Foreign Events, 1900–1950" (Ph.D. Dissertation, University of Minnesota, 1969), 239.
31. Walter Duranty, "Soviet Coercion Won Grain Supply," *New York Times*, 5 Jan. 1929, p. 6.
32. Walter Duranty, *I Write As I Please* (New York: Simon and Schuster, 1935), 288.
33. Ibid., 288.
34. Sheila Fitzpatrick, *The Russian Revolution: 1917–1932* (New York: Oxford University Press, 1984), 127.
35. Maurice Hindus, *Humanity Uprooted* (New York: Jonathan Cape and Harrison Smith, 1930), 166.
36. Ibid., 167.
37. Ibid., 173.
38. Maurice Hindus, *Red Bread* (New York: Jonathan Cape and Harrison Smith, 1931), 360.
39. Duranty, *Duranty Reports*, 90.
40. Walter Duranty, "War on Church Not New in Russia," *New York Times*, 2 March 1930, p. 4.
41. Walter Duranty, "Soviet Sees Error of War on Church," *New York Times*, 15 Sept. 1923, p. 6.
42. Stephen F. Cohen, "Bolshevism and Stalinism," in *Stalinism: Essays in Historical Interpretation*, edited by Robert C. Tucker (New York: W. W. Norton, 1977), 5n.
43. Walter Duranty, "Red Russia of Today Ruled by Stalinism, not by Communism," *New York Times*, 14 June 1931, p. 1.
44. Walter Duranty, *Stalin & Co., the Politburo, the Men Who Run Russia* (New York: W. Sloane Associates, 1949), 63.
45. Duranty, "Red Russia of Today," p. 14.
46. Walter Duranty, "Fifteen Stern Years of Soviet Power," *New York Times*, 6 Nov. 1932, VI: p. 3.
47. Ibid., 4.
48. Filene, *Americans and the Soviet Experiment*, 278.
49. Eugene Lyons, *Stalin: Czar of All the Russias* (New York: Lippincott, 1940), 198.
50. Eugene Lyons, "Stalin Urges U.S. Trade with Soviet in His Only Interview in Four Years," New York *Herald Tribune*, 24 Nov. 1930, p. 2.
51. Ibid., 1.
52. Ibid., 2.
53. Henry Shapiro to SJT, in an interview 15 March 1979.
54. Walter Duranty, "Stalin Sees Capitalists Drifting Surely to War," *New York Times*, 1 Dec. 1930, p. 7.
55. Ibid., 1.

56. Isaac Deutscher, quoting Stalin, *Stalin: A Political Biography* (London: Oxford University Press, 1967), 328.
57. Walter Duranty, "Stalin: Man, Mouthpiece, Machine," *New York Times*, 18 Jan. 1931, V: 1–2.
58. Ibid., 22.

CHAPTER X. *Dizzy with Success*

1. William B. Seabrook, *Jungle Ways* (London: Harrap, 1931), 171–72.
2. William Seabrook, *No Hiding Place: An Autobiography* (New York: Lippincott, 1942), 306; *see also* Marjorie Worthington, *The Strange World of Willie Seabrook* (New York: Harcourt, Brace and World, 1966), 54–57 passim.
3. William Seabrook and Walter Duranty, "You're Telling Me!" *The American Magazine*, July 1926, p. 55.
4. George Seldes to SJT, in an interview 6 June 1979.
5. Mrs. Walter (Jane Cheron) Duranty to H. R. Knickerbocker, 27 March [1928?], H.R. Knickerbocker Papers, Columbia University, New York.
6. Walter Duranty, "Opium Smoking," *Atlantic Monthly*, Feb. 1943, p. 108.
7. Worthington, *Strange World*, 12.
8. George Seldes to SJT, in an interview 6 June 1979.
9. Worthington, *Strange World*, 12–13.
10. George Seldes to SJT, in an interview 6 June 1979.
11. Jane Perry Gunther to SJT, in an interview 21 Feb. 1979.
12. Henry Shapiro to SJT, in an interview 18 April 1979; *see also* Armand Hammer, with Neil Lyndon, *Witness to History* (London: Coronet Books, 1988), 239.
13. Malcolm Muggeridge, *Chronicles of Wasted Time*, Vol. l: *The Green Stick* (London: Collins, 1972), 254.
14. James Abbe, *I Photograph Russia* (New York: Robert McBride, 1934), 35.
15. Ibid., 183.
16. Robin Kinkead to SJT, in an interview 20 April 1979.
17. Walter Duranty, *I Write As I Please* (New York: Simon and Schuster, 1935), 157.
18. Henry Shapiro to SJT, in an interview 18 April 1979.
19. Robin Kinkead to SJT, in an interview 20 April 1979.
20. Hammer, *Witness to History*, 239.
21. William L. Shirer, *Twentieth Century Journey* (New York: Simon and Schuster, 1976), 231.
22. William L. Shirer to SJT, in an interview 15 June 1979.
23. Robin Kinkead to SJT, in an interview 20 April 1979.
24. Robin Kinkead to SJT, in an interview 12 April 1979.
25. Robin Kinkead to SJT, in an interview 20 April 1979.
26. Walter Duranty, "Gold Output Gains Rapidly in Russia," *New York Times*, 26 Dec. 1933, p. 17.
27. Robin Kinkead to SJT, in an interview 12 April 1979.
28. Muggeridge, *Chronicles*, 215–16.
29. Duranty, *I Write*, 254.
30. Seabrook and Duranty, "You're Telling Me!" p. 107.

31. Noel Coward, "Preface" to *Camera Obscura* by William Bolitho, published posthumously (New York: Simon and Schuster, 1930), 2.
32. Walter Duranty to H. R. Knickerbocker (telegram), 20 May 1931, H. R. Knickerbocker Papers.
33. "Musical Play Gets the Pulitzer Award; Mrs. Buck, Pershing, Duranty Honored," *New York Times*, 3 May 1932, p. 1.
34. Ibid., 16.
35. Ibid.
36. John F. Roche, "Uninterpreted News of Russia Puzzles Prejudiced World, says Duranty," *Editor & Publisher* 65 (June 4, 1932) 5.
37. Ibid., 6.
38. Ibid.
39. "Roosevelt Confers on Russian Policy, Consults Walter Duranty in Regard to Suggestions That Our Policy Should Change," *New York Times*, 26 July 1932, p. 1.
40. Duranty, *I Write*, 320.
41. Walter Duranty, "Red Square; A Poem," *New York Times*, 18 Sept. 1932, VI: p. 10.
42. Ibid., 11.
43. Edwin P. Hoyt, *Alexander Woollcott: The Man Who Came to Dinner* (New York: Abelard-Schuman, 1968), 234.
44. Alexander Woollcott, *The Letters of Alexander Woollcott*, ed. by Beatrice Kaufman and Joseph Hennessey (New York: Viking Press, 1944), xvi.
45. Hoyt, *Alexander Woollcott*, 234–35.
46. Ibid., 235.
47. Muggeridge, *Chronicles*, 242.
48. Malcolm Muggeridge, *Winter in Moscow* (London: Eyre & Spottiswoode, 1934), 93.
49. Ibid., 67.
50. Walter Duranty, "The United States and the Union of Soviet Socialist Republics," in *Red Economics* (Boston: Houghton Mifflin, 1932), 311.
51. Walter Duranty, "Untitled," unpublished manuscript, Personal Files of Walter Duranty, Orlando, Florida, n.p.
52. Walter Duranty, "Soviet Limit on Parleys Here," *New York Times*, 5 Nov. 1933, p. 18.
53. Walter Duranty, "America Delights Envoy of Soviets," *New York Times*, 8 Nov. 1933, p. 25.
54. Ibid., 25.
55. *Time*, 20 Nov. 1933, p. 12.
56. Walter Duranty, "United States Recognizes Soviet, Exacting Pledge on Propaganda; Bullitt Named First Ambassador," *New York Times*, 18 Nov. 1933, p. 2.
57. Ibid., 2.
58. Walter Duranty, "Triumph Hailed by Soviet People," *New York Times*, 18 Nov. 1933, p. 1.
59. "Pretty Fat Turkey," *Time*, 27 Nov. 1933, p. 10.
60. "Roosevelt Health Drunk in Moscow," *New York Times*, 20 Nov. 1933, p. 2.
61. "Horse-Trading," *Time*, 20 Nov. 1933, p. 12.
62. "Caviar to Litvinov," *Time*, 4 Dec. 1933, p. 19.
63. "New Peace Force Seen by Litvinov," *New York Times*, 25 Nov. 1933, p. 3.
64. Alexander Woollcott, "A Personal Note on Walter Duranty," in *Duranty Reports Russia* (New York: Viking Press, 1934), v.

65. Walter Duranty, "Stalin Says Japan Is Great Danger; Hopes for Peace," *New York Times*, 28 Dec. 1933, p. 8.
66. "Stalin to Duranty," *Time*, 8 Jan. 1934, p. 22.
67. Duranty, *I Write*, 166–67.

CHAPTER XI. *A Blanket of Silence*

1. British Embassy Dispatch, 21 June 1932.
2. Ibid.
3. Andrew Cairns to Mr. Lloyd, Secretary of the Empire Marketing Board, 7 June 1932, p. 35; Enclosure, British Embassy Dispatch, 21 June 1932.
4. Ibid., n. p.
5. Ibid., 29.
6. Ibid., 90.
7. Cairns to Lloyd (2 draft telegrams), 2 Aug. 1932; Enclosure, British Embassy Dispatch, 3 Aug. 1932.
8. Foreign Office Dispatch, 13 March 1933.
9. Kyril FitzLyon to SJT, in an interview 24 May 1988.
10. British Embassy Dispatch, 5 Oct. 1933.
11. Comments, Lloyd Collier, Foreign Office Papers, 6 Dec. 1932.
12. Record by Mr. Strang of a Conversation with Mr. Duranty; Enclosure No. 1, British Embassy Dispatch, 14 Nov. 1932.
13. Strang on Duranty, British Embassy Dispatch, 14 Nov. 1932.
14. British Embassy Dispatch, 6 Dec. 1932.
15. Ibid.
16. Malcolm Muggeridge, *Chronicles of Wasted Time. The Green Stick,* Vol. I (London: Collins, 1972), 224.
17. William Henry Chamberlin, *Russia's Iron Age* (London: Duckworth, 1935), 149.
18. Ibid., 149.
19. Robert Conquest, *The Harvest of Sorrow: Soviet Collectivization and the Terror-Famine* (London: Hutchinson, 1986), 170.
20. Walter Duranty, "Moscow Purged of Undesirables," *New York Times*, 9 April 1933, IV: 3.
21. Walter Duranty, "3 High Soviet Aides Pay Death Penalty," *New York Times*, 13 March 1933, p. 7.
22. Ian Hunter, *Malcolm Muggeridge: A Life* (London: Collins, 1980), 76.
23. Muggeridge, *Chronicles*, 219–20.
24. Muggeridge, *Winter in Moscow* (London: Eyre and Spottiswoode, 1934), 134–35.
25. Arthur Koestler, *The Yogi and the Commissar* (London: Jonathan Cape, 1945), 142.
26. Ibid., 143.
27. William Stoneman to Harrison Salisbury, 16 May 1979.
28. Harrison E. Salisbury, *Without Fear or Favor: The New York Times and Its Times* (New York: Times Books, 1980), 464.
29. Conquest, *Harvest of Sorrow*, 310.
30. Eugene Lyons, *Assignment in Utopia* (New York: Harcourt Brace, 1937), 561.
31. British Embassy Dispatch, 22 March 1933.

32. Ibid.
33. Ibid.
34. Moscow Chancery Dispatch, 3 April 1933.
35. British Embassy Dispatch, 21 March 1933.
36. [Malcolm Muggeridge], "The Price of Russia's 'Plan'; Virtual Breakdown of Agriculture; Officials Shot; The Problem of Food Supplies," Manchester *Guardian*, 12 Jan. 1933, p. 9.
37. Marco Carynnyk, "The Famine the *Times* Couldn't Find," *Commentary*, Nov. 1983, p. 32.
38. [Malcolm Muggeridge], "The Soviet and the Peasantry; An Observer's Notes; I. Famine in North Caucasus; Whole Villages Exiled," Manchester *Guardian*, 25 March 1933, p. 13.
39. Ibid., 13.
40. [Malcolm Muggeridge], "The Soviet and the Peasantry; An Observer's Notes; II. Hunger in the Ukraine," Manchester *Guardian*, 27 March 1933, p. 9.
41. [Malcolm Muggeridge], "The Soviet and the Peasantry; An Observer's Notes; III. Poor Harvest in Prospect," Manchester *Guardian*, 28 March 1933, p. 9.
42. British Embassy Dispatch, 21 March 1933.
43. Malcolm Muggeridge to SJT, in an interview 27 Oct. 1987.
44. Carynnyk, "The Famine the *Times* Couldn't Find," p. 33.
45. Hunter, quoting Muggeridge, p. 86.
46. Ibid.
47. Hunter, *Malcolm Muggeridge*, 84.
48. Malcolm Muggeridge to SJT, in an interview 27 Oct. 1987.
49. Gareth Jones, "Famine in Russia," Manchester *Guardian*, 30 March 1933, p. 12.
50. Whitman Bassow, quoting Lyons, *The Moscow Correspondents: Reporting on Russia from the Revolution to Glasnost* (New York: William Morrow, 1988), 69.
51. Walter Duranty, "Russians Hungry But Not Starving," *New York Times*, 31 March 1933, p. 13.
52. Ibid., 13.
53. Gareth Jones, "Mr. Jones Replies" (letter), *New York Times*, 13 May 1933, p. 12.
54. Ibid., 12.
55. Carynnyk, "The Famine the *Times* Couldn't Find," quoting Lyons, pp. 34–35.

CHAPTER XII. *The "Famine" Is Mostly Bunk*

1. Walter Duranty to H. R. Knickerbocker, 27 June 1933, H. R. Knickerbocker Papers, Columbia University, New York.
2. William Henry Chamberlin, *The Ukraine: A Submerged Nation* (New York: Macmillan, 1944), 61.
3. Ibid., 61.
4. Marco Carynnyk, "The Famine the *Times* Couldn't Find," *Commentary*, Nov. 1983, p. 33.
5. Walter Duranty, "Stalinism Smashes Foes in Marx's Name," *New York Times*, 24 June 1931, p. 9.
6. Moshe Lewin, *Russian Peasants and Soviet Power* (Evanston: Northwestern University Press, 1968), 502–5 passim.

7. Robert Conquest, *The Harvest of Sorrow: Soviet Collectivization and the Terror-Famine* (London: Hutchinson, 1986), 138.
8. Ibid., 293.
9. Roy A. Medvedev, "New Pages from the Political Biography of Stalin," in *Stalinism: Essays in Historical Interpretation*, Ed. by Robert C. Tucker (New York: W. W. Norton, 1977), 211.
10. Conquest, *Harvest of Sorrow*, 186–187.
11. Vasily Grossman, *Forever Flowing* (London: Deutsch, 1973), 149–50.
12. Conquest, *Harvest of Sorrow*, 75.
13. Grossman, *Forever Flowing*, 143.
14. Ibid., 141.
15. Ibid., 142.
16. Conquest, *Harvest of Sorrow*, 231.
17. Victor Kravchenko, *I Chose Freedom* (New York: Scribner's, 1946), 63.
18. *Khrushchev Remembers* (London: Deutsch, 1971), 73.
19. Ibid., 72.
20. Grossman, *Forever Flowing*, 153.
21. Malcolm Muggeridge, *Winter in Moscow* (London: Eyre and Spottiswoode, 1934), 137.
22. Grossman, *Forever Flowing*, 157.
23. Muggeridge, *Winter in Moscow*, 137.
24. Dana G. Darymple, "The Soviet Famine of 1932–1934," *Soviet Studies* 15 (Jan. 1964): 261.
25. Dana G. Darymple, "The Soviet Famine of 1932–1934; Some Further References," *Soviet Studies* 16 (April 1965): 471.
26. Kravchenko, *I Chose Freedom*, 118.
27. Walter Duranty, "Soviet Peasants Are More Hopeful," *New York Times*, 14 May 1933, p. 18.
28. Moscow Chancery Dispatch, 3 April 1933. Kinkead himself said later that one of the reasons he eventually left Moscow was, "I could see that I was in danger of becoming a drunk." Whitman Bassow, *The Moscow Correspondents: Reporting on Russia from the Revolution to Glasnost* (New York: William Morrow, 1988), 91.
29. Robin Kinkead to SJT, in an interview 20 April 1979.
30. Conquest, *Harvest of Sorrow*, 250.
31. "Semi-Starvation in Russia," *The Times* (London) 30 May 1933, p. 15.
32. Walter Duranty, "Russian Suffering Justified by Reds," *New York Times*, 9 July 1933, IV: 2.
33. Ralph Barnes, "Millions Feared Dead of Hunger in South Russia," New York *Herald Tribune*, 21 Aug. 1933, p. 7.
34. "Moscow Doubles the Price of Bread," *New York Times*, 21 Aug. 1933, p. 1.
35. Walter Duranty, "Famine Report Scorned," *New York Times*, 21 Aug. 1933, p. 8.
36. Ibid., 8.
37. Muggeridge, *Winter in Moscow*, 171.
38. Walter Duranty, "Famine Toll Heavy in Southern Russia," *New York Times*, 24 Aug. 1933, p. 1.
39. Frederick T. Birchall, "Famine in Russia Held Equal of 1921," *New York Times*, 25 Aug. 1933, p. 7.

Notes

40. Walter Duranty, "Huge State Farms Lagging in Russia," *New York Times*, 27 Aug. 1933, IV: 2.

41. British Embassy Dispatch, 16 Sept. 1933.

42. British Embassy Dispatch, 30 Sept. 1933.

43. Walter Duranty, "Abundance Found in North Caucasus," *New York Times*, 14 Sept. 1933, p. 14; the other two stories were published 11 and 15 Sept., both on page 11.

44. Walter Duranty, "Big Soviet Crop Follows Famine," *New York Times*, 16 Sept. 1933, p. 14.

45. (My italics); Carynnyk, "The Famine the *Times* Couldn't Find," p. 35.

46. Duranty, "Big Soviet Crop," p. 14.

47. Walter Duranty, "Big Ukraine Crop Taxes Harvesters," *New York Times*, 18 Sept. 1933, p. 8.

48. British Embassy Dispatch, 30 Sept. 1933.

49. Ibid.

50. The figure of ten million interestingly corresponds with that later suggested by Moshe Lewin for the number of kulaks transported during collectivisation: *Russian Peasants and Soviet Power*, 507–8.

51. Eugene Lyons, *Assignment in Utopia* (New York: Harcourt Brace, 1937), 579–80.

52. Malcolm Muggeridge, *Chronicles of Wasted Time*, Vol. I. *The Green Stick* (London: Collins, 1972), 254–55.

53. Muggeridge, *Winter in Moscow*, 112.

54. Ibid., 90.

55. Alec Nove, *Economic Rationality and Soviet Politics or Was Stalin Really Necessary?* (New York: Frederick A. Praeger, 1964), 20.

56. Walter Duranty, *I Write As I Please* (New York: Simon and Schuster, 1935), 166–67.

CHAPTER XIII. *The Masters of Euphemism*

1. Joseph Alsop, "The Reporter's Trade," *Chicago Sun-Times*, 30 Dec. 1974, p. 29.

2. Joseph Alsop to SJT, in an interview 14 March 1979.

3. Malcolm Muggeridge, *Chronicles of Wasted Time*, Vol. I. *The Green Stick* (London: Collins, 1972), 228.

4. James William Crowl, quoting a letter from Muggeridge, *Angels in Stalin's Paradise* (Lanham, Maryland: The University Press of America, 1982), 35.

5. British Embassy Dispatch, 22 March 1933.

6. John Gunther, Personal Diaries, Green Notebook II, 1934, Personal Files of John Gunther, New York.

7. John Gunther, Personal Diaries, loose entry, n.d., Personal Files of John Gunther.

8. Robin Kinkead to SJT, in an interview 11 April 1979.

9. Muggeridge, *Chronicles*, 232. In *Men and Politics: An Autobiography* (New York: Duell, Sloan, and Pearce, 1941), 62, Louis Fischer said Chamberlin ate his weight in chocolate *daily*.

10. Fischer, *Men and Politics*, 62.

11. Muggeridge, *Chronicles*, 241.

12. Jane Gunther to SJT, in an interview 21 Feb. 1979.

13. Eugene Lyons, *Assignment in Utopia* (New York: Harcourt Brace, 1937), 519.
14. Ibid., 96.
15. Ibid., 214–15.
16. Crowl, *Angels*, quoting Lyons, p. 35.
17. Robin Kinkead to SJT, in an interview 12 April 1979.
18. Ibid.
19. Harrison E. Salisbury to SJT, in an interview 9 May 1979.
20. Linton Wells, *Blood on the Moon* (Boston: Houghton Mifflin, 1937), 340–41.
21. Harrison E. Salisbury, *Russia on the Way* (New York: Macmillan, 1946), 67.
22. Whitman Bassow, *The Moscow Correspondents: Reporting on Russia from the Revolution to Glasnost* (New York: William Morrow, 1988), 82.
23. William Henry Chamberlin, *The Confessions of an Individualist* (New York: Macmillan, 1941), 259.
24. Harrison E. Salisbury to SJT, in an interview 9 May 1979.
25. Robin Kinkead to SJT, in an interview 25 April 1979.
26. Harrison E. Salisbury to SJT, 19 April 1989.
27. Henry Shapiro to SJT, in an interview 13 April 1979.
28. Walter Kerr to SJT, in an interview 15 March 1979.
29. Harrison E. Salisbury, *Without Fear or Favor: The New York Times and Its Times* (New York: Times Books, 1980), 459.
30. Harrison E. Salisbury to SJT, in an interview 21 Feb. 1979.
31. Ibid.
32. Robin Kinkead to SJT, in an interview 20 April 1979.
33. Malcolm Muggeridge, *Winter in Moscow* (London: Eyre and Spottiswoode, 1934), 180–81.
34. Duranty, *I Write As I Please* (New York: Simon and Schuster, 1935), p. 197.
35. Ibid., 167.
36. [William Henry Chamberlin], "Big Crop Harvested in North Caucasus," *Christian Science Monitor*, 13 Sept. 1933, p. 1.
37. [William Henry Chamberlin], "Soviets Remove Lenient Officials in Wheat Areas," *Christian Science Monitor*, 26 Sept. 1933, p. 3.
38. [William Henry Chamberlin], "A Tour of Inquiry I. The Soviet Countryside," Manchester *Guardian*, 17 October 1933. p. 9.
39. Ibid., 10.
40. [William Henry Chamberlin], "A Tour of Inquiry, II. Some Cossack Villages," Manchester *Guardian*, 18 Oct. 1933, p. 9.
41. British Embassy Dispatch, 14 Oct. 1933.
42. Muggeridge, *Chronicles*, 241.
43. Crowl, *Angels*, quoting Fischer, 157.
44. William Stoneman to Harrison Salisbury, 16 May 1979.
45. Eugene Lyons, *Stalin: Czar of All the Russias* (New York: Lippincott, 1940), 16.
46. Peter G. Filene, *Americans and the Soviet Experiment: 1917–1933* (Cambridge, Mass.: Harvard University Press, 1967), 279.
47. Crowl, quoting letters from Lyons, in *Angels in Stalin's Paradise*, 161.
48. For a chilling recital of the rebuffs, *see* Robert Conquest, *The Harvest of Sorrow: Soviet Collectivization and the Terror Famine* (London: Hutchinson, 1986), 311; *see also* James E. Mace's extensive article "The Politics of Famine: American Government and Press Response to the Ukrainian Famine, 1932–1933," *Holocaust and*

Genocide Studies, Vol. 3, No. l, 1988, p. 86, as well as the *Report to Congress* of the Commission on the Ukraine Famine (Washington, D. C.: U. S. Government Printing Office, 1988), 151–67 passim.
49. Marco Carynnyk, "The Dogs That Did not Bark," *The Idler*, Jan. 1985, p. 15.
50. Professor Colonel Gerald Draper to SJT, in an interview 21 July 1988.
51. Stoneman to SJT, 18 Jan. 1979.
52. William Stoneman to Harrison Salisbury, 16 May 1979.
53. Walter Duranty, *Europe - War or Peace?* (London: Hamish Hamilton, 1935), 29.
54. Walter Duranty, *The Kremlin and the People* (New York: Reynal and Hitchcock, 1941), 45.
55. Duranty, *I Write*, 283.
56. Walter Duranty, *USSR: The Story of Soviet Russia* (New York: J.B. Lippincott, 1944), 192.
57. Ibid., 193–195 passim.
58. George Kennan, *Memoirs, 1925–1950* (Boston: Little, Brown, 1967), 71.
59. Filene, *Americans and the Soviet Experiment*, 266.
60. Dana G. Dalrymple, "The Soviet Famine of 1932–1934," *Soviet Studies* 15 (Jan. 1964): 273.
61. Walter Duranty, *Stalin & Co., the Politburo, the Men Who Run Russia* (New York: W. Sloane Associates, 1949), 78.

CHAPTER XIV. *Getting Away with It*

1. Robin Kinkead to SJT, in an interview 11 April 1979.
2. Jane Gunther to SJT, in an interview 21 Feb. 1979.
3. Walter Duranty to H. R. Knickerbocker (telegram), 10 June 1933, H. R. Knickerbocker Papers, Columbia University, New York.
4. Walter Duranty to H. R. Knickerbocker, 27 June 1933, H. R. Knickerbocker Papers.
5. Robin Kinkead to SJT, in an interview 11 April 1979.
6. Henry Shapiro to SJT, in an interview 15 March 1979.
7. J. Dunbar to SJT, 19 March 1979.
8. Walter Duranty, *I Write As I Please* (New York: Simon and Schuster, 1935), 60–64 passim.
9. George Kennan to SJT, 16 April 1979.
10. George Kennan, *Memoirs: 1925–1950* (Boston: Little, Brown, 1967), 59–60.
11. Henry Shapiro to SJT, in an interview 15 March 1979.
12. Walter Duranty to Alexander Woollcott (telegram), n.d., 1933, Private Files of Viking Penguin Inc., New York.
13. Viking Press Inc. to Walter Duranty, 26 Jan. 1933, Private Files of Viking Penguin Inc., New York.
14. The author is grateful to Edwin Kennebeck for this information and for making available the contents of Viking's files concerning their business arrangements with Duranty in 1933 and 1934.
15. Harrison Salisbury to SJT, in an interview 21 Feb. 1979.
16. Robin Kinkead to SJT, in an interview 12 April 1979.
17. "Our Russian Correspondence" (editorial), *New York Times*, 3 April 1934, p. 20.
18. John Gunther, Personal Diaries, n.d., Personal Files of John Gunther, New York.

19. Robin Kinkead to SJT, in an interview 12 April 1979.
20. Irena Wiley, *Around the Globe in Twenty Years* (New York: David McKay, 1962), 2–3.
21. "Walter Duranty Here," *New York Times*, 9 May 1934, p. 17.
22. William Seabrook and Walter Duranty, "You're Telling Me!," *The American Magazine*, July 1926, p. 55.
23. "Duranty Predicts a Major War Soon," *New York Times*, 7 June 1934, p. 7.
24. Ibid.
25. Edwin P. Hoyt, *Alexander Woollcott: The Man Who Came to Dinner* (New York: Abelard-Schuman, 1968), 12.
26. "The Adventures of Mr. Duranty," *New York Times*, 17 Nov. 1935, IV: p. 5, 23.
27. Ibid., 23.
28. Duranty, *I Write*, 255.
29. Harrison E. Salisbury to SJT, in an interview 21 Feb. 1979.
30. Duranty, *I Write*, 311–12.
31. Walter Duranty to Aleister Crowley, n.d., The G. J. Yorke Collection, The Warburg Institute, London.
32. Walter Duranty to John Gunther, 4 Dec. 1935, Personal Files of John Gunther.
33. Walter Duranty to John Gunther, 11 Jan. 1936, Personal Files of John Gunther.
34. Ibid.
35. "Walter Duranty Back," *New York Times*, 24 Jan. 1936, p. 17.
36. Walter Duranty, *Babies Without Tales* (New York: Modern Age Books, 1937) 9–21.
37. Walter Duranty to John Gunther, 24 March 1936, Personal Files of John Gunther.
38. Mrs. Joseph T. Walker to SJT, in an interview 10 May 1979.
39. Ibid.
40. Robin Kinkead to SJT, in an interview 20 April 1979.
41. Walter Duranty, "The Bogey of Moscow," *The North American Review* 241 (June 1936): 232.
42. Walter Duranty to John Gunther, 17 July 1936, Personal Files of John Gunther.
43. James William Crowl, for example, has accepted at face value Duranty's claims that his parents were killed in a train crash, that he lived with his uncle in Norfolk, that he went to Temple Grove Grammar School: *Angels in Stalin's Paradise: Western Reporters in Soviet Russia, 1917 to 1937* (Lanham, MD: University Press of America, 1982), 9. Crowl also missed Duranty's obvious reference to Wythe Williams when he wrote in *Search for a Key* (p. 10) that Duranty had worked for Henry Harborn of the *New York Times*. (Duranty substituted the initials H. H. for W. W. in naming his character.)
44. "Writers Must Work" (portrait), *Saturday Review of Literature*, 5 Dec. 1936, p. 14.
45. Walter Duranty to John Gunther, 14 Dec. 1936, Personal Files of John Gunther.

CHAPTER XV. *Hypocritical Psychologists*

1. William B. Seabrook, *Jungle Ways* (London: Harrap, 1931), 122.
2. Marjorie Worthington, *The Strange World of Willie Seabrook* (New York: Harcourt, Brace and World, 1966), 154.
3. William B. Seabrook, *Asylum* (London: Harrap, 1935), 7.

Notes

4. William Seabrook and Walter Duranty, "You're Telling Me!" *The American Magazine*, July 1936, p. 55.
5. Ibid., 54.
6. Ibid., 108.
7. Ibid., 106.
8. Ernest Hemingway to Arnold Gingrich, 16 Sept. 1936, *Selected Letters 1917–1961*, Edited by Carlos Baker (New York: Granada, 1981), 452. Recalling the actual title of the article inaccurately, Hemingway wrote, "I liked the guy who verified me by Duranty and Seabrook. That was nice."
9. Seabrook and Duranty, "You're Telling Me!," p. 107.
10. Ibid., 108.
11. William Seabrook, *No Hiding Place: An Autobiography* (New York: Lippincott, 1942), 370.
12. Ibid., 394.
13. Worthington, *The Strange World*, 248.
14. Walter Duranty to John Gunther, 26 Feb. 1937, Personal Files of John Gunther, New York.
15. Walter Duranty to John Gunther, 2 Feb. 1937, Personal Files of John Gunther.
16. Ibid.
17. Fletcher Pratt, "Russian Cyclorama," *Saturday Review of Literature*, 14 Aug. 1937, p. 5.
18. Walter Duranty, *One Life, One Kopeck* (New York: Simon and Schuster, 1937), 36.
19. Ibid., 66.
20. Ibid., 44.
21. Walter Duranty, *Solomons Cat* (Grand Rapids, Mich.: Mayhew Press, 1937), 2.
22. Ibid., 19–20.
23. Walter Duranty to John Gunther, 26 Feb. 1937, Personal Files of John Gunther.
24. Ibid.
25. Linton Wells, *Blood on the Moon* (Boston: Houghtin Mifflin, 1937), 348.
26. Walter Duranty, *The Kremlin and the People* (New York: Reynal and Hitchcock, 1941), 119.
27. Ibid., 121.
28. Robert Conquest, *The Great Terror: Stalin's Purge of the Thirties*, Rev. Ed. (London: Macmillan, 1973), 230.
29. "Another Russian Trial" (editorial), *The New Republic*, 3 Feb. 1937, p. 400.
30. Joseph E. Davies, *Mission to Moscow* (London: Gollancz, 1942), 181.
31. Roy A. Medvedev, *Let History Judge: The Origins and Consequences of Stalinism* (New York: Vintage Books, 1973), 178.
32. Davies, *Million to Moscow*, 43.
33. Ibid., 42.
34. Lion Feuchtwanger, *Moscow, 1937: My Visit Described for My Friends* (New York: Viking, 1937), 114.
35. Ibid., 114.
36. "Another Russian Trial," 400.
37. George F. Kennan, *Russia and the West* (Boston: Little, Brown, 1961), 241–42.
38. "Wire Break Balks Trotsky as 6,500 Await Speech Here," *New York Times*, 10 Feb. 1937, p. 4.
39. Ibid., 4.

40. Walter Duranty to John Gunther, 3 April 1937, Personal Files of John Gunther.
41. *See* George A. Stoychoff, "Both Their Houses" (letter) *and* Sidney Hook, "Letter," *The New Republic*, 2 June 1937, p. 104; *and* Waldo Frank, 12 May 1937, pp. 19–20.
42. "Soviet Chills and Fevers" (editorial), *The New Republic*, 23 June 1937, p. 174.
43. Duranty, *Kremlin*, 44–45.
44. Robert C. Tucker and Stephen F. Cohen, eds. *The Great Purge Trial* (New York: Grossett and Dunlap, 1965), xlv.
45. Conquest, *The Grest Terror*, 203.
46. Walter Duranty, "The Riddle of Russia," *The New Republic*, 14 July 1937, p. 272.
47. Duranty, *USSR: The Story of Soviet Russia* (New York: Lippincott, 1944), 217.
48. Ibid., 219.
49. Walter Duranty, *Stalin & Co., The Politburo, The Men Who Run Russia* (New York: W. Sloane Associates, 1949), 186.
50. Duranty, *Kremlin*, 39.
51. Duranty, *Stalin & Co.*, 81.
52. Duranty's figures appear on p. 122 of *The Kremlin and the People*; for an extensive discussion of more reliable casualty figures, *see* Conquest, *The Great Terror*, 713.
53. Duranty, *Kremlin*, 124.
54. Ibid., 115.

CHAPTER XVI. *A Citizen of the World*

1. A. M. Sperber, *Murrow: His Life and Times* (New York: Bantam Books, 1986), 103.
2. William Shirer to SJT, in an interview 15 June 1979.
3. Walter Duranty to John Gunther, 2 March 1939, Personal Files of John Gunther, New York.
4. William L. Shirer, *Berlin Diary: The Journal of a Foreign Correspondent* (New York: Knopf, 1942), 89.
5. "Duranty Discusses Situation in Russia," *New York Times*, 29 Nov. 1937, p. 9.
6. William L. Shirer to SJT, in an interview 15 June 1979.
7. Walter Duranty to John Gunther, 24 July 1937, Personal Files of John Gunther.
8. Henry Shapiro to SJT, in an interview 18 April 1979.
9. Joseph E. Davies, *Mission to Moscow* (London: Gollancz, 1942), 149.
10. Walter Duranty to John Gunther, 12 Aug. 1938, Personal Files of John Gunther.
11. Walter Duranty to H. R. Knickerbocker, 1 Aug. 1938, H. R. Knickerbocker Papers, Columbia University, New York.
12. Sperber, *Murrow*, 120.
13. Shirer, *Berlin Diary*, 152–53.
14. William Shirer to SJT, in an interview 15 June 1979.
15. Walter Duranty to John Gunther, 8 Dec. 1938, Personal Files of John Gunther.
16. Walter Duranty to John Gunther, 2 March 1939, Personal Files of John Gunther.
17. Walter Duranty to John Gunther, 8 Dec. 1938, Personal Files of John Gunther.
18. George Seldes to SJT, in an interview 6 June 1979.
19. Walter Duranty to John Gunther, 2 March 1939, Personal Files of John Gunther.
20. Henry Shapiro to SJT, in an interview 15 March 1979.

21. Henry Shapiro to SJT, in an interview 18 April 1979.
22. Walter Duranty, "The Russo-German Partnership," *Atlantic Monthly*, March 1940, p. 404.
23. Ibid., 406.
24. Henry Shapiro to SJT, in an interview 18 April 1979.
25. Harrison E. Salisbury to SJT, 9 June 1979.
26. C. L. Sulzberger, *A Long Row of Candles* (Toronto: Macmillan, 1969), 145.
27. Harrison E. Salisbury to SJT, 9 June 1979.
28. Drew Middleton to SJT, in an interview 23 Feb. 1979.
29. Ibid.
30. Clare Hollingworth to SJT, in an interview 24 June 1983.
31. Ibid.
32. Cyrus Sulzberger to SJT, 6 June 1979.
33. Robert St. John, *Foreign Correspondent* (London: Hutchinson, 1960), 75.
34. Robert St. John to SJT, in an interview 11 June 1979.
35. Clare Hollingworth to SJT, in an interview 24 June 1983.
36. Ibid.
37. Cyrus Sulzberger to SJT, 6 June 1979.
38. Robert St. John to SJT, in an interview 11 June 1979.
39. Clare Hollingworth to SJT, in an interview 24 June 1983.
40. St. John, *Foreign Correspondent*, 75.
41. Clare Hollingworth to SJT, in an interview 24 June 1983.
42. St. John, *Foreign Correspondent*, 108–9.
43. Ibid., 143–44.
44. "Rumania Expels Duranty," *New York Times*, 25 Sept. 1940, p. 2.
45. *See* Sulzberger's *A Long Row of Candles*, p. 145, where Sulzberger gives the impression he does not hold Geyde in high esteem, in part, it appears, because of his having helped talk the *Times* into withdrawing from Moscow. Also, former Moscow correspondent and associate editor for the *New York Times*, Harrison E. Salisbury, believed that the withdrawal of the *Times* was a poor decision.
46. Harrison E. Salisbury to SJT, 9 June 1979.
47. Ibid.
48. Walter Duranty, "Nazi-Soviet Moves Viewed as 'Dicker,'" *New York Times*, 2 May 1941, p. 4.
49. Walter Duranty, "Stalin Move Held Step Toward Axis," *New York Times*, 8 May 1941, p. 3.
50. Walter Duranty, "Stalin Is Believed Likely to Yield Further Concessions to Germany," *New York Times*, 12 June 1941, p. 6.
51. Walter Duranty, "Soviet-Nazi Deal Held More Likely Than Clash Despite All Rumors," *New York Times*, 17 June 1941, p. 8.

CHAPTER XVII. *Hollywood*

1. Walter Duranty to Marjorie Worthington, 4 July 1941, Personal Papers of Marjorie Worthington, Ft. Lauderdale, Florida.
2. Marjorie Worthington, *The Strange World of Willie Seabrook* (New York: Harcourt, Brace & World, 1966), 244.

3. Ibid., 244–45.
4. Walter Duranty to Marjorie Worthington, 4 July 1941, Personal Papers of Marjorie Worthington.
5. Ibid.
6. Mrs. Sylvan Hoffman to SJT, in an interview 29 May 1979.
7. Worthington, *Strange World*, 246.
8. Walter Duranty to Marjorie Worthington, 16 Sept. 1941, Personal Papers of Marjorie Worthington. The book Duranty was referring to was Huxley's *Grey Eminence*.
9. John Russell Taylor, *Strangers in Paradise: The Hollywood Emigres, 1933–1950* (London: Faber and Faber, 1983), 132.
10. Sheridan R. Morley, *Tales from the Hollywood Raj: The British Film Colony On Screen and Off* (London: Weidenfeld and Nicolson, 1983), 167.
11. Taylor, *Strangers*, 134.
12. Walter Duranty to Marjorie Worthington, 16 Sept. 1941, Personal Papers of Marjorie Worthington.
13. Mary Loos to SJT, in an interview 11 April 1979.
14. Christine R. Barker and R. W. Last, *Erich Maria Remarque* (London: Oswald Wolff, 1979), 23.
15. Mary Loos to SJT, in an interview 12 April 1979.
16. Taylor, *Strangers*, 119.
17. Walter Duranty to John Gunther, 9 September 1941, Personal Files of John Gunther, New York.
18. Walter Duranty, *The Kremlin and the People* (New York: Reynal and Hitchcock, 1941), 213–15.
19. Louis Fischer, "Still the Enigma," *Saturday Review of Literature*, 6 Dec. 1941, p. 14.
20. Eugene Lyons, *The Red Decade: The Classic Work on Communism in America During the Thirties* (New York: Arlington House, 1941), 111.
21. Ibid., 243.
22. Ibid., 10.
23. Ibid., vi.
24. John Gunther, Personal Diaries, Chapt. VIII, Personal Files of John Gunther, New York, p. 7.
25. Mary Loos, Drew Middleton, and John Gunther all speak of Duranty's brief infatuation with a red-haired woman from the Midwest.
26. Worthington, *Strange World*, 247–48.
27. John Gunther, *Procession* (New York: Harper and Row, 1965), 235.
28. Struthers Burt, "The Keenness of Walter Duranty," *Saturday Review of Literature*, 3 April 1943, p. 12.
29. Walter Duranty to Marjorie Worthington, 19 July 1943, Personal Papers of Marjorie Worthington.
30. Walter Duranty to Marjorie Worthington, 27 July 1943, Personal Papers of Marjorie Worthington.
31. Walter Duranty to Marjorie Worthington, 17 Aug. 1943, Personal Papers of Marjorie Worthington.
32. Mrs. Sylvan Hoffman to SJT, in an interview 29 May 1979.
33. Walter Duranty to Marjorie Worthington, 18 Nov. 1943, Personal Papers of Marjorie Worthington.
34. "Walter Duranty Ill," *New York Times*, 2 Dec. 1943, p. 22.

35. John Gunther to Walter Duranty (telegram), 2 Dec. 1943, Personal Papers of John Gunther, New York.
36. Walter Duranty to Marjorie Worthington, 21 Dec. 1943, Personal Papers of Marjorie Worthington.
37. Walter Duranty to Marjorie Worthington, 25 Dec. 1943, Personal Papers of Marjorie Worthington.
38. Walter Duranty to Walter Kerr, 1 Feb. 1944, Personal Papers of Walter Kerr, Santa Fe, New Mexico.
39. Ibid.
40. Walter Duranty, *USSR: The Story of Soviet Russia* (New York: Lippincott, 1944), 156.
41. Ibid., 276.
42. Mary Loos to SJT, in an interview 12 April 1979.
43. Ibid.
44. Federal Bureau of Investigation, United States Department of Justice, File on Walter Duranty, p. 14; made available to the author according to the provisions of the Freedom of Information Act.
45. John Gunther to Walter Duranty, 21 Dec. 1944, Personal Files of John Gunther.
46. Walter Duranty to John Gunther, 5 Jan. 1945, Personal Files of John Gunther.
47. Walter Duranty to John Gunther, 3 Feb. 1945, Personal Files of John Gunther.
48. Mary Loos and Walter Duranty, *Return to the Vineyard* (Garden City, N.Y.: Doubleday, Doran, 1945).
49. Mary Loos to SJT, in an interview 12 April 1979.
50. Walter Duranty to John Gunther, 10 Feb. 1945, Personal Files of John Gunther.
51. John Gunther to Walter Duranty, 23 Feb. 1945, Personal Files of John Gunther.
52. Walter Duranty to John Gunther, 10 Feb. 1945, Personal Files of John Gunther.
53. Mary Loos to SJT, in an interview 12 April 1979.
54. Taylor, *Strangers*, 175.

CHAPTER XVIII. *I Write As* You *Please*

1. Drew Middleton to SJT, in an interview 23 Feb. 1979.
2. Ibid.
3. Walter Duranty to John Gunther, 16 Feb. 1945, Personal Files of John Gunther, New York.
4. Robin Kinkead to SJT, in an interview 25 April 1979.
5. John Gunther, "Diaries," 11 June 1945, Personal Files of John Gunther, n.p.
6. John Gunther, "Diaries," 13 June 1945, Personal Files of John Gunther, n.p.
7. Walter Duranty to John Gunther, 6 Aug. 1945, Personal Files of John Gunther.
8. Ibid.
9. Walter Duranty to Marjorie Worthington, 5 Nov. 1945, Personal Papers of Marjorie Worthington, Ft. Lauderdale, Florida.
10. Walter Duranty to Marjorie Worthington, 14 Nov. 1945, Personal Papers of Marjorie Worthington.
11. Walter Duranty to Marjorie Worthington, 28 Nov. 1945, Personal Papers of Marjorie Worthington.

12. Walter Duranty to Marjorie Worthington, 26 Dec. 1945, Personal Papers of Marjorie Worthington.
13. Malcolm Muggeridge, *Winter in Moscow* (London: Eyre & Spottiswoode, 1934), 165.
14. (Author's italics); "I Write As You Please," *Time*, 25 March 1946, p. 60.
15. W. Colston Leigh to SJT, in an interview 13 March 1979.
16. Mary Loos to SJT, in an interview 12 April 1979.
17. William Shirer to SJT, in an interview 15 June 1979.
18. Robert St. John to SJT, in an interview 11 June 1979.
19. John Gunther, "Diaries: Part II," 10 Oct. 1946, Personal Files of John Gunther, p. 78.
20. W. Colston Leigh to SJT, in an interview 13 March 1979.
21. John Gunther, "Diaries," 9 Oct. 1944, Personal Files of John Gunther, p. 35.
22. Richard Edes Harrison to SJT, in an interview 23 Feb. 1979.
23. Henry Shapiro to SJT, in an interview 15 March 1979.
24. Henry Shapiro to SJT, in an interview 18 April 1979.
25. Mary Loos to SJT, in an interview 12 April 1979.
26. Henry Shapiro to SJT, in an interview 18 April 1979.
27. Mrs. Sylvan Hoffman to SJT, in an interview 29 May 1979.
28. *Encyclopaedia Britannica*, 14th ed., s.v. "Russia" (*in part*) by Walter Duranty, pp. 734–44; 1939 ed. s.v. "Russia" (*in part*) by Walter Duranty, pp. 734–44.
29. Parker F. Enwright to SJT, in an interview 10 Feb. 1979.
30. "Spotlight on Slander: How the Encyclopaedia Britannica Distorts History," *New Times*, 1 Jan. 1948, p. 27.
31. John Gunther, "Diaries: Part I," 18 June 1947, Personal Files of John Gunther, p. 201.
32. John Gunther, "Green Notebook II," nos. 118-119, Personal Files of John Gunther, n.p.
33. Jane Gunther to SJT, in an interview 21 Feb. 1979.
34. John Gunther, "Diaries: Part II," n.d., 1947, Personal Files of John Gunther, pp. 104–5.
35. John Gunther, *Death Be Not Proud* (London: Hamish Hamilton, 1949), 16.
36. Ibid., 25.
37. Ibid., 62.
38. Ibid., 79.
39. John Gunther, "Diaries: Part II," 18 Oct. 1946, Personal Files of John Gunther, p. 86.
40. John Gunther, "Diaries: Part II," 1 Oct. 1946, Personal Files of John Gunther, n.p.
41. John Gunther, "Diaries," 14 April 1947, Personal Files of John Gunther, n.p.
42. John Gunther, "Diaries," 23 April 1947, Personal Files of John Gunther, n.p.
43. Gunther, *Death*, 124.
44. Gunther, *Death*, 137.
45. John Gunther, "Diaries: Part I," 11 June 1947, Personal Files of John Gunther, p. 191.
46. John Gunther, "Diaries: Part I," n.d., 1947, Personal Files of John Gunther, p. 75.
47. John Gunther, "Diaries: Part III," n.d., 1947, Personal Files of John Gunther, p. 89.
48. John Gunther, "Diaries: Part I," 19 June 1947, Personal Files of John Gunther, p. 203.

49. John Gunther, *Death* (The Modern Library ed., 1959), 174.
50. John Gunther, "Diaries: Part I," 30 June 1947, Personal Files of John Gunther, p. 221.
51. Gunther, *Death*, 153.

CHAPTER XIX. *Midnight Minus One Minute*

1. John Gunther, "Diaries: Part II," 15 July 1947, Personal Files of John Gunther, New York, p. 27.
2. John Gunther, "Diaries: Part II," 9 July 1947, Personal Files of John Gunther, p. 19.
3. John Gunther, "Diaries: Part II," 14 Aug. 1947, Personal Files of John Gunther, p. 111.
4. John Gunther, "Diaries: Part II," 19 Aug. 1947, Personal Files of John Gunther, n.p.
5. Ibid., 115.
6. Jane Gunther to SJT, in an interview 21 Feb. 1979.
7. John Gunther, "Diaries: Part III," 17 Oct. 1947, Personal Files of John Gunther, p. 11.
8. Walter Duranty to William Sloane, n.d. 1948, Personal Files of Walter Duranty, Orlando, Florida.
9. William Sloane to Walter Duranty, 7 May 1948, Personal Files of Walter Duranty.
10. Walter Duranty, *I Write As I Please* (New York: Simon and Schuster, 1935), 257.
11. Parker Enwright to SJT, in an interview 9 Feb. 1979.
12. William Sloane to Walter Duranty, 13 April 1948, Personal Files of Walter Duranty.
13. William Sloane to Walter Duranty, 7 May 1948, Personal Files of Walter Duranty.
14. Walter Duranty to Hamish Hamilton, n.d., Personal Files of Walter Duranty.
15. Walter Duranty to M. Lincoln Schuster, 24 June 1948, Personal Files of Walter Duranty.
16. Walter Duranty to John Gunther, 27 Feb. 1950, Personal Files of John Gunther.
17. Katya to Walter Duranty, 2 Feb. 1948, Personal Files of Walter Duranty.
18. [unnamed] to Walter Duranty, 16 Nov. 1948, Personal Files of Walter Duranty.
19. Katya to Walter Duranty, 12 Aug. 1948, Personal Files of Walter Duranty.
20. Harrison Salisbury to SJT, in an interview 21 Feb. 1979.
21. Mrs. Sylvan Hoffman to SJT, in an interview 29 May 1979.
22. Harrison E. Salisbury, *Without Fear or Favor: The New York Times and Its Times* (New York: Times Books, 1980), 460.
23. Walter Duranty to Cass Canfield, 12 May 1948, Personal Files of Walter Duranty.
24. Walter Duranty, "Unpublished Manuscript," Personal Files of Walter Duranty.
25. William Sloane to Walter Duranty, 31 Dec. 1948, Personal Files of Walter Duranty.
26. Albert Rhys Williams wrote two letters to Duranty, giving him a number of fresh anecdotes to use in his book; 2 May and 14 May 1948, Personal Files of Walter Duranty.
27. A. T. Cholerton to Walter Duranty, 3 April 1949, Personal Files of Walter Duranty.
28. John N. Wheeler, 23 June 1949, Personal Files of Walter Duranty.
29. Noel Singer to Walter Duranty, 19 Feb. 1949, Personal Files of Walter Duranty.
30. Noel Singer to Walter Duranty, 13 April 1949, Personal Files of Walter Duranty.

31. Walter Duranty to Noel Singer, 20 April 1949, Personal Files of Walter Duranty.
32. John N. Wheeler, "To Whom It May Concern," 23 June 1949, Personal Files of Walter Duranty.
33. Walter Duranty to John Gunther, 22 Aug. 1949, Personal Files of John Gunther.
34. Walter Duranty to John Gunther, 21 Aug. 1949, Personal Files of John Gunther.
35. Walter Duranty to John Gunther, 22 Aug. 1949, Personal Files of John Gunther.
36. Parker Enwright to SJT, in an interview 10 Feb. 1979.
37. "Author Walter Duranty Died at 72," *Orlando Sentinel*, Oct. 1957, n.p.
38. Parker Enwright to SJT, in an interview 10 Feb. 1979.
39. Walter Duranty to Jane Gunther, 1 Oct. 1949, Personal Files of John Gunther.
40. Stanley J. Kunitz, ed. *Twentieth Century Authors, lst Supplement* (New York: H. W. Wilson, 1955), 292.
41. Walter Duranty, Stalin & Co, MS, pp. 6, 8, 8, 10, 61, respectively, Personal Files of Walter Duranty.
42. William Sloane to Walter Duranty, 15 Aug. 1950, Personal Files of Walter Duranty.
43. [unnamed] (Kemsley House), London to Walter Duranty, 24 July 1950, Personal Files of Walter Duranty.
44. John Gunther to Walter Duranty, 10 May 1950, Personal Files of John Gunther.
45. Walter Duranty to John Gunther, 27 Feb. 1950, Personal Files of Walter Duranty.
46. Walter Duranty to John Gunther, 5 April 1950, Personal Files of John Gunther.
47. Walter Duranty to John Gunther, 6 Nov. 1950, Personal Files of John Gunther.
48. Walter Duranty to John Gunther, n.d., Personal Files of John Gunther.
49. Walter Duranty to John Gunther, 6 Nov. 1950, Personal Files of John Gunther.
50. Ibid.
51. Walter Duranty to John Gunther, n.d., Personal Files of John Gunther.
52. Walter Duranty to John Gunther, 28 Nov. 1950, Personal Files of John Gunther.
53. John Gunther to Walter Duranty, 27 Dec. 1950, Personal Files of John Gunther.

CHAPTER XX. *Death Is the End*

1. Sheila Saint Lawrence, Ann Watkins, Inc., to Walter Duranty, 25 Jan. 1951, Personal Files of Walter Duranty, Orlando, Florida.
2. Walter Duranty to John Gunther, 6 Feb. 1950, Personal Files of Walter Duranty.
3. The letter was found in Duranty's Personal Files, finally working its way to him through other means.
4. Parker Enwright to SJT, in an interview 10 Feb. 1979.
5. Ibid.
6. Walter Duranty to Marjorie Worthington, 18 March 1951, Personal Papers of Marjorie Worthington, Ft. Lauderdale, Florida.
7. Jane Gunther to SJT, in an interview 21 Feb. 1979.
8. Walter Duranty to Marjorie Worthington, 18 March 1951, Personal Papers of Marjorie Worthington.
9. John Gunther to Walter Duranty, 1 Nov. 1951, Personal Papers of John Gunther.
10. Walter Duranty to John Gunther, 13 Nov. 1951, Personal Files of John Gunther.
11. John Gunther to Walter Duranty, 27 Nov. 1951, Personal Files of John Gunther.
12. Walter Duranty to John Gunther, 18 March 1952, Personal Files of John Gunther.

13. Jane Gunther to SJT, in an interview 21 Feb. 1979.
14. John Gunther to Walter Duranty, 9 May 1952, Personal Files of John Gunther.
15. Unsigned Memorandum, Federal Bureau of Investigation, United States Department of Justice, 18 Jan. 1951, p. 3. (The memorandum can be found in the Bureau's File on Walter Duranty.)
16. Walter Duranty to John Gunther, 6 Feb. 1950, Personal Files of John Gunther, New York.
17. Parker Enwright to SJT, in an interview 10 Feb. 1979.
18. Walter Duranty, Orlando *Morning Sentinel*, 6 March 1953, pp. 1, 3.
19. Walter Duranty to Jane Gunther, 25 Jan. 1955, Personal Files of John Gunther.
20. John Gunther to Walter Duranty, 19 March 1955, Personal Files of John Gunther.
21. Walter Duranty to Armitage Watkins, 31 Aug. 1957, Personal Files of Walter Duranty.
22. Ibid.
23. Harrison E. Salisbury to SJT, in an interview 9 May 1979.
24. Harrison E. Salisbury, *Without Fear or Favor: The New York Times and Its Times* (New York: Times Books, 1980), 465.
25. The cap from Emmanuel College was given to the author by Parker F. Enwright in February 1979.
26. Walter Duranty, *I Write As I Please* (New York: Simon and Schuster, 1935), 36.
27. Parker Enwright to SJT, in an interview 10 Feb. 1979.
28. Walter Winchell, "News World Lost Titan in Duranty," *Miami Herald*, 13 Oct. 1947, p. 23-E.
29. Walter Kerr to SJT, in an interview 15 March 1979.
30. *Time*, 14 Oct. 1957, p. 110.
31. Parker Enwright to SJT, in an interview 10 Feb. 1979.
32. Katya to Walter Duranty, 12 Aug. 1948, Personal Files of Walter Duranty.

Select Bibliography

BOOKS AND SELECTED
ARTICLES BY WALTER DURANTY

Articles from Orlando *Morning Sentinel*, Orlando, Florida, Jan.–March, 1947; March 1953.

Dispatches in *New York Times*, 1913–41.

"Introduction," to *Red Economics* by Walter Duranty, W. H. Chamberlin, H. R. Knickerbocker, and Others. Boston: Houghton Mifflin, 1932.

Duranty Reports Russia, Ed. by Gustav Tuckerman, Jr. New York: Viking Press, 1934.

Europe – War or Peace? London: Hamish Hamilton, 1935.

I Write As I Please. New York: Simon and Schuster, 1935.

Babies Without Tails. New York: Modern Age Books, 1937.

One Life, One Kopeck. New York: Simon and Schuster, 1937.

Solomons Cat. Grand Rapids, Mich.: Mayhew Press, 1937.

The Gold Train and Other Stories. London: Hamish Hamilton, 1938.

Encyclopaedia Britannica, 14th ed., s.v. "Russia" (*in part*) by Walter Duranty, pp. 734–44; 1939 ed. s.v. "Russia" (*in part*) by Walter Duranty, pp. 734–44.

The Kremlin and the People. New York: Reynal and Hitchcock, 1941.

Search for a Key. New York: Simon and Schuster, 1943.

USSR: The Story of Soviet Russia. New York: Lippincott, 1944.

[with Mary Loos] *Return to the Vineyard*. Garden City, N.Y.: Doubleday, Doran and Company, 1945.

Stalin & Co., the Politburo, the Men Who Run Russia. New York: W. Sloane Associates, 1949.
The Curious Lottery. Freeport, N. Y.: Books for Libraries Press, 1969.

OTHER SELECTED BOOKS AND ARTICLES

Abbe, James. *I Photograph Russia*. New York: Robert McBride, 1934.
Adams, Samuel Hopkins. *A. Woollcott: His Life and His World*. New York: Reynal and Hitchcock, 1945.
Alsop, Joseph. "The Reporter's Trade." Chicago *Sun-Times*, 30 Dec. 1974, p. 29.
Barker, Christine R., and R. W. Last, *Erich Maria Remarque*. London: Oswald Wolff, 1979.
Barnes, Ralph. "Millions Feared Dead of Hunger in South Russia." New York *Herald Tribune*, 21 Aug. 1933, p. 7.
Bassow, Whitman. *The Moscow Correspondents: Reporting on Russia from the Revolution to Glasnost*. New York: William Morrow, 1988.
Bolitho, William. *Camera Obscura*. New York: Simon and Schuster, 1930.
Bolitho, William. *Twelve Against the Gods*. London: Heinemann, 1930.
Carynnyk, Marco. "The Dogs That Did Not Bark," *The Idler*, Jan. 1985, pp. 14–20; Feb. 1985, pp. 17–21.
Carynnyk, Marco. "The Famine the *Times* Couldn't Find," *Commentary*, Nov. 1983, pp. 32–40.
Chamberlain, John. *A Life with the Printed Word*. Chicago: Regnery Gateway, 1982.
Chamberlin, William Henry. Dispatches in *Christian Science Monitor*, 1933.
Chamberlin, William Henry. Dispatches in Manchester *Guardian*, 1934.
Chamberlin, William Henry. *Russia's Iron Age*. London: Duckworth, 1935.
Chamberlin, William Henry. *The Confessions of an Individualist*. New York: Macmillan, 1941.
Chamberlin, William Henry. *The Ukraine: A Submerged Nation*. New York: Macmillan, 1944.
Chandler, George. *Liverpool*. London: Batsford, 1957.
Chandler, George. *Victorian and Edwardian Liverpool and the North West from Old Photographs*. London: Batsford, 1972.
Channon, Howard. *Portrait of Liverpool*. London: Robert Hale, 1970.
Clements, Barbara Evans. *Bolshevik Feminist: The Life of Aleksandra Kollontai*. Bloomington: Indiana University Press, 1979.
Conquest, Robert. *The Great Terror: Stalin's Purge of the Thirties*. Rev. Ed. London: Macmillan, 1973.
Conquest, Robert. *The Harvest of Sorrow: Soviet Collectivization and the Terror-Famine*. Hutchinson: London, 1986.
Crowl, James William. *Angels in Stalin's Paradise*. Lanham, Maryland: The University Press of America, 1982.

Select Bibliography

Crowley, Aleister. *The Diary of a Drug Fiend.* London: Collins, 1922.

Crowley, Aleister. *The Magical Record of the Beast 666: The Diaries of Aleister Crowley 1914–1920,* ed. by John Symonds and Kenneth Grant. London: Duckworth, 1972.

Crozier, Emmet. *American Reporters on the Western Front 1914–1918.* New York: Oxford University Press, 1959.

Dalrymple, Dana G. "The Soviet Famine of 1932–1934," *Soviet Studies* 15 (Jan. 1964): 250–84.

Dalrymple, Dana G. "The Soviet Famine of 1932–1934," *Soviet Studies* 16 (April 1965): 471–74.

Davies, Joseph E. *Mission to Moscow.* London: Gollancz, 1942.

Deutscher, Isaac. *Stalin: A Political Biography.* London: Oxford University Press, 1967.

Deutscher, Isaac. *The Prophet Unarmed, Trotsky: 1921–1929. London: Oxford University Press, 1959.*⁴

Duncan, Isadora. *My Life.* London: Gollancz, 1928.

Emery, Michael Charles. "The American Mass Media and the Coverage of Five Major Foreign Events, 1900–1950." Ph.D. Dissertation, University of Minnesota, 1969.

Farson, Negley. *A Mirror for Narcissus.* New York: Doubleday, 1957.

Feuchtwanger, Lion. *Moscow, 1937: My Visit Described for My Friends.* New York: Viking, 1937.

Filene, Peter G. *Americans and the Soviet Experiment, 1917–1933.* Cambridge, Mass.: Harvard University Press, 1967.

Fischer, Louis. *Men and Politics: An Autobiography.* New York: Duell, Sloan and Pearce, 1941.

Fitzpatrick, Sheila. *The Russian Revolution, 1917–1932.* New York: Oxford University Press, 1984.

Gibbs, Philip. *Realities of War.* London: Heinemann, 1920.

Goldman, Emma. *Living My Life.* 2 vols. London: Duckworth, 1932.

Grossman, Vasily. *Forever Flowing.* London: Deutsch, 1973.

Gunther, John. *Death Be Not Proud.* New York: The Modern Library, 1949.

Gunther, John. *Death Be Not Proud.* London: Hamish Hamilton, 1949.

Gunther, John. *Procession.* New York: Harper and Row, 1965.

Harriman, W. Averell. *America and Russia in a Changing World.* Garden City, New York: Doubleday, 1971.

Harriman, W. Averell, and Elie Abel. *Special Envoy to Churchill and Stalin, 1941–1946.* New York: Random House, 1975.

Hassall, Christopher. *Rupert Brooke: A Biography.* London: Faber and Faber, 1964.

Hemingway, Ernest. *Selected Letters 1917–1961,* Ed. by Carlos Baker. New York: Granada, 1981.

Hindus, Maurice. *Humanity Uprooted.* New York: Jonathan Cape and Harrison Smith, 1930.

Hindus, Maurice. *Red Bread.* New York: Jonathan Cape and Harrison Smith, 1931.

Hohenberg, John. *Foreign Correspondence: The Great Reporters and Their Times.* New York: Columbia University Press, 1964.
Hoyt, Edwin P. *Alexander Woollcott: The Man Who Came to Dinner.* New York: Abelard-Schuman, 1968.
Hunter, Ian. *Malcolm Muggeridge: A Life.* London: Collins, 1980.
"I Write As You Please." *Time,* 25 March 1946, p. 60.
Ilin, M. [Ilia Y. Marshak]. *New Russia's Primer: The Story of the Five-Year Plan,* trans. by George S. Counts and Nucia P. Lodge. Boston: Houghton Mifflin, 1931.
Jackson, William G.F. *Alexander of Tunis as Military Commander.* London: Batsford, 1971.
Kennan, George F. *Russia and the West.* Boston: Little, Brown, 1961.
Kennan, George F. *Soviet Foreign Policy, 1917–1941.* Princeton: Van Nostrand, 1960.
Kennan, George F. *Memoirs, 1925–1950.* Boston: Little, Brown, 1967.
Khrushchev, Nikita. *Khrushchev Remembers.* London: Deutsch, 1971.
Knightley, Phillip. *The First Casualty: The War Correspondent as Hero, Propagandist, and Myth Maker from the Crimea to Vietnam.* London: Deutsch, 1975.
Koestler, Arthur. *The Yogi and the Commissar.* London: Jonathan Cape, 1945.
Kravchenko, Victor. *I Chose Freedom.* New York: Scribner's, 1946.
Lewin, Moshe. *Russian Peasants and Soviet Power.* Evanston: Northwestern University Press, 1968.
Lyons, Eugene. *Assignment in Utopia.* New York: Harcourt Brace, 1937.
Lyons, Eugene. "Stalin Urges U.S. Trade with Soviets in His Only Interview in Four Years," New York *Herald Tribune,* 24 Nov. 1930, pp. 1, 2.
Lyons, Eugene. *Stalin: Czar of All the Russias.* New York: Lippincott, 1940.
Lyons, Eugene. *The Red Decade: The Classic Work on Communism in America During the Thirties.* New York: Arlington House, 1941.
Mace, James E. "The Politics of Famine: American Government and Press Response to the Ukrainian Famine, 1932–1933," *Holocaust and Genocide Studies,* Vol. 3, No. 1, 1988, pp. 75–94.
MacVay, Gordon. *Isadora and Esenin.* London: Macmillan, 1980.
Marx, Harpo. *Harpo Speaks.* London: Gollancz, 1961.
Mathews, Joseph J. *Reporting the Wars.* Minneapolis: University of Minnesota Press, 1957.
Medvedev, Roy A. *Let History Judge: The Origins and Consequences of Stalinism.* New York: Vintage Books, 1973.1
Merz, Charles, and Walter Lippmann. "A Test of the News," *A Supplement to The New Republic,* 4 Aug. 1920, pp. 1–42.
Montague, C. E. *Disenchantment.* London: Chatto and Windus, 1922.
Morley, Sheridan R. *Tales from the Hollywood Raj: The British Film Colony On Screen and Off.* London: Weidenfeld and Nicolson, 1983.
Mowrer, Paul Scott. *The House of Europe.* Boston: Houghton Mifflin, 1945.

Muggeridge, Malcolm. Dispatches in Manchester *Guardian*, 1933.

Muggeridge, Malcolm. *Winter in Moscow*. London: Eyre & Spottiswoode, 1934.

Muggeridge, Malcolm. *Chronicles of Wasted Time*, Vol. 1: *The Green Stick*. London: Collins, 1972.

"Musical Play Gets Pulitzer Award: Mrs. Buck, Pershing, Duranty Honored," *New York Times*, 3 May 1932, pp. 1, 16.

Nove, Alec. *Economic Rationality and Soviet Politics, or Was Stalin Really Necessary?* New York: Praeger, 1964.

Palmer, Frederick. *With the New Army on the Somme*. London: John Murray, 1917.

Pearce, Brian. *How Haig Saved Lenin*. London: Macmillan, 1987.

Porter, Cathy. *Alexandra Kollontai: The Lonely Struggle of the Woman Who Defied Lenin*. New York: Dial Press, 1980.

Salisbury, Harrison E. *Russia on the Way*. New York: Macmillan, 1946.

Salisbury, Harrison E. *Without Fear or Favor: The New York Times and Its Times*. New York: Times Books, 1980.

Seabrook, William B. *Jungle Ways*. London: Harrap, 1931.

Seabrook, William B. *Asylum*. London: Harrap, 1935.

Seabrook, William. *No Hiding Place: An Autobiography*. New York: Lippincott, 1942.

Seabrook, William, and Walter Duranty, "You're Telling Me!" *The American Magazine*, July 1936, pp. 54–55.

Seldes, George. *Tell the Truth and Run*. New York: Greenberg, 1953.

Seldes, George. *You Can't Print That! The Truth Behind the News, 1918–1928*. New York: Payson & Clark, 1929.

Seldes, George. *The Truth Behind the News, 1918–1928*. London: Faber and Gwyer, 1929.

Sheean, Vincent. *In Search of History*. London: Hamish Hamilton, 1935.

Sheffer, Paul. *Seven Years in Soviet Russia*. New York: Macmillan, 1932.

Shirer, William L. *Berlin Diary: The Journal of a Foreign Correspondent*. New York, Knopf, 1942.

Shirer, William L. *Twentieth Century Journey*. New York: Simon and Schuster, 1976.

Sperber, A. M. *Murrow: His Life and Times*. New York: Bantam Books, 1986.

St. John, Robert. *Foreign Correspondent*. London: Hutchinson, 1960.

Sulzberger, C. L. *A Long Row of Candles*. Toronto: Macmillan, 1969.

Symonds, John. *The Great Beast: The Life and Magick of Aleister Crowley*. London: MacDonald, 1971.

Taylor, A. J. P. *The First World War: An Illustrated History*. Harmondsworth, Eng.: Penguin Books, 1986.

Taylor, John Russell. *Strangers in Paradise: The Hollywood Emigres, 1933–1950*. London: Faber and Faber, 1983.

Thompson, Dorothy. *The New Russia*. New York: Henry Holt, 1928.

Tucker, Robert C., and Stephen F. Cohen, eds. *The Great Purge Trial.* New York: Grossett and Dunlap, 1965.
U.S. Government, Commission on the Ukraine Famine, *Report to Congress.* Washington, D.C.: U.S. Government Printing Office, 1988.
Wells, Linton. *Blood on the Moon.* Boston: Houghton Mifflin, 1937.
Williams, Wythe. *Passed by the Censor.* New York: E.P. Dutton, 1916.
Williams, Wythe. *Dusk of Empire.* New York: Scribner's, 1937.
"Wire Break Balks Trotsky as 6,500 Await Speech Here," *New York Times,* 10 Feb. 1937, pp. 1, 4.
Woollcott, Alexander. *The Letters of Alexander Woollcott,* ed. by Beatrice Kaufman and Joseph Hennessey. New York: Viking, 1944.
Worthington, Marjorie. *The Strange World of Willie Seabrook.* New York: Harcourt, Brace and World, 1966.

MANUSCRIPTS AND ARCHIVES

Annales de la Guerre, No. 76, 1914–1918, part of the Official Documents of the Cinematographic Section of the French Army, made available to the author at the Imperial War Museum in London.
Bedford Grammar School *Register* for 1899.
British Embassy, Foreign Office and Moscow Chancery Dispatches, 1932–33, including letters of Andrew Cairns to Mr. Lloyd, Secretary of the Empire Marketing Board, in Public Record Office, Kew.
Census records in the Land Registry Office, London; records of births, marriages, and deaths, wills and other probate documents in various branches of the Public Record Office in London and in the public archives of Liverpool; indexes in Companies House, London.
Federal Bureau of Investigation, United States Department of Justice, 18 Jan. 1951, File on Walter Duranty. Requested under the provisions of the Freedom of Information Act.
G. J. Yorke Collection at the Warburg Institute in London.
H. R. Knickerbocker Papers, Columbia University, New York.
Louis Fischer Papers, Seeley G. Mudd Manuscript Library, Princeton University, Princeton, New Jersey.
Personal Files of John Gunther, New York; made available by Mrs. John [Jane Perry] Gunther, widow of the late John Gunther.
Personal Files of Parker F. Enwright, Orlando, Florida, son of Mrs. Anna Enwright Duranty.
Personal Files of Walter Duranty, Orlando, Florida; made available by Parker F. Enwright.
Personal Papers of Marjorie Worthington, Ft. Lauderdale, Florida; made available by Mrs. Sylvan Hoffman, sister of Marjorie Worthington.
Personal Papers of Walter Kerr, Santa Fe, New Mexico.

Private Files of Reuters, Ltd., London; made available by P. Cain.

Private Files of Viking Penguin Inc., New York; made available by Edwin Kennebeck.

The Last Will and Testament of Alexander Duranty, dated 1 February 1873, proved 19 June 1876 (Somerset House, London).

Index

(Index covers the main text, not the notes on pages 356–88.)

Alcohol, 178, 255, 257, 280, 288, 301, 313, 318, 322, 339, 349
Alcott, Louisa May, 349
Alexander I (Czar), 292
Alexander, General Harold Rupert, 88–9, 92, 95, 300–1
Algonquin Hotel, 51, 128–9, 334–5
Alsop, Joseph, 224, 230–1, 237
American Magazine, 256–7
Anderson, Sherwood, 156
Aristophanes, 21
Arsenic and Old Lace, 302
Asquith, H. H., 288
Associated Press, 86, 110, 217, 236, 266, 288–9
Atlantic Monthly, 112, 132, 282
Attlee, Clement, 314

Balashova, 122
Barnes, Joe, 266, 280
Barnes, Ralph, 202, 204, 216–17, 233, 235, 237
Barry, Philip, 318
Battle of Britain, 286
Beard, Charles A., 157
Beatty, Bessie, 122
Bedford Grammar School, 20–22, 26
Benchley, Robert, 296
Berkman, Alexander, 91

Berlin, 3, 40, 64, 141, 145–6, 153, 173, 175, 182, 185, 217–18, 226, 229, 237, 250–1, 274, 336–7
Berliner Tageblatt, 149, 199
Bernhardt, Sarah, 37
Berry, Major, 68
Bibesco, Prince Antoine, 288
Bierce, Ambrose, 67
Birchall, Frederick T., 144, 159, 218–19, 246–7
Blivens, Bruce, 157
Bogart, Humphrey, 318
Bolitho, William, 19, 52–3, 92–4, 104, 120–1, 126, 130–1, 133–4, 138, 141, 180–1, 184, 232, 248–9, 271, 331
Brest-Litovsk, Treaty of, 72, 84, 87
British Embassy (Moscow), 180, 193, 196–8, 203, 205–6, 218, 225–6
Broun, Heywood, 51, 128
Brown, Jim, 266
Bucharest, 34, 286–90, 317
Bukharin, Nikolai, 137–8, 144, 162, 269
Bullitt, William Christian, 191, 239, 244, 266
Burt, Maxwell Struthers, 301
Butchkavitch, Father, 109–11, 128

Caillaux, Mme Henriette, 38–40, 43
Cairns, Andrew, 193–6, 212

Index

Cambridge, *see* Emmanuel College
Campbell, Julie, 12
Canfield, Cass, 335–6
Carol II, King of Rumania, 287
Carynnyk, Marco, 220
Catherine the Great, 87, 188
Chaikovsky, Nikolai, 84
Chamberlain, Neville, 277
Chamberlin, Sonia, 186, 226–7
Chamberlin, William Henry, 138, 146,
    175, 186, 210, 217, 226, 228, 233–7,
    314
Cheka, 100, 107, 125, 138, 160
Chekhov, Anton, 186
Cheron, Jane (WD's wife), 30–34, 49–50,
    117–18, 132, 173–4, 242, 254, 256,
    311
China, 142–4, 147–9, 160, 183, 238–9,
    344, 351
Cholerton, A.T., 144–5, 174, 203, 225–6,
    337
Christian Science Monitor (Boston), 138,
    186, 210, 233–4
Churchill, (Sir) Winston, 65, 295, 314,
    321
Clemenceau, Georges, 58, 65–6
Coffee House (New York), 318–19
Collier's Weekly, 58
Columbia Broadcasting Service (CBS),
    176, 273, 302, 314
Conquest, Robert, 265
Cooke, George Frederick, 9
Cooper, Colonel Hugh L., 191
Coote, Edmond, 218–19
Counts, George S., 156
Coward, Noel, 181
Crowley, Aleister, 28–38, 50, 118, 172,
    249–50, 311
cummings, e. e., 157
Current History Magazine, 70

Daily Chronicle (London), 56
Daily Express (London), 56, 286
Daily Herald (London), 86
Daily Mail (London), 56
Daily Mirror (London), 56
Daily News (Chicago), 57, 86, 151, 158,
    202
Daily News (London), 56
Daily Telegraph (London), 56, 174, 225,
    286
Daladier, Edouard, 277
Davidson, Jo, 38
Davies, Joseph E., 266–7, 276
Davis, Richard Harding, 55, 147
Denikin, Anthony, 84

Denny, Harold, 247, 249–50, 264, 266,
    276, 280–1, 283–4
Deuel, Norman, 266, 280
Dewey, Stoddard, 57
Dickens, Charles, 15
Dietrich, Marlene, 296
Dos Passos, John, 157
Dostoyevsky, Feodor Mikhailovich, 267
Doubleday, Nelson, 318
Douglas, Lord Alfred, 31
Dreiser, Theodore, 156
Duchin, Eddy, 296
Duncan, Isadora, 121–7
Duranty, Alexander (WD's grandfather),
    10–13
Duranty, Anna Enwright (WD's second
    wife), *see* Enwright
Duranty, Catherine Emily (WD's aunt),
    10–11
Duranty, Charles (WD's uncle), 10–12,
    15
Duranty, Emmeline [née Hutchins]
    (WD's mother), 12–13, 20, 26–27,
    182
Duranty, Frances Emmeline (WD's
    sister), 18, 20, 27, 181–2, 242
Duranty, Jane (WD's grandmother), 10–
    12, 18
Duranty, Jane Cheron (WD's wife), *see*
    Cheron
Duranty, Michael (WD's son), 230–1,
    241–2, 252, 261, 274–5, 320, 324,
    333–4, 337–8, 355
Duranty, Selina Jane (WD's aunt), 10
Duranty, Walter, *passim*
    birth, family, education, 9–27; first
        assignment, 34–35; war
        correspondent, 58–79; correspondent
        in Moscow, 96 *et seq.*; loses leg, 45,
        130–4; maxim on omelettes, 185,
        207, 222–3; part in U. S. recognition
        of U.S.S.R., 184, 188–93, 198, 203–4,
        223, 258–9; Russian soul thesis, 267–
        9, 299; dismissal from *New York
        Times*, 290–1; death, 354; *see also*
        Alcohol, Opium, Pulitzer Prize,
        Ukraine Famine
    dispatches and articles, *passim*
    Duranty Reports Russia, 245–6
    Encyclopaedia Britannica articles, 321
    Europe—War or Peace?, 238
    The Kremlin and the People, 270, 297–
        8, 305
    I Write As I Please, 238, 248–9, 254–5,
        269, 278, 332
    One Life, One Kopeck, 252, 261–2

"Red Square" (poem), 184–5, 207
Return to the Vineyard, 308–10
Search for a Key, 27, 132, 254, 279, 291, 299, 301
short stories, 114–15, 127–8, 142, 144–6, 149, 153, 252, 263, 313, 353
Solomons Cat, 262–3
Stalin & Co., 330–1, 337, 342
USSR, 301, 305–6, 331
Duranty, William Steel (WD's father), 10–13, 18, 20, 26–27, 182, 242
Dzerzhinsky, Felix Edmundovich, 112

Editor & Publisher, 183
Elizabeth I, 24
Emmanuel College, Cambridge, 22–26
Enwright, Anna (WD's second wife), 329, 335, 340–1, 348–9, 351–5
Enwright, Parker F. (WD's stepson), 355
Esenin, Sergei, 122–8, 165
Estonia, 84, 86, 92, 279, 283
Evans, Ernestine, 112, 122
Evening Post (New York), 57, 141, 182
Evening Standard (London), 189, 203

Fabian Society, 16
Fadiman, Clifton B., 156
Fascism, 5, 160, 236, 251, 331
Federal Bureau of Investigation, 351
Ferdinand, Archduke Franz, 39
Feuchtwanger, Lion, 267, 296
Figaro, Le, 38
Finland, 85–86, 283, 292
Fischer, Louis, 146, 175, 227, 235–6, 298–9, 336
Five-Year Plan, 5, 154–71, 182, 185, 196, 222, 227, 239, 245, 354
Foch, General Ferdinand, 65–67, 69–70, 77–78
Forbes, Lord, 290
Foxe's *Book of Martyrs*, 14–15
Franco, General Francisco, 251
Frank, Waldo, 156

Gade, Commander, 84, 87, 92
Gannett, Lewis, 310
Garbo, Greta, 296
Gedye, G.D., 283–4
Gell, Sir William, 24
Gemier, Firman, 37
Gerson (physician), 324
Gibbons, Floyd, 55–6, 67–8, 101–5, 133
Gibbs, Philip, 56–7, 59–60, 64–5
Gil Blas, 42
Gilles, Beth, 178
Goddard, Paulette, 296

Goldman, Emma, 91, 120, 173
Goltz, Graf Rudiger von der, 87, 92
GPU, *see* OGPU
Grasty, Charles C., 65–6, 80, 85
Greenshields, Jeanette (WD's great-aunt), 12
Greenshields, Mary (WD's great-aunt), 12
Grisha (WD's chauffeur), 177, 264
Guardian (Manchester), 52, 61, 86, 92, 138, 180, 200, 204–6, 234, 266, 289
Gunther, Frances, 324–7
Gunther, Jane (née Perry, Vandercook), 133, 328–30, 335, 341, 345, 349–50, 353
Gunther, John, 133, 151–2, 158, 176, 225, 246–7, 250–2, 254, 261–4, 268, 274–6, 279, 296–7, 299, 303, 308–10, 313–15, 317–18, 322–30, 335, 339–41, 343–51, 353
Gunther, Johnny (Jr.), 324–7

Hamilton, Hamish ("Jamie"), 251, 254, 332
Hammer, Armand, 175
Harper & Brothers, 335
Harriman, W. Averell, 139–40
Harris, Frank, 31
Harrison, Richard Edes, 319
Harrods, 253
Harrow School, 18–20, 88, 327
Hartzel, Lieutenant Oscar, 68
Harvard, John, 24
Hawtrey, Clifford, 132
Haywood, "Big Bill", 119–20
Hearst, William Randolph, 55
Hemingway, Ernest, 53, 133, 259
Henry, O., Prize, 153, 182
Herald Tribune (New York), 202, 244, 266, 280
Herald Tribune (Paris), 303
Hibbard, Fred, 289–90
Hicks, Granville, 156
Hindus, Maurice, 165–6
Hitchcock, Alfred, 295
Hitler, Adolf, 233, 238, 251–2, 276–7, 282, 292, 294, 331
Hoffman, Della (Sylvan), 320–1
Hollingworth, Clare, 286–8
Hollywood, 293–311, 349
Hoover, President Herbert, 98
Howard, Cecil, 38
Howard, Leslie, 295
Howard, Willie and Eugene, 312
Hutchins, Charles (WD's maternal grandfather), 12, 15
Huxley, Aldous, 295–6

Industrial Workers of the World (IWW), 91, 119
Inland Revenue Service, 338–9, 343
International News Service, 141, 228
Izvestia, 107, 152, 266, 305, 331, 337

James, Edwin L. ("Jimmy"), 65–6, 73, 80–1, 99–100, 182, 246, 248–9, 279, 281, 284, 290–1
Japan, 5, 83, 197–8, 236, 238–9, 251, 265–6, 269–70, 275, 291, 294, 314, 344
Jews: anti-Semitism and the Holocaust, 239–40, 277, 282, 331, 339–40, 342
Jones, Gareth, 206–9, 235–6, 240
Joffre, General Joseph J.C., 53

Kalinin, Mikhail Ivanovich, 136
Kamenev, Leo, 112, 137–8, 265, 267
Katya (WD's mistress), 118–19, 176, 199, 227, 230–1, 241–2, 244, 252–3, 261, 275, 312–13, 319–20, 332–5, 348, 355
Kennan, George, 239, 244
Kerensky, Alexander Feodorovich, 150
Kerr, Walter, 303–4, 323, 327, 355
KGB, 224, 227, 230–2, 313, *and see also* Cheka, NKVD, OGPU
Khrushchev, Nikita, 214
Kinkead, Robin, 177–9, 215–16, 232, 241–2, 313
Kipling, Rudyard, 14
Kirov, Sergei, 264–5
Kitchener, Lord, 54
Knickerbocker, Agnes, 182, 252–3, 317
Knickerbocker, H.R. ("Red", "Knick"), 140–2, 144–6, 149, 153, 155, 161, 173, 175, 182, 210, 225–6, 241, 252–3, 255, 262, 274, 277, 312–13, 316–18, 322–3, 332, 338–40, 343, 353
Knickerbocker, Hubert Conrad, 255
Knickerbocker, Laura, 144, 182
Knox, John, 18
Koestler, Arthur, 202
Kolchak, Alexander, 84
Kollontai, Alexandra, 116, 124–5
Korda, Alexander, 295
Korean War, 343–5
Krock, Arthur, 267
Kronstadt Mutiny, 113
Krylenko, Nikolai V., 151
Kulaks, 137–9, 162–6, 185, 199, 208, 211–13

Labour Party, 16
Lamoureux, Haidée, *see* Cheron

Latvia, 84–92, 98–100, 104, 161, 168, 216, 279, 283
Law, Bonar, 46
Lawrence, D.H., 348
Leigh, Vivien, 295
Leigh, W. Colston, 276, 280, 316, 318, 332, 340, 343
Lenin, N. (Vladimir Ilich Ulianov), 5, 71–2, 96, 99, 111–12, 116–17, 128, 135–7, 139, 145, 150, 155, 158–9, 166–7, 169, 190, 192, 200, 250, 269
LeRoy, Mervin, 296
Lewis, Sinclair ("Red"), 145–6, 149, 323
Lippincott, J.P., 301, 305, 331–2, 338
Lippmann, Walter, 96
Lithuania, 84, 87, 170, 283
Litvinov, Ivy, 228
Litvinov, Maxim, 3, 86, 98–99, 101, 109, 188–91, 218, 222, 228, 280–2
Liverpool, 9–16
Lloyd George, David, 46, 65, 78, 208
Lockhart, (Sir) Robert Hamilton Bruce, 321
Loos, Anita, 295–6, 306, 310
Loos, Mary, 306–10, 313, 320, 331
Ludendorff, General Erich Friedrich Wilhelm, 64–5, 69, 72–73, 77
Lunacharsky, Anatoly Vasilievich, 121
Lyons, Billie, 229
Lyons, Eugene, 168–9, 171, 179, 202, 206–9, 222, 227–30, 235–6, 298–9

MacArthur, General Douglas, 343–5
McCarthy, Senator Joseph, 235, 299, 343, 350
McCormick, Anne O'Hare, 221
McCoy, Bessie, 55
Mann, Heinrich, 296–7
Mann, Thomas, 296
Mao Tse-Tung, 343
Mariengov, Anatoly, 121–2
Markel, Lester, 314–15
Markov (Soviet press officer), 98
Marne, First Battle of the, 43–44
Marne, Second Battle of the, 73–77, 243
Marquand, J.P., 318
Marx, Harpo, 129
Massock, Dick, 266
Maunoury, General Michel Joseph, 43
Maupassant, Guy de, 142, 263
Mayakovsky, Vladimir Vladimirovich, 121
Medvedev, Roy A., 212
Mencken, H.L., 55
Merz, Charles, 96
Metro-Vickers trial, 203, 207–8, 216

Metropol Hotel (Moscow), 3, 100, 175, 186, 244, 252, 275
Meyerhold, Vsevolod Emilevich, 121
Middleton, Drew, 285–6, 312–13
Mironov (Soviet censor), 178
Molot, 202
Molotov, Vyacheslav, 280–2, 289, 327
Montague, C.E., 61–2
Morning Post (London), 56
Morning Sentinel (Orlando), 352
Moscow, *passim*
Mowrer, Edgar, 322
Mowrer, Paul Scott, 57, 249, 322
Muggeridge, Kitty, 200, 206
Muggeridge, Malcolm, 180, 187–8, 200–6, 217, 222, 225, 231–7, 240, 316, 337
Murrow, Edward R., 273–4, 277, 312, 318
Mussolini, Benito, 277

Napoleon, 41, 89, 181, 292
Nation, The, 227
Nazis, 196, 206, 217, 238, 251, 265, 277, 296, *and see also* Fascism, Hitler
Neuburg, Victor, 37
New Economic Policy (NEP), 99, 113–21, 137, 139–40, 154, 158, 162, 167, 197
New Republic, 96, 157, 267–9
New Times (Moscow), 321
New York, 4, 13–14, 30, 82–83, 90, 111, 128–30, 142, 154–5, 158, 182, 184, 187, 218, 223, 229, 247, 251, 255, 257, 268, 291, 294, 299, 301, 303, 311–12, 318–20, 322–3, 325, 328–30, 338, 348, 351
New York Times, 3, 5, 34, 36, 42, 46, 50, 57, 64–65, 68, 71, 84–85, 87, 91–92, 96, 99, 101, 106, 108–10, 129, 144–5, 159–60, 170, 174–5, 178, 182, 184–5, 188–90, 192, 208, 218, 221, 230–1, 237, 240, 245–8, 250, 252, 255, 266–7, 275–6, 279–81, 283–8, 290–1, 303, 312–14, 318–19, 334, 348, 352–4, *et passim*
New York Tribune, 51
New Yorker, 51
News Chronicle (London), 174, 225
Newsweek, 354
Nicholas II (Czar), 71
NKVD, 212, 230, 264, 270
North American Newspaper Alliance (N.A.N.A.) 147, 252, 275–7, 280, 287, 291–2, 317, 338–9
Nove, Alec, 222–3
Nutter, Charles, 266

Odessa, 94, 215
OGPU, 163, 202, 230
Olivier, (Sir) Laurence, 295
Opium, 5, 30–32, 34, 49, 131–3, 173, 179, 257, 288
Orlando, Florida, 335, 340–3, 348–50, 352, 354
Osborne, Fairfield, 318
Oulahan, Richard V., 80–1
Oumansky, Constantine, 178, 204, 207, 235–6, 310
Overseas Press Bulletin, 354
Ovey, Sir Edmund, 193–4, 205–6

Palmer, Attorney General A. Mitchell, 91
Palmer, Frederick, 54, 60, 62
Paris, 3, 30, 34–48 *passim*, 52–3, 57–8, 80–1, 86, 128, 130, 133, 144, 158–9, 172–3, 175, 198, 229, 249, 259, 322, 327, 348
Parker, Dorothy, 128, 295
Parrott, Lindesay, 176, 215
Pearson (millionaire), 322–3
Pégoud, Alphonse, 35–36
Perris, G.H., 65–6
Pershing, General John J., 65
Pétain, General Henry Philippe, 68
Peters, Karl, 125
Peters, Mary, 125
Petit Parisien, Le, 39
Phillips, Joe, 266
Phillips, Percival, 56
Piatakov, Grigory, 265
Pilgrim's Progress, 14
Podolsky (Soviet censor), 178
Pratt, Fletcher, 262
Pravda, 99, 107, 159, 161, 196, 291, 305, 337
Prohme, Rayna, 147–9, 317–18
Public Ledger (Philadelphia), 141, 182
Pulitzer Prize, 3, 182, 184, 224, 240, 316
Pyle, Ernie, 304

Radek, Karl, 137, 144, 265
Rapallo, Treaty of, 251
Rathbone, Basil, 318
Rawlings, Marjorie, 341
Red D. Steamer Line, 10
Reed, John, 3, *and see* 190
Remarque, Erich Maria, 296–7
Reuben, curse of, 26
Reuters, 56
Reynal and Hitchcock, 295
Richardson, Stanley, 217, 236
Robinson, H. Perry, 56
Robinson, T.P. Gordon, 22

Index

Rogers, Will, 175
Romm, Vladimir, 266–7
Roosevelt, President Franklin Delano, 3, 184, 188–90, 258
Rose, W., and Company, 10
Ross, Harold, 51, 128–9
Ruete, Theodore (WD's uncle by marriage), 10–11
Russell, Herbert, 56
Rykov, Alexei, 112, 269

St. John, Robert, 288–9, 317
St. Tropez, 3, 5, 49, 132–3, 173
Saki (H.H. Munro), 25, 114
Salisbury, Harrison E., 231, 284, 334–5, 355
Saturday Evening Post (Philadelphia), 187
Saturday Review of Literature (New York), 255, 262, 298, 301
Savinkov, Boris Viktorovich, 150–1
Schiller, Dr. Otto, 193, 196
Schopenhauer, Arthur, 331
Schuster, Lincoln, 332
Seabrook, William ("Willie"), 172–4, 256–61, 284–5, 293–4, 300, 320, 330, 335
Secker and Warburg, 337
Selden, Charles A., 80–3
Seldes, George, 98–100, 107–8, 110, 117–18, 173–4, 279
Shapiro, Henry, 242, 244–5, 266, 275–6, 280–3, 292, 319–20, 332–3
Shaplen, Joseph, 159
Shatoff, Bill, 120
Shaw, George Bernard, 16
Sheean, Vincent ("Jimmy"), 146–9, 295, 317–18
Sheffer, Paul, 149–50, 199, 225–6
Shirer, William L., 175–6, 273–5, 277–8, 285, 317
Shiroshikh, Natalya Petrovna, 202
Simon and Schuster, 254, 332
Simon, Sir John, 193, 197, 205, 218
Sloane, William, 330–2, 337, 342
Sokolnikov, Grigory Iakovlevich, 265
Somme, Battle of the, 53
Soviet Union, *passim*
  Bolshevik revolution, 71–72, 301; Civil War, 83–84, 94, 97–98, 125, 161; collectivization, 6, 156–8, 162–6; United States recognition of the Soviet Union, 4, 6, 184, 188–93, 198, 203–4, 223, 258–9; German

invasion, 292, 294; *see also* Five-Year Plan, Lenin, New Economic Policy, Stalin, Ukraine Famine
Spain, 252–3
Spectator (London), 343
Stalin, Joseph, 3, 5–6, 112, 137–40, 144, 154–6, 158, 162–3, 165–71, 173–4, 179, 183, 186–7, 190, 192, 196–8, 205, 212, 222–3, 227–8, 235–6, 238–9, 250–2, 269–70, 286, 292, 298–9, 305, 314, 320, 336, 343, 352; Stalin's purges and show trials, 6, 264–72, 284, 298; *see also* Five-Year Plan, Ukraine Famine
Stars and Stripes, 51
Steffens, Lincoln, 157
Stoneman, William, 202, 204, 216, 233, 235, 237
Strang, William, 196–9
Strunsky, Simeon, 159, 182
Sulzberger, Arthur Hays, 353–4
Sulzberger, Cyrus, 287–8, 291
Sun (Baltimore), 227
Sunday Times (London), 343
Svartsman, Alexander, 175
Swing, Raymond Gram, 325

Tallents, (Sir) Stephen, 88
Tannenberg, Battle of, 53–4
Tass, 107, 168
Thanatopsis Club, 51, 128–9
Thomas, W. Beach, 56
Thompson, Dorothy, 145–6, 148–9
Thurber, James, 176
Time, 189, 192, 316, 354–5
Times (London), 56, 203, 352, 354
Tribune (Chicago), 55–56, 86, 98, 101, 176, 273
Trotsky, Leo Dividovich, 5, 72, 95–6, 112, 135, 137–40, 143–4, 149–50, 153, 162, 170, 265, 268–70
Truman, President Harry, 344
Tuckerman, Gustav, 245–6
"21" (New York), 129, 294, 299–300, 302, 318–19, 328, 335

Ukraine Famine of 1921, 97–116, 239, 259, 342
Ukraine Famine of 1932–33, 6, 193–240, 259
United Press, 146, 229, 244, 266, 320

Van Anda, Carr, 57, 65, 80, 92, 96, 98, 110
Verdun, Battle of, 53, 220

Index

Versailles, 81–2, 289
Viking Press, 245
Vyshinsky, Andrei Ianuarevich, 327
Vyvyan, S.M.K., 203–4

Wall Street Crash, 155–6
Wallgren, Albian A., 51
Walpole, Hugh, 25
Warburg, Fred, 337
Warshawsky, A. G., 38
Watkins, Ann, 353
Waugh, Alec, 318
Webb, Beatrice and Sidney, 16, 196, 200,
    206, 224
Weininger, Otto, 33–34, 330
Wells, Bombadier, 34
Wells, H. G., 16
Wells, Linton, 203, 228–9, 264
Whitaker, John, 304, 323, 327
Wicksteed, Alexander, 177
Wilde, Oscar, 34, 249
Wiley, Irena, 247, 251, 274, 279
Wiley, John, 247, 251, 274, 278–9
Williams, Albert Rhys, 337
Williams, Spencer, 266, 289–90

Williams, Wythe, 34–42, 45–46, 51, 53,
    57–8, 142, 178
Wilson, Edmund, 156–7, 224
Winchell, Walter, 354
Wodehouse, P.G., 318
Wood, Junius, 151
Woolcott, Alexander, 34, 38, 50–2, 128–
    30, 142, 185–7, 191, 245, 248, 354
Worker's Gazette, 154
World War I, 38–79, 106, 164, 243, 300,
    322, 349
World War II, 214, 282–3, 285–6, 291–2,
    294–5, 300–1, 309, 313–14
Worthington, Marjorie, 173–4, 256–7,
    260, 293–6, 299–303, 319–21, 328,
    330, 335, 339, 349
Wren, Sir Christopher, 24

Yezhov, Nikolai Ivanovich, 270, 336
Young, Thomas, 24
Ypres, Battle of, 52–53, 78–9
Yudenich, General Nikolai, 84–5

Zepliak, Archbishop, 110
Zinoviev, Grigory Evseevich, 137–8, 265,
    267